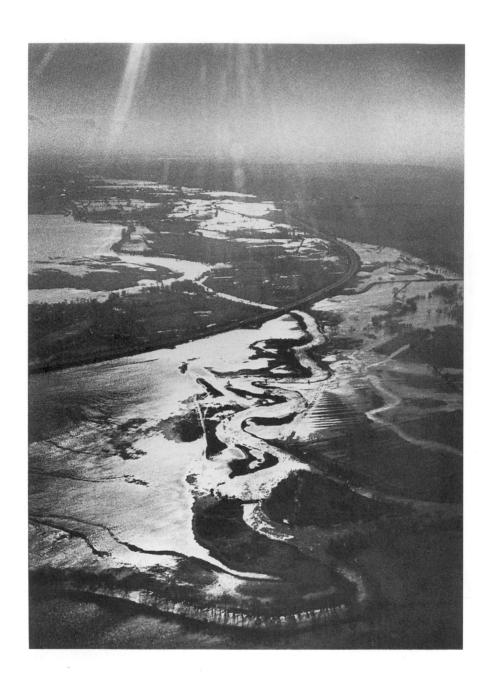

Land, water and development

The management of the environment is under increasing pressure to conserve systems and to pursue a sympathetic approach. This, despite the increasing demands of population, agriculture, industrialisation and public awareness. Historically, the sector of the environment most effected by human development has been the river.

Land, Water and Development reviews the evolution of river basin management and the history of applied hydrology to contextualise a global study of river basin systems and their contemporary management. Case studies are drawn from across the world. Technical coverage includes the basin as a geomorphological system, the influence of land-use on hydrology, soil erosion and the problems of river modification and regulation. Physical laws are set in the context of their boundary conditions at a variety of size and time scales. River basin systems and their management are also assessed within both physical and social frameworks. The book stresses the need for appropriate consultation when considering water management in a variety of institutions and areas throughout the world.

Providing a systematic review of both policy and practice, *Land, Water and Development* argues for a sustainable approach to the management of the world's rivers.

Routledge Natural Environment –
Problems and Management Series
Edited by Chris Park
Department of Geography, University of Lancaster

The Roots of Modern Environmentalism
David Pepper

Environmental Policies: An International Review
Chris C. Park

The Permafrost Environment
Stuart A. Harris

The Conservation of Ecosystems and Species
G. E. Jones

Environmental Management and Development in Drylands
Peter Beaumont

Chernobyl: The Long Shadow
Chris C. Park

Nuclear Decommissioning and Society: Public Links to a New Technology
Edited by Martin J. Pasqualetti

Green Development:
Environment and Sustainability in the Third World
W. M. Adams

Environmental Policy and Impact Assessment in Japan
B. Barrett and R. Therivel

Radioactive Waste: Politics and Technology
Frans Berkhout

The Diversion of Land: Conservation in a Period of Farming Contraction
Clive Potter, Paul Burnham, Angela Edwards, Ruth Gasson
and Bryn Green

Waste Location: Spatial Aspects of Waste Management,
Hazards and Disposal
Edited by Michael Clark, Dennis Smith and Andrew Blowers

Land, water and development

River basin systems and their sustainable management

Malcolm Newson

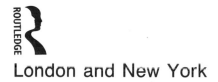

London and New York

First published 1992
by Routledge
11 New Fetter Lane, London EC4P 4EE

Simultaneously published in the USA and Canada
by Routledge
a division of Routledge, Chapman and Hall, Inc.
29 West 35th Street, New York, NY 10001

© 1992 Malcolm Newson

Typeset in 10/12 Times by
Mathematical Composition Setters Ltd,
Salisbury, Wiltshire
Printed and bound in Great Britain

British Library Cataloguing in Publication Data
A catalogue record for this title is available from the
British Library.

Library of Congress Cataloging-in-Publication Data
Newson, Malcolm David.
    Land, water, and development : river basin systems and their
sustainable management / Malcolm Newson.
        p.   cm. – (Routledge natural environment – problems and
management series)
    Includes bibliographical references and index.
    ISBN 0–415–05711–6. – ISBN 0–415–08031–2 (pbk.)
    1. Watershed management. 2. River engineering. 3. Water
resources development.   I. Title.   II. Series.
TC409.N49   1992
333.91'62 – dc20   91-39206
                                                                CIP

Contents

Plates

Figures

Tables

Preface

'It stands to reason,' said the farmer, 'we've only had these quick, high floods since the foresters ploughed those hills up there.'

This man's knowledge of, dependence on, and reaction to his local river made his reasoning easy. Yet to a government hydrologist, as was the author at the time of the conversation, proof of a link between preparing upland soils for successful afforestation and a change in the unit hydrograph for the basin would take a decade of expensive research. After its completion the logical outcome of the proven link, between land there and water here, i.e. modifying forestry practice, compensating the farmer or afforesting a less sensitive hillside, would not translate into public policy. There were simply no river-related land planning policies in many countries; the UK was no exception.

The outcome was that local authority engineers built the farmer a bridge over the newly flood-prone stream. Perhaps it is the heroic talent of the civil engineer to solve in this way point problems where they arise which has discouraged the 'look upstream' mentality of the local, the peasant, the river enthusiast. Societies have built dams, canals, flood walls, bridges and other structures to 'stabilise' river systems without questioning the cause of the instability. Rather like early technical medicine, we have used the equivalents of drugs and pain-killers to cure 'now problems' whereas some claim the true human talent lies with holism and the longer term.

This book tries to assemble a body of knowledge which supports a very broad approach to river problems; physically destabilised river systems will be a major theme but polluted and biologically sterilised systems are all amenable to 'the treatment'. At the other extreme, there is increasing demand to conserve, by management intervention, those relatively few pristine wilderness river systems which remain.

'The treatment' as a concept comes relatively easily to the geographer. Fluvial geomorphology, a major feature of geographical research in the second half of this century, has provided chapter and verse on the natural dynamics of the river basin, which function to transfer water and sediments to the ocean, leaving a characteristic morphology – river channel, floodplain, valley side – to form the basis of river habitat. Whilst the engineer has applied knowledge of precise physical laws to the 'now' problems of river basins for millennia, the geomorphological view puts these laws into the context of their boundary conditions in a variety of global environments, at a variety of scales, and, most critically for enlightened management, over a range of timescales.

Seen as a total transport system in the longer term it becomes axiomatic that Mankind's use of land settlement, agriculture and forestry will have an eventual impact on water. In some cases governments appreciate this link quickly, particularly if impacts are rapid, spectacular and very damaging. This book will draw out the particular case of flooding and erosion following deforestation; in countries such as New Zealand public policies were reactive but science-driven. Proactive river policies are scarcer!

No scientific research finds its way directly into public policy; the democrat reader would not wish it. However, scientists become considerably frustrated by the political filters through which their results are put and so this book also pays attention to those ideas, attitudes, policies and laws which relate land practice to river management and which derive from the people. It is perhaps variability across the globe in this cultural, ethical approach to river basins which sustains another element of the geographer's interest. This internationalism finds particular contrasts between the developing and developed world. The developed world consultant can do well to remember that, whilst the laws of physics are universal, relativity has a new perspective when their application lies for example in the hands of an Ethiopian peasant woman. 'Where is the river?' asked the consultant 'I have designed a weir for it which will help you to grow your crops.' 'It has not been here for thirty years', said the African, 'and we grow excellent crops because it no longer floods us.' Seldom is the misunderstanding this great but on many river basin development schemes it might as well be so.

This book is idealistic but idealism is tempered by practicalities. Upon what kind of knowledge base should we mount a river basin management programme and how is such knowledge derived? If we are to forsake direct and heroic interventions in favour of a greater willingness to make indirect approaches, through land planning and management, what are the risks? What sorts of institutions provide successful regulation of river basins? The clear message must be that people should identify with both the basin as a unit and the river itself. Furthermore they must participate, as in Ontario, Canada, and not merely be moved around to fit the right river scheme, as in Indonesia. Scale, another geographical tool, can help us to understand the problem of identity; the circulation of information around units of different sizes is critical, be they drainage basins or institutions managing them.

Fortunately, the international movement to conserve ecosystems and those concerned with human amenity have recently adopted river systems much more actively than in the past. The International Rivers Network is part of this 'new wave' and it may well recruit support in the developed world from the host of 'yuppie' riverside dwellers, the millions enjoying water sports and those who regularly walk river banks or fish for recreation.

This book is undertaken some twenty years after the author drew great inspiration from *Water, Earth and Man* (Chorley, 1969). Geographers have, since then, become widespread in research, education and administration in connection with rivers; at the very least this volume will record their progress. Since 1969 our knowledge of the rate of environmental change has exploded; among those ecosystems whose response to extrinsic change is critical for human occupation of the planet, river basin systems take a high priority, having been the first to be exploited by settled human societies. Can science help?

A note to readers from other disciplinary backgrounds

If you have had no experience of the workings of the hydrological cycle it may be necessary to begin your reading of this text at Chapter 3, reversing through to Chapter 1! Years of experience of teaching this material to final year students with a background in hydrology (though a growing minority join us from social science!) makes me feel that the chapter order as presented sets up the questions to be answered by the book (see Prologue and Chapter 1) and that the placing of transfer systems ahead of hydrology forces attention to the morphological condition of the river basin.

If you have had no background in river systems please consult the many simple texts available at school or college level (e.g. Newson, 1979 and Newson, in press).

Acknowledgements

The author wishes to acknowledge the many contributors over the years to the set of ideas presented here; as a work of synthesis it necessarily contains much imported material – too much to acknowledge by individual citation. As an avid bibliophile the author is indebted to those who have produced the books which are stacked in piles all round every room he works in! There is a particular debt to those who, in their river writings, dared to break fresh ground – all the way from Richard Chorley's *Water, Earth and Man* in 1969 to Stan Schumm's *The Fluvial System* in 1977 to John Gardiner's *Manual for Holistic Appraisal* in 1991.

The author also acknowledges a life-long debate with engineers; levels of mutual appreciation have grown as the contribution of geographers has become clearer and less self-effacing, but the engineers known to me have also been faced with environmental and social problems with which they have found it hard to cope – I believe they have responded with great flair.

Acknowledgement is due, by name, to Lynne Martindale for producing the typescript and Ann Rooke for the artwork, both to punishing schedules – one marvels at the accuracy. The gatekeeper for those 'gremlins' that got through was Ros Ramage who also worked at great speed and with stunning accuracy.

Finally I acknowledge the tolerance of all those whom I have failed for about two years, whilst wandering around with what Laurens van der Post once described as 'the river look' on my face!

Malcolm Newson, Newcastle upon Tyne

Prologue

RIVER BASIN IMAGES

Figures i–viii illustrate a range of published images of river basins. Any hydrologist asked to draw one will produce a prototype 'hot air balloon', slightly crumpled and with a very simple stream network, possibly second or third order according to Strahler's (1957) classification (Figure i). This is the small *catchment* beloved of water supply engineers and one over which land use control is relatively easily practised; it is also the scale most used by experiments in hydrology – again because of the suitability of such units (say 10 km^2) for controls and experimental treatments.

If we consider, however, that at another extreme the Amazon river basin may be fourteenth order on the Strahler scale, has a basin area of 5 Mkm^2 and is in desperate need of efficient management under changing political and environmental circumstances, the hydrologist's simplicity of concept may be dangerously illusory. The river manager, even on a small island like Great Britain, may turn up the alternative image shown in Figure ii. The

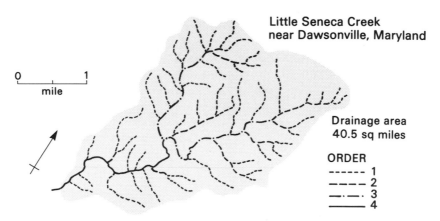

Little Seneca Creek near Dawsonville, Maryland

0 — 1 mile

Drainage area 40.5 sq miles

ORDER
- - - - - 1
- - - - 2
— · — · 3
——— 4

Figure i The geomorphologist's view of the river basin: ordered stream network within a defined boundary (Leopold, 1974)

Figure ii The water manager's view of the river basin: control systems without natural boundaries

reader should note, however, that the dangerous illusion in this image is that the basin's boundary is not shown. Certainly 'land and catchment use' is noted as a label but, along with the other labels, this connotes the manager as something of a hero, coping with problems thrown at the channel network by land use on the banks. Engineers, particularly, tend to use 'responsibility', 'dirty' and other anthropocentric and value-laden terms when dealing with river basin management. Figure ii admits that water management itself imposes certain further 'duties' of planning and engineering, although a river system as completely controlled as the Tennessee example

(Figure iii) would, to the tidy mind of the traditional engineer, perhaps need no further intervention. Such pictorial 'overkill' would not nowadays be a feature of the PR for a river scheme but the tidy-minded, rather simplistic, positivism of the river engineer is still represented in Figure iv. Here management problems are presented as amenable to mathematical or physical solution. Once again, any suggestion of the catchment boundary, or of indirect influences on the river, is missing.

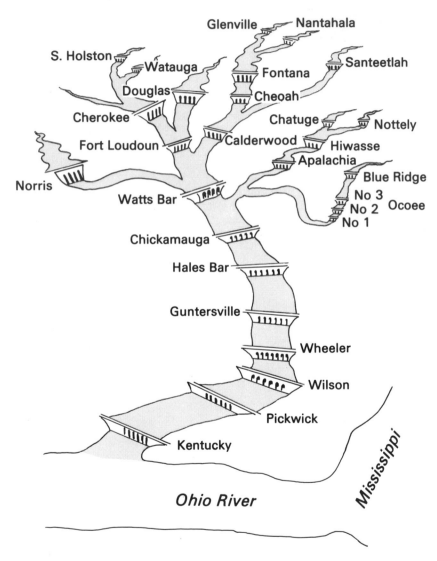

Figure iii The Tennessee Valley Authority view of the river basin: total control by dams (Huxley, 1943)

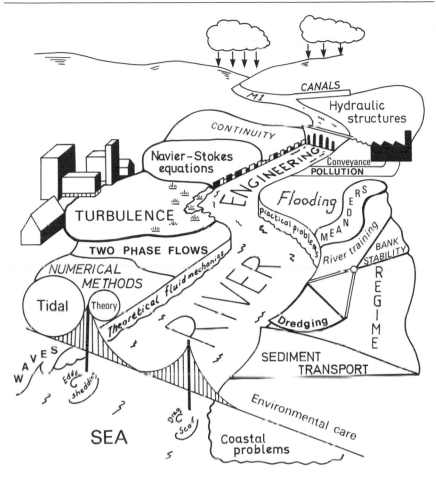

Figure iv The engineer's view of the river basin: a series of hydraulic problems (Knight, 1987)

Can the clever geographer come up with an improved image? One is sought to convey the spirit of this book. To bring in human activity after the fashion of traditional human geography (Figure v) is clearly insufficient and largely outdated. In fact Figure vi, a recent offering from geomorphology, is more useful because it is not scale-dependent and because it emphasises sources, transfers and transformations in the drainage basin. Schumm (1977) applied the original version of this image to the basin sediment system but it is relevant, too, to water flows and pollution. Headwater areas are largely sources for the types of river management problems which this book addresses. In the transfer zone, riparian land use is no less critical but efforts in planning and management can be largely directed to

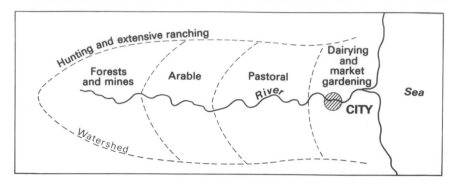

Figure v The view of the river basin of traditional geography: zones of economic development

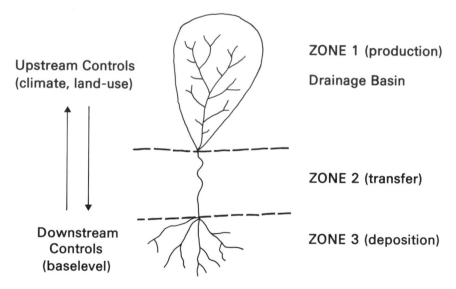

Figure vi S. A. Schumm's river basin as a sediment transfer system (Schumm, 1977)

specific sites, e.g. on floodplains and valley floors. At some stage in the system water, sediments or a pollutant will be deposited, or used, or will enter the food chain.

The beauty of Schumm's image is that it is educational but very simple. The full message, involving elements of the hydrologist's, manager's and engineer's images requires complex annotation, such as that of Figure vii. This Figure is a child of its time; stressing the sensitivity of the drainage basin to change, emphasising risks and vulnerability. A definition which

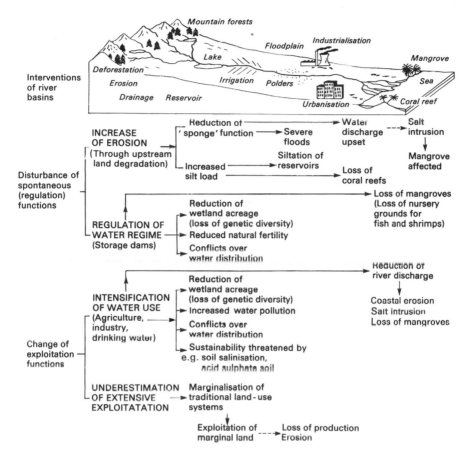

Figure vii The basin 'slice' of environmental assessments: sensitivity table
(Marchand and Toornstra, 1986)

further emphasises this sensitivity is found in Black (1970):

> The watershed is a natural unit of land which collects precipitation and delivers runoff to a common outlet. It may be represented by an electrical analogy which consists of elements which may be containers for storage or resistances to movement of water; storage-runoff components of which there are four primary types; modules which consist of at least one of each type of storage and which represent the smallest complete watershed, and an array of modules which describes watershed complexity and permits extensive evaluation of the principles of watershed characteristics, behavior, and management.
>
> The watershed is a system in dynamic equilibrium and is more easily influenced by man in later stages of its evolution.

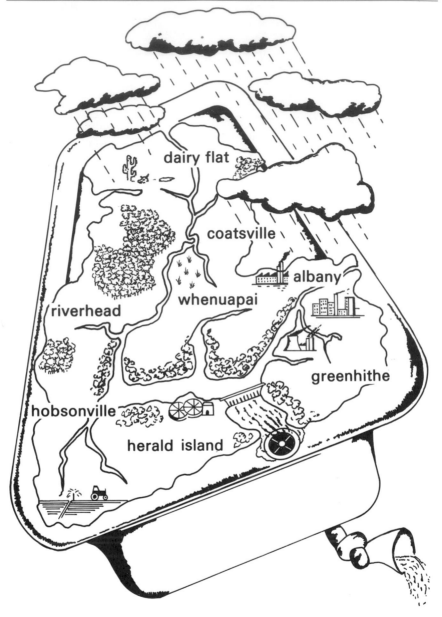

Figure viii Public relations view: your river basin (modified from The Upper
Waitemata Harbour Catchment Study, National Water and Soil
Conservation Authority, Wellington, New Zealand, undated)

The watershed is more easily influenced by man through manipulation of factors which dominate the local scene and which mask broad regional patterns of watershed reactions and stream behavior.

The watershed is most efficiently managed through careful manipulation of key elements of its environment which have effects beyond their apparent limits.

The watershed is an intricate natural resource which demands varied practices, complex management decisions, and manifold research efforts in order to ensure its efficient utilisation.

(Black, 1970, p. 161)

Readers may like to note the convention used in terminology in this book. The large management units over which we shall try to specify outcomes (e.g. sustainable development, ecosystem equilibrium and human welfare) are described as river basins. 'Watershed' or 'catchment' are taken as much more specific terms referring to the 'hot air balloon' of Figure i. They are small scale, identifiable, sources of water and less desirable products, and amenable to treatment (in this case positive land-use allocation or accommodation).

Possibly the humorous image deriving from New Zealand (Figure viii) most closely summarises the unit for which we have here most to say. Furthermore it is intended to deliver the management problem, at a basin scale, to those who live in it.

Chapter 1

History of river basin management

The purpose of this chapter is to explore briefly the nature of Man's occupation of river basins; the adoption of a conscious modern attempt at holistic management will almost certainly involve cultural attitudes to the problems, with their roots in history. Too often scientists ignore the importance of such elements in the translation of research results into policy and practice. For example, religious attitudes to the significance to water and its uses date back to the dawn of recorded history, as recently portrayed for the British Isles by Bord and Bord (1986).

The first hominids of 6–8 million years ago emerged as a savanna species and therefore into a seasonal climate; elements of our species as fundamental as bipedalism and communication are attributed to this environmental context. The savanna forced adaptation to finding, harvesting and storing food and water. Settlement, when it developed, inevitably produced advantages for the evening out of supplies; in the case of water, however, considerable technological intervention was required. Societal repercussions of the need for efficiency and some equity in the distribution of water included the highly structured 'hydraulic civilisations' of the Indus, China, Egypt and the first of all: 'the fertile crescent'.

1.1 HYDRAULIC CULTURES: MANAGEMENT IN ADVANCE OF SCIENCE

The closest and probably the most widespread association of past human activity with the hydrological balance, relief, slopes and stream networks of the drainage basin has been achieved through the operation of irrigation systems.

(Smith, 1969, p. 107)

Irrigation began to form a strong bond between humans and river basins in the sixth millenium BC; two important river basin civilisations, Mesopotamia and then Egypt, manipulated water to sustain settled agriculture. Both irrigation and elementary flood control were practised. The food surpluses which were generated by the success of these elementary management strategies were the basis for excess labour to be put into creating the architecture and other artefacts from which we have come to know so much about the Tigris–Euphrates and Nile valleys between 5000 and 3000 BC (Hawkes, 1976). The Sumerians built temples to the gods whom they considered responsible for the success of agriculture, whilst the Egyptians built memorials to the kings who were paramount in the strongly structured societies essential to primitive water management.

Toynbee (1976) describes the Sumerian achievement as the source from which Egypt and later the Indus civilisation drew their basic water technologies; he also stresses the importance of *social structures*:

> Before this alluvium (of the Tigris and Euphrates) was drained and irrigated for human occupation and cultivation it was inhospitable to Man and to his domesticated plants and animals. It was a maze of waters threading their way through reed-beds – the marshland to which the district around the lower course of the Euphrates has now reverted.
>
> The mastering of the jungle swamp was a social, far more than a technological achievement. The human conquest of alluvium must have been planned by leaders who had the imagination, foresight and self-control to work for returns that would be lucrative ultimately but not immediately. The one indispensable new tool was a script. The leaders needed this instrument for organising people and water and soil in quantities and magnitudes that were too vast to be handled efficiently by the unrecorded memorising of oral arrangements and instructions.
>
> (Toynbee, 1976, pp. 45, 51)

Toynbee sees in this dependence on social structures and *flows of information* the reason for the eventual demise of the Sumerian culture: 'The Sumerian civilisation depended for its survival on an effective control and administration of the lower Tigris–Euphrates basin's waters; this control could not become fully effective unless and until it was brought under a unitary command' (p. 61). Instead Sumerian society became partitioned into a number of local city-states. Smith (1969) also stresses the tight structures responsible for any successful hydraulic culture; summarising Wittfogel (1957) he suggests that:

> the construction and maintenance of large-scale irrigation systems require the assembly of a considerable labour force which may be most efficiently created either by the institution of forced labour or the levy of tribute and taxation or both. A centralised administration is also needed for the maintenance of canals and to control water distribution. The administration in control of the distribution of water is, in effect, in complete control of agricultural activity, and is thus in a position to demand complete authority and complete submissiveness, subject only to mass

revolt and rebellion in the face of desperate conditions. Society becomes polarised, in fact, into an illiterate, dependent peasantry and an élite, as in the traditional bureaucratic governments of China.

(Smith, 1969, p. 108)

Biswas (1967) tabulates a chronology of hydrological engineering works by the Sumerians, the Egyptians and the Harappans who, by 2500 BC, had developed a very powerful (though less creative) civilisation in the Indus basin (Table 1.1). Among the most interesting artefacts remaining is the Sadd el-Kafara ('Dam of the Pagans') built *c.* 2800 BC just south of Cairo. It was apparently built without a spillway and with a capacity so small in relation to its catchment area that it failed early in its lifetime. Distribution of water was clearly more successful than collection; it requires, after all, much more organisation than understanding and it was to be 2000 years before the study of nature began and 4500 years before scientific hydrology! According to Vallentine (1967) the Egyptians had more success in their diversion of the Nile into a huge flood storage scheme (Lake Moeris), which was excavated, according to Herodotus, in the nineteenth century BC. Smith (1972), however, concludes that Lake Moeris is entirely natural and that Herodotus is an unreliable source for the record of Egypt's water engineering. Figure 1.1 illustrates the origins of river basin mapping; the reader may wish to compare it with Figure 5.5.

Irrigation practice along the Nile floodplain required the subdivision of land into embanked plots to be flooded during the annual flood cycle of the river between July and September. The Tigris and Euphrates were much less predictable and systems of canals and ditches, fed by diversion structures, took water directly to small plots. It is suggested by some writers that the need for efficient irrigation prompted the development of geometric ground

Table 1.1 Key dates in the development of hydraulic civilisations

Date (BC)	Event
3000	King Menes dammed the Nile and diverted its course.
3000	Nilometers were used to record the rise of the Nile.
2800	Failure of the Sadd el-Kafara dam.
2750	Origin of the Indus Valley water supply and drainage systems.
2200	Various waterworks of 'The Great Yu' in China.
1050	Lake Moeris and other works of Pharaoh Amenmhet III.
1750	Water codes of King Hammurabi.
1050	Water meters used at Oasis Gadames in North Africa.
714	Destruction of quanat systems at Ulhu (Armenia) by King Saragon II. Quanat system gradually spread to Persia, Egypt and India.
690	Construction of Sennacherib's Channel.

Source: After Biswas (1967)

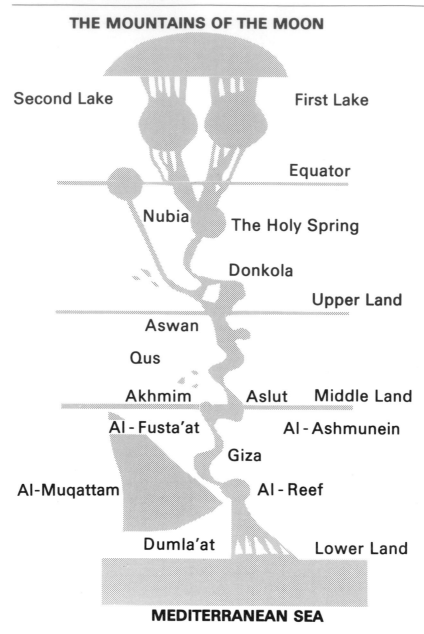

THE MOUNTAINS OF THE MOON

Second Lake

First Lake

Equator

Nubia

The Holy Spring

Donkola

Upper Land

Aswan

Qus

Akhmim   Aslut   Middle Land

Al-Fusta'at   Al-Ashmunein

Giza

Al-Muqattam   Al-Reef

Dumla'at   Lower Land

MEDITERRANEAN SEA

Figure 1.1 Ptolemy's map of the Nile basin (from T. E. Evans, 1990)

survey techniques. A tablet in the British Museum illustrates algebraic calculations for the design of dikes, dams and wells. The story of Noah almost certainly derives from the biggest flood to affect the Sumerian civilisation and therefore flood protection was highly developed. Rulers were extremely interested in legislating for efficient river management. The Code of Hammurabi is a codification of Sumerian and Babylonian water law. Flood damage due to negligence was particularly feared:

> Sec 53. If any one be too lazy to keep his dam in proper condition, and does not keep it so; if then the dam breaks and all the fields are flooded, then shall he in whose dam the break occurred be sold for money and the money shall replace the corn which he has caused to be ruined.
> Sec 55. If any one open his ditches to water his crop, but is careless, and the water flood the field of his neighbor, then he shall repay his neighbor with corn for his loss.
> Sec 56. If a man let out the water, and the water overflow the land of his neighbor, he shall pay 10 gur of corn for every 10 gan of land flooded.
> (Biswas, 1967, p. 128)

One must not neglect the military significance of water engineering at this time. Sennacherib the Assyrian destroyed Babylon in 689 BC by damming the Euphrates and then destroying the dam (Smith 1972). Sennacherib became the agent of some extremely well-surveyed and constructed dams and irrigation schemes.

Another important prehistoric achievement in the Middle East was the building of quanats, underground channels conveying water from springs to consumers (over a distance of more than 20 miles in some cases) at a constant gradient and free from pollution or losses by evaporation. Groundwater exploitation and underground storage of water are also recorded for both Egypt and Mesopotamia. Clearly, therefore, potable water supplies to urban centres were also a feature of these hydraulic civilisations. It is, however, from the archaeological record of the Indus civilisation that houses served by both water supply and drainage systems have been found, dating from 2200 BC (Vallentine, 1967).

At about the same stage of prehistory the legendary Emperor Yu in China began to control rivers in the interests of land reclamation. As Biswas (1967, p. 120) recorded, 'He studied the rivers ... he mastered the waters'; it is clear from the Chinese literature that mapping of river networks and, consequently, some concept of river basins, had been born.

At the dawn of Western civilisation the hydraulic cultures of the Middle and Far East were still strong; but rival military fortunes produced fluctuating prosperity and eventually Western influences became all-pervading. However, uniquely it seems, the Indus civilisation ended as a result of profound *environmental change* – climatic extremes of damaging floods and extensive droughts overcame the sophistication of the engineering. The evidence for wetter conditions at the height of the Indus culture is mainly faunal (chiefly rhinoceros) and it has been criticised by Raikes (1967) as giving a false impression; hydrological responses, he argues, are complex when climate changes and we may make reference to current arguments over desertification and salinisation (Chapter 6) in his support. The Indus civilisation, claims Raikes, 'could have survived and prospered on zero rainfall with or without irrigation, for the Indus complex of rivers enjoys a well-marked seasonal flood that would have inundated vast areas of the flood-plain' (p. 113). Even with today's barrages and levees, he claims, uncontrolled flooding still occurs. Toynbee stresses the magnitude and scale of the Indus civilisation, with its two principal cities 400 miles apart; he does not consider the management problems of such a scale: possibly management failed to respond in a coordinated way to environmental change, however caused.

1.2 THE RISE OF HYDROLOGY AND HYDRAULICS

Having tentatively concluded that water distribution can occur in advance of hydrological knowledge, how can empirical knowledge and theoretical understanding be put to work in support of engineering? The dichotomy between the reasoning science of the Greeks and the practical application of the Romans is traditionally drawn in deriving the origins of Western science.

Empirical records of river levels can be traced for the Nile back to 3000 BC; the famous Roda 'nilometer' (Figure 1.2) recorded the annual flood. A system of flood warning may have been developed, using watch towers and 'extremely good rowers' (Biswas, 1967, p. 125) who propelled their boats ahead of the flood wave. The same author records the 3000-year history of simple water metering for irrigation supplies in North Africa.

Greek philosophers were not able to advance our knowledge of hydrology, though Archimedes' observations led to the foundation of hydrostatics. The engineering skill of the Romans, however, led to great progress in urban water supply and drainage systems. Nevertheless, Xenophanes of Colophon (570–470 BC) stated that, 'the sea is the source of the waters and the source of the winds without the great sea, not from the clouds could come the flowing rivers or the heaven's rain'. By contrast Nace (1974) dismisses the Romans' contribution to hydrology: 'Despite their great hydraulic works, no evidence has been found that Roman engineers as a group had any clear idea of a hydrological cycle' (p. 44).

Under the very different environmental conditions of these Western civilisations irrigation was obviously less important; distribution systems took water from constant, pure sources, such as large springs in the countryside, to the streets and houses of Roman cities. The remains of Corstopitum (Corbridge) in Northumberland show supply pipes, fountains and road

Figure 1.2 The Roda nilometer, upon which the heights of the annual Nile flood have been measured from antiquity (from Biswas, 1967)

drainage (Plate 1.1). One may speculate that for the Roman Empire the humid conditions of Europe encouraged drainage, which led to sewerage and therefore to the use of remote sources of water supply to avoid pollution.

The largest technical problems of achieving the most impressive Roman feats, such as the Pont du Gard aqueduct (supplying Nîmes in southern France), would have been the design of capacity for flow and gradient. In an interesting review of the Pont du Gard's hydraulic design, Hauck and Novak (1987) stress the subtleties of conveying a steady flow of water down only 17 m of fall in 50 km. The Romans made a clear trade-off between the expense of a higher aqueduct (i.e. a longer span across the Gardon valley) and the need to maintain a steady gradient. In 19 BC the most precise level was a 6 m-long bar, levelled by water in a groove or plumb bobs. Simple

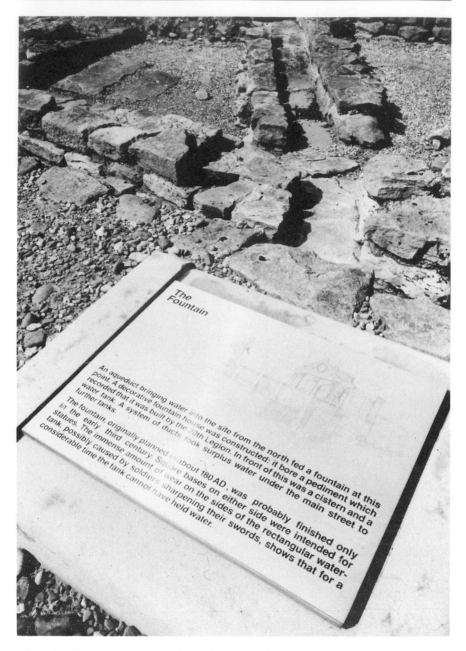

The Fountain

An aqueduct bringing water into the site from the north fed a fountain at this point. A decorative fountain house was constructed: it bore a pediment which recorded that it was built by the 20th Legion. In front of this was a cistern and a water tank. A system of ducts took surplus water under the main street to further tanks.

The fountain, originally planned in about 180 AD, was probably finished only in the early third century. Square bases on either side of the rectangular water-tank, possibly caused by soldiers sharpening their swords, shows that for a considerable time the tank cannot have held water.

Plate 1.1 Roman water supply engineering, Corbridge, Northumberland

geometry and a knowledge of the flow rate would have provided the cross-sectional area of the aqueduct's channel. The authors report that the limestone spring water continually encrusted the channel and regular maintenance was clearly essential; in every other way the work was a masterpiece of applied hydraulics.

Applications spawned both empirical knowledge and theoretical contributions; Vitruvius (first century AD) designed the undershot water wheel but also stated that groundwater, providing the most constant supply of water power, must derive from rain and snow by slow infiltration from the ground surface.

At the downfall of the Roman Empire we enter a thousand-year period of little or no recorded progress in either empirical or theoretical hydrology and hydraulics. The next important step was the establishment of the *hydrological cycle.*

Nace (1974) suggests that acceptable definitions of the hydrological cycle were published at a very early stage of recorded history, for example in the Bible (Ecclesiastes 1:7):

> All the rivers run into the sea; yet the sea is not full; unto the place from which the rivers come, thither they return again.

These words were written in the tenth century BC and a dynamic concept of the hydrological cycle arose in China at the same time. However, the route by which 'they return again' was not established and it was to take nearly 3,000 years of a multitude of conceptual links between oceans, atmosphere and rivers (for example an underground cycle was popular from time to time) before empirical measurements came to the aid of the true picture.

It is hard to document scientific progress during the Renaissance without reference to Leonardo da Vinci; of him Popham (1946) says, 'water played a very important part in his life. A great deal of his energies and his intellect were absorbed in directing and canalising rivers and in inventing or perfecting hydraulic machinery' (p. 70). He was obsessed with depicting water movement in his art (Plate 1.2) and careful observation aided his design of water wheels and pumps. However, his was not merely a brilliant combination of water engineering and art: he formalised the relationship between catchment and flow properties in his study of the Arno above Florence (Plate 1.3). The Arno catchment map (1502–3) shows very great care with both the stream network and the contributing slopes; mountains are not shown as isolated hills in the medieval tradition but by contour shading. To record so precisely the relationship between slopes and channels and between events over the river basin and those at a site (i.e. Florence) sets up the combination of hydrology and hydraulics which was eventually to guide modern river management.

Plate 1.2 Leonardo da Vinci's perception of river turbulence: *Deluge* (Windsor Royal Library no. 12382)

Plate 1.3 Leonardo da Vinci's map of northern Italy showing the watershed of the Arno (Windsor Royal Library no. 12277)

There can be little wonder that in the same century Palissy (1580) is acknowledged as having the first accurate insight into the general process of runoff (as credited by Ward, 1982).

We have noted the antiquity of river level measurements on the Nile; rain gauging was not necessary in the dry climates of the river-fed hydraulic civilisations. It had developed in China by 200 BC; in India rain was measured as an index of tax liability for agricultural production. Not until John Dalton presented a paper to the Philosophical Society of Manchester in 1799 had rainfall and runoff been brought together quantitatively.

It is interesting to note both the title and first paragraph of Dalton's paper:

> Experiments and Observations to determine whether a Quantity of Rain and Dew is equal to the Quantity of Water carried off by the Rivers and raised by Evaporation; with an Enquiry into the origin of Springs.

> Naturalists, however, are not unanimous in their opinions whether the rain that falls is sufficient to supply the demands of springs and rivers, and to afford the earth besides such a large portion for evaporation as it is well known is raised daily. To ascertain this point is an object of importance to the science of agriculture, and to every concern which the procuration and management of water makes a point, whether for domestic purposes or for the arts and manufacturers.

> (from Dooge, 1974)

Ward (1982) brings the development of hydrological concepts up to date in a review of the changing conclusions as to the sources and routes followed for runoff to streams. Most of the controversy of the twentieth century has concerned the balance between surface and subsurface runoff routes; most of the evidence has come from the fully instrumented catchment. We return to this source of scientific guidance to basin management in Chapter 8.

The rise of hydraulics and hydrology has clearly been slow and at each stage the simpler conceptual and theoretical advances were applied first (and almost universally). Hydrology, arguably, is more relevant to river basin management. The fact that it did not enter its main phase of numerical data collection until this century and become applied by river management agencies illustrates how meagre is the scientific guidance available for the management of complex systems. It is particularly unfortunate that our knowledge of runoff routes is so recent; ignorance has curtailed our appreciation of the importance of the catchment, its soils and land use.

1.3 MONKS, MILLS AND MINES: ORIGINS OF RIVER COORDINATION IN ENGLAND

C. T. Smith (1969) offers a variety of reasons why a river network can integrate the activity of societies within a drainage basin; irrigation is subordinate in most humid climates to direct water power, accessibility by water or by land along the valley floor, supplies of fish and game and supplies of water for humans and stock.

Through the careful work of Rowland Parker (1976) it is possible to reconstruct a 2000-year history of human settlement on the banks of a tributary of the River Rhee in Cambridgeshire. Up to the period of Anglo-Saxon conquest it is clear that navigation was an important function of even the smaller elements of the river network; indeed, invasion was by that route. However, Parker interprets the settlers as constructing a water mill which must have interrupted future navigation (since no mention is made of a mill leat). Later, with forest clearance on the interfluves, settlements moved from flood- and invasion-prone riversides to the terraces and low hills nearby. Those which did not were protected by the digging of moats and diversion channels.

The Domesday Book of 1086 enables us to gain insights into the distribution of mills (6,000 of them) and also of freshwater fisheries, a traditional water use by the very powerful monastic landowners of the time. After the Norman Conquest the rise of manorial estates and the use of milling tolls as part of a feudal structure ensured a rapid increase in obstructions to our rivers, but also protections against selfish behaviour. The chaotic picture of mills and fisheries recorded by Domesday is shown in Figure 1.3.

The next step in Parker's record of The Brook, not surprisingly, involves some form of legislation from manorial courts to control private use by

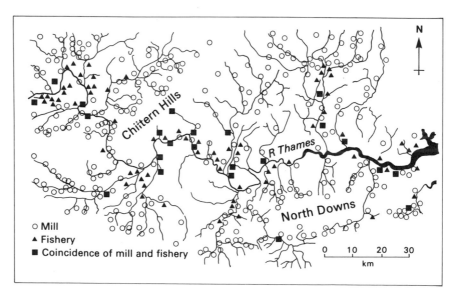

Figure 1.3 Domesday (i.e. AD 1086) mills and fisheries on the River Thames, England (compiled by Sheail, 1988)

tenants of the channel to create ponds for stock watering, human bathing, etc. Parker presents an almost continuous record of 'river offences' from 1318 until 1698. Gradually, with the obvious hiatus of the Black Death, pressure on the stream increases and the domination of ponding and diversion offences in the fourteenth century gives way to efficient land drainage ('cleaning and scouring') in the fifteenth and sixteenth and to pollution ('noysome sinkes and puggell water') in the sixteenth and seventeenth centuries. A selection of these offences is worthy of quotation to illustrate the ways in which English society was dealing with this two-mile stretch of minor stream.

In 1318 the following entries occur:

All the capital pledges of Foxton fined for not putting right the brook which was stopped up by Thomas Roys.
John Kersey fined 12d. for diverting the brook which flows through the middle of the manor, to a width of half a foot, and causing a nuisance.
Simon le Roo diverted the brook; fined 12d.
Roysia Kelle widened the stream by half a foot; fined 12d.
Ate Reeve did the same alongside his yard, widening the brook by letting the other bank fall in to a width of two feet; fined 3d.

1492 John Everard, butcher, allowed his dunghill to drain into the common stream of this village, to the serious detriment of the tenants and residents; fined 4d.; pain of 10s.

1541 Each tenant of this manor henceforth shall be ready and present at the cleaning and scouring of the watercourse called 'le Broke' whenever it shall be necessary, and they shall be warned to do so by the village officials or other inhabitants; pain of 12d.
No person shall wash linen called 'Clothes' in the common Broke; on pain of 20d. for everyone caught in default.

1590 Whoever has not appeared within one hour after the ringing of the bell to clean out the common brook shall forfeit 4d. to the Lord.
And whoever shall not clean out the brook fronting his land within the time appointed by the Heyward shall forfeit 12d.
No one shall wash any cloth in the brook before 8 of the clock at night on pain of forfeiting 12d. for every offence.

1594 No man shall lett out there sesterns or other noysome synkes untill eight of the clock at night uppon payne for every one doinge the contrary to forfeite unto the Lord for every tyme xiid.

1698 Item that any person who shall suffer any ducks to come into the Common Brooke shall fforfeit for every such offence 6d. to the Lord of the Manor.
Item that every inhabitant that shall not cleanse the Brooke or

> rivulet which runns through the towne of ffoxton soo far as is abutting upon their grounds att such time or times as shall bee appointed by the Churchwardens of the said towne shall fforfeit for every such offence 3*s*. 4*d*. to the Lord of the Manner.
>
> Item that any parson that shall lett out or suffer to runn any of their sinkes or puddles out of their yards into the Common Running Brooke of the town of ffoxton shall fforfeit for every such offence (if it bee att any time from ffoure of the clock in the morning until eight of the clock at night) 6*d*. to the Lord of the Manner.

(Parker, 1976, passim)

Whether manipulating streamflow for milling, stock watering, abstraction or fisheries, some form of obstruction to the natural regime was required and we have the origins of what we now call river regulation. Sheail (1988) reviews the history of river regulation in the UK; much of the available documentary evidence refers to drainage schemes in the Fens, Lincolnshire and Romney Marsh but the conclusion is universally applied:

> Whatever the purpose of river regulation, no scheme could fulfil its potential without the cooperation of all the interests involved. A balance had to be struck between the protection of individual rights and the furtherance of the common good.

(Sheail, 1988, p. 222)

Central government became involved in drainage issues in 1427 with the establishment of a Commission of Sewers; a General Sewers Act followed in 1531. Interestingly, a complex hybrid of statute and common law was applied to water management, the presence of common law implying progress by precedents rather than a completely technocratic application of principles and hence standards (in the scientific sense).

The very extensive lowland drainage, under Dutch direction, of the seventeenth century has a literature of its own, particularly in the Fens (e.g. Darby, 1983). Less attention has been paid to the more hydrologically complex task of irrigation and drainage (of the same land) as was practised extensively in chalkland valleys from the seventeenth to the early twentieth century. The water-meadow farming system has much to commend it in an age of low-intensity production with plentiful labour whilst drainage of land in the Fens was considered to be of regional and national benefit, threatening only those who took the annual harvest from the flood (duck, reeds, fish). River regulation elsewhere quickly led to conflicts of interests between upstream and downstream users of water. Whilst corn-millers frequently fought for effective use of low river flows, it was the arrival of industry, extractive then manufacturing, from the eighteenth century, with its demands on water for power, transport and processing, which put strain on the available structures for coordinating the use of the linear resource of the river.

The common law of riparian rights, datable to the Chasemore v. Richards case of 1859, gives the following rights to those who own land adjacent to rivers.

It has been now settled that the right to the enjoyment of a natural stream of water on the surface *ex jure naturae* belongs to the proprietor of the adjoining lands as a natural incident to the right to the soil itself; and that he is entitled to the benefit of it, as he is to all the other advantages belonging to the land of which he is the owner. He has the right to have it come to him in its natural state, in flow, quantity and quality, and to go from him without obstruction, upon the same principle that he is entitled to the support of his neighbour's soil for his own in its natural state. His right in no way depends on prescription or the presumed grant of his neighbour.

(Wisdom, 1979, p. 83)

Dams were built for a variety of purposes: for hydraulic mining (called 'hushing' in the Northern Pennines), ore processing and separating, and to supply the canal network which expanded in the late eighteenth century.

Binnie (1987) traces the origins of dams in Britain back to the Roman occupation; the occupants of fortifications along Hadrian's Wall clearly used reservoir storage on small streams. The Romans also used dams in connection with metal mining. The first modern dams were the mill and fishing weirs; in 1788 cotton milling alone accounted for 122 weirs on relatively large streams. More than 150 canal reservoir dams were built, the precursors of the modern water-supply reservoirs.

Industrial use of water power made mill operators a powerful voice in legal pressures for coordinated use of water. Finally, the growth of manufacturing and of large urban populations led to the construction of dams for domestic water supply. The conflict of interests between water storage and industrial water use led to the concept of 'compensation water', a minimum flow allowed out of reservoirs to maintain the rights of downstream users. Setting these flows was not easy in the absence of modern hydrological data. As Sheail comments:

Parliamentary committees spent more time considering the issues of compensation flows than any other aspect of reservoir development. Much controversy stemmed from lack of data on, and understanding of, the hydrological processes involved in determining the reliable yield of catchment areas and the need to take account of the changing economic use of the river water.

(Sheail, 1988, p. 228)

A detailed history of technical aspects of compensation flows is provided by Sheail in Gustard *et al.* (1987). Careful debate and evaluation was hardly necessary in the case of North Pennine lead mining. The 'hushing' technique, in which artificial flood waves were created (by the construction and subsequent breach of dams on small tributaries) to expose metal ores, produced sudden and often fatal flooding of the valley floors below.

Lead mining was also involved in early pollution litigation, an interesting example being that of Hodgkinson v. Ennor (1863) in which the owner of a paper-mill using pure water resurging in a limestone spring brought a successful case against a lead mine and works 7 km away. This was, effectively, a case of groundwater pollution and the defendant attempted to escape the clutches of riparian rights by claiming that these pollutants percolated through the ground. The very dirty refuse from the mine washings was, however, its own 'tracer' material and the case was won.

1.4   THE RISE OF ENVIRONMENT

The early hydraulic civilisations perfected, with relatively simple science, but with highly structured management systems, the major distributional systems of irrigation and water supply. They carried out flood protection but very empirically, on the basis of common experience. Whilst the Romans built sewer networks to collect waste and must therefore have understood the public health problems associated with river pollution, it is to the 'Workshop of the World', Britain during its Industrial Revolution, that we can look for an emerging approach to rivers as collection systems. Two elements of urbanisation and industrialisation prompted the need: the huge toll of life in epidemics of water-borne diseases (e.g. cholera in 1832), which forced attention to the classic source−pathway−target pollution system, and the need to establish 'gathering grounds' in the uplands to feed reservoirs of abundant pure water to be supplied under gravity to the developing lowland conurbations.

Binnie (1981) records the personal achievements of those Victorian water engineers who carried forward the heroic skills of Sennacherib or Vitruvius into an era of new design requirements. Aspects of coordinated management were quickly added to the agenda of social reformers of the time; we have already considered legislation related to compensation flows from the new upland reservoirs. Of much more profound importance in any historical review of river basin management was the rapid development of statutory law in relation to river pollution. Table 1.2 offers a brief history of this development. Two important elements are noteworthy.

The early emphasis on both water supply and sewerage was municipal, i.e. part of local government of towns and cities, and was a determined alternative to private enterprise because of the importance of both issues to public health. The technical shortfall in understanding river pollution, matched with a political desire not to halt development, led to a regulatory concept of the 'best practicable' solution.

Howarth (1988) provides an illuminating history of the development of

Table 1.2 Significant dates in the development of river management legislation in England and Wales

Date	Legislation	Target	Notes
1388	Act for Punishing Nuisances which Cause Corruption of the Air near Cities and Great Towns	Dung, filth, garbage, entrails not to enter ditches, rivers and other waters	£20 fine
1489	Act to prohibit slaughtering of animals within cities		
1492–1698	By-laws of village of Foxton, Cambs	Villagers to clean brook; no dunghill drainage into brook; no washing in brook; no discharging of cisterns	Fines of 4d. to 3s. 4d.
1531	Act to prevent tin operations silting harbours; General Commissions of Sewers	General Act was to 'cleanse and purge the trenches, sewers and ditches'	
1535	Act for the Preservation of the River of Thames	Prevented 'annoying of the river of Thames'	100 shillings fine
1830/3	Lighting and Watching Acts	To prevent washing of gasworks waste into streams	
1835	Municipal Corporations Act allows 179 towns to make by-laws and to levy rates		
1847	Waterworks Act	Made an offence to bath in, allow animals into or dump filth into any waters used for supply	
	Town Improvement Clauses Act	Drainage of towns, hitherto referring only to kitchen waste, now including foul waste, to be led to sea, river or for agricultural use	
	Cemetries Act	Cemetries to prevent offensive matter entering streams	
1858/61	Local Government Act/Amendment Act	Sewage works could be constructed outside Board of Health districts but no local board to construct sewage outfall to streams 'until such water be freed from all excrementious matter' which would reduce purity of streams	
1859	Chasemore v. Richards	Lord Wensleydale's judgement on the common law of riparian rights to water in 'natural state, in flow, quantity and quality'	

water pollution law in England and Wales (Scottish law is a separate system). He cites the earliest enactment as that of 1388 'for Punishing Nuisances which Cause Corruption of the Air near Cities and Great Towns'. Clearly, from contemporary accounts, even the pre-industrial cities of England treated their streams badly:

> so much dung and other filth of the garbage and entrails as well of beasts killed, as of other corruptions, be cast and put in ditches, rivers and other waters, and also many other places, within, about, and nigh unto divers cities, boroughs, and towns of the realm, and the suburbs of them, that the air there is greatly corrupt and infect, and many maladies and other intolerable diseases do daily happen, as well to the inhabitants and those that are conversant in the said cities, boroughs, towns, and suburbs, as to others repairing and travelling thither, to the great annoyance, damage, and peril of the inhabitants, dwellers, repairers, and travellers aforesaid.
>
> (Howarth, 1988, p. 2)

The subsequent acts dealing with water pollution were apparently of little success in combating the public attitude to streams as dumps for all excrement and filth, not an unusual attitude in burgeoning developing-world cities of today.

> Sweepings from butchers' stalls, dung, guts and blood,
> Drowned puppies, stinking sprats, all drenched in mud,
> Dead cats and turnip tops, come tumbling down the flood.
>
> Swift 'Description of a city shower'

By the arrival of the main phase of the Industrial Revolution, England and Wales had a plethora of legislation relating to the clearance of filth from towns using water-borne systems (e.g. Town Improvement Clauses Act, 1847, Public Health Act 1848) and to the mitigation of the effect of these domestic and industrial wastes on rivers. One of the principal of the latter class of enactments was a Salmon Fisheries Act (1861); because the hard-working Victorian water engineers were busy bringing clean, fresh supplies from the upland streams, concern for urban lowland streams was directed mainly at the loss of livelihood from fisheries. In our major urban centres none of this legislation had a comprehensive effect as is revealed by Engels' account of the Irk in Manchester during the 1840s:

> Above the bridge are tanneries, bone mills and gasworks, from which all drains and refuse find their way into the Irk, which receives further the contents of the neighbouring sewers and privies. It may be easily imagined, therefore, what sort of residue the stream deposits. Below the bridge you look upon the piles of debris, the refuse, filth, the offal from the courts on the steep left bank.

The principle of riparian rights, though set out again by Lord Wensleydale in 1859, did not bring the common law into any greater efficiency than statute in dealing with the relationship between towns on the same river. Clearly the next stage was to change the geographical reference scale for administration of the water cycle, rather than to perfect new legislative principles, though the Royal Commission on Sewage Disposal provided chemical and physical principles for pollution control by 1912.

The Rivers Pollution Prevention Act, 1876, was eventually implemented under the administration of the County Councils, independent bodies neither operating sewerage systems nor organised deliberately around river basin units. Ironically such a spatial organisation came about through progress in flood protection, still a mainly rural preoccupation, in the 1930 Land Drainage Act. Local drainage boards were established on a catchment basis and the 1948 River Boards Act set up similar bodies to deal with water resources (see Chapter 7). From this point onward we see a steady move towards the addition of pollution control responsibilities to these authorities (called various names by the 1963, 1973 and 1989 water legislation; see Chapter 7).

Patterson (1987) sees in the last 100 years of river basin management in England and Wales a grave political symptom, the removal of the *democratic* element of municipal control in favour of, firstly, a *technocratic* element in the river basin authorities and, latterly, an increasing *commodification* of water. Regional state institutions in England and Wales, he claims, are particularly inaccessible to non-dominant groups such as consumers. As we have learned throughout the history of river basin management, such social issues are by no means irrelevant.

Since the 1960s the rise of environmentalism, aided by industrial stagnation and diversification, has led to a general desire to improve the purity of rivers. Toxicological studies reveal hidden dangers from impure water; fishing and boating have become major recreations and residential accommodation has returned to river waterfronts. It is the 600-year record of attempting to control the river environment which is now under most scrutiny in the 'New Environmental Age'. Not just water pollution is involved; flood protection causes environmental damage (Purseglove, 1988) and, elsewhere in the world, irrigation does so too. As a result of enormous resource pressures, Man's attitude to the water cycle and to river basin management is now as critical as it was in prehistoric Mesopotamia.

1.5   THE LESSONS OF HISTORY AND THE CHALLENGES OF THE FUTURE

This chapter has analysed the historical record of Man's intervention in the land phase of the hydrological cycle in order to draw out fundamental cultural attitudes to river management under a very wide variety of circumstances. A central aim has been to reveal that aspect of cultural attitude which may be labelled rational: what we would now call the scientific approach. This element is essential if we are to know the value of knowledge as a guide to management. If river management is now to extend to the basin scale and is to take a broader role in global schemes of sustainable environmental intervention, what are the lessons of history? In summary, we have determined that:

(a) Social aspects of both coordination and control have been as important as, if not more important than, technical aspects (the Sumerian lesson).
(b) Distributional aspects of water management (e.g. early irrigation drainage and flood control) are capable of highly efficient development using relatively simple scientific foundations (the Roman lesson).
(c) Collection systems including flows into reservoirs but also flows of pollutants to streams are much more difficult to understand without a contribution from science. This contribution is only now becoming coherent.
(d) Laws which societies employ to control human use of river basins contain elements of statute and common law. The fundamental legal principles upon which a society bases its approach to water management will powerfully determine and constrain the environmental outcome.
(e) Scale issues are critical (the Indus lesson) because they control the distribution of information in the system, both technical and social. Whilst riparian rights are relatively simple to apply to a short, linear system of an English river they are much more problematic to extend to land remote from the river (and therefore to diffuse sources of pollution).
(f) Response to environmental change is a key aspect of river basin management. On the verge of an era of heavier intervention in resource systems it will pay to consider the social, legal, political and institutional aspects as carefully as the knowledge base provided by science. The humans need to be consulted as well as the river.

This, I submit, is a matter for Geography.

This book seeks to form a bridge between past and future at the river basin scale by taking lesson (c) above as central to other physical and social issues of the day as well as the challenge of rapid changes, likely in both physical and social environments. It therefore addresses the following themes:

(a) The essential need to consider the linkages inherent in the 'cascade' of water, sediment and pollutants from divisions of land to divisions of the river system when developing the resources of river basins.
(b) The requirement to match this kind of thinking to river basin outlines as management units and to carry out active management of key parts

or whole basins through interdisciplinary, interagency and international understanding.

(c) The consideration of the impact of today's decisions over longer times-cales, requiring an understanding of the time-dependency of the sensi-tivity of each aspect of the basin's environment. An immense problem under this heading is that we make our evaluations under conditions of the 'moving goalposts' of climate change.

(d) the role of modern science as a provider of information rather than a solver of problems and the degree to which democratic principles will 'allow out' the information so that planning decisions may be supported and lived with by the majority, even where they are sub-optimal.

These challenges are perhaps best laid bare by a river system such as the Nile (Section 5.3) and the Ganges (Section 5.5); here the scale of the basins and the political kaleidoscope of their national boundaries mean that the com-petition to develop simultaneously both land and water resources leads to great tensions. However, these are no less acute (and may become worse as a result of climate change) in the smaller basins and highly developed nations of, for example, the UK and New Zealand. In such nations the current emphasis is on restoration and pollution control but the sustained effort needed to educate and regulate land users towards new objectives is no less arduous than that needed to bring Egypt and Ethiopia to a conference table!

Chapter 2

Natural river basins
Transfer systems

In this chapter the aim is to set down those patterns and processes which lead us to the view of the drainage basin as a *systematic physical whole*. It is the key concept in the wider education of politicians, planners and the public that river systems are an *interconnected transport system*, albeit often working invisibly (as in the transfer of dissolved salts) or over extremely long timescales (as in the evolution of floodplains). Professional perceptions are not without fault in their view of the basin system, particularly in terms of the timescales over which it comes to steady states and can therefore be managed by relatively simple, sustainable controls. Although remote sensing and interactive, real-time, mathematical modelling can now allow reactive as well as proactive control, the latter, as in river channel 'training' to improve land drainage, is still the least-cost solution in many cases to our exploitation of rivers or to protect ourselves from their extremes. There are, understandably, new professional viewpoints which see control of any kind as undesirable and river basin systems have become a focus for a variety of conservation approaches.

In formalising the importance of timescales in perceptions of the river basin system Hickin (1983) has demarcated the following groups of research interests in the field of river sediment dynamics:

Geologists	1,000,000 years
Geomorphologists	100–100,000 years
Engineers	100 years

Newson (1986) and Newson and Leeks (1987) take this a stage further and Figure 2.1 illustrates a corollary of the timescale criterion for river professionals – in this case a differentiation based upon the preferred spatial scale of research. These divergences lead to considerable problems of mutual understanding at conferences or, more expensively, in the design and carrying out of river development or control programmes. We return to this theme, therefore, in treating the importance of river basin management institutions in Chapter 7.

It is not surprising that much of the more holistic thinking about the

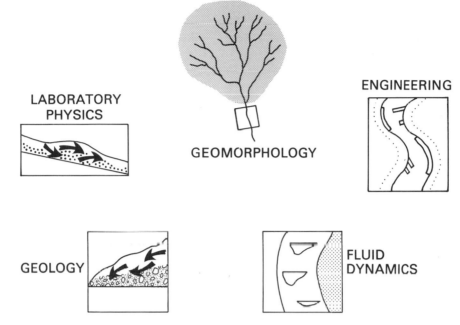

Figure 2.1 The scales of investigation adopted by river research specialisms

practical management of rivers has come from geomorphologists. There is no superiority in the geomorphologist's viewpoint, we merely say that a conjunction of long-term and large-space scales has as many advantages for managing complex systems realistically and sustainably as it has disadvantages for conducting scientific experiments under controlled conditions.

In the last analysis, however, a river basin which is *physically destabilised*, through natural or man made perturbation of its morphological and sediment transfer elements, is extremely difficult to stabilise through management intervention; the current scientific and political consensus over the desirability of longer-term aims tends, therefore, to play into the geomorphologist's hands. There is, therefore, a bias in this chapter to the sediment transfer system, although solutes are extremely important, not only for their contribution to geomorphological evolution but also as pollutants and nutrients. The transfer system for water itself and solutes is dealt with mainly in Chapter 3 where a hydrology bias is appropriate.

2.1 FLOW OF WATER AND TRANSPORT OF SEDIMENT

Whilst hydrologists now have a variety of predictive models for runoff at the catchment scale, prediction of flows for river basin management is more difficult, requiring a general reduction of sophistication (or the incorporation of more sophisticated statistical components) as areal scales increase. If the basin manager then requires in addition to a successful prediction of river flow a precise estimate of the sediment transport, we simply do not have the robust techniques of the hydrologist.

Why should runoff prediction prove relatively easy but sediment transport more difficult? To answer this, one must attempt to unravel the complex interrelationships between the hydraulics of streamflow and the ability of flow to power transport. The most important aspect of sediment transport at the river basin scale is its supply from source areas, including headwater catchments, and the beds and banks of the channel network.

The concept of separated supply and transport components of the basin sediment system has only recently been found to be analytically and practically helpful, particularly in the formulation of geographical zonations of river basins. The American geologist W. M. Davis (1899) proposed a threefold subdivision of river basins into 'youth' (headwaters), 'maturity' and 'old age' (downstream reaches) – a classification helpful for the very long timescales over which the Davisian cycle of landform development was hypothesised to occur. However, for the last thirty years geomorphologists have become orientated towards active processes and the energy levels implied by terms such as 'youth' are misleading.

Schumm (1977) has proposed the subdivision of *supply*, *transfer* and *deposition* zones which is much more in tune with contemporary knowledge of processes (see Figure vi). Further, classification schemes for river morphology within the transfer zone, also by Schumm (1963; see Table 2.1), emphasise the nature of the sediment load being transferred in the reach.

2.1.1   Elementary hydraulics and sediment transport

In the headwater, sediment-supply zone of a river basin, particularly where this is mountainous, the coupling between slopes and channels controls the amount and timing of sediment removed from the system. Largely governed by natural conditions (but often exacerbated by development), slope transport of sediments occurs by the slow, progressive production of weathered rock and its gravitational movement, progressive or sudden, towards the nearest stream channel.

In the polarised case of a supply-zone river valley, slope inputs are almost direct to river channels: there is not the extensive floodplain and valley floor which intervenes to store sediments in the transfer zone. Clearly, therefore, there can be mismatches in time between the rate of slope-derived sediment supply and the rate of removal by the channel at its foot. Obviously, extreme events such as rare floods provide energy to both slope and channel environments but, even within the spectrum of extreme floods, there are

Table 2.1 Classification of alluvial channels

Mode of sediment transport	Channel sediment (M) %	Proportion of total load		Channel stability		
		Suspended load %	Bedload %	Stable (graded stream)	Depositing (excess load)	Eroding (deficiency of load)
Suspended load	3C–100	85–100	0–15	Stable suspended load channel. Width–depth ratio <7; sinuosity >2.1; gradient relatively gentle.	Depositing suspended load channel. Major deposition of banks cause narrowing of channel; streambed deposition minor.	Eroding suspended load channel. Streambed erosion predominant; channel widening minor.
Mixed load	8–30	65–85	15–35	Stable mixed-load channel. Width–depth ratio >7 and <25; sinuosity <2.1 and >1.5; gradient moderate.	Depositing mixed-load channel. Initial major deposition on banks followed by streambed deposition.	Eroding mixed-load channel. Initial streambed erosion followed by channel widening.
Bedload	0–8	30–65	35–70	Stable bedload channel. Width–depth ratio >25; sinuosity <1.5; gradient relatively steep.	Depositing bedload channel. Streambed deposition and island formation.	Eroding bedload channel. Little streambed erosion; channel widening predominant.

Source: Schumm (1963)

also populations of *effectivenes*. Newson (1980) divides 'slope floods' from 'channel floods' on the basis of rainfall intensity and duration; later (Newson, 1989) he includes floods which are effective in both environments.

If we consider the stream channel transport process, we need to demarcate the different calibre or size of the grains supplied to the channel. Grain size determines, within broad limits, the process of transport within the flow. Figure 2.2 illustrates the components of *bedload* and *suspended load*, with an intermediate status of bouncing or saltating transport. This is a gross generalisation, particularly in the case of the saltation process, where the time effects of turbulent water flow are simply not known, other than at the statistical level or in experimental flume conditions. It is occasionally assumed that the suspended load, because of its fine grain size under most natural conditions, equates to the 'wash load' and derives from the surface washing of weathered material into the channel, e.g. from soil erosion. However, all forms of sediment transported in channels may derive from either the bed material of the channel itself or from bank erosion and inwash from slopes (or, in extreme events, from landslides or ephemeral gullies).

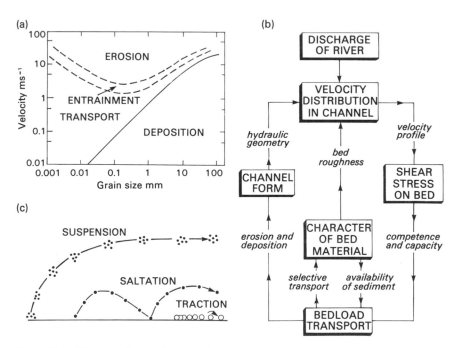

Figure 2.2 River sediment transport:
　　　　(a) The curves of Hjulstrom (1935)
　　　　(b) Feedback diagram between river flow, bed material transport and channel form (Ashworth and Ferguson, 1986)
　　　　(c) The major sediment transport processes in cartoon

From whatever source, how are grains transported by river flows? Whilst it is axiomatic that water flows downhill, the distribution of the energy so gained and its loss in overcoming friction, both internal and external, and in achieving work by transporting sediment are not yet fully described. Under most conditions of sediment transport during which there is an effective development of channel form, river flow will be turbulent. Turbulent flow is characterised by chaotic patterns of currents and vortices which, however, can be simplified within a treatment of the simple properties of flow; the most important of the properties for effective sediment transport is streamflow velocity and its variability with depth, across the channel and in distinct currents within the flow.

'Velocity' (with little further specification) has been used as the predictive variable for many basin approaches to understanding — and thereby predicting — sediment transport. The best-known pictorial representation is that of IIjulstrom (1935), shown in Figure 2.2; these have educational value in that they:

(a) Differentiate conditions leading to entrainment by erosion of the particle, transport of the particle and deposition.
(b) Emphasise the importance of inter-particle relationships in the finer grain sizes where cohesion leads to a steep rise in the necessary velocity for erosion.

The curves do not, however:

(u) Extend sufficiently towards the coarser grain sizes which are important in sediment supply zones and during floods.
(b) Reveal the existence of inter-particle effects within coarser grades of sediment and in sediment mixes across the whole range of bed and bank materials and those delivered from slopes.

Alongside the effects of the normal mix of sediments available for transport by a known streamflow velocity we have also the quandary as to the location, within the turbulent mass of water, of that energy: average velocities may be plotted during a period of measurement with a current meter but these simple patterns demonstrate only the energy loss by friction at the channel boundaries and these patterns, too, are complex, as the measurements in mountain streams illustrate.

Much of the morphological development of river channels occurs as a result of the *sinuous planform* and uneven longitudinal profile of natural channels; in this connection, therefore, it is important to research:

(a) The existence, pattern and strength of *secondary currents* or flow cells which distribute the primary, downslope, energy of the flow into effective pathways.
(b) The distribution of velocity throughout a reach, as between high and

low points ('*riffles*' and '*pools*' in the alluvial reaches) and between high and low flows.

These are major items which remain on the research agenda of those interested in refining our knowledge of fluvial systems. However, there is a clear ongoing need for predicting sediment transport rates, particularly of the coarser elements of bed material which are transported as bedload (by rolling or saltation), because this form of transport can produce the channel instability which threatens erosion of structures and flooding of property.

Bedload formulae (equations) have been developed and used for engineering applications for over a century.

They are of four main types:

(a) Those based on calculation of the shear stress produced by the flow on this stream bed.
(b) Those using stream discharge as an integrating prediction.
(c) Statistical/probabilistic approaches to the movement of grains.
(d) Stream power calculations − a generalised energy approach.

As a review by Gomez and Church (1989) illustrates, many transport formulae are vindicated by the use of data gathered in flume experiments or from field situations of unspecified relevance to the assumptions of the method in question. As the authors suggest,

> It remains a matter of some concern that there appears to be more bed load formulae than there are reliable data sets by which to test them. In consequence, no one formula, nor even a small group of formulae, has either been universally accepted or recognised as being especially appropriate for practical application.
>
> (Gomez and Church, 1989, p. 1161)

Much scientific effort, therefore, has gone into both the comparative testing of the available formulae on standardised data and the collection of large data sets from the field using innovative samplers (e.g. Helley and Smith, 1971 and Figure 2.10b).

Gomez and Church conclude that for general river applications, where detailed hydraulic knowledge is normally impossible to gain, the stream power approach of the formula derived by Bagnold (1977) − using the analogy of an engine working at varying degrees of efficiency − is the most accurate, despite the fact that it lacks physical vigour and that actual operating efficiencies (commonly less than 10 per cent) are hard to predict.

2.1.2 Slopes, channel, storage zones

Because, in many regions of the world and under relatively frequent flood conditions, the sediment transport system can be shown to be *supply limited* (i.e. stream power to transport is not fully utilised), it becomes of critical importance to river basin management to understand the supply processes themselves.

Sediment supply occurs, in the Schumm model, mainly in the headwater zone where slopes and channels impinge closely and where gravitational energy is high and weathering processes active. This emphasises that there are at least two sources of sediment supply which may limit (or not) the transport of sediment out of the basin:

(a) Direct inputs from the slope weathering/transport system (which include man-made additional losses such as cultivation-induced soil erosion – see Chapter 6).
(b) Areas (and volumes) of stored sediments resulting from past phases of erosion under different climatic conditions or from an extreme flood in the recent past. The widespread Quaternary glaciations have meant that storage legacies are a common complication to the prediction of overall fluvial processes throughout large areas of the world.

At the statistical level of analysis there is clearly good adjustment, over long timescales, between sediment transport and sediment supply. Simplistically any shortfall of supply is made up by increased erosion of bed and bank materials, leading to either incision of the transporting channel or its migration across the valley floor; the latter outcome produces the probability of undercutting an adjacent slope. The incision or migration of the channel therefore leads to conditions favouring supply. These links are often easiest to appreciate over the long term when, as Playfair wrote,

> Every river appears to consist of a main trunk, fed from a variety of branches, each running in a valley proportioned to its size, and all of them together forming a system of vallies, communicating with one another, and having such a nice adjustment of their declivities, that none of them join the principal valley, either on too high or too low a level; a circumstance which would be infinitely improbable, if each of these vallies were not the work of the stream that flows in it.
>
> (Playfair, 1802, p. 102)

or during individual flood events when landslides, debris flows and other slope developments are shown to feed a wide range of sediment sizes into a channel system swollen by floodwaters and capable of transporting the resulting load considerable distances downstream.

This impression of perfect adjustment is at least partially illusory. Clearly, measurements of sediment transport loads in the field have shown that stream power, whilst it is a good indicator, is seldom fully utilised in transport and that the very existence of *storage zones* of fluvial material in the river basin indicates that the transport system is not a smooth one. As

Ferguson (1981) puts it:

> Rivers exist to carry water to the sea and they develop channels able to contain their normal flow. The form of the river channel affects the flow of water in it and, through erosion and deposition, the flow modifies the form. The channel (and if it migrates, the whole valley floor) acts as a jerky conveyor belt for alluvium moving intermittently seawards.
>
> (Ferguson, 1981, p. 90)

Nevertheless, at the scales of measurement used in a morphometric approach to river basins (i.e. form indices largely from topographic maps), the 'nice adjustment' is demonstrated by close correlations, both positive and negative, which allowed Melton (1957) to set up the balanced system, inferring process adjustments from the interrelationships of forms such as channel slope and valley-side slope. There is a further, utilitarian, justification for such a view in the high levels of predictability of flow, phenomena such as flood peaks and low flows from morphometric, cover and climatic variables measured from basin maps (see for example NERC, 1975; Institute of Hydrology, 1980).

2.1.3   Timescales of river basin development in nature

The introduction to this chapter has outlined the differences of spatial and temporal scales in the perceptions and research agendas of the professionals involved in river basin management. These differences are critical to the concept of equilibrium states in the physical development of basins via the sediment transport system. Schumm and Lichty (1965) have tabulated (Table 2.2) the pattern of status changes between variables controlling (independent) or controlled by (dependent) river basin evolution.

In a more practical form, Knighton (1984) has illustrated the time and space scales over which various features of the river basin landscape may be said to evolve (and therefore attain some sort of equilibrium or steady-state condition). Not only are conditions and concepts of equilibrium essential to successful, sustainable management techniques in natural systems but they, too, change with different timescales. Once again Schumm (1977) comes to the rescue by expressing this diagrammatically; Figure 2.3 combines the Knighton and Schumm approaches.

Traditionally geomorphologists, locked into the cyclic thinking of W. M. Davis, have considered the concept of *grade* as being appropriate to the time span over which humans study river systems, implying that 'nice adjustment' of Playfair. Engineers, too, have employed a steady-state concept in their design of new river channels (e.g. for irrigation) or their 'training' of eroding or depositing, i.e. unstable, channels. For nearly twenty years now, however, geomorphologists have moved away from

Table 2.2 The timescale dependency of control – and controlled – variables in river basin evolution

River variables	Timescales		
	Geologic	*Modern*	*Present*
1 Time	Independent	Not relevant	Not relevant
2 Geology (lithology and structure)	Independent	Independent	Independent
3 Climate	Independent	Independent	Independent
4 Vegetation (type and density)	Dependent	Independent	Independent
5 Relief	Dependent	Independent	Independent
6 Paleohydrology (long-term discharge of water and sediment)	Dependent	Independent	Independent
7 Valley dimension (width, depth and slope)	Dependent	Independent	Independent
8 Mean discharge of water and sediment	Indeterminate	Independent	Independent
9 Channel morphology (width, depth, slope, shape, and pattern	Indeterminate	Dependent	Independent
10 Observed discharge of water and sediment	Indeterminate	Indeterminate	Dependent
11 Observed flow characteristics (depth, velocity, turbulence, etc.)	Indeterminate	Indeterminate	Dependent

Source: Schumm and Lichty (1965)

notions of stability in river systems to those of *metastability*, or periods of quasi-stability interrupted by episodes of rapid change which appear to managers as challenging demonstrations of instability. The new approach is best summarised in the term *thresholds*.

Threshold phenomena are widespread in science (Newson, in press), particularly in materials where failure phenomena (rapid change between two stable states) abound. The importance of threshold concepts to river geomorphology is that they permit a 'middle road' between two previously dominant philosophies of landscape development   those dominated by catastrophes and, in contrast, by (slow) progressive processes. There are also practical reasons for the recent popularity of threshold phenomena; in their recent move towards process investigations, geomorphologists have inevitably worked in field situations where the engineering approach through regime designs for channels has failed (see Section 2.2.2).

What perturbations to steady state, elucidated by field studies, have become worthy of incorporation within the threshold concept? The major

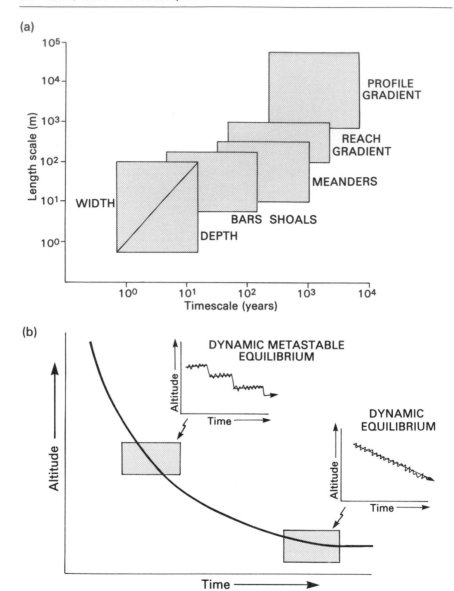

Figure 2.3 Timescales of river system sediment transport and morphological
response:
   (a) The characteristic length and timescales of major river forms
   (after Knighton, 1984)
   (b) Two major forms of equilibria adopted by river systems during
   the geological cycle (Schumm, 1977)

cases are as follows:

(a) River basins affected by artificial developments such as river regulation (Petts, 1984) or urbanisation (Roberts, 1989).
(b) Semi-arid river basins where sediment supply is little constrained by soil and vegetation cover and where the alternation of flood and drought extremes is commonplace. Basins affected by fire are also included (see Graf, 1985).
(c) River basins affected by 'rare, great' floods have been said to exhibit a range of threshold phenomena.
(d) Model-scale experimental river basins in which input conditions are held steady (by the operation of artificial rainfall simulators) but in which sediment output occurs as a series of discrete episodes – much of Schumm's early work was on such a model system.

The important basic points about threshold behaviour in river basin sediment systems by geomorphologists are that it changes our philosophy of timescales of change (see Figure 2.3) and that an important type of threshold is intrinsic to river systems and therefore operates without the need for a large external change such as climate change or an extreme flood. The geomorphic threshold therefore develops by the slow, progressive processes of weathering on slopes or storage of sediments on valley floors to the point where the morphology of the feature in question makes it inherently unstable even under the 'normal' range of conditions. The threshold is crossed when the weathered material on the slope fails, e.g. as a rotational slump, or the valley floor steepens to the point where gullying develops.

Slope angle has been used as a successful geomorphological predictor of intrinsic threshold behaviour in semi-arid terrains, notably in the west of the United States. Graf (1985) illustrates that the instability apparent to managers of the Colorado River basin derives from the superimposition of intrinsic thresholds, occasionally crossed by gullying in the headwaters, compounded by extrinsic thresholds imposed by climatic variability and traditional engineering interventions such as dam construction and floodplain development.

Clearly Ferguson's 'jerky conveyor belt' is therefore a valuable perception of the river basin sediment transport system. Whilst thresholds should be strictly defined and should not be applied to patterns and processes which are merely threshold-like, the educational value to river basin management systems is clear. Short-term management devices which merely 'set up' future threshold behaviour are the equivalent of sweeping dust under the carpet. Furthermore, surveys to investigate signs of symptoms of instability indicative of the state of a river basin, or river reach, are relatively easy to operationalise before inappropriate regime-based designs are employed by engineers (Lewin et al., 1988). When engineers ask, 'what is the alternative design procedure?', one is forced to admit that here the unpalatable choice may be between doing very little (or using low-cost, 'soft' engineering), implying a conservation philosophy and a retreat from the river, and placing emphasis on very indirect forms of river engineering, e.g. erosion control on sensitive slopes and valley floors.

We should not escape from this extremely broad approach to river sediment systems without a view of the entire system. The workings of the 'conveyor belt' are perhaps best demonstrated by diagrammatic and tabular illustrations of where sediments are stored in the system and their average residence time in those stores before 'moving on' by rejoining the channel system. Once in the channel, depending on its length, sediment size is extremely important in determining residence time. In short rivers the suspended load may well reach the estuary on one flood but coarser sediments may become incorporated in the floodplain at several sites downstream. Sediments from process legacies (such as glaciation) may also leave storage to the channel and therefore complicate the assessment of contemporary sediment budgets (see Section 2.4).

2.2   CHANNEL MORPHOLOGY

At every site on a river system which is transporting water and sediment the channel's morphology is adjusted, or is in the process of adjusting, to these downstream fluxes. Characteristic *planform* channel morphologies typify transport systems for different calibres of sediment (see Figure 2.4); relationships between planforms and flow regimes are known to exist but are poorly quantified because of the influence of sediments and of other factors to which we may pay only brief attention.

It is, for example, clear that channel erosion and deposition to bring about adjustment of form to flow cannot occur if the bounding materials are too resistant. Therefore bedrock or glacially derived deposits may confine the channel to a non-equilibrium pattern. The content of silt and clay in channel boundary materials is also effective in determining the width/depth allocation in an individual cross-section (see Schumm, 1977, Ch. 5). Of perhaps greater importance to modern forms of management orientated towards conservation is the importance of bank vegetation (in-channel vegetation also influences flow capacity).

Whereas the stability and roughness of inert materials in the channel is taken as invariable, except by massive and costly works, that attributable to vegetation has traditionally been considered manageable, and a large part of river management work is to that end.

However, there is a dual attitude to the value of vegetation in rivers. On the one hand, its role in preventing scour and protecting bed and banks is recognised, both through the binding action of roots and through the streamlining of flexible leaves and stems. The UK Hydraulics Research

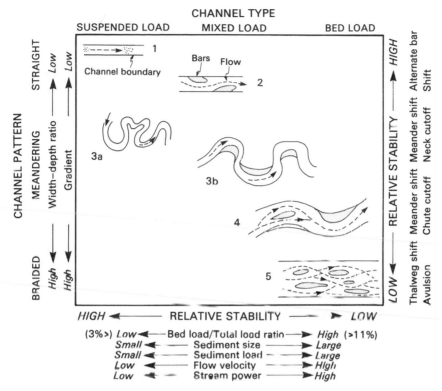

Figure 2.4 A classification of river channel planforms based upon sediment load, cross-section and stability (Schumm, 1985)

Station (Charlton *et al.*, 1978) have established, for example, that unvegetated and short grass channels are, on average, 30 per cent wider than their tree-lined counterparts. On the other hand, there are, in lowland rivers, known flood risks resulting from additional roughness of profuse 'weed growth', the reduction of channel capacity by the bulk of plants, the possibility of increased turbulence around trees in floods, the risk of sudden bank failure if a tree falls, and the possibility of log-jams or weed-jams at bridge points damming the flow.

The balance would appear to favour removing everything except short perennial grasses – and, sadly, miles of watercourses in lowland areas have been reduced to that. But, fortunately, many river managers are glad to retain and even develop varied river vegetation, for its beauty, its landscape value and for the wildlife it harbours.

Traditional methods of river management frequently used the attributes of native plants to stabilise banks and deflect flows where needed. Routine, regular maintenance by hand labour ensured that plant cover did not degenerate. Thus, sallows and alders were planted on rivers, reedbeds along canal banks, and turf walls packed down as toe protection along dikes. However, traditional practices have, in many places, been forgotten or are seen as a 'luxury' under present financial and staffing arrangements. In the rush to capitalise (in more ways than one) on the products of the last fifty years of technology in machinery and materials, river managers have tended to forget the advantages of utilising vegetation to stabilise river sections.

2.2.1 Stable/unstable channels and channel change

It is the river engineer's job to treat problems of river instability at a specific site, yet it is important to have a synoptic view of the river from source to mouth, as a continuous transport system subdivisible, as shown above, only by sediment size and availability which, in turn, control morphology. Nevertheless, it has been traditionally thought in Britain that 'upstream' controls on river form had little influence on what happened in a given reach: average flows of both water and sediment have been considered unvarying in the long term. Consequently the engineer has used empirical data, often from such non-dynamic environments as canals, to guide him on the selection of the basic channel dimensions of width and depth and the stream's velocity. The anticipated success of such channel designs can be judged from the terms 'regime' and 'grade' which are used to describe a 'trained' river in perfect equilibrium with its dominant flow, usually taken to be the annual flood. However, rivers respond over different timescales to different influences. Over geological timescales rivers can clearly cut down to sea level. Davis deserves credit for working out this long timescale, but it coloured much of his argument and eventual classification. At the timescale over which riparian owners these days expect the river to be stabilised, it is the lateral migration of the channel and not downcutting which is of most concern.

Furthermore, it is lateral migration which is best recorded as a pattern, if not a process, by geomorphologists. The sinuosity of river planforms has always excited the interest of a number of sciences but key factors in our present knowledge based on channel patterns have been the ability to make measurements of bank erosion relatively simply and our access to relatively long periods of data from old plans, maps and aerial photography (see compilations by Gregory, 1977 and Hooke and Kain, 1982; also Figure 2.5).

As a result of this concentration in fact we have tended to underestimate the contemporary importance, at least locally, of *vertical* morphological development. This imbalance is, however, being corrected (Schumm *et al.*, 1984; Lewin *et al.*, 1988).

The tendency of rivers to follow curved rather than straight courses is another systematic problem of river engineering. The Davis classification, by linking meanders to the 'mature' or 'old age' river, has tended to give

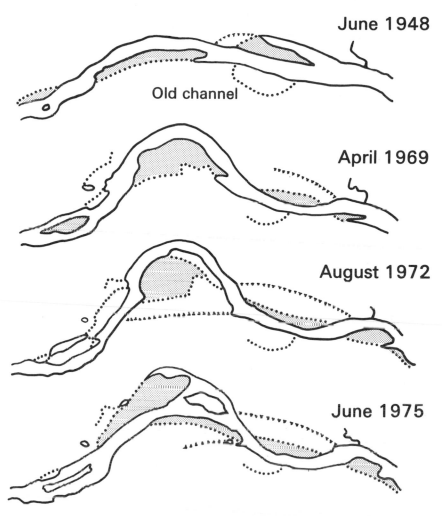

June 1948

Old channel

April 1969

August 1972

June 1975

Figure 2.5 Channel planform change identified from historic maps and aerial photographs: River Severn, Maesmawr, mid-Wales (Thorne and Lewin, 1982)

the impression that a river wanders aimlessly without energy for erosion. This is a fallacy, since meanders develop in floods, when the river has maximum available energy. Energy not used to overcome bed and bank friction is far from equally distributed across a river. Instead, turbulence breaks up into a number of cells, producing currents which act laterally with as much force as the main thread of downstream flow. These secondary flows are generated in any stream and with a regularity which relates to the stream's width, i.e. to the space available for the cells to develop.

In streams where banks are compact and unerodable, secondary flows create midstream shoals, or riffles, and pools at fairly regular intervals; where the banks are erodable, riffles and pools still occur, but the secondary cells produce a sinuous river planform by lateral erosion and deposition. Cut-banks occur opposite shoals and together they create the familiar pattern of the meandering river. Given further development, rivers may also exhibit a form in which both banks are cut and the shoals are mainly in midstream; this is the braided river typical of streams in recently glaciated areas.

This natural tendency to sinuosity, and the tendency for meanders and other less regular river bends to migrate by erosion and deposition, means that the equilibrium regime approach which is mostly indexed from data on straight reaches is seldom successful in coping with sinuosity. Much expense and environmental degradation is involved in forcing a river to flow where it is put when the designed planform is inappropriate to the reach's position within the system. Clearly, however, river engineers would willingly use a new empirical method of predicting river planform pattern, if one existed. The most hopeful method is that based upon the secondary flow pattern itself, because it describes the pattern with which energy is expended within the channel. Current meters now exist which can measure cross currents such as these; even simple photography will identify the locus of maximum stress on the banks and reveal just where any necessary structural or vegetative bank protection can be positioned.

A key question in interpreting our knowledge of river planform changes in relation to management is whether they represent 'natural' equilibrium conditions, in which case intervention can be costly and does not best utilise natural forces, or an instability of a short-term but dangerous nature in which society must take a 'curative' role. Riparian cultures have tended to intervene without judging the degree of instability displayed by rivers, deploying a range of *river training* techniques. Stability is clearly culturally defined but, since the rise of environmental values in management of terrestrial systems, research has sought 'natural' definitions of stability.

In river systems there is still argument over the form of equilibrium adopted by rivers (see Section 2.1). Formerly Schumm's concept of threshold change was widely applied to river planforms, especially to the segregation of meandering and braided forms on the basis of channel slope and discharge, which was originally proposed by Leopold and Wolman (1957) and widely used as an indication as to 'what the planform should be' in a given reach. However, the boundary line has been regarded as a threshold condition implying costly instability in planforms. This view is widely challenged at present (Carson, 1984; Ferguson, 1987), with the result that managers will need new guidance as to the natural stability or instability of channels.

There are form guides to river instability (Lewin et al., 1988) but there are also good grounds for assuming that man-made changes to flow and sediment systems evoke morphological change which may occur over relatively short timescales.

Flow changes can be expected following changes in land use, land management (e.g. drainage) and the manipulation of river flows by the water industry (e.g. abstraction for water supply). The developments occurring in upland areas today – afforestation, timber harvesting, and farm improvements – mean that changes in sediment supply can also be expected. Such changes are already being monitored in a few catchments and give some guide to the scale of change to be expected in others (Chapter 3). However, the complexity of interrelated factors suggests that accurate predictive models for a particular system cannot yet be confidently extrapolated from data derived elsewhere. Erosion rates and stream loads need to be monitored as well as water flows so that in river management and project planning the system's degree of metastability can be taken into account.

2.2.2   Hydraulic geometry, regime and channel design

Whilst the trajectory of much current geomorphological research favours a generally metastable interpretation of channel form developments, it is essential to review briefly the equilibrium (steady-state) approaches which continue to guide management of the world's river channels.

Hydraulic geometry and *regime* approaches represent, respectively, the geomorphological and engineering approaches to the adaptation of channel width, depth and velocity of flow to water discharge. The former is empirical, involving data collection foremost; the latter is theoretical and therefore more flexible and capable of extension to include channel slope, roughness, and sediment load. Both assume that in the longer term (timescales are not specified) there is an adjustment of channel dimensions to flow which is predictable. Thus regime theory is ideal for the construction of new conveyance channels (needed for flood relief or irrigation) and was largely 'proved' in practice with low-gradient canals lined by cohesive materials.

Because hydraulic geometry research represents an important phase in the quantification of fluvial geomorphology there are many compilations. After its widespread popularisation in the formative text of Leopold *et al.* (1964) numerous studies were carried out, either of changes at-a station with varying flows or downstream as flow builds up.

Park (1977) compiled the first international review of the results (Figure 2.6). This indicated little consistency in the exponents (rate of change) reported for width, depth and velocity changes with discharge at-a-station or downstream; the downstream problem appeared to be inconsistent choice of an indicative discharge for the basin channel network. Park concluded that alternatives to simple linear relationships should be explored or

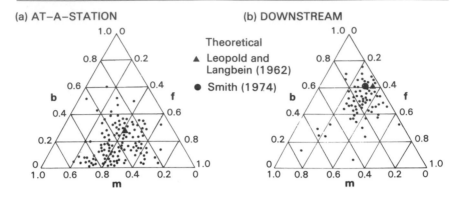

Figure 2.6 Summary diagrams of major findings of hydraulic geometry in terms of triaxial plots of the exponents in equations linking river width, depth and velocity to discharge (respectively **b**, **m**, **f**):
(a) At-a-station
(b) Downstream
(from Park, 1977)

the conclusion drawn that 'maladjustment' could not be proven for flow transmission.

Regime channel design begins with a clear problem – that of producing an active channel which may well scour or fill temporarily but which, during its design lifetime, will transfer its charge of water and sediment without profound morphological change. The design lifetime of an engineered channel varies but may be up to a century and it should be emphasised that the nature of river engineering schemes presents opportunities to reinforce or maintain regime channels as they adjust; geomorphologists argue, therefore, that the steady-state assumption of such designs is seldom fairly stated or tested. The regime approach selects a stable width and depth and, therefore, a velocity (together making up water discharge); the hydraulic resistance, slope and sediment transport properties are also chosen from deterministic equations (Table 2.3).

Slope is rarely adjustable in channel design since bridges, sewer outfalls and other structures cannot (except in new irrigation schemes) be adjusted a posteriori to channel slope. Here regime is at its most vulnerable and there is abundant evidence that straight channel planforms built in good faith to provide flood protection are liable to adjust to a meandering or even to a braided pattern without considerable structural protection (Figure 2.7).

Recognising this interdependence of form and process in fluvial systems, streams in North America have been experimentally designed to form and maintain riffles, pools and meanders where desired (principally by fisheries interests). No structures were used; control of bank slopes and variation in channel cross-sections resulted in the emergence of point bars and pools

Table 2.3 Regime approaches to stable channels, geomorphological
approaches to changing channels

(a) Regime equations for engineering design

Equations for straight sand-bed channels *Blench (1952)*	*Equations for straight gravel-bed channels* *Kellerhals (1967)*

$w = (F_b/F_s)^{0.5} \, Q^{0.5}$

$d = (F_s/F_b)^{1/3} \, Q^{1/3}$

$s = \dfrac{F_b^{5/6} \, F_s^{1/12} \, v^{1/4}}{3.63gQ^{1/6}(1 + C_b/2330)}$

$F_b = 0.58D_{50}^{0.5} \, (1 + 0.012C_b)$

$F_s = 0.009$ (sandy loam) to
    0.028 (clay)

v = velocity of flow
R = hydraulic radius (cross-sectional
    area/wetted perimeter)
C_b = bankfull cross-sectional area
Q = discharge
w = channel width
g = gravitational acceleration
s = slope of water surface
τ_{0c} = critical shear stress for sediment
    transport
ρ_w = density of water
d = depth of flow

(F_b and F_s are Blench's bed and side
factors)

$w = 3.26 \, Q^{0.5}$

$\dfrac{v}{\sqrt{(gRs)}} = 6.5 \left(\dfrac{d}{D_{90}}\right)^{1/4}$

$\tau_{0c} = \rho_w gRs = 15.79 D_{90}^{0.8}$

$d = 0.1830 Q^{0.4} \, D_{90}^{-0.12}$

$v = 1.68 Q^{0.1} \, D_{90}^{0.12}$

$s = 0.086 Q^{0.4} \, D_{90}^{0.92}$

D_{50} are sediment sizes at which
D_{90} 50%/90% are coarser

(b) Qualitative models of channel metamorphosis, illustrating the direction of
morphological response to particular combinations of changing discharge and
sediment yield (after Schumm, 1969)

(a) Increase in discharge alone
    $Q^+ \quad w^+ d^+ F^+ L^+ s^-$

Decrease in discharge alone
    $Q^- \quad w^- d^- F^- L^- s^+$

(b) Increase in bed material
    discharge
    $G_b \quad w^+ d^- F^+ L^+ s^+ P^-$

Decrease in bed material
    discharge
    $G_b \quad w^- d^+ F^- L^+ s^- P^+$

(c) Discharge and bed material load increase together; e.g. during urban
    construction, or early stages of afforestation
    $Q^+ G_b \quad w^+ d^= F^+ L^+ s^= P^-$

(d) Discharge and bed material load decrease together; e.g. downstream from a
    reservoir
    $Q^- G_b \quad w^- d^= F^= L^- s^= P^+$

(e) Discharge increases as bed material load decreases; e.g. increasing humidity
    in an initially sub-humid zone
    $Q^+ G_b \quad w^= d^+ F^- L^= s^- P^+$

(f) Discharge decreases as bed material load increases; e.g. increased water use
    combined with land-use pressure
    $Q^- G_b \quad w^= d^- F^! L^- s^+ P^-$

Q = a suitable streamflow index; G_b = bedload transport expressed as a percentage
of total load); w = width; d = depth; F = width:depth ratio; L = meander wavelength;
s = channel gradient; P = sinuosity

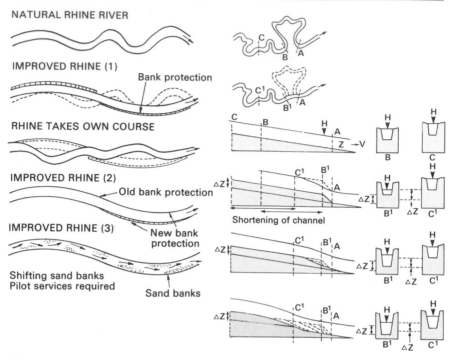

Figure 2.7 Engineering problems of meandering channels:
(a) The response of the Rhine to 'training'
(b) Reaction of a meandering channel to cut-off
(Ryckborst, 1980)

after the first above-normal flow, in the required locations, even in straight reaches. It is too much to expect that there could be similar research before all new channelisation projects in the UK. However, computer modelling has enabled more complex designs to be attempted and tested, with encouraging results in the field for 'natural' habitats and landscapes.

2.3   FLOODPLAINS

It is perhaps invidious to select only one piece of characteristic river morphology for separate treatment in this chapter. The floodplain, and a set of both narrower and wider valley features, are, however, of critical importance to a range of human river-use systems and to the conservation of nature (Newson, 1992 [a]). Therefore, it is essential to know how floodplains form, what are their natural regulatory functions and how our use of them involves costs as well as benefits.

A cross-section through a river valley in the transfer zone indicates several important features (Figure 2.8). The *valley floor* is the broadest

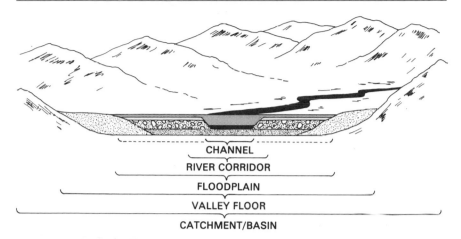

Figure 2.8 Zones of the valley floor within the basin

definition, encompassing all the landforms dominated by processes of deposition, including legacies such as those of glacial deposits. At the narrowest level is the *river corridor,* recently defined officially for conservation purposes in the UK and governed by interactions with channel flow and sediment regimes via the agency of flora and fauna dependent on the channel itself (we can also include human recreation).

The floodplain represents that area across which the river escapes during floods and therefore may be subdivided by the frequency of the flood concerned. Since the discharge which fills the channel (*bankfull discharge* of hydraulic geometry; *dominant discharge* of regime) occurs between once a year and every other year, floodplains appear captivatingly suitable for human settlement, agriculture and communications. There is considerable surprise and anxiety when, subsequently, damaging, costly and fatal inundations occur.

2.3.1 Floodplain formation and functions: floods, aquifers

Much of the damage caused by inundation of floodplains occurs by relatively concentrated flows down features resembling infilled remainders of river channels; these so-called palaeochannels also provide the best indication of floodplain formation processes. These processes are closely linked to lateral mobility of active river channels. As sinuous patterns evolve and migrate, valley sides become eroded; the active channel therefore creates a wider valley in which both flood waters and sediments can be stored. The storage of sediments is, as we observed in Section 2.1, a salient property of the transfer system and in confined river reaches there is clearly a throughput of both flow and load until spreading can occur. In regions which have experienced climatic fluctuations, particularly glaciation, valleys tend to have adjusted to the flow of ice or to substantial meltwater streams. The present channel is therefore often a 'misfit' in a wide valley. This makes the confinement which our occupation of floodplains usually implies (by flood- or erosion-protection engineering) even more intensive.

Sediments enter floodplain storage in two principal ways: by deposition in the channel (e.g. as bars and shoals) followed by abandonment, through migration, of that channel, or by out-of-bank flows. Clearly the former mechanism favours coarse clasts of sediment and the latter fine clasts; the result is that floodplains are frequently composite, with coarse material below, topped by fines. A further environment for the deposition of fines is the 'backwater', partially abandoned, channels of alluvial (silt/clay) reaches.

The coating of fines, often carrying organic and chemical nutrients, makes a fertile parent material for soil development – one of the original reasons for the 'hydraulic civilisations', notably that of the Nile, whose floodplain is seasonally inundated and 'fertilised' with silt.

There are two dimensions in which floodplain sediments act as aquifer deposits. First, the down-river flow of water is seldom restricted to the channel itself; large volumes can move 'invisibly', close to the open channel but having leaked into the coarser deposits of the floodplain, often following the palaeochannels described above. There are two notable demonstrations of this phenomenon: the successful abstraction of relatively large amounts of quite pure water for supply from floodplain deposits (including those of former river courses in the semi-arid zone) and the 'loss', through temporary leakage, of volumes of water released from regulating reservoirs (Chapter 6).

In the other dimension, at right-angles to the down-valley flow, all the runoff contributed from valley-side slopes enters the channel via the floodplain deposits. Therefore considerable modification of flow patterns occurs across the floodplain and we now know that this is accompanied by beneficial chemical changes such as nutrient stripping (Pinay and Decamps, 1988).

2.3.2 Floodplain modifications by Man

The typical river valley of the developed world is now a wide corridor of intensive land use and water use. Since settlements and infrastructures cannot continually move in response to flood or drought, floodplains have become regulated with more or less respect for natural dynamics according to culture, cost and severity of natural impacts. In a polarised case the following developments may have occurred:

(a) Channel straightened and erosion-proofed.
(b) Extensive flood protection structures.
(c) Extensive irrigation and/or drainage.

(d) Removal of natural vegetation and wetlands.

(e) Encroachment of buildings and structures towards the channel.

(f) Use of floodplain and channels/palaeochannels for waste disposal.

These all result from the exploitative nature of the development process and it is only in recent years that a more cautious approach has been necessitated by the competing objectives of conservation and recreation and by the high costs of the more heroic defence of our occupation of floodplains against natural processes.

There is now a developing field of 'fluvial hydro systems' centring on the natural relationship between the flow and sediment transfer functions of the active channel in terms of interrelationships with floodplain processes. French geomorphologists and biologists have championed this development (see Amoros *et al.*, 1987 and Figure 2.9) and are supporting it with research

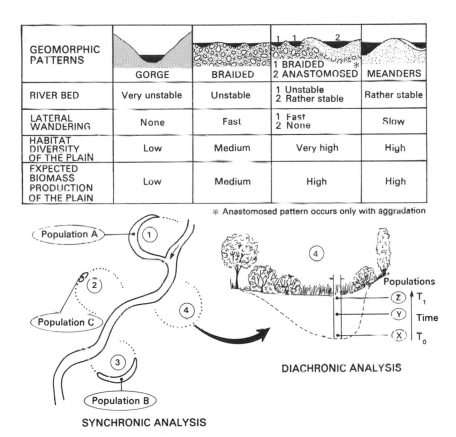

GEOMORPHIC PATTERNS	GORGE	BRAIDED	1 BRAIDED * 2 ANASTOMOSED	MEANDERS
RIVER BED	Very unstable	Unstable	1 Unstable 2 Rather stable	Rather stable
LATERAL WANDERING	None	Fast	1 Fast 2 None	Slow
HABITAT DIVERSITY OF THE PLAIN	Low	Medium	Very high	High
EXPECTED BIOMASS PRODUCTION OF THE PLAIN	Low	Medium	High	High

* Anastomosed pattern occurs only with aggradation

DIACHRONIC ANALYSIS

SYNCHRONIC ANALYSIS

Figure 2.9 The importance of 'wild' river channel migration for the creation of a variety of habitats in space and through time (Amoros *et al.*, 1987)

into the timescales of stability necessary for valley floors to carry out their natural functions of wildlife corridors, water storage and filtration. In Figure 2.9 the biological populations A, B and C are sequentially incorporated in the stream ecosystem, as are those at depths X, Y and Z, providing natural stream migration rates are permitted. Biota have high survival rates in fluvial storage zones.

In the USA there is also a trend towards the zoning of floodplains so as to permit a graded land use with less vulnerable uses adjacent to the channel and more vulnerable uses at a 'safe' distance. In the UK new research

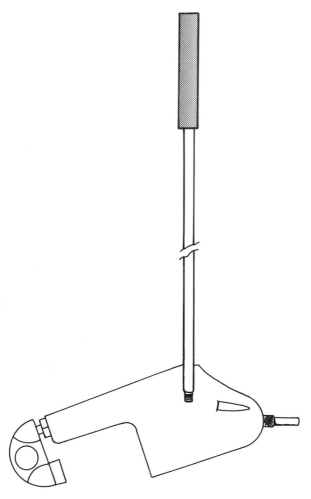

Figure 2.10a Sampling equipment for river sediment loads: the 'USDH' suspended load sampler (water intake to right; sampler contains US milk bottle when in use)

points to the desirability of considerable floodplain 'retirement' to allow nutrient-stripping from the effluent of productive agriculture on valley sides and interfluves. There is also a considerable interest in the natural use of floodplains to store flood waters, a use to which farmers have apparently become adjusted as in the case of Lincoln.

2.4 BASIN SEDIMENT SYSTEMS

It is perhaps surprising that even in those nations which face severe river basin management problems as a result of soil erosion, river instability, or other factors promoting high rates of sediment transport, measurement networks are generally sparse or absent. Consequently it is virtually impossible to calculate either average or extreme transport rates other than by compiling lists of those measurement results which are available (e.g. Holeman, 1968). This assemblage of data leads to attempts to predict the sediment *yield* of rivers (i.e. the rate of output per unit area) on the basis of climate or geology (e.g. Jansen and Painter, 1974). Notwithstanding such predictive tools it is usually essential to make on-the-spot measurements (for major sampling techniques see Figure 2.10a and b) in those cases where a specific problem of erosion or sedimentation is present.

The available techniques are far from satisfactory, particularly because none of the routine ones produces a continuous record of either suspended

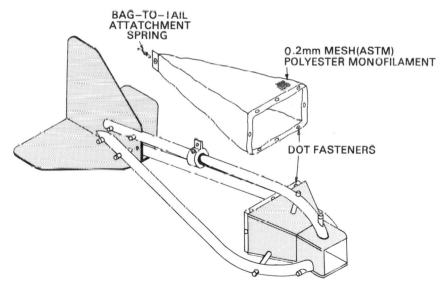

Figure 2.10b Sampling equipment for river sediment loads: the 'Helley-Smith' bedload sampler

or bedload yields, especially during flow extremes. The need for simultaneous measurements of river flow also conspires to make sediment yield and transport rate measurements difficult. Progress is, however, under way towards, for example, the use of turbidity sensors to measure suspended sediment loads (Walling, 1977) and the installation of pressure-sensing or weighing traps for bedload (Reid and Frostick, 1986).

2.4.1   Sediment budgets

The last thirty years of research in drainage basin sediment systems has been one of process studies backed by less detailed calibrations of the magnitude of inputs and outputs of the system, parallelling the measurement of water balances in hydrology. A recent international symposium (Bordas and Walling, 1988) indicates a considerable geographical spread of research effort but a continuing anxiety over techniques and over the ability to construct satisfactory budgets given the 'jerkiness' of the sediment conveyor from source to sink and the fact that many sinks are, albeit temporary, in mid-basin. The much shorter turnover times in hydrology make budgeting on an annual basis much more satisfactory.

The most severe practical problem confronting the measurements of sediment budgets for management (e.g. to determine the rate at which a new reservoir will fill with sediments) is that temporal and spatial discrepancies in throughput of sediments leads to mismatch of, for example, soil erosion rates and sediment yields further down the basin (see also Chapter 6, pp. 206–7). This discrepancy is, however, considered to have certain regularities and the basin *sediment delivery ratio* defines the proportion of headwater sediment supply which reaches the outlet of river basins of increasing area. The delivery ratio requires much more research, particularly because it implies a smooth operation for processes we know to be disjointed (see Section 2.1). Nevertheless, for small basins it is now common to see the sediment budget compartmentalised into all the relevant sources and sinks (see Foster *et al.*, 1988 and Figure 2.11).

The problem of delivery processes becomes much more severe when in certain glaciated or eroded regions a considerable legacy of stored sediments becomes re-mobilised after hundreds or even thousands of years. On the eastern seaboard of the USA the era of European settlement led to massive soil erosion; much of the resulting sediment was, however, stored as *colluvium* (a basal slope deposit).

2.4.2   World sediment yields

Given the requirement posed by the concept of sediment delivery to assess sediment yields much more thoroughly than has been the case to date, it is

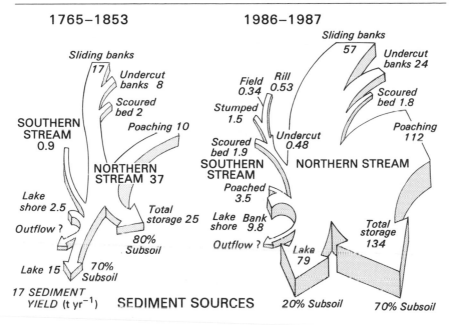

Figure 2.11 Source components of the sediment inflow to two Midland lakes
(Foster *et al.*, 1988)

essential to conclude this chapter with a brief coverage of the major factors
which control sediment yields and of how, within a typical large basin, we
may refer yields back to their controlling processes.

Jansen and Painter (1974) provide a simple assessment of 'the global
denudation rate': 26.7×10^9 tonnes per year; the range of other published
estimates which they review is from 12.7×10^9 tonnes to 58.1×10^9 tonnes.
Such estimates are of most use to geologists making comparisons with
estimated rates of 'new rock' production. For river basin managers it is
necessary to assess the geographical variability of yield for standard
areas. Holeman (1968) does this by continent:

	tonnes. $km^{-2}.yr^{-1}$
North America	97
South America	63
Africa	27
Australia	33
Europe	35
Asia	600

Jansen and Painter (1974) by climate:

	$tonnes.\ km^{-2}.yr^{-1}$
Tropical rainy	71.5
Dry	169.0
Humid, mediterranean	714.4
Humid, cool	46.5

and Fleming (1969) by vegetation type (see Figure 2.12). This latter approach emphasises a key component for management – the importance of the cultural impact. Clearly, from the Figure, deforestation or desertification can, without changing annual river flows, result in a huge increase of sediment yields. This effect is demonstrated in every continent, either by careless contemporary development or in the sediment record or archaeological record as the imprint of major settlement phases.

A major review of all the component processes of continental denudation, produced by Saunders and Young (1983), concluded that acceleration of natural erosion rates by human activities ranges from two to three times

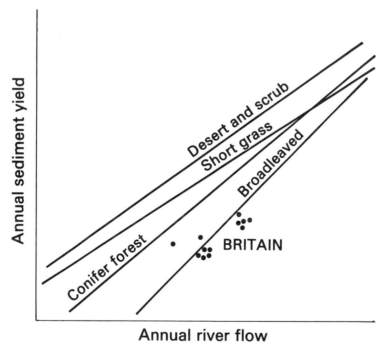

Figure 2.12 Annual sediment yield of world river basins by flow, stratified by vegetation type with British data shown for comparison (from data in Fleming, 1969)

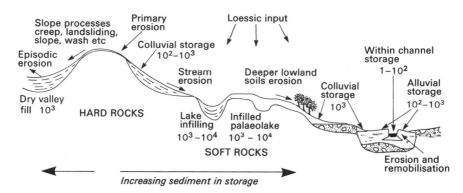

Figure 2.13 Duration and location of long-term sediment storage in the fluvial landscape (Brown, 1987)

with moderately intense land use to ten times with intense land use. However, in any such estimation it is necessary to recall the local, partial and unsophisticated nature of most geomorphological measurements; bedload transport is frequently merely 'added on' as a token 10 per cent and solutes, ignored in this chapter (see Chapter 3) are likely to equal or exceed sediment yields in many large river basins.

The most integrative concept with which to leave this chapter on the basic physical stability of the river basin is perhaps that of sediment residence times. Figure 2.13 shows a section through a typical humid, cool river basin and indicates the location of the key sediment storages and an estimate of the average duration of that storage. This illustration stresses:

(a) The division of the transfer system into supply and transport.
(b) The importance of storage of sediments.
(c) The vulnerability of stores to mobilisation through river instability or land-use change.
(d) The importance of taking longer timescales into account in basin management.

2.5 SUMMARY: KEY ELEMENTS OF THE NATURAL SYSTEM, A SENSITIVITY ASSESSMENT

The confidence of the geomorphologist in seeking a role in river basin management springs from the fact that, when the sediment transport system of any basin becomes destabilised, that basin 'falls apart' in more than one sense (see White 1982). The advantages of the basin to human settlement and resource-utilisation patterns disappear as the system degrades. In many senses river sediments, once the source of wealth for the hydraulic civilisations, are the worst pollutants. Their sources are so widespread that control is far less rapidly achieved than for most chemical pollutants, not that they can be divorced from chemical pollutants since many of the latter are bound to sediment particles (Slaymaker, 1982).

Whilst the river floodplain has many advantages to human resource utilisation and newly discovered values for conservation and for moderating and modulating the transport system, a destabilised river system will suffer from irregular and largely unpredictable extremes of flow which in some environments can remove the entire floodplain. At a much more modest level the expenditure necessary to 'clean up' such a system by removing the sedimentation from reservoirs, navigation-ways and even nature reserves puts an unbalancing burden on the broad base of holistic river basin management. Our new knowledge of the prevalence of threshold reactions by the river basin system, especially the potential of intrinsic thresholds, further adds to the dismal recovery prospects of a basin destabilised by poor land management, poor flow management or over-development.

As will be revealed in Chapters 5 and 6, the most sensitive world environments for such destabilisation to occur are precisely those in the semi-arid and mountainous marginal environments where population and development pressures are most likely to produce it. Whilst the river managers of moderate humid–temperate and long-developed nations are learning only slowly the importance of the system of fluvial geomorphology, it is imperative that those in charge of the process of development programmes in these sensitive environments do not engineer the ultimate failure of their ambitious programmes.

Preservation of river systems is impossible because of their dynamism; however, conservation of a few wilderness rivers is equally misguided. The fundamental physical integrity of river basins must be respected by any management scheme which claims to be long-term; against this claim some of the most immediately alarming effects of chemical pollution pale into insignificance.

Chapter 3

Land and water
Interactions

As we have previously observed, 'water and land' best represents the driving force behind the hydraulic civilisations, their use of the land being controlled by the availability of water and the efficiency of the distribution network. Just as the controlling variables of fluvial geomorphology may change their status as dependent or independent according to timescales (see Chapter 2) so land and water have become reversed in order of influence — at least in the humid zones in which development has been rapid.

An example will illustrate the rapidity with which the balance may change. One of the preoccupations of water resource managers in the UK between 1930 and 1970 was that human recreational pressure might damage reservoir and river water quality and lead to the spread of disease, e.g. typhoid. During the 1970s recreational facilities were slowly developed on both reservoirs and rivers, with the purification costs borne by the water suppliers. By 1990 the situation had reflexed totally and recreational water users were being warned that reservoir and river water threatened them as the result of algal blooms!

The need now to address 'land and water' as a prelude to sustainable basin management puts pressure on scientists to identify and quantify those relationships of cause and effect which link the vast majority of the area of a river basin — its land surface — to the highly significant minority area — its rivers. The problems of environmental science in this situation are considered in Chapter 8; for the moment we must proceed as though hydrology were an exact science and its axioms worthy of operationalising. The hydrological cycle, quantified for river basin units, is an ideal starting point.

3.1 VEGETATION, SOILS AND HYDROLOGY

The UK is a humid, temperate land surface with a dense network of surface stream channels. However, even in mountainous parts of the UK, less than 2 per cent of the surface area of a river basin is occupied by stream channels. Clearly, therefore, with the exception of some lake and reservoir catchments, the huge majority of rainfall is translated to river flows via a canopy of vegetation and a mantle of soils, weathered bedrock or drift and via underground routes.

Whilst it is now known through our experience with acid rain that precipitation itself may carry the pollution resulting from poor environmental management, we may assume for most of this chapter that vegetation and soils have had their naturally benign influences on the quantity and quality of groundwater and river flow severely corrupted by their development for productive uses. Whilst it may 'stand to reason' to the casual rustic observer that this is so, it has taken hydrological experiments more than a century to elucidate the detail and to extend initial rural preoccupations to an urban and suburban context.

Chapter 1 relates the slow historical progress towards a cyclic concept of balancing components of the global water mass. For three hundred years, however, it has been axiomatic to hydrology that the hydrological cycle (Figure 3.1) links the important storages and fluxes of global moisture. The land surface is one of the important switching points in the cycle and a large number of land surface variables act to control the routeing of precipitation through the land phase of the cycle (see Figure 3.2). Although major 'fixed' controls are operated by relief and climate, the hydrological cascade of storages and flows in the surface zone is important, critically important in many relief and climate zones. In fact land-use hydrology is very much a regional science, with the exact effects (particularly their magnitude) of land use dependent largely on regional conditions; for instance, precipitation and evaporation volumes and seasonality in the case of forest effects on water quantities reaching rivers (Newson and Calder, 1989).

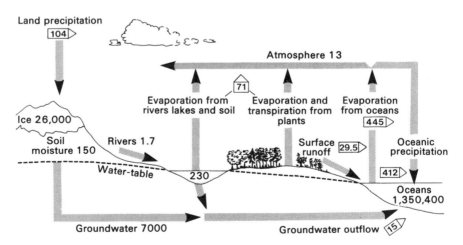

Figure 3.1 The global hydrological cycle; all volumes in thousands of cubic kilometres

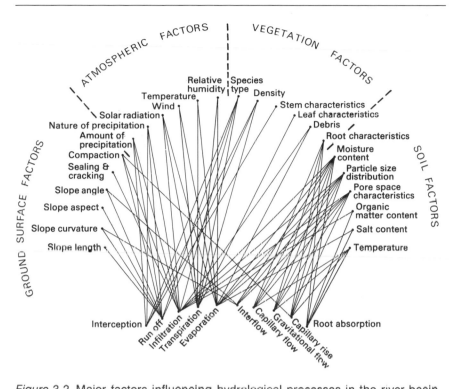

Figure 3.2 Major factors influencing hydrological processes in the river basin (from Ward, 1967)

3.1.1   The hydrological cycle in nature and the role of vegetation

The most telling demonstration of the relationship between fluxes and storages in the land phase of the hydrological cycle is that, whilst biological, domestic and industrial demand for water is almost constant, precipitation occurs for a relatively small proportion of the time; even in the humid conditions of the UK there are few places in which rain or snow falls more than 15 per cent of all time and many important regions where the figure is less than 5 per cent. 'Storage is the answer', both *artificial*, in obvious masses called reservoirs and, more importantly, *natural*, in the pores between soil and rock particles, faults and joints in aquifers, in ponds and lakes and in the channel network. These storages have been calculated as shown in Table 3.1; they can be represented at the river basin scale as a hardware model or as a conceptual model such as that shown in Figure 3.3. The latter device can be used to illustrate the potential impacts on the volume and quality of storages and the flows between them of land-use developments and land management techniques.

Table 3.1 Storages and fluxes in the global hydrological cycle

	Values (km³ × 10³)	Percentage of total
STORAGE		
Ocean	1350000.0	97.403
Atmosphere	13.0	0.00094
Land	35977.8	2.596
Rivers	1.7	0.00012
Freshwater lakes	100.0	0.0072
Inland seas, saline	105.0	0.0076
Soil water	70.0	0.0051
Groundwater	8200.0	0.592
Ice caps/glaciers	27500.0	1.984
Biota	1.1	0.00008
ANNUAL FLUX		
Evaporation	496.0	
Ocean	425.0	
Land	71.0	
Precipitation	496.0	
Ocean	385.0	
Land	111.0	
Runoff to oceans	41.5	
Rivers	27.0	
Groundwater	12.0	
Glacial meltwater	2.5	

Land-use hydrology has at its core the solution of the water balance equation for a particular unit of land, normally a river basin but often at much smaller 'plot' scales where measurements can be more accurate and control more secure:

P	$- Et$	$\pm S$	$= Q$
Precipitation	Evapotranspiration	Changes in storage	Discharge in stream

It can be solved for any time period but generally an annual or flood hydrograph base is chosen so that initial and final conditions are similar, reducing the need to make comprehensive storage measurements. Even without this difficulty the measurement of evapotranspiration has proved very difficult to make directly and climatic calculations of the potential rate are much more common than those of actual rate. The ability to measure actual rates of evapotranspiration on small numbers of plants in plots or lysimeters has made these small-scale experiments popular but more recently methods of direct measurement of the vapour flux from plant surfaces have been devised.

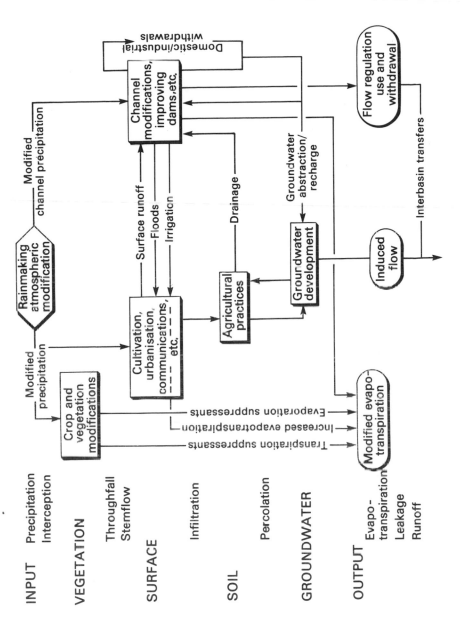

Figure 3.3 The river basin hydrological cycle shown as storages and flows, with artificial influences identified (original by J. Lewin)

The other dilemma in evaporation studies is that of how to separate two controlling processes in the loss of moisture from vegetated surfaces:

(a) *Interception* is the detention of precipitation on plant surfaces and its re-evaporation from that location.
(b) *Transpiration* is the 'use' of water by the plant physiological system linking roots and leaf stomata (variable openings).

It was Dalton who, in 1801, demonstrated that evaporation rates from containers of warmed water were proportional to the vapour pressure difference between water and air; this resistance or aerodynamic approach to the phenomenon became less easy to solve for field sites where climatological data made the energy balance approach through measurements of radiative power for evaporation more popular. In 1948 the late Howard Penman combined the two approaches in an equation which was to facilitate vastly estimation of water balances, particularly in the humid temperate zone.

To allow for reduced actual evaporation via the transpiration process when soil moisture is depleted, Penman introduced a concept of the *root constant*, fixed differently according to crop rooting depth. We may take simplistic guidance from this concept that deeper-rooted plants (such as trees) 'use' more water than shallower-rooted plants (such as grasses), a difference which may well hold for warm, dry climates with a plentiful supply of water to roots (e.g. riparian trees or phreatophyte species).

Calder (1990) traces the isolation and solution of a more difficult problem with the original Penman equation − one of canopy height, not rooting depth. Penman's aerodynamic calculations are appropriate for short, but not tall crops, especially in windy climates when the canopy is wet. Under dry conditions the Penman approach has some mutually compensating errors between aerodynamic and radiative terms but the errors are so large ($\times 2$) for wet, tall crops such as forests that a separate approach to evaporation under these conditions (i.e. of interception) is now the norm for evaporation equations and models.

The issue of relative rates of evaporation achieved under different conditions in different climates by interception and transpiration by species of different heights has dominated land-use hydrology this century.

3.1.2   Important canopy processes

In terms of our knowledge of their hydrological effects, the above-ground portions of natural plant, crop and forest covers have grown in importance since the processes they control have been investigated more closely. As Figure 3.3 demonstrates, the canopy is itself a temporary store in the hydrological cycle. Whilst not constituting a large depth of storage in terms of incoming precipitation (commonly <5mm), the lateral extent of plant cover is considerable and therefore volumes are by no means negligible. Whilst storage is only temporary the individually small volume of each storage site and its comparatively large surface area mean that both evaporative and chemical (solute) transfers are efficient in the canopy under most conditions.

It is important to list the properties of vegetation canopies which influence their hydrological behaviour (Table 3.2). In the early days of qualitative observations on, for example, the hydrological influence of natural forests (see Chapter 8 and Kittredge, 1948) canopies were seen as exercising a simple, single, umbrella-like influence on rainfall and a generally protective, beneficial outcome was assumed for river behaviour. Nevertheless, even at that stage, failure to separate the precise canopy processes and their variability with canopy properties led to controversy and misunderstanding. Issues of canopy effects were often confused with those of soils and soil management (see Section 3.1.3). No rapid improvement was produced by quantified observations; here catchment experiments involving a manipulation of canopy cover, such as afforestation or deforestation/harvesting, were found to produce different effects on streamflow (or different magnitudes of effect), depending on plant species, climate and other variables.

It is perhaps not surprising that ignorance prevailed so long in the field of canopy hydrology; one of the dominant processes operating at canopy level, evaporation, is the most difficult to measure or predict in the hydrological cycle. Ultimately, therefore, clarification has come from a wide variety of scales of research carried out by several disciplines in numerous climates (even so, neglecting the importance of vegetation management). Vegetation changes may be accidental (fire, disease) or deliberate, but in each case the 'before and after' covers may be different (e.g. trees may follow bracken, or heather, or scrub rather than short grass).

It has been clear that during the short life of the International Hydrological Decade and Programme (1965–74 and subsequently) forest hydrology

Table 3.2 Vegetation canopy properties having an influence on the hydrological performance of vegetation cover

Interception (a)	Transpiration (b)	Evaporation (a + b)
'ARCHITECTURE'	'PHYSIOLOGY'	'SITE'
Crop height	Stomatal cover	Exposure – regional
Canopy depth	Seasonal growth	– local
Leaf area (per plant)	Growth stage of plant	Ventilation
Leaf shape	Health of canopy	Albedo
Crop spacing		Radiation climate
		Seasonality of site

has dominated studies of land-use effects. In the proceedings of the first international symposium on the subject in this period, held in Wellington (IAHS-UNESCO, 1970), it is clear that, whilst a very large majority of papers are on techniques and problems of extrapolation (indicating a youthful stage?), a significant number reported results from forest studies. Ten years later in Helsinki the organisers were confident enough to call the meeting 'the influence of man on the hydrological cycle' (IAHS, 1980); again forests dominated with fourteen pages (regulation effects were next with nine) and by 1981 the Vancouver Symposium was devoted entirely to 'Forest hydrology and watershed management' (Swanson *et al.*, 1987). Table 3.3 shows the categorisation and country of origin of papers in this volume. It is also indicative of the maturing state of forest hydrology that watershed management appeared in the title of the Vancouver Symposium.

3.1.3   Patterns of soil hydrological processes

One of the major pieces of empirical progress in twentieth century hydrology has been in determining the spatial pattern of runoff processes. Geographers have played a prominent part in the retreat from a concept of catchment surface runoff to a variety of spatially orientated runoff zones in which permutations of surface and sub-surface runoff occur at various times during a runoff event, for example the flood hydrograph.

Two prominent variants of the newer conceptual framework are proposed: the *partial contributing area* (PCA) and the *dynamic contributing area* (DCA). Their strengths and validity are both determined by the pattern of rainfall (or snowmelt) interaction with the surface of the soil. Figure 3.4 illustrates an earlier different view of this interaction, assembled from observations in the semi-arid rangelands of the USA by R. E. Horton (1933). The Horton model at its simplest states that runoff occurs from the surface of the soil when rainfall intensity exceeds the infiltration capacity

Table 3.3 The broadening scope of forest hydrology as represented by the topic and origin of papers in *Forest hydrology and watershed management* (IAHS, 1987)

Topic	Papers	Nations
Acid precipitation	10	4 (USA 4; UK 3)
Erosion and sedimentation	14	10 (none dominant)
Snow in forested basins	4	2 (USA 3)
Evapotranspiration	7	7 (none dominant)
Soil moisture	7	4 (USA 3; UK 2)
Whole watershed studies	11	7 (USA 3; New Zealand 3)
Simulation models	6	5 (USA 2)

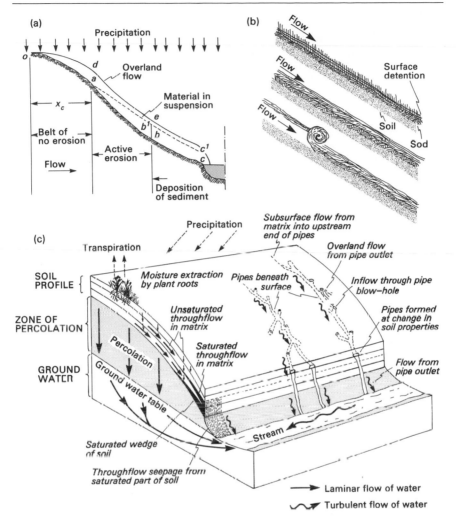

(a)

Precipitation

o

d   Overland flow

a

x_c

Belt of no erosion

Flow

Active erosion

Material in suspension

e

b^1 *b*

c^1

c

Deposition of sediment

(b)

Flow

Flow

Flow

Surface detention

Soil

Sod

(c)

Precipitation

Subsurface flow from matrix into upstream end of pipes

Transpiration

Overland flow from pipe outlet

SOIL PROFILE

Moisture extraction by plant roots

Pipes beneath surface

Inflow through pipe blow–hole

ZONE OF PERCOLATION

Unsaturated throughflow in matrix

Percolation

Saturated throughflow in matrix

Pipes formed at change in soil properties

GROUND WATER

Ground water table

Flow from pipe outlet

Stream

Saturated wedge of soil

Throughflow seepage from saturated part of soil

Laminar flow of water

Turbulent flow of water

Figure 3.4 The overland flow model of R. E. Horton and its replacement by a view incorporating a much larger role for soil throughflows:
(a) The basic Horton model showing the profile of overland flows on slopes (Horton, 1945)
(b) Breakdown of grass cover during intense rains (Hortonian flow) (Horton, 1945)
(c) Slope section and plan to emphasise saturated zones built up by subsurface flow processes (after Atkinson, 1978)

of that soil. It is a rate-exceedance rather than a capacity-exceedance, an important distinction to make when considering the regional and local application of the model. 'Overland flow' or 'surface runoff' was assumed to have universal applicability in hydrology and had the further advantage, as conceived by Horton, of explaining many of the geomorphological features of the drainage basin by focusing attention on soil erosion (see Figure 3.4b). Under overland flow conditions (i.e. at the critical rainfall intensity) we assume that river flow is derived from every part of the river basin, a concept largely supported by the predictive power of basin area data.

The Horton runoff model went largely unquestioned during thirty important years in the development of applied hydrology in which techniques of prediction such as the unit hydrograph were developed. However, field measurements of infiltration capacity in soils proved difficult to make compared with the relative ease of rainfall intensity gauging; the model was therefore difficult to apply in detail at a river basin scale. Those attempts to link infiltration capacity to soil type suggested that, for the humid temperate zone, rainfall intensities seldom exceeded infiltration capacities for the majority of soils. Direct observations of runoff phenomena on slopes in the field also revealed an important role, in terms of both volumes and rates of runoff, for subsurface flows within the soil profile.

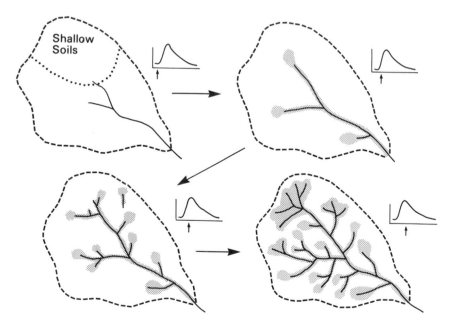

Figure 3.5 Expansion of the dynamic contributing area of a drainage basin into ephemeral channels and areas of saturated soils during the passage of a flood hydrograph (Hewlett and Nutter, 1970)

As the section of hillslope shown in Figure 3.4c demonstrates, we now understand a variety of routes for runoff on slopes, especially in vegetated, humid landscapes with a good development of soil horizons. Control passes from the soil surface in Horton's model to the state of soil moisture storage in, and rate of filling of, successive layers of soil. Vegetation and crop covers, together with management practice, therefore assume an even greater significance than in the Hortonian model; surface flows remain effective but mainly where soils are saturated, a phenomenon typical of the base of slopes (as shown) and one which can clearly extend upslope in any soil horizon during a rain storm. This extension is the basis of the dynamic contributing area concept. Figure 3.5 illustrates how the saturated areas of catchment at the start of a small flood event expand during the event.

A further feature of Figure 3.4c worthy of note in connection with land use and management is the existence in many soil profiles of natural 'pipe' networks which clearly promote efficient soil drainage; subsurface runoff or *throughflow* is not, therefore, an invariably slow phenomenon.

If canopy processes in hydrology largely underlie the importance of crop

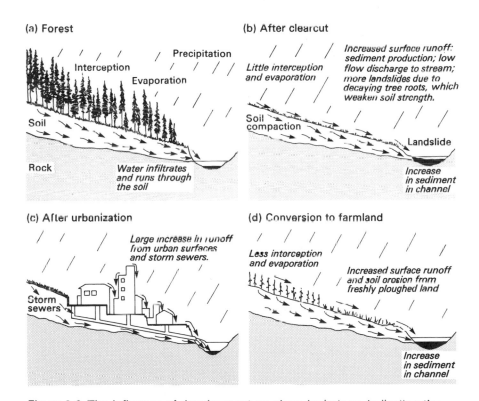

Figure 3.6 The influence of development on slope hydrology, indicating the role of agriculture and urbanisation

choice, dominated by research on forest hydrology, soil processes justify the attention of river basin managers to surface treatments, of which urban covers have achieved a similar dominance in research terms.

Figure 3.6 illustrates the major river basin influences of forest, bare, cultivated and urban covers. Table 3.4 confirms a considerable variability of impermeability of urban covers but the most obvious urban effect on the natural system of Figure 3.4c is that of re-routeing precipitation at the surface.

Table 3.4 demonstrates a measure of flexibility in urban design and it has become standard practice in North America to mitigate the urban influence on both runoff and sediment yields by innovating with materials to reduce urban impermeability. Another aspect of urban hydrology which promotes hydrological change is the channelling of the extra runoff from an impermeable surface into an efficient system of drains and sewers; this drainage system is also being modified with the introduction of storage tanks, hydraulic 'brakes' in sewers and surface balancing ponds.

Research in urban hydrology has been dogged by the sheer complexity of the system (much of which disrupts the flow paths of the natural surface catchment), the need to develop special instrumentation and the difficulty of finding experimental sites for 'urban v. rural' comparisons or 'before and after' studies at a catchment scale. The most recent phase of urban hydrology has, therefore, tended to concentrate on smaller scale investigations of elements of the urban runoff system, such as roofs and gutters, pavements and streets (Hollis, 1988).

Agricultural disruption to soil processes in the runoff cascade are also imperfectly understood; again the difficulties of finding experimental sites and of innovating techniques abound – to which one may add the problem of generalising between national and even regional differences in cropping and cultivation techniques. As an example of the problems of generalising

Table 3.4 Approximations of the impermeability of various surfaces

Type of surface	Impermeability (%)
Watertight roof surfaces	70–95
Asphalt paving in good order	85–90
Stone, brick and wooden block pavements:	
with tightly cemented joints	75–85
with open or uncertain joints	50–70
Inferior block pavements with open joints	40–50
Macadam roads and paths	25–60
Gravel roads and paths	15–30
Unpaved surfaces, railway yards, vacant lots	10–30
Parks, gardens, lawns, meadows – depending on the	
surface slope and character of the subsoil	5–25

land-use effects on hydrology we may cite the long debate in the British Isles about the effects of farm and forest drainage on the flood hydrograph. Are streams in heavily drained areas more prone to rapid and high flood hydrographs? Empirical studies yield both 'yes' and 'no' answers. At first a separation appeared between sites on peat soils (enhanced response) and mineral soils (reduced response); see Newson and Robinson (1983). Subsequently, for clay soils, detailed investigations revealed that two conditions exist within the same drained area: under wet conditions undrained land responds more rapidly to rainfall than drained land because soil cracks become closed (Robinson and Beven, 1983). Furthermore Robinson *et al.* (1985) revealed the importance of mechanically cracking the soil when draining land and Reid and Parkinson (1984) the importance of landform in controlling soil moisture and hence drainage flow response. There is clearly not one single answer!

Knowledge of runoff zones, such as those proposed by protagonists of PCAs, DCAs, or even the traditional surface runoff models, is essential to those who wish to control land use and land management in support of river basin management (Dunne and Leopold, 1978). For example, surface drainage channels installed in areas of a catchment prone to either Hortonian surface runoff or seasonal saturation are unlikely to be effective in increasing soil moisture storage. Instead these drains merely channel surface runoff more quickly to natural channels, increasing flood peaks by acting as extensions to that natural network.

Guidance to planners and others without hydrological knowledge can be obtained from patterns of natural vegetation which often mark very clearly the zones of runoff generation in a catchment. Plants tolerant of saturated soils clearly delimit the partial contributing area. Mapping vegetation communities also reveals variations which indicate soil piping zones, seeps and other diagnostic features.

3.2   RUNOFF MODIFICATIONS IN DEVELOPED RIVER BASINS

Despite the evidence offered in Section 3.1 of the potential for hydrological effects of land use, it is essential to be highly specific when suggesting links between land use or land management and properties of the river hydrograph: merely 'that land use has altered the river flow' will not suffice without a wealth of detail about both the land use and the flow properties which are alleged to have been affected. Clearly coincidental changes in both must not be ruled out and statistical 'proof' will be of limited application without a knowledge of causal processes.

In the case of land use we need to subdivide crop from the infrastructure to grow and harvest it, stages of the *crop cycle* and the cover effects of the urban surface from those of infrastructure, e.g. sewerage.

In terms of the river flow properties influenced by land use, these may be

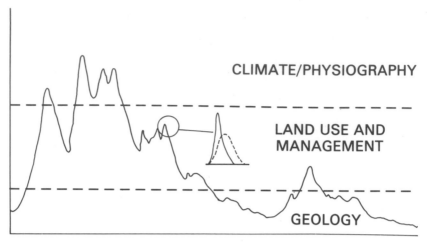

Figure 3.7 Influences on the annual regime of river flow

be extreme and obvious in some climates (e.g. a dry river bed) but in many cases the influences are very much more subtle, possibly seasonal and possibly variable between patches of the same land use because of physiographic, climatic or management differences.

One must not neglect the operation of natural controls on the runoff process; for example, basins may differ profoundly in their flood or drought behaviour because of physiographic or geological differences. Figure 3.7 offers a simple guide, based on the annual hydrograph of a hypothetical humid zone surface river, to those aspects of flow liable to be influenced by land use; clearly the land use and management influence may make its biggest impact in the mid-range of flows where subtle changes in volume or timing may become exaggerated over longer timescales.

3.2.1 Modifications to runoff volume

The dried-up river bed resulting from over-abstraction is a clear and extreme version of an artificial volumetric change in river flows! Nevertheless changes of river flow could also be the result of timing changes – a less equable temporal spread of an unaltered volume. The two properties are obviously linked but the emphasis in this and the following sections will be on those links with land use where the major influence is on one of these properties (see also Table 3.5).

Land use and land management effects on runoff volume are clearly most likely where a change is brought about in:

(a) Evaporative loss from an identical precipitation volume.
(b) Surface characteristics of a basin which influence the detention and storage of runoff.

Table 3.5 Land-use/management effects on the flow of rivers

	Volume of runoff	Timing of runoff
FORESTS		
Planting	Increase if previous cover cleared	More rapid if cultivation/drainage required
Mature cover	Decrease in climates favouring interception or transpiration; increase where snow trapped in forests	More rapid if cultivation/drainage required
Harvesting	Increase until cover re-established	Location and extent of harvesting critical
URBAN		
Surface	Increase in surface volume and totals where replacing crop/forest cover	More rapid as more precipitation retained on surface
Drain/sewer systems	No influence except on groundwater volumes	Most flood flows made more rapid; extreme floods may be ponded in urban area
AGRICULTURE		
Drainage	May reduce long-term storages and reduce low-flow volume	Effect depends on primary soil permeability
Cropping	Evaporative use by irrigated crops reduces net runoff volume	Little direct effect in humid, temperate climates; elsewhere critical to surface runoff and erosion
QUARRYING/MINING		
Surface water	Little affected	Restored open-cast often yields rapid runoff
Groundwater	Stored/pumped; boosts low-flow volumes	Little affected

Both cropping (including the crops) and urban/industrial land uses may be expected to cause such changes — at key switching points in the land phase of the hydrological cycle — at the canopy level and the soil surface level.

At the canopy level, there is now an emerging empirical consensus amongst hydrologists that a forest cover reduces runoff volume under most climatic conditions. Bosch and Hewlett (1982) review results from 94 catchment experiments involving timber harvesting from climates ranging from <300 mm to >3000 mm of annual precipitation. There is a consistent

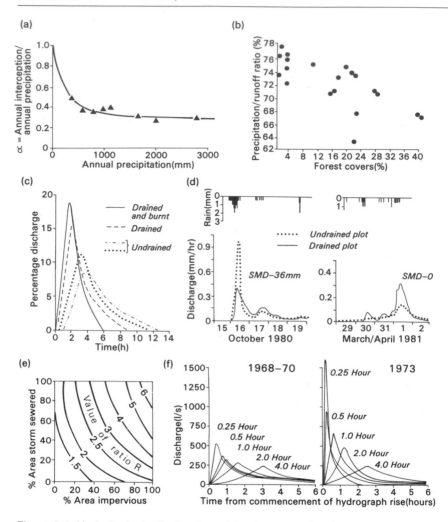

Figure 3.8 Hydrological effects of rural land use and land management:
  (a) Interception ratios of mature forest canopies in the UK (Calder and Newson, 1979)
  (b) Reduction of annual runoff coefficient with increasing forest cover, Wales (Mas'ud, 1987)
  (c) Moorland drainage and the flow hydrograph (Conway and Millar, 1960)
  (d) Farm (under-) drainage and the flow hydrograph, indicating the role of antecedent conditions as soil moisture deficit (SMD) in routeing rainfall through/over the soil (Robinson and Beven, 1983)
  (e) Mean annual flood increments (cf. natural floods) with increasing urban cover and sewerage (Leopold, 1968)
  (f) Flood hydrograph changes after urbanisation (Walling, 1979)

increase in catchment yield when tree cover is removed, though the magnitude varies (positively) with annual rainfall and, obviously, the proportion of the forest cover removed. Forest types are difficult to compare within the same climatic zone but, broadly, conifers and eucalypts cause 40 mm change in annual yield for the loss of 10 per cent cover, deciduous hardwoods 25 mm and brush 10 mm.

The intensive research programme on forest hydrology in Britain has yielded further details of the interception process and of the essentially exclusive operation of the two components of forest moisture loss: interception and transpiration. Calder and Newson (1979) conclude that in the British uplands interception ratios for plantation conifers converge at 30 per cent of annual precipitation (Figure 3.8a). During periods in which the forest canopy is moist, interception entirely dominates transpiration but when the canopy is dry the reverse is true. Consequently, in drier climates the tree's own physiological control of transpiration may come to dominate its comparative water usage in relation to adjacent land covers; in practice understorey vegetation in forests also uses moisture and Roberts (1983) has concluded that overall forest transpiration is essentially a conservative process with similar annual rates across Europe (approx. 333 mm/yr).

Outside catchment experiments very little work has been performed on catchments monitored for water supply or pollution control purposes. Figure 3.8b reveals the utility of such a sample, from Wales, in which there is a clear negative relationship between the volume of annual runoff (as a proportion of rainfall) and the forest cover of the catchment. Nevertheless, results of this type, together with those of Bosch and Hewlett (1982), are much more rare than those from process-based or catchment studies and it should be emphasised that predictive techniques for runoff volume used at national and international scales do not, as yet, incorporate forest or other land-use variables – physiographic and climatic variables are much more effective in statistical predictions of runoff volume. This apparent mismatch between small-scale findings on process and large-scale, statistical predictions is followed up in Chapter 8.

3.2.2 Modifications to runoff timing

Figure 3.4c shows the multitude of processes and routes by which precipitation reaches the humid zone surface stream. We have already considered this as a cascade of storages and clearly timing of runoff is proportional, in a simplistic system, to the number of storages through which each molecule of runoff passes. Response times vary accordingly as Figure 3.8c, d and f demonstrates. Any land-use or management strategy which significantly re-routes runoff will alter its timing: the simplest example is surface drainage of the soil. It should once again be emphasised, however, that timing changes will also bring about volume changes in another part of the system, e.g. urban storm sewers will deprive the underlying aquifers of recharge.

Table 3.6 illustrates the range of velocities characteristic of different runoff routes in the river basin; however it would be simplistic to consider changes in runoff timing to be merely a function of re-routeing between these categories: the volumes re-routed and the destination of the re-route are also important. Two examples illustrate this point: soil pipes (and drainage pipes) appear to be rapid routes for runoff but often small volumes only are involved and, in the case of soil pipes, the destination of the runoff involves storage delays and slower routeing; in extreme floods urban drainage systems overflow and the resulting inundation tends to reduce the velocity of the floodwave as a whole.

Despite these caveats, artificial processes which gather runoff efficiently into hydraulically smooth channels and which reduce the distance to the stream or increase the pathway gradient will promote faster flood responses. This is particularly true if some other change has also occurred to promote a higher volume of runoff, e.g. in Figure 3.8c where a small peat catchment has been both burned (sealing the surface) and drained. In the case of subsurface drainage the condition of the soil between surface and drainage pipes has a subtle control on the timing of responses. As already described above, hydrologists in the UK have discovered that a dry, cracked clay soil promotes a more rapid response by drained farmland but when the same soil is wet (and only slowly permeable), undrained farmland responds more quickly because it routes more rainfall across the surface (Figure 3.8d).

The combination of increased volumes of runoff and more efficient drainage from traditionally planned urban areas is shown by Figure 3.8e, in which the peak of the annual flood is increased in proportion to both the

Table 3.6 Estimated flow velocity of various hydrologic processes

Flow medium	Velocity range (m/h)
Open channel	300–10000
Overland flow	50–500
Pipeflow	50–500
Matrix throughflow	0.005–0.3
Groundwater flow:	
Sandstone	0.001–10
Shale	0.00000001–1.0
Jointed limestone	10–500

Source: Weyman (1975)

impervious area and the extent to which it is drained. The evolution of the more rapid urban response through time is shown in Figure 3.8f.

3.2.3 Regulated rivers, an introduction

It is a paradox of our subject area in this chapter that, whilst the intention is to substantiate a planned approach to the joint management of land and water, it is water engineering which has produced a more identifiable, and in many cases more marked, effect on river flows than has land use or management. The regulation of river flows, either by design to ameliorate the natural regime, or as a secondary impact of water use, dates back to the first dams and irrigation schemes.

The extent of river regulation by dams has been gauged by several authors; it extends into areas outside the effects of land use and management for development because it is to pristine, remote, wilderness or mountainous sites that dam builders look for good foundations, abundant runoff and good water quality.

Beaumont (1978) plots the growth of international dam construction since 1840 (Figure 3.9); building continues undiminished although rather

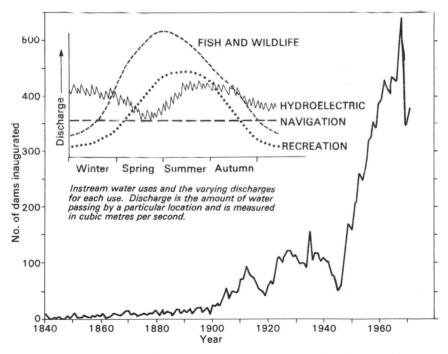

Figure 3.9 Direct control of river flows: river regulation. Growth of world dam construction (Beaumont, 1978) and (inset) the seasonal flow regime suitable for natural and exploitable purposes

fewer and larger schemes are now the norm. Between 400 and 700 dams are currently being built every year round the world.

To the obvious effects of damming rivers on their downstream flow patterns we may add the following water uses which effectively alter the volume and timing of river flows downstream in ways which resemble damming:

(a) Major industrial users of river water; few are consumptive but even a use for cooling will modify river flows.
(b) Irrigation use of river water is both consumptive and switches the river water to a slower return flow route.
(c) Water use by human settlements both imposes demands on flow from dams by direct supply, from natural or regulated rivers, and returns this water as sewage which places quality demands on the downstream river.

Some indication of the extent of the last of these categories can be gained from the fact that up to 34 per cent of the flow volume of the River Trent (England) during average conditions is provided from sewers, not by 'natural' sources (Farrimond, 1980). Because the sources of water for human consumption are often remote from the settlement and yet sewers discharge to the nearest river, such systems often effect a transfer between basins.

The major technical problems raised by river regulation from reservoirs are given special attention in Chapter 6. For the moment we remain purely with the magnitude of artificial influences on the regime of river flow (volume, timing) in order to contrast those of land use and direct regulation.

Figure 3.9 presents the conflicting requirements of different river users for particular patterns of flow. To these may be added the needs of riparian consumers and the need to protect settlements from both floods and droughts. It is clearly wrong to consider that the 'best' river regime for settled, civilised human life is a constant flow! Ecologically the pattern of fluvial systems and habitat derives just as much from flow variability through time as from the physiographic and nutritional features of river systems.

Table 3.7 lists the magnitude of changes in volume and timing of flow occasioned by a variety of regulating activities both direct and indirect (cf. Table 3.5, land use effects).

One of the grave difficulties in making quantitative assessments of regulating effects is that many of the causes are of long standing and pre-date our official flow measuring networks. Thus, for example, many UK upland reservoirs date from the nineteenth century but, despite protests over their 'compensation flows' (see Chapter 1), their precise effect on downstream volumes and timing could not be assessed effectively until recently. In the case of less localised effects such as sewerage outfalls, they are so numerous in developed regions that even with flow measurement stations installed,

Table 3.7 River regulation: magnitude of effects on flow regime

	Volume	Timing	Downstream distance
DIRECT EFFECTS			
Direct supply reservoir	Reduces	Delays flood peak by storage	
River regulating reservoirs	Reduces and increases according to conditions	Tends to delay natural floods	
Hydro-power (dam)	Diurnal or seasonal pulses	Towards artificial regime	Depends on position and size of unregulated tributaries
Run-of-river	Little impact	Little impact	
Flood control	Reduces/ removes peaks	Delays	
INDIRECT EFFECTS			
Irrigation return flows	Reduces	Little effect	
Sewerage return flows	Redirects/ transfers	More rapid if includes storm drain	

reduction of total flow to 'naturalised' flow is difficult; flow measurements are made on the larger sewers but, for many, flow rates are an approximation.

Clearly, too, impacts become reduced and blurred in terms of a unique hydrological signal as one moves further downstream from the point of maximum activity, be it dam site, plantation or city. Scaling these decay factors is as difficult with direct regulating influences as it is with those of land use/management. As Table 3.7 shows, the location of unregulated tributaries in the system makes almost every case unique.

3.3   VEGETATION, SOILS AND WATER QUALITY

Knowledge of the hydrological cycle (Figure 3.1) prepares us for the links between land use/management and changes in runoff timing and volume. During the last decade, however, possibly reflecting an increased human perception of environmental degradation and of mankind's controlling role, hydrologists have developed detailed programmes of research on river basin water chemistry and its variation with land use (see Table 3.2). They have been joined by ecologists anxious to investigate links between water quality and habitat; much of this latter research has been done at smaller scales and, once again, we find forests, both natural and exploited, exciting the interest of many research programmes.

In Chapter 2 we emphasised the role of the basin sediment system in controlling the basic physical systems of river basins, particularly in the longer term. Sediment transport is also a feature of water quality changes brought about by land-use activity; in this case it is fine sediments (sands, silts and clays) which we consider. Nevertheless the emphasis in this section will be away from sediments and towards water chemistry.

Before continuing it is appropriate to make a simple subdivision between two types of basin effect in this category. Whether the problem is *contamination* (the introduction of new materials and compounds to the system) or *pollution* (the introduction of damaging loads or concentrations of material or compounds), we separate two sources:

(a) Point sources are identifiable, such as the obvious outfalls of irrigation return flows or sewerage systems.
(b) Diffuse sources are much more difficult to identify, such as nutrients and pesticides added evenly to agriculture or forestry.

These are difficult intermediate categories such as the farm slurry-store which, if it is emptied carefully and spread on the land, becomes a diffuse source of nutrient chemicals but which, if it spills to a stream, becomes a point source. It is obvious to those managing river basins that scientific detection of, and legal controls on, diffuse pollution are much more problematic than the equivalents for point sources.

The difficulties associated with diffuse sources mean that proving links between rural land use/management and water quality are much greater than for urban links. Furthermore, scientific studies will find difficulties of extrapolation beyond the boundaries of research sites, in this case far more insuperable than those of scaling a universal physical process such as interception. Studies of river sediment systems or water chemistry systems have additional problems of downstream changes in processes and of the importance of local conditions of culture, climate, soils and rock types.

3.3.1   Land use and the fine sediment system

Archaeologists have revealed in many regions of the world an association between the human artefacts of a datable civilisation and characteristics of the sediments which contain them, indicating a major erosion phase associated with typical land use of the era. In semi-arid lands the land-use effect is via settled irrigated agriculture. In humid regions of North America, Europe and Asia there are clear deforestation- and overgrazing-related erosion horizons. Often a rival climatic explanation is available but, with close analysis of how basins route the products of soil erosion, it is clear that in certain major areas of basins, notably in hollows and at the base of slopes, land-use practices themselves can account for impressive thicknesses of deposit. We may therefore hypothesise a link between 'land-use sediments' in colluvium and 'climate sediments' in alluvium (see further debate in Chapter 6).

A much more detailed analysis than this is available for the eastern seaboard of the USA. Meade (1982) describes how soil erosion was increased ten-fold by European settlement; large quantities of the resulting sediment are still stored on hillslopes and valley floors, exaggerating contemporary sediment yields. The impact of modern man in the region has been to trap the same sediment in reservoirs; the remainder is stored in estuaries and coastal marshes. Knox (1989) has pointed to the fact that river valleys act as huge stores of alluvium from such periods, demonstrating the evidence of prehistoric clearances in Wisconsin (see Figure 3.10c).

On a world scale the interplay of climatic and land-use (in this case natural vegetation) covers is available through the work of Schumm. Figure 3.10a shows how, because transport processes in river systems are critical for moving fine sediments in suspension from river basins, the broad characteristics of hydrology determine sediment yields at a given time.

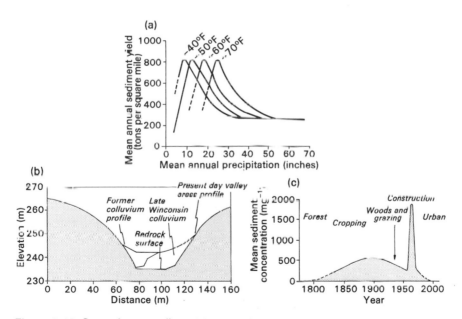

Figure 3.10 Controls on sediment transport:
    (a) Climate, on a world scale (Schumm, 1977)
    (b) Storage of historically eroded material (Knox, 1989)
    (c) General development processes on pristine landscape (Wolman, 1967)

However, the feedback of moisture availability to vegetation cover means that humid climates have a far lower yield than the potential indicated by their high runoff.

Not surprisingly, therefore, it is disruption to vegetation covers in climates of intense rainfalls which leads to rapid deterioration of water quality and river habitats through soil erosion. Urbanisation produces the worst impact during construction and the urbanisation of semi-arid lands is especially damaging; however, tropical deforestation exposes the most sensitive soils on earth to some of the most intense rainfalls on earth and has a very serious impact on water quality downstream.

For those particles of soil released from soil erosion the route to the ocean may occur as a complex and lengthy set of paths via storages (see also Chapter 6 for technical discussion). The path lengths between storages, once entrained by channel flows, is much greater. Lambert and Walling (1988) conclude that channel storage of fine sediment in the Exe basin, UK, is minimal and the channel efficiently conveys suspended material direct to the coast.

The question to pose next is whether fine sediments entrained by rivers represent a significant contamination or pollution of the environment (implications for reservoir sedimentation, flood control, etc. are discussed in Chapter 6). The concentration of fine sediments in suspension is referred to, and can be measured as, turbidity – an occlusion of the natural clarity of the pure substance to various degrees. Turbid water requires expensive filtration for all human users of water.

At Holmestyles Reservoir in Yorkshire, forestry ploughing and draining operations created severe pollution by suspended sediments, costing £23,000 to cure because filtration equipment needed replacement. At Cray Reservoir in Wales a public water supply was out of commission for some days as the result of forestry operations.

Turning to biotic conditions in turbid streams, some research indicates very little damage from, for example, quarry waste materials. However, fine waste material has geomorphological implications, as Richards (1982) demonstrates for Cornish streams contaminated by china-clay waste; width/depth ratios of polluted channels are under half of those for 'natural' streams, showing an adjustment to the finer load carried. A series of laboratory experiments conducted by Alabaster (1972) indicates that the presence of fine materials in suspension seriously exacerbates the toxic effect of certain chemicals in water. Cross-linkages between solid and soluble phases of river flows are emerging from many land-use related river pollution studies. For example, phosphates become preferentially adsorbed to fine sediments (Walling, 1990). The loss of organic and mineral nutrients from eroded soils can become an accumulating pollution hazard in lakes and reservoirs.

In studies of sedimentation from 'hydraulic' mining (in which water is used to expose and sort ores and dispose of waste), the fine fraction of the sediment mix released appears to be an important carrier of the metal pollution downstream (Macklin and Dowsett, 1989) to lakes, slack-water sites on the river and to floodplains where poisoning of vegetation and cattle may continue for decades.

3.3.2   Solute processes, mineral and nutrient

A protestor arguing against the fluoridation of public water supplies was once heard to object to 'the addition of a chemical to pure water'. Nature conspires to add many chemicals to river water; in some cases the concentration or loading of wholly 'natural' chemicals pollutes water to the extent that it is undrinkable and the stream lifeless. In the case of crystalline limestone terrains the chemical solution of the landscape actually creates the typical river network (an underground one flowing through caves).

Figure 3.11 shows both systematically and pictorially the origins of natural stream water quality (in rural areas). There are both mineral and nutrient cycles, often largely controlled by soil/vegetation systems and agricultural practices, which explain chemical content at any point in the hydrological cycle. Two elements of this system are often neglected by field monitoring campaigns: the chemical characteristics of precipitation and the chemical modifications produced by 'instream' processes, often controlled by stream biota. Indeed it is upon the in-stream processes of purification that we depend across the world when using rivers as conveyor belts for the waste products of housing, farming and industry.

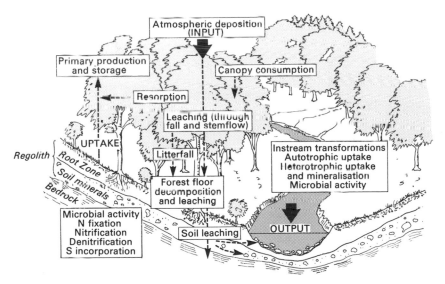

Figure 3.11 Processes leading to the production of stream solute loads in a natural catchment

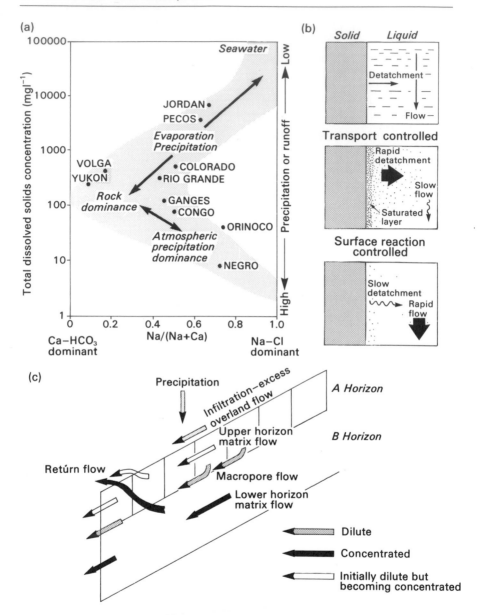

Figure 3.12 Details of controls on solute load:
(a) Rainfall quality and evaporation rates (Gibbs, 1970)
(b) Kinetics of the soil water reaction (Trudgill, 1986)
(c) Flow routes through the soil profile/slope profile (Burt, 1986)

'Natural' water quality is governed by two great sources of mineral salts, the ocean and ocean-deposited sediments containing abundant sodium and chloride, and by rock types consisting of lithified marine organisms, rich in calcium and carbonate (dissolved as bicarbonate); Figure 3.12a illustrates a spectrum of river water quality on the basis of concentration and the ratio of sodium content to sodium and calcium (see also Walling and Webb, 1986). These ions are merely discriminators; the full list of major ions in river water is shown in Table 3.8.

Whether introduced by 'natural' processes or by land-use related modifications, the soil is a primary site for geochemical reactions and the concentration of ions is influenced by both the rate of solution (or production of soluble chemical) and the rate of removal by soil moisture movement; Figure 3.12b illustrates this two-stage process. An understanding of hydrological patterns, flow paths and flow velocities (e.g. Figure 3.12c) is therefore of immense importance in managing water quality problems resulting from land use. For example, nitrate pollution arising from intense production on well-cultivated, freely draining soils can be mitigated as the throughflow drains to the channel via saturated floodplain soils where de-nitrification occurs (Pinay and Decamps, 1988; Hill, 1990).

In the case of urban and industrial land use, the soil plays a much less prominent role unless waste products are applied to land – an increasingly popular option for sewage sludge, the solid product of urban sewage purification. Mostly, however, urban industrial water quality problems are not routed by the national hydrological pathways but originate in an industrial process at a site with a clear point discharge direct to a stream (see Table 3.9).

Other diffuse water quality changes related to land use or land management occur as the result of the following processes:

(a) Hydrological changes occurring as a consequence of canopy processes,

Table 3.8 Average composition of world river water

Author	Concentration (mgl^{-1})								
	Ca^{2+}	Mg^{2+}	Na^+	K^+	Cl^-	SO_4^{2-}	HCO_3	SiO_2	Total
Livingstone (1963)	15.0	4.1	6.3	2.3	7.8	11.2	58.4	13.1	120[a]
Meybeck (1979)	13.4	3.35	5.15	1.3	5.75	8.25	52.0	10.4	99.6[b]
Meybeck (1983)	13.5	3.6	7.4	1.35	9.6	8.7	52.0[c]	10.4	106.6[b]

[a]Total content of all solutes.
[b] Total listed constituents.
[c] HCO_3 not listed in Meybeck (1983); Meybeck (1979) value used.

Table 3.9 Some sources and causes of water quality deterioration

Effluent	Factors affecting water quality deterioration
Domestic sewage	BOD, suspended solids, ammonia, nitrate, phosphate
Vegetable processing	BOD, suspended solids, colour
Chemical industry	BOD, ammonia, phelons, non-biodegradable organics, heat
Iron and steel manufacture	Cyanide, phenols, thiocyanate, pH, ammonia, sulphides
Coal mining	Suspended solids, iron, pH, dissolved solids
Metal finishing	Cyanide, copper, cadmium, nickel, pH
Brewing	Suspended solids, BOD, pH
Dairy products	BOD, pH
Oil refineries	Heat, ammonia, phenols, oil, sulphide
Quarrying	Suspended solids, oil
Power generation	Heat

resulting in, for example, increased evaporation and therefore concentration of solutes trapped from the air, excreted by the plant or released by weathering from the soil below.

(b) Hydrological changes resulting from the route(s) taken by water through the soil column, e.g. towards or away from reactive zones such as weathering horizons or via more or less rapid routes downslope to the nearest collecting channel itself; that channel may itself be an artefact of the land management system.

(c) Chemical changes resulting from the burning or decay of a crop, the removal of a crop or stronger or weaker livestock pressure on land.

(d) Chemical changes resulting from the use of artificial chemicals such as fertilisers and pesticides.

(e) Chemical changes occurring in transit through the stream channel system because that system mixes reactive chemicals or because reactive sites such as metabolising organisms are encountered in the stream ecosystem.

It is, however, the diluting power and biological vitality of streamflow from the upper parts of river basins which allows such point discharges to be made. Thus it is not merely the practice of land-disposal of sewage sludge which links urban to rural water quality; the loss of 'purification power' which occurs as the result of rural pollution is highly significant to urban land use since the world's popular city sites are often riparian and downstream.

Rural water quality changes are caused by a number of natural phenomena, including the seasonal march of temperature and moisture, operating through their effects on micro-organisms and, as already demonstrated, on flow routes and velocities of runoff. A graphic demonstration of change in a non-polluting characteristic of water quality is shown in Figure 3.13, derived from a felling experiment performed on a natural forest at Hubbard Brook in the USA. Felling produces a change in runoff volume and soil temperatures (due to loss of canopy). As a result, both the production and transport of ions such as nitrate, potassium, magnesium and hydrogen are increased (though the phenomenon is transient, declining as forest regrowth occurs).

Figure 3.14 illustrates a much more pressing rural water quality problem, that of the increasing activity of nutrient cycling (in this case nitrogen) which is an inevitable corollary of optimised agricultural production

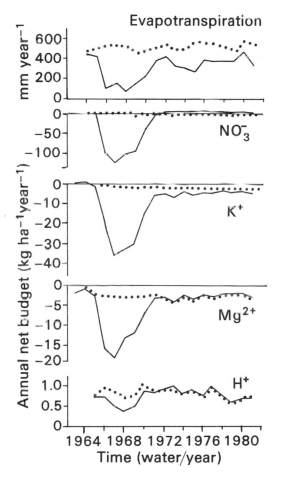

Figure 3.13 Annual net budgets for the Hubbard Brook forest catchment after clear felling (Likens et al., 1978)

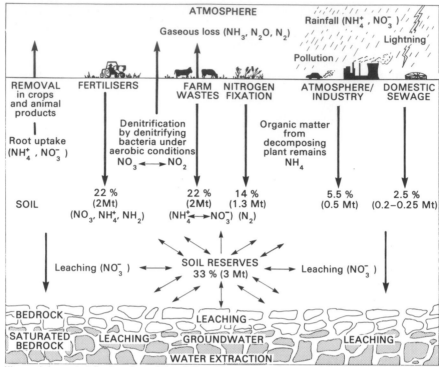

Nitrogen is in constant flux in and out of the soil. Part of it enters groundwater, and thus into our drinking supplies. (Figures come from French research.)

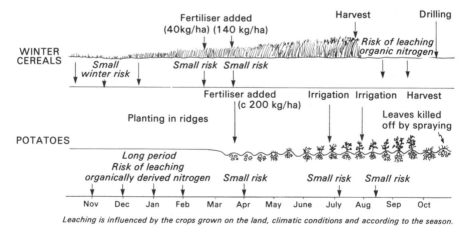

Leaching is influenced by the crops grown on the land, climatic conditions and according to the season.

Figure 3.14 The nitrogen cycle for developed land surfaces and the seasonal risk of nitrate leaching for two crops, winter cereals and potatoes

systems. Industry and domestic waste are also implicated as Figure 3.14 shows but the major and obvious source illustrated for the developed humid temperate zone illustrates is 'bag nitrogen' or artificial fertiliser. Nevertheless, the relative role of and time-dependence of fertiliser inputs are not fully understood; Figure 3.14 indicates considerable scope for altering crops, crop patterns or crop cycles to minimise the seasonal mobilisation and loss of nitrate to water courses.

The loss of pollutants from the surface of urban areas is a more difficult problem. As Figure 3.15 shows, pollutants collect on urban surfaces such as roads as the direct result of 'normal' urban activity. The British proclivity to dog ownership, for example, leads to an annual deposition of 17g per square metre of dog faeces which, together with waste oils, litter, de-icing salt and other pollutants, finds its way to streams by virtue of the need to provide efficient road drainage.

The developed and fast-developing economics of the world are currently experiencing very extensive problems of water quality, not only from the perspective of purification needs for human consumption – a measurable cost if health standards are to be maintained – but also in relation to the recreational use of freshwaters, either directly by bathing and boating or

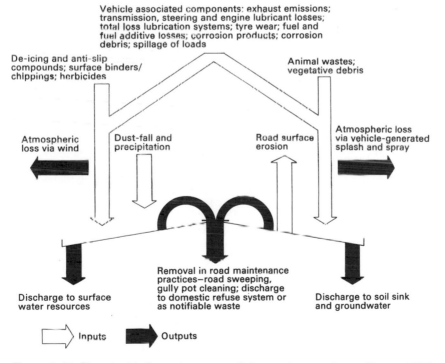

Figure 3.15 Chemical influences on runoff from urban surfaces (Pope, 1980)

indirectly via fisheries. A loss of fisheries also bespeaks a further indefinable cost to species diversity, i.e. declining water quality is a conservation threat. In addition to the impact on surface waters it is now concluded that, despite the filtration capacity of many aquifers, groundwaters are now suffering extensive pollution; furthermore, most rivers discharge into the world's oceans whose capacity to absorb polluting loads is huge but finite.

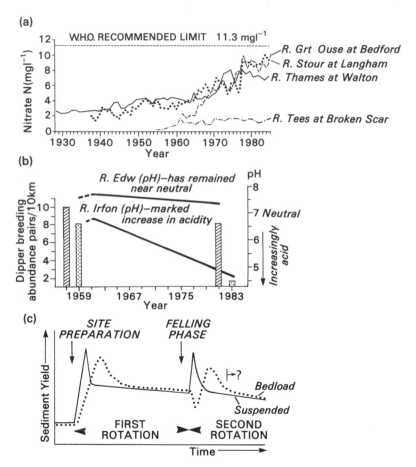

Figure 3.16 Changing river water quality as a result of land use:
(a) Increasing nitrate concentrations in England and Wales (Roberts and Marsh, 1987)
(b) Decreasing pH (increasing acidity) revealed by bird numbers breeding by two streams in Wales; vertical bars refer to inferred pH for the two streams (Tyler, 1987)
(c) Variations in sediment discharge during forest rotation (coniferous plantations, upland UK) (Leeks, personal communication)

Two time trends illustrated in Figure 3.16 are becoming relatively common in Europe and North America. In the richer agricultural and highly populated areas nitrate concentrations are increasing at an alarming rate (Figure 3.16a); in upland areas of low agricultural productivity (especially after afforestation in the UK) pH measurements are declining. In the case shown by Figure 3.16b, the decline of pH is indicated by a decline in the numbers of a bird of conservation significance whose food consists of invertebrates which are intolerant of industrially derived acidity which is scavenged from the atmosphere by recent conifer plantations.

It is of interest to long-term planning that certain adverse land-use effects on water quality are temporary; the hydrological system recovers to a new equilibrium following an initial disturbance. This behaviour is clearly most common where no increase in inputs is occurring but where new sources or pathways for contaminants occur through land-use change, for example the behaviour of bedload and suspended sediments during the forest crop cycle in the uplands of Britain. The eventual recovery demonstrated for these basin outputs does not, however, free land managers from responsibility for pollution. In many cases the transient high concentrations of sediment or solute may be costly; in others any addition to an accumulative problem (such as reservoir or lake sedimentation) is undesirable.

3.4   CONCLUSIONS

The severe problems encountered in constructing a generalised body of scientific results, operable in river basin management, from a series of mainly small-scale, short-term empirical studies of land-use effects are featured in Chapter 8. In an inexact, environmental science such as hydrology we must at the very least be sure about the errors involved in field studies. Of overriding concern and crucial to the design of catchment experiments, particularly those concerned with the water balance, is the requirement that the experimental error attached to the effect being studied is not larger than the effect itself.

Calder's (1990) volume is one of the few in hydrology to follow a forty-year 'story' of scientific investigations into the effects of commercial forestry plantations in the uplands of the UK. Figure 3.17 illustrates the necessary shifts in scale and technique which his programmes experienced during part of that time. At no stage could the detection of the processes involved be left to one technique or field site. The scientific agenda moved on remorselessly; Calder had to follow and he in turn had to justify funds to extend.

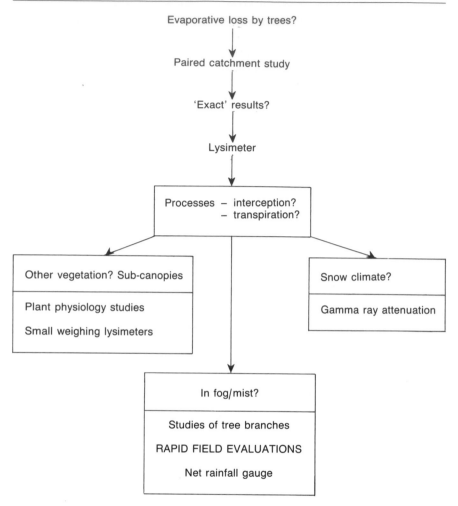

Figure 3.17 The progress of UK studies of the hydrological effects of conifer canopies

Nevertheless, his efforts and those of others (e.g. those reported by Bosch and Hewlett, 1982) have taken us at least to the stage where Calder (in press) can write:

These two results, that interception losses from tall vegetation are likely to be higher than those from short vegetation and that, when soil moisture is non-limiting, forest transpiration is likely to be similar but less than 'grass', have a general significance and can, with a few qualifications, explain the results from the majority of the world's forest/grass catchment experiments.

Despite this optimism in one area of land-use hydrology, the level of investment needed for scientific programmes in this topic means that we remain
in ignorance of key relationships in certain types of land-use practice such
as those in the developing world (Chapter 5); Calder's optimism is not, for
example, vindicated in the case of the many species of Eucalypts being
considered as crops by poor farmers in some regions of the world.

In some nations, however, there are particular reasons for acting quickly
and providing 'watershed protection' by varying natural plant covers, deliberate choice of crops in the interests of water management or protective
laws against urbanisation. In as many others, however, doubts as to
whether science can correctly identify and measure causes are used as a perfect recipe for policy delay.

Finally, it is essential to bear in mind the fact that long timescales are
involved both in the adaptation of hydrological regimes and water quality
by land-use change or regulation and in recovery from any transitory
effects. This problem has been addressed very little because of the prevailing
short-termism in scientific investment; nevertheless, both the afforestation/
deforestation impact and the urbanisation impact have attracted long-term
studies. These indicate that the general concept of reaction relaxation
and recovery periods should be adopted in implementing the findings of
land-use hydrology.

Chapter 4

Managing land and water in the developed world

An international survey

4.1 DEVELOPMENT AND THE RIVER BASIN

Geographers and politicians argue over definitions of development and over maps of where it has occurred, is occurring and will occur and over rates of development. Perhaps the most commendable classification to emerge in recent years separates off the Least Developed Countries (LDCs). However, virtually all definitions imply some form of 'cultural colonialism' by suggesting that development patterns are laid down immutably by the 'First World' (Bissio, 1988). To anyone based in a small nation on an island, developed for habitation over thousands of years, the two most startling aspects of river basin development are the size of the river basins tackled by both ancient and modern management schemes (consider those shown on Figure 4.1) and the rapidity with which technology transfer is now leading to convergence of schemes. Two important new questions then emerge: Are large

1 Yukon
2 Mackenzie
3 St Lawrence
4 Mississippi
5 Colorado
6 Rio Grande
7 Orinoco
8 Amazon
9 Parana

10 Rhine
11 Danube
12 Senegal
13 Volta
14 Niger
15 Lake Chad
16 Nile
17 Congo
18 Zambezi
19 Okavango
20 Orange

21 Tigris–
   Euphrates
22 Indus
23 Ganges

24 Volga
25 Ob
26 Yeni-sei
27 Lena
28 Amur
29 Hwang-ho
30 Yangtse
31 Mekong

Figure 4.1 The world's largest river basins

Table 4.1 River basin development: prioritising the issues of water-based schemes

	'Developed'		'Developing'
Life-permitting	Priorities often domestic and industrial supplies	WATER RESOURCES	Priorities often irrigation and hydro-electric power
	Priorities normally urban centres	FLOOD PROTECTION	Priority is food security
	Major influence associated with property rights	FISHERIES	Subsistence only: little enhancement
	Reacts to 'chemophobia'	POLLUTION CONTROL	Eradication of disease
Life-enhancing	Increasingly Increasingly	RECREATION CONSERVATION	Little known Little known

schemes good schemes? Does convergent technology negate local variation in environment? These cannot be answered until the end of Chapter 5.

A simplistic definition of development in river basin terms (presented in Table 4.1) establishes the priority of life-permitting water schemes over life-enhancing ones. Ideally we would move towards fully comprehensive schemes across the globe but one aspect of local variability is that politicians and budgets are prone to listing priorities. One contribution made by Table 4.1 is that, for the 'developed world', the subject of this chapter, the list represents an approximate chronological sequence of river basin management themes.

The basis for a selection of nations in this chapter inevitably involves literature in the English language but also includes the potential for the 'national experiences' of river basin development in the USA, Canada and New Zealand to exemplify both physical and cultural influences on public policy with regard to rivers. These influences are drawn together in Chapter 7 with the addition of the UK pattern of river basin development.

4.2 RIVER BASIN MANAGEMENT IN THE USA

The USA is essentially two nations in terms of water resource development; although the Mississippi basin (Figure 4.2) appears to integrate a vast internal drainage system, the division between 'humid' and 'dry' America is too profound in terms of history, attitude, law and contemporary problems to be ignored. The problems of water-based development in

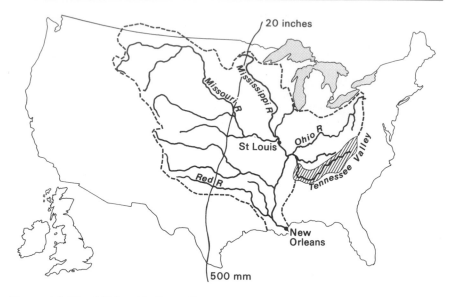

Figure 4.2 The USA, with Great Britain at the same scale, showing the extent
and central position of the Mississippi basin

the West are well and colourfully documented from the days of the earliest
exploration of 'The Interior'. Government finance was used to hold and
populate the West against natural hazards and indigenous cultures, making
a study of river basins in that region highly instructive. By contrast, in the
humid east the water agenda is dominated by issues of national planning
and environmental protection.

4.2.1   Exploration, development, destabilisation

In 1803 the USA completed the diplomatic coup of doubling its land area
by the purchase from Napolean of Louisiana; 'at four cents an acre'
(Cooke, 1973), the opening of an interior for the young nation was a critical
development for the President, Thomas Jefferson. We know that by 1804
Jefferson had despatched Lewis and Clark on an expedition, largely routed
along rivers, to explore the new hinterland, to survey and to make records
of all natural resources (de Voto, 1953).

Extracts from the journals of Lewis and Clark in 1804 (provided by de
Voto) make plain the priority their expedition showed to issues of land and
water development. For example:

[21 July 1804]
about 10 Leagues up this river on the S Side a small river comes into the

Platt called Salt River, the water so brackish that it can't be drank at some seasons

[23 July 1804]
I commence coppying a Map of the river below to send to the P. [President]

Whilst Lewis and Clark's three-year expedition contributed an essential knowledge base to the 'Go West' mentality which continues to pervade the USA (*vide* the continued growth of the 'Sun Belt'; see below), a more important journey in terms of water development was that made by the Civil War veteran John Wesley Powell. It is a tribute to the Powell expedition's use of photography that Stephens and Shoemaker (1987) have recently been able to assemble a compelling visual record of a century of environmental changes in the basins of the Green and Colorado Rivers. Powell it was who first spoke of 'reclamation' for the harsh habitats of the West; he favoured a careful and conservational application of damming and irrigating but the US Government reacted slowly. However, in the year of Powell's death (1902) the Reclamation Act was passed by Congress, paving the way for Federal intervention in the financing of water schemes in the West. The Mormons' settlement of Salt Lake City provided, perhaps, too inspiring a vision of what could be achieved by irrigation. James Michener's epic historical novel *Centennial* (1975) contains abundant factual evidence of the impacts of 'reclamation' on the lives of settlers in the Colorado township which gives the book its name. The development of water resources is at first a private venture, steered by Russian immigrant Brumbaugh; he immediately concludes that the eastern seaboard's law of *riparian rights* is totally inappropriate for his grandiose scheme for diverting water from the River Platte ('too thick to drink; too thin to plough') on to his land so as to convert from an extensive livestock to an intensive arable economy.

> The average rainfall in parts of England where Riparian Rights were codified was more than thirty-five inches a year, and a farmer's big problem was getting excess water off his land.... 'We must have a new law', Brumbaugh grumbled ... And [Beck] the seedy lawyer proceeded to do so. He devised a brilliant new concept of a river,...: 'The public owns the rivers and all the water in them. The use of that water resides in the man who first took it onto his land and put it to practical purposes. ... First-in-time, first-in right.'
>
> (Michener, 1975, pp. 683–4)

Michener colourfully collapses the evolution of the law of *Prior Appropriation* in the American West but correctly identifies the attitude and environment behind it; as noted below it is the current battle between attitude and environment which disfigures water planning in relation to land resources in the West.

Even Michener can record Brumbaugh, near death, as becoming attuned to the hydrological cycle and a more egalitarian outlook: 'There is no rest, neither for the river nor for the man. And the man is entitled only to as much water as he can borrow from this endless cycle' (p. 927).

Another service provided by Michener's researches in writing *Centennial* is to emphasise the very high level of climatic risk (blizzard, drought, dust-storm) involved in settling the high plains; we may extend this concept of hazard across the Rockies to the shores of the Pacific.

The USA's colonisation of the more extreme climatic zones of its land led in the 1930s to disaster: successive droughts led to the Dust Bowl which forced millions of farming people to migrate, often to other dry areas without a soil erosion problem.

4.2.2   The Colorado basin

Reisner (1990) has labelled the Colorado an 'American Nile' because the river, despite its moderate size (Figure 4.3), is 'the most legislated, most debated, and most litigated in the entire world' (p. 125). It has the largest population and industrial base of other world rivers of a similar level of exploitation and management. It is, in most years, all used (Figure 4.3e), its delta being dry. Its unhappy record of allocation to competing states resembles that of the Nile and the growth of the American West this century, superimposed upon considerable environmental change (both natural and resulting from water management itself) makes a fascinating, if distressing, geographical study (see Graf, 1985).

The waters of the Colorado were first used for a major irrigation project in the Imperial Valley of California in 1901. Dams were built on tributaries from 1910 but by 1922 there was sufficient competition for the relatively modest annual flow of the Colorado itself that the Colorado River Compact was arranged to split this resource between the upper and lower (altitude) states along its steep, often gorge-like course. In 1928 approval was given for the Boulder Canyon Project in which the Hoover Dam was built by 1935. Since that moment, and largely as a result of Federal activity (by the Bureau of Reclamation or US Army Corps of Engineers), the river has been comprehensively dammed (Table 4.2) and diverted, at first to feed the irrigation of high-value arable crops in the south-west but also in the interests of 'high altitude' irrigation (mainly for livestock farming) in the upper basin; clearly the result of Federal projects is cheap water. Reisner (1990) remarks that 'in the West water flows uphill towards money' – and in this case the money is that of the taxpayer or of those paying for the expensive electricity produced by the dams. Graf (1985) likens the Colorado to 'the world's largest plumbing system' because of the dams.

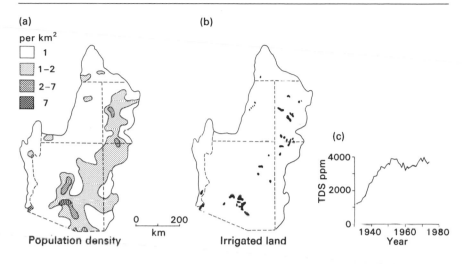

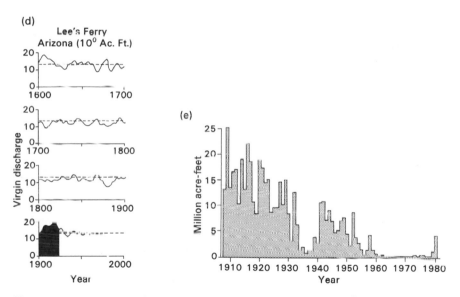

Figure 4.3 Features of the Colorado basin, an 'American Nile':
  (a) Population density
  (b) Irrigation schemes
  (c) The rise of total dissolved solids (TDS) in the river as irrigation schemes have developed
  (d) Time series of natural ('virgin') discharge, illustrating the wetter period preceding the negotiation of the Colorado Compact (all from Graf, 1985)
  (e) Annual flows of the Colorado below all major abstractions, 1910–80 (Englebert and Scheuring, 1984)

Table 4.2 Major high dams in the Colorado system

River	State	Dam	Reservoir	Date	Height (m) completed	Capacity (acre-feet)[a]
Colorado	AZ CA	Parker	L. Havasu	1938	98	807615
Colorado	AZ NV	Davis	L. Mohave	1950	61	2267487
Colorado	AZ NV	Hoover	L. Mead	1936	221	37103436
Colorado	AZ	Glen Canyon	L. Powell	1964	216	33668298
Colorado	CO	Granby	L. Granby	1950	91	673218
Los Pinos	CO	Vallecito	Pine L.	1941	49	161523
Blue	CO	Green Mtn	Green Mtn L.	1943	94	155359
Aqua Fria	AZ	Waddell	L. Pleasant	1927	78	203445
Gila	AZ	Coolidge	San Carlos L.	1928	76	1506726
Verde	AZ	Horseshoe	Horseshoe L.	1949	43	173853
Verde	AZ	Bartlett	Bartlett L.	1939	87	224406
Salt	AZ	Stewart Mtn	Saguarto L.	1930	63	87543
Salt	AZ	Mormon Flat	Canyon L.	1938	68	72747
Salt	AZ	Horse Mesa	Apache L.	1927	93	305784
Salt	AZ	Roosevelt	Roosevelt L.	1911	85	1723734
Green	WY	Flaming Gorge	Flaming Gorge	1964	153	4724856
Strawberry	UT	Strawberry	Strawberry L.	1913	22	286056
Price	UT	Scofield	Scofield L.	1946	38	690480
San Juan	NM	Navajo	Navajo L.	1963	123	2130624

Total storage 86721822

Source: Graf (1985)
[a] 1 acre-foot = 1233 m³.

In the lower parts of the Colorado a continuing battle occurs between California and Arizona over rights to the Colorado. Arizona, inhabited by a successful Indian culture based on irrigation (the Hohokam) between 300 BC and AD 1400 (Figure 4.4), experienced a quadrupling of population between 1920 and 1960.

Graf (1985) undermines the basis of allocating the average flow of the Colorado between competing states on the grounds of a number of natural instabilities in the basin, many of which are exacerbated by the existing management (largely based on dam construction). There is inherent climatic variability in the south-west USA, the result of oscillating positions of the jet stream (Figure 4.3d). For example, the period for calculating discharge averages prior to the Compact was wetter than long-term figures now available; the 1940–60s, a period of the urbanisation of floodplains, were largely flood-free. As Graf puts it, 'Planning for variability rather than for averages is therefore the most likely route to success' (p. 154).

Amongst the variability detailed by Graf, the Colorado suffers from:

(a) The periodic formation of deeply incised (21 m deep) channels known as *arroyos* which severely damage agricultural land and release tonnes of sediment downstream to hinder basin management.

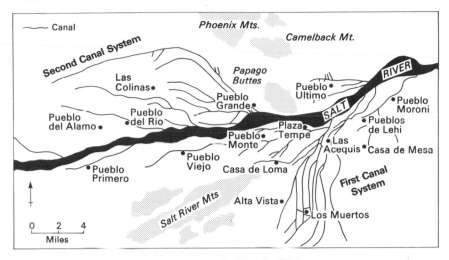

Figure 4.4 The irrigation schemes of the Hohokam Indians, Arizona (Graf, 1985)

(b) Channel changes which threaten irrigated agriculture, settlements and communications, with narrow, single-thread channels widening and braiding after 'rare' floods (e.g. those in the late 1970s and 80s in Arizona which produced channels 1.5 km wide).

(c) Colonisation of floodplain and channel bars by phreatophyte vegetation such as willow, cottonwood and tamarisk which evaporates much-needed river water and produces more extensive flooding than would occur with a 'clean' floodplain.

Each of these inherent variabilities may be climatically driven or may result from threshold behaviour of the geomorphological system (see Schumm, 1977) or else is conditioned by factors such as overgrazing, the introduction of non-native species such as tamarisk or thoughtless 'channelisation' of problem rivers.

The dams and irrigation systems are also responsible for unwelcome changes such as sedimentation (not only in reservoirs but also in upstream channels), habitat changes (especially below dams with a heavily controlled flow regime) and salinisation (Figure 4.3c). The latter problem threatened to wreck the political structure of basin management when polluted, saline water, the result of crop and reservoir evaporation, was supplied over the border to give Mexico its legitimate share of the Colorado's water.

Despite these problems, Graf (1985) asserts that 'a factor common to the ancient and modern approaches is a perspective on the river basin as an holistic entity, a complex grouping of individual parts that function together' (p. 3).

Table 4.3 Significant dates in the development of environmental
river basin policy in the USA

Date	Event
300 BC	Hohokam Indians' irrigation, Arizona (Figure 4.4)
1623 AD	European migrants build dam for sawmill, Maine
1717	First levees, New Orleans (flood protection)
1750	First municipal water supply, Philadelphia
1799	Army Corps of Engineers formed
1842	New York City builds its first water supply dam
1869	John Wesley Powell explores the Colorado
1902	Bureau of Reclamation formed
1908–13	Hetch Hetchy Dam controversy
1922	Colorado River Basin Compact
1933	Tennessee Valley Authority
1948	First Water Pollution Control Act
1965	Water Resources Planning Act
1968	Wild and Scenic Rivers Act
1968	National Water Commission Act
1969	National Environmental Protection Act
1972	Water Pollution Control Act
1973	President Carter suspends work on a dam project
1974	Safe Drinking Water Act
1976	Teton Dam Disaster
1977	Soil and Water Resources Conservation Act
1977	Clean Water Act
1983	Water Resources Commission disbanded

Source: Modified from Palmer (1986)

There is, in fact, little evidence in the Colorado that such an holistic outlook is substantiated by institutions and technology. Indeed, it was the continuing inability to coordinate the exploitation of the Colorado and to reconcile it with conservation that forced the US Government to set up the National Water Commission in 1968 (see Table 4.3).

4.2.3   The Tennessee Valley Authority (TVA)

The Tennessee River is a tributary of the Ohio, itself a tributary of the Mississippi which occupies half of the continental USA (Figure 4.2). The Tennessee is itself huge, comprising an area of 80 per cent of that of England and Wales, with a flow which is 24 times that of the Thames or 70 per cent of that of the Nile.

There are many tensions in American public policy but two of the greatest, between Federal and State action and between private and public investment in projects, have joined to threaten the success of a model river basin project, much imitated the world over, begun in the south-eastern

USA in 1933. A hydro-electric power dam, on the River Tennessee at Muscle Shoals, was to be the first act of the Tennessee Valley Authority (TVA), a powerful river basin institution, charged with both land and water management, which President Theodore Roosevelt called 'a corporation clothed with the power of government, but possessed with the flexibility and initiative of a private enterprise' (Palmer, 1986, p. 34). As Palmer writes, 'New dams were at the cutting edge of the TVA and the national attitude about rivers was reflected and shaped by the agency' (p. 35 and see Figure iii, in the Prologue, this volume). Later, President Truman tried to create similar authorities for the Missouri and Columbia rivers but Congress refused. The dams on the Tennessee (9 major sites) and on tributaries (42 sites) created a longer lake shoreline than on the Great Lakes; however, despite the heroic achievements of this conservation scheme (in the sense of the word 'conservation' in vogue at the time), it has been much criticised.

Chandler (1984) points out that the costs were far more than the 1.5 billion dollars spent on capital schemes: 10 per cent of the Valley's best farmland was drowned and most of the benefits of flood control were enjoyed by a single city – Chattanooga. Saha and Barrow (1981) dismiss the TVA as 'a massive electricity generating utility' and have drawn attention to the use of that power for polluting activities such as fertiliser manufacture and to the subsequent generation by the TVA of coal-fired and nuclear power. The availability of local power has, however, led to a regeneration of regional prosperity; the navigation improvements built into each dam scheme have also aided the connectivity of a 'backwoods' area (originally isolated by the 37-mile long rapids at Muscle Shoals).

However, the TVA had become an exploratory concept in soil and water management because of its approach to erosion control; 'watershed management' was a term first used there and an agency spawned by the approach – the US Soil Conservation Service – was to have a major influence throughout the world, often by reversing TVA scales of operation and concentrating on small dams and on-farm techniques. The reach of the TVA, via government agencies, to farmers has been impressive by way of:

(a) Land reclamation from gullying.
(b) Soil conservation.
(c) Use of fertilisers (many produced at Muscle Shoals).
(d) Demonstration farms – crop diversification.
(e) Cooperatives for marketing.

In addition, the TVA needed to manage reservoir water levels to control malarial mosquitoes; this it does by keeping water levels raised during the period April to June when plant growth and stagnant shallows would encourage breeding. The results have been good and further success has come from reducing water levels in winter so as to store floodwaters in the

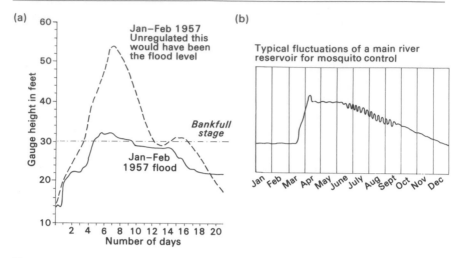

Figure 4.5 Tennessee Valley Authority reservoir regimes for:
(a) Containing flood runoff
(b) Controlling mosquito life cycle (malaria control) (TVA)

system (see Figure 4.5); despite drowning land beneath its dams the TVA has, however, freed much good land from flooding and yet more through erosion control in the uplands.

In a recent review of the environmental effects of dams, Brown and Shelton (1983), both employees of the TVA, strongly support the record of their dams in making the Tennessee River 'one of the most useful in the world' (p. 139). The TVA 'means as much in meeting the challenge of the future as it did in helping to overcome the problems of the 1930's' (p. 150). However, they also admit to problems in responding to 'environmental and societal effects in the planning and decision-making process' (p. 150), a point taken up in Chapter 7 here.

4.2.4 Dams and river basin management

Palmer (1986) takes the environmentalist position against the USA's talent for dam-building:

> Reservoirs have flooded the oldest known settlement in North America, the second-deepest canyon, the second most popular whitewater, the habitat of endangered species, one of the first national parks, tens of thousands of homes, rich farmland, desert canyons and virgin forests. In building dams we have blocked the best runs of salmon and broken the oldest Indian treaty – one that George Washington signed.
>
> (Palmer, 1986, p.1)

Palmer describes the USA as having a 'culture of rivers', free-flowing and luxuriant with habitat; an attitude which, whilst latent all this century, peaked in the successful campaigns to prevent dams in Grand Canyon and the Green River Canyons in the 1960s. He sets up a chronology of river abuse up to this time (summarised here as Table 4.3), including the activities of the US Army Corps of Engineers in the East through their flood-control dams as well as the Bureau of Reclamation in the West.

By 1980 all agencies and private developers had built fifty thousand dams of 25 feet or more. Conservationists had begun to oppose dams in the celebrated Hetch Hetchy of Yosemite National Park; at this stage they faced other conservationists who interpreted the term as meaning careful, rational exploitation of resources (American civil policy enshrined this latter definition throughout the early years of this century). The protests failed; in 1908 the Hetch Hetchy dam was approved.

In the 1950s the biggest environmental conservation issue in the USA concerned a proposal under the Upper Colorado River Storage Project to dam the canyons on the Green River in Dinosaur National Monument. In this case the objectors won, only to lose the battle for Glen Canyon, upstream of Grand Canyon on the Colorado in Arizona, as the Bureau of Reclamation took up their charge to 'build it elsewhere'.

Palmer writes that in the 1960–70s:

> A revolution in attitudes about rivers moved through the country and touched every stream. The late 1960s and early 1970s brought powerful ingredients for change: a growing sense of scarcity, the environmental movement, activism by conservationists and landowners, applications of science and economics coupled with publicity, recreational use, and tight money – all contributing to a national movement to save threatened rivers.
>
> (Palmer, 1986, p. 93)

The new spirit had an unexpected outcome in the case of the Tellico Dam, proposed for the Little Tennessee by the TVA in 1966 but delayed by protests from fishermen; in 1973 a zoologist discovered a rare fish, the snail darter, in the river near the dam site and it was placed on the 'endangered species list'. Progress on the dam was halted but, despite an excellent case against the dam for many other reasons (President Carter had long opposed dam construction), the conservationists' case based on the snail darter was lost and the Tellico Dam was completed.

In 1965 the Wild Rivers Act was passed to bring a measure of protection to the rivers of the West; by 1968 the National Wild and Scenic Rivers Act extended protection for eight rivers, with a reserve list of twenty-seven. The Act prohibits dams or other Federal projects which would damage listed rivers; the list has been extended through the surveys of the Department of the Interior.

Another problem with the American proclivity to dam-building has been the relatively scant attention paid to safety, despite the excellence of the national standing in hydrological research. By 1984, in spite of variable uptake of legislation, 2,900 non-Federal dams had been declared unsafe, most because of poor spillway design. The American Society of Civil Engineers responded by establishing a Task Force which first classified dam safety into three levels of importance depending on the damage caused by dam failure; design is relatively straightforward in the very large and very small damage categories but a cost–benefit approach, with much consideration of social and environmental consequences of failure, needs to be taken in-between these extremes (ASCE, 1988a). In the same year the US Committee on Large Dams prepared an update of its survey of the type, frequency and trends in US dam failures (ASCE, 1988b). The 'narrative description of incidents' makes exciting, if distressing, reading. Over 500 incidents are on record, including 125 major failures and 125 'accidents' (Figure 4.6). The failure of the Teton Dam in Idaho in 1976 killed 14 people and cost $400 million.

The USA's experience with dams and dam disasters draws out the following features to be borne in mind when dealing with river basin

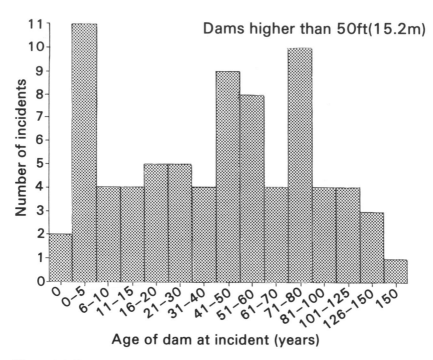

Figure 4.6 Dam incidents, USA, including damage and disaster (American Society of Civil Engineers, 1988b)

management schemes elsewhere, particularly in the developing world:

(a) Dams have a finite lifetime and a risk assessment is a necessary part of any scheme, for both social and environmental reasons.
(b) Dam-building is a scale element of river basin development and can be aimed at small, e.g. farm, scale developments as well as the larger, riskier, but more prestigious structures.
(c) Dam construction at any scale bespeaks maintenance, safety checks and a well-resourced system of disaster warnings if downstream communities are in danger.

A major change of outlook on dam-building and one which also affected land-use policy occurred in 1968 with the passing of the National Flood

Plate 4.1 Devastation resulting in the valley of the Roaring River, Colorado, USA from the failure of the Lawn Lake Dam, July 1982

Insurance Act. This Act sought to change the balance of the Federal approach to flood protection from one reliant upon dams, levees, diversion channels, etc. (structural approaches) to one seeking to identify the use of flood-prone land and to charge an insurance premium consistent with the risk of flooding. In 1973 the Flood Disaster Protection Act forced developers to arrange such insurance cover before becoming eligible for any federally related finance for development. By 1980 over $95 billion of insurance had been taken out but with an emphasis on coastal, not river, flooding (Platt *et al.*, 1983).

4.2.5 Land-use issues in American river basin management

We have not, so far, mentioned an important US agency which maintains the network of basic hydrological observations in the country as a whole – the US Geological Survey (USGS). The Survey exists to:

(a) Collect and analyse data for water resources planning and control
(b) Assess the physical, biological and chemical characteristics of surface and ground water
(c) Coordinate all Federal activity in water-resource data gathering and provide advice to other agencies
(d) Operate State institutes and grant programmes for water resources research.

The Survey's data-gathering activity dates from John Wesley Powell's day; from 1888 Powell sought to train Survey staff to make the necessary measurements to enable satisfactory irrigation and flood control schemes to be devised. He began on the Rio Grande in northern New Mexico; velocities were measured with floats and depths surveyed from log rafts. By 1900 the United States had 160 flow gauges and by the centenary of the Rio Grande site, 7,000 continuously recording sites.

The USGS is therefore technically well-equipped to carry out research on the effects of land use; however, since the USA occupies such a huge land area, the gauge records are dominantly indicative of climatic and geological differences expressed at the scale of large river basins. As we observe in Chapter 8, this is not ideal for detecting land-use effects at a scale where local land planning and management can be varied as part of basin management.

The research catchment programme, run at a much smaller scale, is very active in the USA (see Chapter 3); the USGS participates largely through involvement with State water resource institutes. Additionally the US Department of Agriculture, especially the Forest Service, carries out its own research into farming and forestry effects. Because such agencies also own and manage land there is a good deal of immediate practical benefit from land-use hydrology. For example, in the American Society of Civil

Engineers' *Watershed Management 1980* volume (see Snyder, and McClimans references below), the following farm and forest issues are covered:

Farming $\begin{cases} \text{Soil erosion and tillage} \\ \text{Range management and stocking rates} \end{cases}$

Forestry $\begin{cases} \text{Water yield} \\ \text{Erosion} \\ \text{Roading} \\ \text{Fire} \end{cases}$

These show some characteristic American 'big issues', thanks to the climatic and settlement characteristics of the nation, e.g. irrigated agriculture and forests liable to extensive fires. Attention to the management of snow is also prominent. The major land-use issue so far given relatively little attention in Europe is the impact of 'strip mining' (opencast) for coal and minerals such as phosphate.

Watershed management principles may well, albeit slowly, enter the control of water quality – particularly of non-point pollution – in the USA. The US Environmental Protection Agency (1986) has divided the nation into 76 'ecoregions', representing statistically significant combinations of natural controls on water quality. State quality control programmes then monitor the physical, chemical and biological background quality of indicator watersheds in order to set local standards. In some states (e.g. Illinois; Polls and Lanyon, 1980) homogeneous land uses receive similar monitoring. The Illinois study has tabulated the characteristic pollutant loads contributed from each major land use.

The US approach to forest management and water resources has the benefit of many years of continuous detailed research dating back to the early years of the century, through one or more forest cycles (American forestry has an added environmental issue to address on felling since much of the forested land is pristine). By now forest management is very carefully controlled to meet water resources and pollution objectives. For example, the US Environmental Protection Agency requires the Forest Service to carry out evaluations of non-point sources of pollution including soil erosion/man movement, water temperature, dissolved oxygen, nutrients and pesticides. Snyder (1980) summarises these impacts whilst McClimans (1980) develops the practical aspects of forest management via 'best management practices' for forestry activities; these were instituted by amendment to the Federal Water Pollution Control Act 1972. The BMP procedures link pollution or other damage hazards to slope angle and distance to streams (Figure 4.7).

Heede and King (1990) address the problem that to harvest timber as part of watershed management may lead to more problems (of pollution and

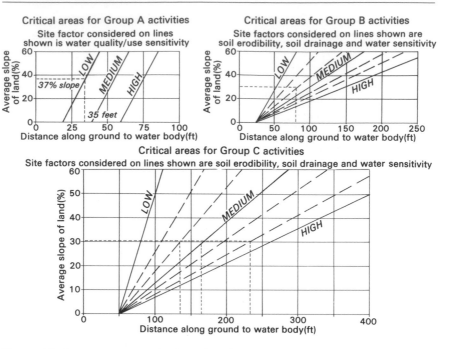

Figure 4.7 Assessment graphs for mitigating the damage from forestry operations close to streams. Group A activities include aerial spraying, Group B cultivating and road work, Group C ground skidding (McClimans, 1980)

sedimentation) than it solves (in water yield). In their study area of Arizona the use of 'state of the art' machinery and of strict rules on its use created no extra surface runoff or soil erosion problems. In the East, Douglass (1983) has demonstrated how the use of simple predictive models can coordinate a felling programme to augment water yield steadily, though he claims that interventionist policies to bring about such a programme are not yet needed in the eastern states.

The ill-fated National Water Commission (1968–83) carefully considered the benefits of the land-use management option in a national water resource strategy (US National Water Commission, 1973). Table 4.4 shows the extra water capable of being made available in each region and the costs of so doing. The major control options were said to comprise:

(a) Forest and brush management, critical because of the 1000 mm average rainfall of the US forests (cf. 610 mm on other land uses). There is, for example, a strong case for a 'joint product' (timber and water) from the sub-alpine forests of the Upper Colorado.

(b) Phreatophyte management, already referred to in connection with the

Table 4.4 Potential annual increase in water supply from watershed land management

Area and source		Potential annual increase under present forest conditions (1,000 acre-feet)[a]	Direct financial cost per acre-foot[a]
Northeast (New England, Middle Atlantic, Great Lakes, and Central States) Commercial forests		2350	2.18
Southeast (South Atlantic and Gulf States) Commercial forests		2750	2.64
Eastern United States	Total	5100 Average	2.41
Pacific Northwest (Eastern portions of Oregon and Washington) Commercial forests		160	3.17
California (excluding North Coast)			
Commercial forests		130	2.13
Phreatophyte areas		10	10.50
Chaparral		410	20.45
Woodlands-grasses		370	45.00
Northern Rocky Mountains (Idaho, Montana, W. South Dakota and Wyoming) Commercial forests		1000	0.89
Other		40	90.00
Southern Rocky Mountains (Arizona, Colorado, Nevada, New Mexico and Utah) Commercial forests		530	1.07
Phreatophyte areas		900	14.00
Chaparral		290	18.00
Other		300	128.00
Western United States	Total	4140 Average	21.42
48 Continuous United States	Total	9240	

Source: US National Water Commission (1973)
[a] 1 acre-foot = 1233 m^3.

Table 4.5 Measured evapotranspiration rates reported
for phreatophytes and other riparian
vegetation in the Southwestern United States

Species	Rate (mm water per year)
Bare Ground	640–810
Phreatophytes	
Cottonwood	1540–2480
Mesquite	1014
Tamarisk	340–2800
Willow	770–1390
Shrubs	
Arrowweed	2440
Fourwing Saltbush	1090
Grasses	
Bermuda	1070–2760
Blue Panic	1240–1330
Alta Fescue	1820
St Augustine	1660
Alkalai Sacaton	430
Saltgrass	540
Crops	
Alfalfa	1750–2130
Barley	300–1120
Cotton	650–1050
Wheat	660–1120

Source: Graf (1985)

Colorado but comprising 6.5 million hectares in the south-west. (For comparative evaporation rates see Table 4.5.)

(c) Management of snow packs by vegetation (largely forest) management; in Colorado 20 per cent of the state's water resources come from snow and in California the proportion stands at 51 per cent.

(d) Soil surface treatments to improve runoff characteristics.

The Commission's other recommendations include institutional changes to permit more rational planning but in practice most of the compliance by land owners and managers is coming from the threat of pollution legislation than from proactive rural planning. Whilst California has watershed planning systems to coordinate the work of agencies in support of the State Wild and Scenic Rivers Act (Watson, 1980), other states have not followed suit and the other examples of basin planning are either urban or part of the brief of interstate and interagency planning for large basins (see below).

There have been several phases of interest in river basin planning authorities subsequent to the Colorado Compact in 1922 and the Tennessee Valley Authority in 1933. In the 1940s the Federal Interagency River Basin Commission provided advice based upon 'layering' the individual activities of a number of agencies in some of the larger basins (Figure 4.8). This scale and type of activity was abolished in 1966; the Water Resource Planning Act 1965 (Black, 1982) had established River Basin Commissions as much more proactive in planning; these paid the penalty of being recommended by the National Water Commission as 'new and unique' regional institutions and clearly regional institutions figure very little in American policy.

Much more enduring have proved to be the river basin compacts between states where the Federal government is also involved, e.g. the Delaware River Basin Compact (see Majumdar *et al.*, 1988). The Commission comprises the Governors of Delaware, New Jersey, Pennsylvania (and New York, which has created 90 per cent of the water storage capacity as dams in the upper basin), together with the Secretary of the Interior. Goodell (1988) describes its functions as:

> to encourage and provide for the planning, conservation, utilisation, development, management and control of the water resources of the basin and to apply the principle of equal and uniform treatment to all water users who are similarly situated and to all users of related facilities, without regard to established political boundaries.
>
> (Goodell, 1988, p. 286)

It successfully saw the basin through the drought of 1961–7 when it took over the operation of several agency schemes (having been instituted after

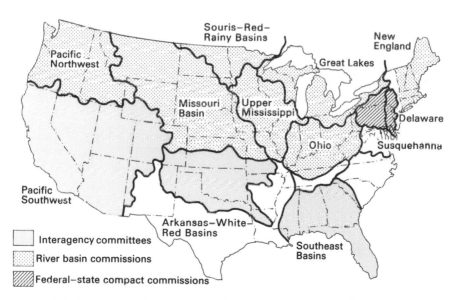

Figure 4.8 Agency structures surrounding the management of major US river basins

devastating floods in 1955!). It has also arranged referenda on further dam projects and cancelled two following adverse votes. Despite very serious problems of industrial waste water quality it has largely 'lost out' to the Environmental Protection Agency in this sector and has failed to reconcile differences in the planning styles and structures, e.g. between New Jersey and Pennsylvania. Polhemus (1988) concludes:

> the Commission is tightly controlled by the states and has not been permitted to develop an innovative operating programme. Although the Commission could evolve into a significant control factor in the basin, influencing growth, economic development and the balance of power in the region, it has been compromised to a limited water management role.
>
> (Polhemus, 1988, pp. 317–8)

4.2.6   Cultural, political, legal attitudes

The contrast we have observed between river basin management issues and structures west and east of the Mississippi supports an earlier division in this book between cultures concentrating on distribution strategies for water and those needing to know more of collection strategies (simply labelled hydraulic and hydrologic cultures).

As Reisner (1990) puts it, the venture West by high density settlement creates the dilemma for water distribution there:

> Any place with less than twenty inches of rainfall is hostile terrain to a farmer depending solely on the sky, and a place that receives seven inches or less − as Phoenix, El Paso and Reno do − is arguably no place to inhabit at all.
>
> (p. 3)

Writing of the heroic efforts of those who succoured the hydraulic civilisation of the West (including meteorologists who claimed that 'Rain follows the plow' [*sic*]), Reisner takes a fatalistic line:

> Such a surfeit of ambition stems, of course, from the remarkable record of success we have had in reclaiming the American desert. But the same could have been said about any number of desert civilizations throughout history − Assyria, Carthage, Mesopotamia; the Inca, the Aztec, the Hohokam − before they collapsed.
>
> (p. 6)

Pricing and legislating water exploitation is something which successive US Governments have found it desperately hard to do; a number of Presidents have begun their political careers with 'pork barrel' water projects won in Washington for local electors. President Jimmy Carter was extremely bold for a US President in standing up to the Bureau of Reclamation over its budget.

Reisner is again fatalistic:

the tragic and ludicrous aspect of the whole situation is that cheap water keeps the machine running: the water lobby cannot have enough of it, just as the engineers cannot build enough dams and how convenient that cheap water encourages waste which results in more dams.

(Reisner, 1990, p. 494)

The Ogallala aquifer underlies the High Plains between South Dakota and Western Texas. From the close of World War II, in an era of cheap energy, its waters have been pumped on to the drought-prone lands; by now, as Reisner (1990) puts it, the aquifer is overdrawn by an amount equivalent to the flow of the Colorado. Groundwater protection and management are likely to be high on the agenda of US water management policy-making in the next decade. Already 27 states have statutes allowing intervention to control 'groundwater mining' but, significantly, those states with a large irrigation need have relied on a 'good neighbour policy' amongst local users (Bowman, 1990). In New Jersey, by contrast, the state has a groundwater strategy, targeted at pollution control as well as water resource allocation (Whipple and Van Abs, 1990).

The most recent estimates (Solley, 1989 and Figure 4.9) are that withdrawals of water declined by 10 per cent in the USA between 1980 and 1985. The USA's five-yearly survey, begun in 1950, had hitherto always shown a rise in consumption; the downturn is ascribed to depressed commodity prices in agriculture and increased use of recycled water in industry. Nevertheless, average public and domestic use remains extremely high at over 350 l/person/day when the water is privately supplied and almost 480 l/person/day under public schemes (illustrating the effects of costs and pricing).

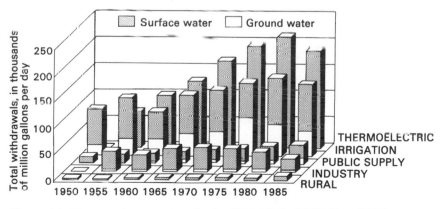

Figure 4.9 Changes in water use in the USA 1950–85 (Solley, 1989)

Table 4.6 Streamflow compared with current withdrawals and consumption (billion US gallons^2 per day)

Region	Mean annual runoff	Runoff in 95% of the years	Freshwater consumptive use 1970	Projected total consumptive use 2000	2020	Withdrawals 1970	Projected total withdrawals 2000	2020
North Atlantic	163.0	112.0	1.8	5.0	8.5	55.0	113.9	236.3
South Atlantic–Gulf	197.0	116.0	3.3	5.7	8.3	35.0	87.4	130.2
Great Lakes	63.2	42.4	1.2	3.2	5.5	39.0	96.6	191.0
Ohio	125.0	67.5	0.9	2.5	3.6	36.0	65.1	90.2
Tennessee	41.5	24.4	0.24	0.8	1.1	7.09	13.9	18.1
Upper Mississippi	64.6	28.5	0.8	0.8	2.6	16.0	30.6	41.3
Lower Mississippi	48.4	24.6	3.6	4.5	6.3	13.0	28.0	39.4
Souris–Red–Rainy	6.17	1.91	0.07	0.5	0.5	0.3	2.0	2.8
Missouri	54.1	23.9	12.0	15.0	16.4	24.0	27.9	31.6
Arkansas–White–Red	95.8	33.4	6.8	10.6	12.3	12.0	25.3	31.6
Texas–Gulf	39.1	11.4	6.2	10.9	12.3	21.0	57.3	92.6
Rio Grande	4.9	2.1	3.3	5.0	5.5	6.3	9.5	11.7
Upper Colorado	13.45	7.50	4.1	3.1	3.1	8.1	6.6	6.7
Lower Colorado	3.19	0.85	5.0	4.6	5.3	7.2	8.4	8.9
Great Basin	5.89	2.46	3.2	3.6	3.8	6.7	7.6	7.8
Columbia–North Pacific	210.0	138.0	11.0	17.3	21.6	30.0	90.1	156.7
California	65.1	25.6	22.0	32.7	38.2	48.0	120.5	244.8
Alaska	588.0		0.02	0.1	0.2	0.2	0.9	4.2
Hawaii	13.3		0.8	1.0	1.4	2.7	4.7	8.6
Puerto Rico			0.17	0.5	0.6	3.0	8.3	13.7
Total United States	1793.7		86.5	127.4	157.1	370.59	804.6	1368.2

Source: US National Water Commission (1973)
[a] 1 million US gallons = 3785 ML.

Given that the 1980s have witnessed seven droughts in the USA, the discrepancy between supply and demand in some regions (Table 4.6) is likely to grow. The most extensive water scheme of all for the western USA remains a gleam in the eyes of dam-builders; the North American Water and Power Alliance (NAWAPA) was devised by a Los Angeles water and power engineer in the early 1950s. Environmentalists are appalled by its scope to bring water south from the Canadian Rockies; Canadians feel threatened by it, especially in the light of their own shortages in British Columbia and Alberta. Reisner (1990) remarks that, if built, the NAWAPA network will destroy what is left of the natural West and require the taking of Canada by force!

Clearly some form of national planning is needed for water resources in the USA, particularly when options other than further dam-building or NAWAPA are so obvious but require institutional changes, e.g. the land-use options referred to in Section 4.2.4. These would help to yield more water and, importantly, help to raise water quality. Approaches to water quality control are little and late in the USA. As the US National Water Commission (1973) concluded:

> One major impediment to an adequate assessment of water quality is that existing monitoring and surveillance programs are inadequate to provide the database required for a comprehensive analysis of water quality conditions, except in a limited number of waterways.
>
> Water quality planning should be a composite of water supply planning, other water resource planning, sewage disposal and storm water drainage planning, land use planning and planning efforts of other environmental agencies handling air quality and solid waste problems.
>
> (US National Water Commission, 1973, pp. 68, 83)

Nevertheless, the US Government's attitude to institutional change can be summarised by the action of Secretary of the Interior James Watt's dismissal of the NWC in 1983; one of his associates described the Commission as 'just another layer of government that you didn't need' and 'another review board that could never make up its mind on anything'. Watt reinstated many agency water projects, especially in the West, linking these to employment needs. Despite the jibes over indecision, the major findings of the Commission (US NWC, 1973) are salutary in the light of our survey here of America's dilemma:

(a) Develop an adequate data base.
(b) Conduct further research into the environmental impacts of water resource development.
(c) Utilise planning techniques which are sensitive to ecological processes and environmental values.

(d) Develop rigorously and present as clearly as practicable the environmental impacts associated with a proposed water resources project and
the available alternatives.
(e) Reach a decision.
(f) Monitor environmental consequences.

Muckleston (1990) points out that in the dismemberment of Federal water
coordination the finances to implement the wise counsel of the Commission
have not followed the responsibilities to State level. The requirement under
the new regime for beneficiaries in water schemes to finance them appeals
directly to private enterprise rather than to coordinated public action.
Muckleston labels the most recent phase in American legislation over water
as 'counterenvironmentalism, devolution and dismemberment of institutions, facilitated by fiscal austerity for domestic programs' (p. 29).

Lack of integration in the Federal water programme also angers Palmer
(1986) from the conservation standpoint. He writes:

> Twenty five government agencies now spend $10 billion a year on water
> but they do not work in unison. The Department of Agriculture drains
> wetlands while the Fish and Wildlife Service of the Department of the
> Interior tries to preserve them. The Bureau of Reclamation in the
> Department of the Interior irrigates new farmland while the Department
> of Agriculture pays farmers to leave the land idle. The Fish and Wildlife
> Service tries to halt channelization while the Federal Emergency
> Management Administration pays for bulldozers to plough through
> streams in attempts to push gravel away after floods.
>
> (Palmer, 1986, p. 40)

Nevertheless it seems unlikely that, despite its success against many development standards and despite its many imitations abroad, the Tennessee
Valley Authority is unlikely to be imitated in the USA . The US NWC
(1973) concluded:

> It does not appear to be either advisable or feasible in the foreseeable
> future to establish additional federally-owned and operated regional
> water resources corporations of the scope and type of Tennessee Valley
> Authority.
>
> (US National Water Commission, 1973, p. 427)

It would appear that America has thrown the coordination baby out with
the Federal bath water!

Black (1982) points out the paradox that, whilst deeply in need of a
powerful and centralised agency for coordinating land and water planning,
the people of the USA have come to distrust such large and powerful
agencies through the historical activity of some of the autonomous
contemporary agencies which might participate.

4.3   CANADIAN RIVER BASIN MANAGEMENT

Canada is a land of rivers and lakes, surface water comprising 8 per cent of Canadian territory. Rivers, referred to as 'lordly' in the national anthem, were the routeways through which the nation was explored and integrated (unlike the waggon trains of the USA to the south). Nine per cent of global runoff serves a population of only 25 million people. Nevertheless, Canada has problems of water being abundant in 'the wrong places' (e.g. the cold North) but scarce by season in the West, on the prairies and in the urban agglomerations of the East (Figure 4.10). Like the United States, Canada has the problem of having developed water supply (and more notably hydropower) schemes at a large capital scale but, unlike the USA, there have been no 'pork barrel' politics with powerful Federal agencies. The Provinces have controlled water development, though Federal agencies have more say in land issues. Federal interests have retained control of fisheries and navigation.

In 1970 the Canada Water Act sought to provide integrated planning between Federal and Provincial agencies; one of the aims was to improve public consultation and awareness. The enormous scale of Canadian Water projects made this a dire necessity. For example, the La Grande project in Quebec involved a work site the size of England, under almost tundra conditions, lasting over 13 years during which four dams were built to divert and double the flow of the La Grande in order to generate 70,000 GWh of

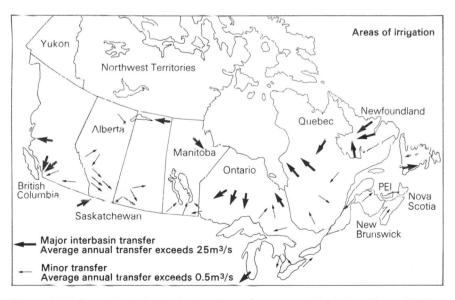

Figure 4.10 Canadian interbasin transfer schemes and irrigation (Day, 1985)

electricity. By excluding the St Lawrence and Mackenzie Rivers, roughly one-third of all Canadian flow is transferred across basin boundaries (see Figure 4.10).

4.3.1   Water transfers: a Canadian speciality

As an indication of the scale of projects for which the Water Act was implemented we may select two further examples. Table 4.7 lists the water transfer schemes under construction in 1980 and indicates the domination of hydro-electric power generation as a driving force. The dominant schemes comprised the La Grande, the Churchill Falls project ($665 million) completed in 1974, using two diversions, and the Lake Winnipeg, Churchill and Nelson project completed in 1977 ($1.36 billion). By this time Canadian water transfer flows had exceeded those of the USA and the Soviet Union combined.

These schemes had a number of undesirable social and environmental effects. For example, the Lake Winnipeg scheme threatened the environment of the Lower Churchill and South Indian Lake; a considerable change of lifestyle was implied for the communities affected. A representative body was established for discussion of implementation of the scheme, a northern development programme was established and a wide range of ecological monitoring was carried out.

Day (1985) concludes that yet more attention is needed on biophysical and social questions in Canadian transfer schemes. 'Enormous overbuilding of diversion-related hydroelectricity capacity has been costly to the Canadian public' and native groups need more equitable treatment, he claims. Institutional reforms would help secure a more sustainable

Table 4.7 Canadian water transfers existing or under construction, 1980

Province	No. of transfers	Average annual flows in m^3/s	Major use
Newfoundland	5	725	Hydro
Nova Scotia	4	18	Hydro
New Brunswick	2	2	Municipal
Quebec	6	1854	Hydro
Ontario	9	564	Hydro
Manitoba	5	775	Hydro
Saskatchewan	5	30	Hydro
Alberta	9	67	Irrigation
British Columbia	9	367	Hydro
Canada	54	4402	Hydro

Source: Day (1985)

approach to water use without such heavy reliance on the 'boom-and-bust' construction industry. The French Canadian perspective in Quebec has implications for such projects as the James Bay scheme. As Hamley (1990) reminds us, Quebec has pretentions to autonomy but little oil, coal or gas; the Province has worries about becoming industrially unattractive. To be regarded as 'electricity Arabs' in the north-east corner of the continent would be more useful to Quebec than the beaver pelt exports of the Cree Indians, now reduced to 1.3 per cent of their national lands because of the 'dated gigantism' of the James Bay project, 'Quebec's monument to a faded vision of modernism'.

Canada's relationship with the USA, soured by the acid rain issue and with the remaining threat of NAWAPA (Section 4.2.6), is of considerable day-to-day importance when managing the Great Lakes along their frontier. The International Joint Commission dates back to 1909; the IJC acts as neutral adviser and factfinder whilst many of the problematic issues of boundary cooperation are retained by individual States and Provinces.

Improvements to municipal waste treatment has considerably reduced the phosphate content of the Great Lakes but their waters are still said to contain 800 toxic solutes. During the 1980s high lake levels caused hundreds of millions of dollars' damage to both sides of the border. Proposals were made to curtail Canadian transfer schemes in Ontario and to augment the Lake Michigan transfer out to the Mississippi. The issue remains unresolved. However, boundary issues are critical to integrated water management, not only with regard to the USA but also because no Canadian Province or Territory has complete control of its water (excepting Prince Edward Island).

The Water Act 1970 has had little impact on such boundary (territorial and agency) problems except where specific missions such as those covered by the Flood Damage Reduction Program or Heritage River System have provided inspiration. By far the biggest stimulus for basin-scale integrated management has come from Provincial governments.

The Provincial government of Ontario has long favoured river basin authorities to develop local initiative, to promote cooperation with municipalities and to encourage conservation and recreation. The Conservation Authorities Act developed from a conference in Guelph in 1941. The Conservation Authorities themselves (38 in number) are formed by purely local initiative, are largely municipal, and have the power to purchase land in order to promote rational management of the river resources. Unfortunately, the addition of a third layer of organisation to national and provincial interests has proved problematic; Conservation Authorities have tended to become active in recreation but not in the 'big issues' of basin management (see Figure 4.11 and Table 4.8). What the map and table do not illustrate, however, is the role of Conservation Authorities in flood

Table 4.8 Recreational provision by S. Ontario Conservation Authorities

Authority	Area no.	Name	Area (ha)	Entrance fee	Campsites	Campsites with hydro	Group camping	Reservations	Parking	Picnic facilities	Drinking water	Washrooms	Showers	Dump station	Boat launching	Motor boat restriction	Fishing	Swimming	Walking trails – summer (km)	Walking trails – winter (km)	Interpretive/historical facilities	Handicap facilities
Central Lake Ontario (416) 579–0411	102	Lynde Shores	189						35	*		*			*	*	*			3		
	103	Heber Down	238		50				30	*	*	*		*					9	6.5	*	*
	104	Harmony Valley	28						76	*	*	*	*				*		2	2.4	*	*
	105	Enniskillen	65						185	*	*	*					*		3	3	*	*
	106	Long Sault/ Authority Forest	286						30	*		*							17	17	*	
Ganaraska Region (416) 885–8173	107	Sylvan Glen	2						20	*		*				*	*		0.4	0.4	*	
	108	Port Hope	37						100	*	*	*				*	*		5	5		
	109	Ganaraska Forest Centre	8	*					100	*	*	*							18	18		
	110	Garden Hill	22						50	*	*	*			*	*	*	*	0.4	0.4		
Lower Trent Region (613) 394–4829	111	Goodrich-Loomis	208						35	*		*					*		17	17		
	112	Trenton Green Belt	10						50	*					*		*	*				
	113	Hastings	0.5						25	*					*	*	*					

Kawartha Region												
114	Ken Reid	110			70	*		*	*		9	6
Otonabee Region (705) 745–5791												
115	Squirrel Creek	111	*		2	*	100	*	*	*	2	2
116	Larg Mill	17	*			30	*	*	*		*	*
117	Hope Mill	50	*	60	20	1	*	100	*	*		
118	Warsaw Caves	224	*	65		3	*	60	*	*	16	16
119	Selwyn	29	*			1		*	*	*	2	2
120	Crowebridge	29	*			1		*	*	*	2	
Crowe Valley (613) 472–3137												
121	The Gut	162					20	*	*	*	1.6	1.6

Figure 4.11 Ontario Conservation Authority areas in the Lake Ontario area
(Ministry of Natural Resources, Ontario, 1986)

control. They have mapped flood hazard areas, they provide flood warnings
and they have carried out structural works. Their success in two fields of
water management, recreation and flooding, illustrates that these schemes
are not duplicated by other interests and both attract the considerable local
interest which the Authorities are able to mobilise.

The most recent extension of this policy of 'intervention with care' in the
planning system states that one of the aims of development planning in the
river basins of Ontario is 'to encourage a coordinated approach to the one
of the land and the management of water'. The Conservation Authorities,
where they exist, are given the hub role of providing information and
reviewing proposals. For example, the Grand River Conservation Authority
has a Master Watershed Planning Committee (Thomson, personal communication) which sees as its role 'the promotion of watershed management

of small tributary watersheds in an effort to facilitate orderly development and the most suitable types of development whilst not compromising environmental quality'.

Ontario has also developed a keen approach, through Provincial environmental legislation, to reducing the discharge of toxic chemicals from industry both to rivers direct and to sewer systems. 'MISA', the Municipal–Industrial Strategy for Abatement, forces industry to curtail emissions at source according to a 'Best Available Technology' clause and to monitor for its own compliance; in some cases monitoring may be for well over 150 chemical determinands (Environment Ontario, 1988).

4.3.2   Land-use issues in basin development

O'Riordan (1986), addressing land-use issues in British Columbia, is yet another Canadian author bemoaning lack of integration and the dangers of overlapping Federal and Provincial functions: 'Although water and land issues are closely inter-related, few administrations have managed to coordinate them effectively into a single planning process' (p. 193).

The Cabinet of British Columbia, however, has established an Environment and Land Use Committee which encourages all Resource Ministries to develop strategic plans prior to trading-off and integration of goals. O'Riordan cites three examples of land-use pressure on basin management: water shortage for irrigation (Nicola Basin), hydrological effects of urbanisation (Serpentine–Nicomekl) and logging effects on runoff quantity and quality (Slocan Valley). In each case the land-use/management decisions are taken at a much larger regional scale than that of the basin whose hydrology is affected. He stresses the need for comprehensive information flows up and down a hierarchy of decision and implementation levels (Figure 4.12). He says:

> In the age of the computer, the massive amounts of data that must be sorted and sieved in such an approach are now manageable. The missing ingredient continues to be man's imagination, innovation and the will of institutions − too often vertically oriented − to make it work.
>
> (O'Riordan, 1986, p. 210)

Controlling water quality in Canada has been facilitated by the selection of new water quality guidelines. A government task force reviewed the practices current across the Provinces, in the USA and elsewhere. The review demarcated important distinctions between quality and standards:

(a) Quality
$\begin{cases} \text{criteria} & - \text{ the type of data considered.} \\ \text{guidelines} & - \text{ recommended general limit values.} \\ \text{objectives} & - \text{ recommendations to support specific uses at} \\ & \quad\ \text{ specific sites.} \end{cases}$

(b) Standards – enforceable objectives.

They then proceeded to rule on these lines for five principal water uses:

(a) Drinking water supplies.
(b) Recreational water/aesthetics.
(c) Freshwater aquatic life.
(d) Agricultural uses.
(e) Industrial water supplies.

Interestingly the report of this exercise (Canadian Council of Resource and Environment Ministers, 1987) is loose-leaf and has already been updated with respect to pesticides. No guidance is, however, provided on abatement

Figure 4.12 Scaled structure for an idealised Canadian water management scheme (O'Riordan, 1986)

by land *management*. Indeed the nitrate problem is reported as insignificant, 85 per cent of Canadian waters containing < 1 mg.1^{-1} of nitrate nitrogen; certain Ontario, Manitoba and Saskatchewan groundwaters, however, contain > 10 mg.1^{-1} and this may be a sign of impending problems for surface water management.

The most compelling recent water pollution problem in Canada has, however, been acidification. As an issue, acidification draws out two dimensions of the Canadian water management problem – relationships with the USA, a continuing source of acid emissions, and the need for effective monitoring systems. On the latter count the Canada Land Inventory of Environment Canada is making rapid strides in the use of geographical information systems to collate, display and relate data on land-related issues. Its survey of the impact of acidification in Eastern Canada (Lynch-Stewart *et al.*, 1986) uses land capability classes for agriculture, forestry, outdoor recreation and wildfowl to determine the extent to which sulphate depositions of > 20 kg.ha^{-1}.yr^{-1} are likely. Canada's own emission standards attempt to reduce deposition to this level, or lower, but 84 per cent of prime land for agricultural land, 96 per cent for forestry, 70 per cent for recreation and 74 per cent for waterfowl are susceptible to excess deposition.

This painstaking approach to data compilation for extensive territories, followed by classifications designed to elucidate environmental sensitivities of river basins, wetlands and lakes, which is carried out by Environment Canada's Lands Directorate, makes it all the more frustrating that institutional arrangements appear to hold back joint planning approaches to land and water.

Developing the state of Canadian knowledge on land/water interactions, Hare (1984) concentrates attention on forestry activity since most of those basins coming under management attention are forested; 43 per cent of Canada's surface is in fact forested and in Hare's words 'forest hydrology is becoming a well developed art in Canada'. In Canada forest hydrology is often snow hydrology since the felling of timber exposes snowcover to direct solar radiation, accelerating spring melting; tightly managed forests offer an opportunity to manipulate streamflow directly in Canada.

The prairie Provinces of Canada also have land management problems in relation to river flows; the prairies lose many millions of tonnes of soil by both wind and water erosion. Seepage of salinised groundwater to hollows is also a problem: in some areas 15 per cent of irrigated land is salinised. Lake Manitoba is alkaline and brackish from prairie runoff and the sedimentation rate has increased in the last 100 years.

Hare concludes that Canada, despite its abundance of water, faces severe local problems of management. As a British expatriate he writes:

Having grown up in a densely-populated European country where denser population and more intensive industry are well-served by supply less abundant than that of Southern Ontario I remain unrepentantly of the opinion that Canada's water problems arise from human misuse, not from poverty in the resource.

(Hare. 1984, p. 4)

4.3.3 Bringing about improved integration of policies

In 1985 Canada reviewed its Federal Water policy once more; the Pearse Inquiry (Pearse *et al.*, 1985) announced two goals for policy:

(a) To protect and enhance the quality of the water resource.
(b) To promote the wise and efficient management and use of water.

These goals effectively mark the end of a public policy of cheap water, begun as early as 1889 with the first mains supply to Vancouver from dams on the Fraser, and the beginning of 'the polluter pays' principle. The review

Table 4.9 Canadian Federal water policy

Specific policy statements

 1 Management of toxic chemicals
 2 Water quality management
 3 Groundwater contamination
 4 Fish habitat management
 5 Water and sewer infrastructure
 6 Safe drinking water
 7 Water use conflicts
 8 Interbasin transfers
 9 Water use in irrigation
10 Wetlands preservation
11 Hydro-electric energy development
12 Navigation
13 Heritage river preservation
14 Management of Northern water
   resources
15 Native water rights
16 Transboundary water management
17 Interjurisdictional water conflicts
18 International water relations
19 Droughts
20 Flooding
21 Shoreline erosion
22 Climatic change
23 Water data and information needs
24 Research leadership
25 Technological needs

Source: Environmental Canada (1989)

led on to five strategies and made 25 specific policy statements (Table 4.9). The strategies are:

(a) Water pricing.
(b) Science leadership.
(c) Integrated planning.
(d) Legislation to span jurisdictions, e.g. on water quality.
(e) Public awareness and consultation.
    (Canada has environmental impact assessment procedures.)

However, Shrubsole (1990) is not optimistic that the strategies can be achieved because they rely on the nebulous concept of 'cooperation' (subtitle: bargaining) between Federal desires and Provincial expertise and opinion. There is clearly a 'Canadian way' in the integrated management of river basins but until its processes can be unpicked with the somewhat wounding honesty of those south of the border, the revolution of the inevitable conflicts caused by 'bargaining' is a very slow process. Neither the integrated plans of the Canada Water Act nor an Environmental Assessment Review Process appear capable of dealing with the scale of Canadian water resource manipulation or the panoply of agency and regional scales of interest. The Canadian approach to water quality control is, however, more optimistic and may well extend the integration of interests around river basin units in a way which has been impossible in a nation obsessed with water transfers *between* basins.

4.4   NEW ZEALAND: WISE MANAGEMENT DETERMINED BY HAZARD

New Zealand is recent both geologically and as a developed economy. Johnston (1985) has summarised the major phases of the country's development and the environmental policy response (see Figure 4.13); development has included forest clearance and mining, both of which have combined with the hazards of a steep landscape, cloaked in weak sediments, and a wet climate to force considerable government attention to river management (see Moore, 1982 for a broad review). Over 12 per cent of New Zealand's land area suffers from fluvial erosion (7 per cent gullied; 2 per cent tunnelled; 3 per cent bank erosion); erosion surveys are one part of a very large national effort put into land survey.

It is not, therefore, surprising to find New Zealand's geomorphologists reporting some of the world's largest rates of fluvial erosion, for example in the Western Southern Alps, even without the intensive land exploitation found elsewhere in the islands. Soons (1986) reports source-area rates of between $96\,\mathrm{m^3.km^{-2}.yr}$ and $8380\,\mathrm{m^3.km^{-2}.yr}$ during the post-glacial period.

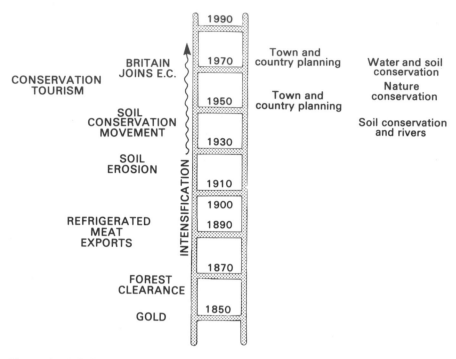

Figure 4.13 Salient dates in New Zealand's colonisation, development and government affecting river basin policy (modified from Johnston, 1985)

During the period since forest clearance, landslides have cost large areas of New Zealand's 'hill country' almost all of their original 2.5 m of soil; the remaining 10–30 cm soils are much less able to store storm rainfall and one result is that flooding is a further hazard to both islands. Plate 4.2 identifies the problem in the Taranaki Hill country and Figure 4.14 shows how an equilibrium soil depth under today's pasture farming is controlled by the landslip hazard.

The *flood hazard* in New Zealand is described in detail by Ericksen (1986). Table 4.10 indicates the options available for adjustment to floods, assuming that upstream mitigation such as *erosion control* and reafforestation are already in the brief of Catchment Authorities (see below). Historically, New Zealand has attempted to modify the floods but continuing disasters led to a programme of modifying the loss burden. However, now that town and country planning and soil and water legislation have begun to line up in New Zealand it is becoming more common to modify the losses. The use of popular devices such as cartoons is very prevalent in New Zealand public life; Figure 4.15 illustrates the desirable features of regulated floodplain development; in order to implement such regulation

Plate 4.2 Landslide resulting from cyclone Bola, Napier, North Island, New Zealand

Catchment Authorities are using a computer model of flood losses developed by the Australian National University in Canberra (ANUFLOOD; Ericksen *et al.*, 1988). ANUFLOOD calculates damage at specific flood heights in relation to known land use and the flood record; it then maps damage under various scenarios of modified floodplain usage.

4.4.1   Catchment Authorities: the New Zealand approach

New Zealand began to organise its river management along catchment lines as early as 1868 with River Boards; Acts were passed in 1884, 1893 and 1908 to strengthen these bodies. However, it was the floods and erosion problems of the 1930s which led to a truly formative piece of legislation, the Soil

(a)

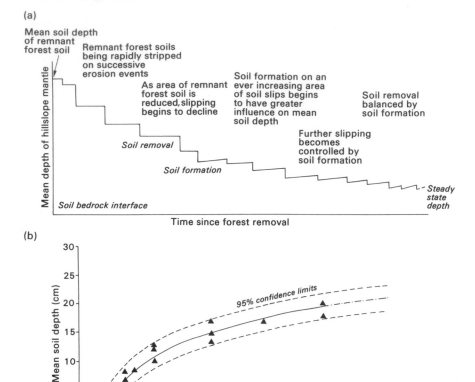

Figure 4.14 Soil slipping – a major hazard in New Zealand river basins:
(a) Development through time
(b) Relationship between time since last slip and soil depth
(NWASCA, 1987)

Conservation and Rivers Control Act 1941, subtitled as follows: 'An act to make provision for the conservation of soil resources and for the prevention of damage by erosion, and to make better provision with respect to the protection of property from damage by floods'.

By 1967 the speed of development and intensification of land use in New Zealand forced the incorporation of wider aims in the Water and Soil Conservation Act, subtitled:

An act to promote a national policy in respect of natural water and to make better provision for the conservation, allocation, use and quality of natural water, and for promoting soil conservation and preventing damage by flood and erosion and for promoting and controlling multiple uses of natural water and drainage of land, and for ensuring that adequate account is taken of the needs of primary and secondary industry, community water supplies, all forms of water based recreation, wildlife habitats and of the preservation and protection of the wild, scenic and other natural characteristics of rivers, streams and lakes.

Table 4.10 A typology of human adjustments to floods

I Modify the flood
  1 Weather modification
    (a) Cloud seeding
  2 Land treatment
    (a) Afforestation
    (b) Conservation farming
    (c) On-site ponding
  3 River control
    (a) Dams
    (b) Levees
    (c) Channel improvements

II Modify damage susceptibility
  1 Land-use management
    (a) Encroachment lines
    (b) Zoning lines
    (c) Subdivision regulations
    (d) Building codes
    (e) Land acquisition
    (f) Floodplain development policies and plans
    (g) Urban renewal policies and plans
  2 Flood-proofing buildings
    (a) Permanent
    (b) Contingent
    (c) Emergency
  3 Community preparedness
    (A) Evacuations
    (b) Flood-fighting
    (c) Flood-forecasting and warning systems
    (d) Rescheduling activities

III Modify the flood-loss burden
  1 Insurance
  2 Tax deductions
  3 Loans
  4 Relief funds
  5 Feeding and sheltering victims
  6 Rehabilitation services: public and private agencies

Source: Ericksen (1986)

(a) Non-regulated floodplain development

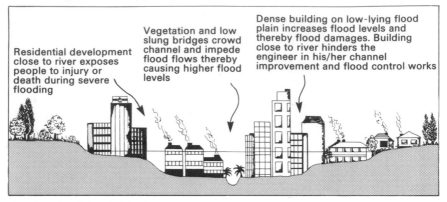

Residential development close to river exposes people to injury or death during severe flooding

Vegetation and low slung bridges crowd channel and impede flood flows thereby causing higher flood levels

Dense building on low-lying flood plain increases flood levels and thereby flood damages. Building close to river hinders the engineer in his/her channel improvement and flood control works

(b) Regulated floodplain development

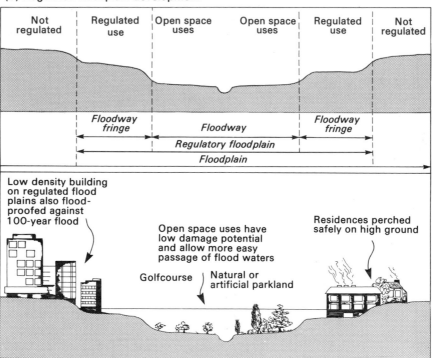

| Not regulated | Regulated use | Open space uses | Open space uses | Regulated use | Not regulated |

Floodway fringe — *Floodway* — *Floodway fringe*

Regulatory floodplain

Floodplain

Low density building on regulated flood plains also flood-proofed against 100-year flood

Open space uses have low damage potential and allow more easy passage of flood waters

Golfcourse | Natural or artificial parkland

Residences perched safely on high ground

Figure 4.15 New Zealand floodplains:
(a) Non-regulated development of an urban community
(b) Means of regulation and regulated development of an urban community
(Ericksen, 1986)

The regional authorities for water and soil resource management are the twenty Catchment Authorities (see Figure 4.16) whose functions are set out in Table 4.11; they include the function of Regional Water Boards. A vivid pictorial account of the work of the Catchment Authorities is provided by Poole (1983).

The 1967 Water and Soil Conservation Act delegated responsibility to the National Water and Soil Conservation Authority (NWASCA) for coordinating the work of Regional Water Boards and Catchment Authorities. By 1976 NWASCA anticipated a move to proactive catchment planning at a regional scale as an alternative to awaiting development proposals before seeking to coordinate activities.

However, the preparation of Water and Soil Management Plans has not become a statutory process and, being expensive to carry out, few are complete. One of them, the Waitara River Catchment Management Plan, has attempted to preclude future construction of dams on the river; it exemplifies the fact that planning only occurs where existing conflict has drawn funds. New Zealand is apparently on the verge of the need to integrate town and country planning with soil and water management.

In 1981 an amendment to the Water and Soil Conservation Act was resurrected to permit the conservation of the natural characteristics of New Zealand's rivers and lakes. Popularly labelled the 'Wild and Scenic Rivers Legislation', this legislation can be used to maintain the flow regime of, and curtail development in the catchment of, both nationally and locally impor-

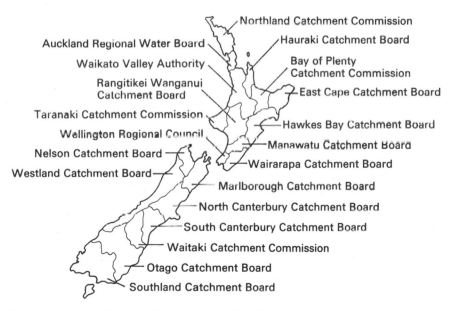

Figure 4.16 New Zealand Catchment Authorities

Table 4.11 New Zealand Catchment Authority functions

I Soil conservation
   1 Preventing/mitigating soil erosion
   2 Promoting soil conservation
      (advice from Catchment Authority Soil Conservators;
      financial assistance for protection planting, destocking, water control,
      etc.)

II River control and drainage works
    1 Investigation, survey, design and construction
    2 Encouraging development in areas of lesser flood risk

III Water management
     (Catchment Authorities also function as Regional Water Boards)
     1 Water rights
     2 Water monitoring

IV Resource planning
    (including water and soil management plans)
    1 Water and soil resource surveys
    2 Collection of public submissions to management plans

V Associated environmental activities
   1 Issue of Safeguards Notices
   2 Burning control (grass fires)
   3 Windbreak schemes
   4 Willow control (phreatophyte growth)
   5 Gravel extraction (permits)
   6 Protection forestry

tant reaches. Interpretations of the amendment give less cause for optimism by calling for multiple use rather than solely conservation of instream values. However, further support for river conservation has come from the interpretation by some authorities of the 1977 Town and Country Planning Act which allows specific attention to river and lake margins. Guest (1987) quotes from the Waimarino County Council's plan which includes the Wanganui River Scenic Protection Zone:

> Although some of the land in this zone was in the past considered to be suitable for farming and exotic forestry, other values such as the quality of the landscape, historic and scenic features and water and soil considerations are now regarded to be of more importance.
>
> (Guest, 1987, p. 11)

The protection of all New Zealand's rivers is a developing issue, involving elements of simple pollution control as well as a growing recreation and conservation interest, fisheries and Maori rights. To the Maori, the essence of life is water and the river or lake of the home area is effectively the address as well as the identity of each individual. Maori culture is threaded with quasi-religious resource management and anti-pollution concepts which are easily offended by European technocratic approaches to wealth and purity (Taylor and Patrick, 1987).

A survey of over half of New Zealand's twenty Regional Water Boards (Quinn and Hickey, 1987) has assessed the degree to which the basic water quality criteria laid down in the Water and Soil Conservation Act 1967 are adhered to. Approximately 50 per cent of New Zealand's rivers are classified waters under the Act and the most common discharges are from dairy farms and domestic sewage plants. Quinn and Hickey report disparities in, for example, the application of the suspended solids criteria by some Regional Water Boards to emissions and by others to receiving waters.

Table 4.12 Principal toxicants discharged to New Zealand rivers

Source	Principal toxicants	Number to river
Point sources		
Meatworks	Ammonia, sulphide, organics	18
Pulp and paper	Various organics, heavy metals	6
Tanneries	Chromium, organics	1
Woolscours	Detergents, sulphide	11
Timber preservers	Arsenic, chromium, copper, PCBs, boron	?
Tip leachates	Zinc, other heavy metals, organics	numerous
Mining	Evanide, various heavy metals	?
Petrochemical	Solvents, biocides, heavy metals	1
Pharmaceutical by-products	Chromium, organics	1
Bore drilling	Chromium, lignasulphonate	?
Geothermal (power)	Mercury, arsenic, lead, boron, biocides sulphide, lithium	4
Municipal sewage	Organics, ammonia, (others depending on industrial output)	96
Dairy shed	Organics, ammonia	7850
Piggeries	Copper, zinc, organics, ammonia	220
Diffuse sources		
Geothermal (natural)	Mercury, arsenic, lead, boron, sulphide, lithium	?
Agricultural and horticultural runoff	Pesticides, herbicides, fungicides	widespread
Urban stormwater	Lead, zinc, copper, cadmium, pesticides, herbicides, petrochemicals, organics	widespread
Weathering and erosion	Heavy metals	?

Source: Quinn and Hickey (1987)

Despite eutrophication problems there have not, as yet, been any controls applied to organic discharges or to nitrate or phosphate runoff. A recent upsurge in horticulture as the result of difficulties in the livestock sector has led to problems with pesticides and herbicides. There has been insufficient research to establish the extent of pollution and to develop guidelines or remedies; this is surprising in a nation so dependent on agriculture (see Table 4.12) but reflects the previous domination of erosion control and flood protection. Of the available research on, for example, fertiliser pollution, that by McColl and Gibson (1979) concludes that for hill-country improved grazing lands very little nutrient runoff reaches streams. In

Table 4.13(a) Analysis of questionnaire no. 2 part 2 by number of 'include' requests

Determinand	Index			
	General (16)	Bathing (16)	Supply (13)	Fish (16)
Dissolved oxygen	16	16	11	16
pH	16	15	10	16
Suspended solids	9[a]	9[a]	8[a]	13.5[a]
Temperature	13	13	3	16
Nitrate	9	5	10	8
Oil and grease	11	13	9	11
BOD (unfiltered)	12	12	4	12
Ammonia	8	7	11	14
Faecal coliforms	11	15	13	4
Turbidity (FTU)	11[a]	12[a]	7[a]	6.5[a]
Phosphate (RDP)	8	4	3	6
Conductivity	6	3	4	4
Colour (Hazen)	2	4	4	3
Phosphate (total P)	2	1		3
Colour (Hue)	1	6	1	
Hardness	1		4	1
BOD (filtered)	1		3	1
Alkalinity			2	
Total coliforms		3	1	1
Fe (as Fe^{2+})	1		4	
Chloride			1	
Organic carbon			1	
COD			1	
Mn (as Mn^{2+})			1	
Magnesium			1	
Calcium			1	
Dissolved solids			1	
Substrate chlorophyll-a	1	1		1
Substrate carbon				1
Standard plate count			1	

Source: Smith (1987)

certain 'source areas', particularly of surface runoff, there is, however, a clear need for management of agricultural practices (cf. UK – p. 312). Quinn and Hickey identify a channelisation problem in conserving stream habitat, emphasising that Catchment Boards have good control in headwaters but less over riparian activity downstream. The 82 hydropower dams throughout New Zealand have also posed problems for fish migration. Detention dams on farmland are now replacing some of the traditional 'hard engineering' solutions to rural flooding.

In an effort to improve water quality control in New Zealand's rivers recent research has attempted to define water quality indices and criteria by expert consultation and by contacting river users. Four groups of quality index, depending on river use (general, bathing, supply and fish), were put to consultation. Table 4.13a shows the frequency of replies on a range of determinands, physical, chemical and biological. From there, numerical values were assessed with a view to weighting scores in simple integrative indices for the four river functions (Table 4.13b).

By 1988 the New Zealand Government had recognised the need for 'Resource Management Law Reform' because of the proliferation of new laws and institutions superimposed on some earlier approaches such as Soil Conservation and Rivers Control. The situation, they maintained, had become cumbersome, hard to understand by the public, had led to costly delays and did not respect Maori rights. Interestingly, because of the prominence of land and water issues, the public consultation undertaken in New Zealand focused upon.

(a) The scale of bodies best able to manage resources.
(b) The role of Government in control of ownership.

Table 4.13(b) Relative importance and final determinand weightings for the four water quality indices

Determinand	General(G) Rel. imp.	Wt	Bathing(B) Rel. imp.	Wt	Supply(W) Rel. imp.	Wt	Fish(F) Rel. imp.	Wt
Dissolved oxygen	1.33	0.30	2.16	0.15	2.13	0.18	1.00	0.34
pH	3.13	0.13	3.10	0.10	2.79	0.15	2.81	0.12
Suspended material	2.57	0.15	1.73	0.19	2.82	0.15	2.41	0.14
Temperature	3.15	0.12	3.78	0.09	3.59	0.12	1.35	0.26
BOD$_5$	2.20	0.18	2.23	0.15			2.48	0.14
Faecal coliforms	3.18	0.12	1.00	0.32	1.78	0.24		
Ammonia					2.59	0.16		

Source: Smith (1987)

(c) The voice of local communities.
(d) The role of indigenous culture and values.

Ericksen (1990) also refers to a problem of bureaucratic confusion at the regional level. The proposed reforms would unify the regional councils (i.e. local government) and Catchment Boards to produce fourteen new authorities. NWASCA has already been disbanded, representing a sad loss of central information, education and synthesis of policy. Nevertheless the Ministry for the Environment (1989) is convinced of the benefits of devolution and of grouping agencies by legal function rather than by resource.

In conclusion we may suggest that the scale of the erosion and flood problems in the 1930s, clearly exacerbated by poor land management, led to heavy intervention at a national scale, for instance, riparian rights were handed over to national ownership of water resources. However, whilst land inventories have remained a national operation, the Catchment Board policy has ensured good local representation and decision-making. Ericksen (1990) has the last word: 'New Zealand has a reputation for throwing hastily-prepared legislation at its problems then making corrective amendments as experience highlights the shortcomings' (p. 83).

4.5   CONCLUSIONS: NATIONAL PRIORITIES IN THE DEVELOPED WORLD

To characterise the nations whose approaches to river basin management have been outlined in this chapter one would say that:

(a) The USA was the victim of the rapidity of its colonisation and of the ability of the financial resources thereby created to 'hold' hazardous environments, particularly drylands, in settlement and in productive use. Superimposed on this resource picture is the cultural and legal battle between an enormous national technological skill to operate rational planning and the private enterprise culture of a Gold Rush. Politically, there are continuing tensions between the national view and that of the individual states.
(b) In Canada a more sympathetic view to resource management might well prevail for a number of physical and cultural reasons but the plentiful water is badly distributed and the issue of clean energy generation also contributes to the 'gigantism' of the many water-transfer schemes. The resource problems of the neighbour to the south are intricately bound up with those of Canada and it is possible that the Canadian policy, replete with centralist mission statements on the environment, will not settle down until the future of US use of Canadian water has taken shape, possibly following climate change. Canada also has its own political battle between nation and provinces, notably Quebec.

(c) New Zealand, uniquely, appears to have experienced a relatively stable period of careful water management policies, made necessary by earlier misdeeds and by a very unstable natural background. The ability of the New Zealand system to combine central strategy with local planning and implementation seems, however, to be crumbling in the face of devolved policies.

To the reader in the UK, many of the aspects and approaches described above may be familiar during various stages of the evolution of UK policies. The UK may be characterised by: poor distribution of water in time and space, a drastic neglect during early industrialisation of water quality, and over-simplified 'free resource' approaches to water consumption.

The current direction of UK policy shares with the USA, Canada and New Zealand a number of other cultural and political controls, for example the development of a national position on all aspects of environmental management, the enforced cutback on public expenditure and the degree to which the population is consulted about policy development. These work against each other and produce tensions which may or may not be creative in all four developed nations we have considered. For example, the dismemberment of centralised strategic planning may have the advantage of encouraging more local action, but not if that action is financially driven or constrained; in that case the increasing feeling in the developed world that environmental matters require a strategic overview swings the argument back towards central action − or possibly towards international action.

Chapter 5

River basins and development

5.1 GENERAL CHARACTERISTICS AND NEW PHILOSOPHIES

There are many characteristics of developing world water projects which are reminiscent of the 'distribution philosophies' of the early hydraulic civilisations; a principal difference may be summarised by the word 'identity'. Modern schemes have tended to lack the identity of communal national effort which seemingly characterised earlier eras, partly because of marked regional disparities in technological expertise but mainly because of lack of popular national involvement. The strong social structures which upheld prehistoric irrigation economies are imitated by bureaucratic resettlement schemes and innovative, but rarely successful, land tenure arrangements. What are the remedies?

Indigenous tribal peoples have little incentive to bring forward their own water development schemes at a scale which could improve national economic performance; some form of imposition, if only of development alternatives by extension workers, is clearly inescapable. Equally clearly, *indigenous people* have both human rights and huge reserves of adaptive strategies involving local environmental management (see Section 5.6.2).

5.1.1 Pre-empting exploitation

Is there a rationale with which the technology of water development could have a more acceptable social focus when viewed both from the centre and periphery of a developing nation? Marchand and Toornstra (1986) advocate an ecological concept in which both perspectives admit to the *spontaneous functions* of river basins at the same time as the development occurs of *intensive exploitation functions*. Marchand and Toornstra first demand the treatment of the entire river basin as an ecosystem and define the essential functions as follows:

> River systems fulfil *spontaneous functions* for human society, i.e. functions fulfilled without any need of intervention. Examples include the natural regulation of erosion and sedimentation, the spongelike action of

wetlands and the water-purifying capacity of lakes and marshes. At the present time, the derangement of these functions is perhaps the major problem in river basin management, something that is due partly to unfamiliarity with the importance of these functions, as well as to underestimation thereof.

A second group of functions whose importance is often underrated are the *extensive exploitation functions*; all those practices involving human 'harvesting', but requiring few or no outside inputs. Examples include extensive forms of herding, traditional paddy farming in wetlands, fishing etc, activities widespread in the tropics and with far greater potential than is often appreciated. Floodplains in particular, as producers of high value protein, should be incorporated in plans more often than is presently the case.

(Marchand and Toornstra, 1986, p. i)

The authors develop these themes through to a set of impact matrices for specific intervention by development agencies, one of several such matrices now available (see Chapter 8, plus Horberry, 1983; Hellawell, 1986). Table 5.1 summarises Marchand and Toornstra's guidelines, items of which (but seldom their whole agenda) are now part of the 'project cycle' of development plan, appraisal, finance and intervention.

The problem remains, however, of what sort of institutions are capable of delivering the refined, ecological model of river basin development to the people whose efforts will ensure success (or failure). We return to this theme in Chapter 7.

Table 5.1 Guidelines for river basin management

1 Preservation or improvement of the spontaneous functions fulfilled by the river, by:
  (a) Restoring erosion/sedimentation processes, through countering increased silt loads caused by upstream erosion (improvement of watershed management!).
  (b) Preserving genetic diversity, through conserving natural areas and threatened species.
  (c) Preserving the self-purifying capacity of the river, through combating pollution (water-treatment plants, at-source anti-pollution measures).
2 Conservation of the natural values of the river basin, by:
  (a) Preventing deterioration/destruction of natural resources, by means of legislation (incl. compulsory environmental impact assessments) directed towards industrial development, impoldering schemes and drainage activities.
  (b) Establishing reserves in the most vulnerable ecosystems, with surrounding buffer areas.
  (c) Establishing environmental education programmes.
  (d) Initiating programmes to promote sound, durable exploitation of ecosystems (particularly fisheries, herding and forestry).

(continued)

Table 5.1 (Continued)

3 Conservation of the river basin's extensive exploitation functions, by:
   (a) Guaranteeing the protection of productive zones, such as floodplains, estuaries and lakes, by allocating appropriate quantities of water (in relation to para. 4) and by means of the programmes mentioned in para. 2).
   (b) Implementing reafforestation schemes for supply of firewood, in relation to sound watershed management (cf. para. 1).
4 Development of sustainable intensive exploitation functions, by:
   (a) Drawing up a water allocation plan for the entire river basin, to achieve a better match between water demand and supply; this should give due consideration to the water requirements of the spontaneous functions (para. 1), natural values (para. 2) and extensive exploitation functions (para. 3).
   (b) Developing small-scale projects, e.g. irrigation, fishponds, forestry.
   (c) Improving product processing, sales and marketing, e.g. by making better use of the river as a transport route.
   (d) Ensuring that detailed plans for the above objectives are thoroughly checked against the other criteria (paras 1–3 and 5) within the framework of an environmental impact assessment procedure.
5 Improvement of the overall health situation in the river basin, by:
   (a) Combating water-borne diseases.
   (b) Improving the food situation, both quantitatively and qualitatively.
   (c) Establishing a drinking-water programme for rural areas, with the objective of making clean, healthy water available for the whole population.
   (d) Ensuring that detailed plans for the above objectives are thoroughly checked against the other criteria (paras 1–4) within the framework of an environmental impact assessment procedure.
6 Guiding principles for regional planning:
   (a) Work with, not against the environment.
   (b) Start work from the existing situation, i.e. existing infrastructure, technical know-how, perceptions of subsistence security, cultural needs, etc.
   (c) Protect the authentic evolution of local culture, institutions and know-how.
   (d) When undertaking action or introducing social change, prefer those actions involving decision-making at the lowest possible level.
   (e) Assess the carrying capacity of extensive agricultural and water-use systems, as well as their present value.
   (f) Assess the required inputs for intensive systems of land and water use and their value if a growing number of people are to be fed.
   (g) Intensify or introduce intensive land- and water-use systems at locations with the best soil and superior climatological and market conditions.
   (h) Preserve, develop and utilise nature's spontaneous functions.
   (i) When planning reserves for species or ecosystems, endeavour to make them as large, as varied and as interconnected as possible.
   (j) Preserve rare species and ecosystems in their authentic ecological setting, giving due consideration to the long-term effects of isolation.
   (k) Avoid land- and water-use systems exhibiting irreversible dependence on a single crop or market (especially narrow or foreign markets), also on the input side.

Source: Marchand and Toornstra (1986)

5.2   PROBLEMS OF FOOD, POWER AND TRADE IN DRYLANDS

The 42 LDCs (least developed countries) on earth show a high correlation with the tropical arid and semi-arid lands; 340 million people live in these countries (Figure 5.1). Many of the major river basins of the world impinge on the arid and semi-arid lands and the exploitation of their basins has a disproportionately vital effect on indigenous peoples. Most of the important basins are also international – they cross the boundaries of sovereign nations (Figure 5.1). Whilst the population of most of the LDCs is rising fast, much of the land within their boundaries is limited by drought (Table 5.2a,b) and it is very difficult to increase food production for the home population as well as creating exportable surpluses of cash crops; Africa has the most formidable problem of all continents in this respect (Figure 5.2a). Drought years place an unmanageable burden upon food production systems by both delaying the crop cycle and curtailing the period of growth (Figure 5.2b). Whilst acknowledging along with Brandt and Bruntland (Independent Commission on International Development Issues, 1980; World Commission on Environment and Development, 1987) that the 'world order' of trade and militarism are responsible for the dilemma of development, the management of individual river basin projects and the cross-boundary allocation of water resources and hazard mitigation is a necessary focus of the hydrologist.

A much wider group of world population is, in fact, threatened by low levels of water resource development. The UN's International Drinking

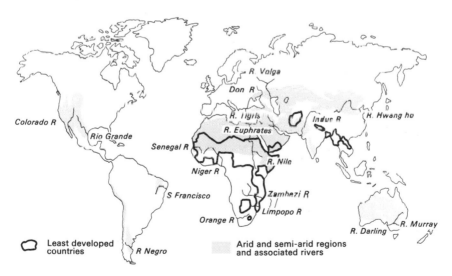

Figure 5.1 Major river basins, least developed countries and the world's arid and semi-arid lands

Table 5.2(a)   Areas of land limited by drought

Region	% of land limited by drought
North America	20
Central America	32
South America	17
Europe (mainly Spain)	8
Africa	44
South Asia	43
North and Central Asia	17
South East Asia	2
Australia	28

Source: Finkel (1977)

Table 5.2(b) Distribution of drylands by country

Group	Description	No.	% of nation arid/semi-arid	Countries
1	Arid	11	100	Bahrain, Djibouti, Egypt, Kuwait, Mauritania, Oman, Qatar, United Arab Emirates, Saudi Arabia, Somalia, South Yemen
2	Predominantly arid	23	75–99	Afghanistan, Algeria, Australia, Botswana, Burkina Faso, Cape Verde, Chad, Iran, Iraq, Israel, Jordan, Kenya, Libya, Mali, Morocco, Namibia, Niger, North Yemen, Pakistan, Senegal, Sudan, Syria, Tunisia
3	Substantially arid	5	50–74	Argentina, Ethiopia, Mongolia, South Africa, Turkey
4	Semi-arid	9	25–49	Angola, Bolivia, Chile, China, India, Mexico, Tanzania, Togo, USA
5	Peripherally arid	18	<25	Benin, Brazil, Canada, Central African Republic, Ecuador, Ghana, Lebanon, Lesotho, Madagascar, Mozambique, Nigeria, Paraguay, Peru, Sri Lanka, USSR, Venezuela, Zambia, Zimbabwe

Source: Paylore and Greenwell (1979)

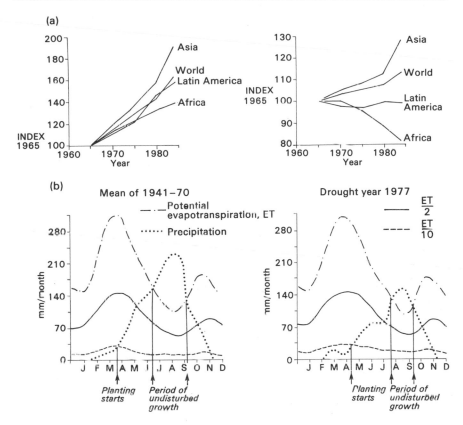

Figure 5.2 Problems of the developing semi-arid world:
(a) The growth of population (*left*) and food supplies (*right*)
(Higgins *et al.*, 1988)
(b) The sensitivity of the growing season to the water balance,
both depths and timings, 'normal' and drought (Falkenmark,
1986)

Water Supply and Sanitation Decade (1981–90; see Figure 5.3) set out to
reduce the appalling statistics of inadequate or polluted water supplies for
human use (Agarwal *et al.*, 1980): 30,000 children die each year because of
inadequate water supply or sanitation and half of the world's hospital beds
are occupied by patients with water-related diseases. At the close of the
Decade, 700 million extra people had been supplied with clean water but
nearly 2 billion people remained in danger – a vanishing perspective.

The special problems of the world's drylands (comprising one-third of the
earth) have recently been highlighted by Beaumont (1989). His comprehensive survey of all aspects of development highlights that this is
not a rural problem; rural communities in drylands have shown superb

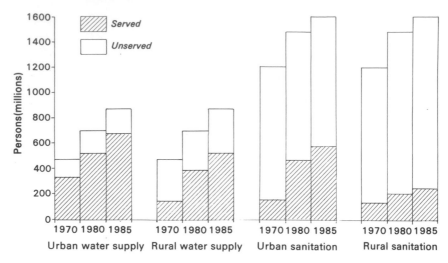

Figure 5.3 The UN's International Drinking Water Supply and Sanitation
Decade: growth of water supply, urban and rural, and sanitation,
urban and rural

adaptations including primitive, yet sophisticated, technologies based upon
folk knowledge of environmental variables (e.g. Australian Aborigines),
but today's use of drylands is more intensive and urbanised, as Table 5.3
shows.

There is but one water lifeline for such an intensive use of drylands –

Table 5.3 Major urban dryland centres with more than 2 million people

Continent	Estimate date	City proper	Urban
Africa			
Cairo (Egypt)	1974	5,715,000	—
Alexandria (Egypt)	1974	2,259,000	—
Asia			
Peking (China)	1970	7,570,000	—
Tientsin (China)	1970	4,280,000	—
Teheran (Iran)	1973	4,002,000	—
Delhi (India)	1971	3,287,900	3,647,000
Karachi (Pakistan)	1972	3,498,634	—
Lahore (Pakistan)	1972	2,165,372	—
America			
Los Angeles (USA)	1975	2,727,399	7,032,075
Santiago (Chile)	1970	3,273,600	3,350,680
Lima (Peru)	1972	2,833,609	3,303,523

Source: Cooke *et al.* (1982)

irrigation, but only 15 per cent of the world's land area is irrigated, producing 40 per cent of the crop food. Despite this impressive productivity ratio
the irrigated area is a relatively small proportion, especially in areas which
are in serious need of food (e.g. Africa at 4.7 per cent; see Table 5.4).

The proportion of urban and rural areas unserved by water supply and
sanitation measures is also extremely small (see Figure 5.3).

5.2.1   Desertification

Paradoxically, despite this need, the drylands of the world are mismanaged
to the extent that in the Sahel zone of Africa as much land is lost to food
production by the processes known as 'desertification' as is gained by new

Table 5.4(a) Continental distribution of irrigated area, 1984

	Irrigated area (10^6 ha)	% of world total
Asia	136.865	62.30
North America	20.461	9.31
Soviet Union	19.485	8.87
Europe	15.710	7.15
Africa	10.390	4.73
South America	7.979	3.63
Central America	6.914	3.15
Oceania	1.869	0.85
Developing countries	157.198	71.56
Industrial countries	62.475	28.44
World	219.673	100.00

Source: FAO (1986)

Table 5.4(b) Countries with major involvement in irrigation: irrigated areas in
1984 (10^6 ha)

China	45.42	Spain	3.14	Sudan	1.70
India	39.70	Italy	2.97	Argentina	1.66
United States	19.83	Afghanistan	2.66	Australia	1.63
Soviet Union	19.48	Romania	2.61	Philippines	1.43
Pakistan	15.32	Egypt	2.47	Chile	1.26
Iran	5.73	Brazil	2.20	Bulgaria	1.21
Indonesia	5.42	Turkey	2.14	Nigeria	1.20
Mexico	5.10	Bangladesh	1.92	Peru	1.20
Thailand	3.55	Iraq	1.75	South Korea	1.20
Japan	3.25	Vietnam	1.75	France	1.16

Source: FAO (1986)

irrigation schemes. The term 'desertification' and the extent of 'the problem' are both hotly debated by hydrologists, agriculturalists and development specialists. Promoted vigorously by the 1977 UN Commission on Desertification meeting in Nairobi, the phenomenon is said to affect 21 m ha yr^{-1} at a cost of $26B yr^{-1}. Desertification is defined as: 'the diminution or destruction of the biological potential of land that can lead ultimately to desert-like conditions' (UNCOD, 1977).

Spectacular schemes to halt desertification, such as tree-planting in Mali and Algeria, to 'halt the Sahara' have forced a re-think. It is possible that UNCOD's estimates of the extent of desertification risk were based on a poor database, mainly comprising early remote sensing images.

Desertification as a theme to discourage profligate rural development is still intensively pursued. For example, Grainger (1990) considers the causes as overcultivation, overgrazing, poor irrigation management, and deforestation.

Table 5.5 UNCOD plan of action: checklist of priority measures to combat desertification

---

A Land Use and Rehabilitation
  1 Introduce methods of planning land use in ecologically sound ways.
  2 Improve livestock raising by means of new breeds of livestock and better range management.
  3 Improve rainfed cropping by introducing more sustainable techniques.
  4 Rehabilitate irrigated cropping schemes that have failed owing to water-logging, salinisation and alkalinisation.
  5 Manage water resources in environmentally sound ways.
  6 Protect existing trees, woodlands, and other vegetative cover and restore tree cover and vegetation to denuded lands.
  7 Establish woodlots as sustainable sources of fuelwood and encourage the development of alternative energy sources.
  8 Conserve flora and fauna.
  9 Ensure the fullest possible public participation in measures to combat desertification.

B Socio-economic and institutional measures
  1 Investigate the social, economic and political factors connected with desertification.
  2 Introduce measures to control population growth, as appropriate.
  3 Improve health services.
  4 Improve scientific capabilities.
  5 Expand local awareness of desertification and skills with which to combat it by training and education, both by means of mass media and courses at various educational institutions.
  6 Assess the impact of settlements and industries on desertification, and keep desertification in mind when planning or expanding new settlements and industries.

Source: Summarised from Grainger (1990)

Among the outcomes are wasted water, disease, erosion, salinisation, pollution by pesticides. As such UNCOD's recommendations (Table 5.5) remain valid.

Most authorities, however, now see desertification as an issue utterly complicated by climatic change. Mensching (1986) emphasises the need, therefore, for the population of the Sahel to have a flexible response and for exploitation potentials to be reviewed downwards to reflect the inherent variability of environmental controls.

> The main requirement is to maintain the natural regenerative capacity of the vegetation. This calls for far-sighted settlement and development plans which, in the last analysis, can be prepared only by the desert countries themselves.
>
> (Mensching, 1986, p. 17)

Binns (1990) concludes that:

> The evidence seems to suggest that the idea of the Sahara desert sweeping southwards on a broad front, as Stebbing postulated in 1935 and others have argued more recently, is no longer tenable. However, *land degradation* of varying degrees does exist and the causes and possible remedies of this problem must be understood. The search for better systems for indigenous participation and co-operative management of resources is also important.
>
> (Binns, 1990, p. 112)

It would appear that river basin management to integrate land and water resources is an overriding preoccupation for such policies.

5.3   THE NILE: A DEFINITIVE CASE OF HYDROPOLITICS

The Nile (Figure 5.4) is the world's longest river (6825 km); its catchment area (3M km^2) covers one-tenth of Africa and its annual flow is measured in cubic kilometres but the scale of the Nile basin is not the cause of its river management problems, except in so far as its scale stretches its boundaries across several climatic zones, nine sovereign states and a number of racial and religious boundaries. Moorehead (1983) describes just one of the boundaries, on the Blue Nile, in this way:

> No one crosses this border with impunity. When the Arab invades Ethiopia his camels die in the mountains and he himself loses heart, in the fearful cold. When the Ethiopian comes down into the desert his mules collapse in the appalling heat, and he is soon driven back to the hills for the lack of water. It is the conflict between two absolutely different forms of life, and even religion seems unable to make a bridge since Christianity falters as soon as it reaches the desert and Islam has

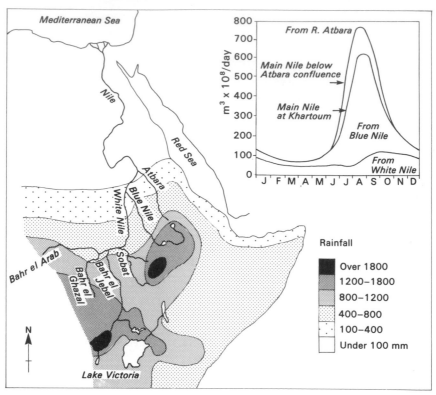

Figure 5.4 Nile basin annual rainfall and the Nile flood hydrograph, subdivided by contributing catchment

never been really powerful in the mountains. Only the river binds these two conflicting worlds together.

(Moorehead, 1983, p. 16)

Moorehead (1973; 1983) has given us a very graphic insight into the physiography and exploration of this river's two main branches − the Blue Nile which carries the majority of the flow and the White Nile whose source proved so elusive to men like Burton and Speke. Moorehead's books also weave the themes of exploration and exploitation closely; once European nations had discovered the wealth of Egypt (notably from Bonaparte's invasion in 1798) they became launched inevitably on controlling the rest of the basin. This destiny has never proved attainable and the cost in lives, reputations and failures was enormous in the nineteenth century alone.

5.3.1 Egypt: product of the river

Modern Egypt has a severe population problem; 48 million people live there, sustained only by the waters of the Nile. Unlike some Middle Eastern

Table 5.6(a) Estimated present water use in Egypt

	Volume in billion cubic metres
INFLOW	
Aswan release	55.5
OUTFLOW	
Edfina to sea	3.5
Canal tails to seas	0.1
Drainage to sea	13.2
Drainage to Fayoum	0.7
Sub-total	17.5
WATER USE	
Municipal and industrial	2.4
Evapotranspiration (irrigation)	33.6
Evaporation from water surfaces	2.0
Sub-total	38.0

Source: Chesworth (1990)

Table 5.6(b) Growth of Egyptian population and cultivated and cropped land

	Estimated population (million)	Cultivable area (000 feddans)[a]	Cropped area (000 feddans)[a]	Cropping intensity (%)
1821	2.51 – 4.23	3053	3053	100
1846	4.50 – 5.29	3746	3746	100
1882	7.93	4758	5754	121
1897	9.72	4943	6725	136
1907	11.19	5374	7595	141
1917	12.72	5309	7720	146
1927	14.18	5544	8522	154
1937	15.92	5312	8302	156
1947	18.97	5761	9133	159
1960	26.09	5900	10200	173
1966	30.08	6000	10400	173
1970	33.20	5900	10900	185
1975	37.00	5700	10700	188
1986	49.70	6000	11400	190

Source: Chesworth (1990)
[a] One feddan = 4,200 m^2.

states Egypt's oil resource is small by comparison with its size; furthermore its population continues to grow by >2.5 per cent per annum. Egypt's situation is dire as Table 5.6 indicates.

Egypt's need for water has had violent political repercussions already in modern times; in 1956 when the USA refused finance for the construction of the Aswan High Dam, Egypt nationalised the Suez Canal to raise the capital herself. Aswan is now complete, financed after all by outside capital from the former Soviet Union. It is a controversial dam (see below) but its existence has both saved Egypt from famine and constantly posed the problem of providing guaranteed inflows from upstream.

Another historian with a fascination about the Nile is Robert Collins, who uses the word 'hydropolitics' to connote the sequence by which the basin has reached its present level of development. Collins (1990) traces history through the lives of those who harnessed the river's water in both Egypt and Sudan. For more than six thousand years the benign flood of the Nile (compared with the flashy snowmelt regime of Tigris and Euphrates) provided simple gravity irrigation to the cereal-growing flood basins of Egypt. However, rulers and occupiers of the nineteenth century needed to extend the area of cultivation and to diversify into cash crops such as cotton; from 1843 barrages were built on the delta to raise water throughout the year for perennial irrigation. The size of this task is demonstrated by the river's markedly seasonal regime (see Table 5.7).

Table 5.7 Monthly average discharge for the major rivers in the Nile basin

	White Nile	Blue Nile	Atbara	Nile–Aswan
	(m^3/sec)			
October	1200	3040	340	5200
November	1200	1030	79	2270
December	1100	499	25	1400
January	829	282	8	1100
February	634	188	2	1020
March	553	156	0	834
April	525	138	0	819
May	574	182	1	698
June	742	461	35	1340
July	897	2080	640	1910
August	1030	5950	2100	6570
September	1130	5650	1420	8180
Annual average	868	1638	388	2612

Source: UNESCO

5.3.2   Control of the river

A new phase of development on the basis of dam-building began with the first Aswan Dam in 1902. Collins (1990) records the history of the long British engineering/hydrological involvement with the river; Garstin's hydrological surveys between 1899 and 1903 heralded the modern phase, although flow records at the ancient 'nilometers' date back to AD 672. Throughout the centuries Egypt had established its claim to Nile waters by historic use. However, by 1929 it proved essential to reconcile the Egyptian needs with the growing use of irrigation in Sudan; the Egyptians were suspicious of the ruling British in that country. The Nile Waters Agreement of 1929 merely partitioned the annual flow between the two countries, it did nothing to develop the basin's resources as a whole. After the resignation of the most famous engineer/hydrologist, MacDonald, in 1921 the basin entered what Collins calls 'the years of indecision', in which a huge extra effort went into river gauging and the analysis of records but very little into proactive planning.

> They were terrified of not having sufficient data but few were able to forge the enormous amount of information they gathered into a rational, coherent, holistic view of the Nile. They were also dull, rigid and unimaginative. Reports they could write; dreams they suppressed.
>
> (Collins, 1990, p. 162)

H. E. Hurst was the first hydrologist to combine data with dreams and he labelled the product 'century storage', a proposal to smooth out the regular variability in Nile flow by increasing storage (principally on the White Nile) to the point where 100-year mean discharges could be guaranteed. Figure 5.5 compares Hurst's design with the existing management and utilisation pattern in the Nile Basin.

One major obstruction has, however, always thwarted the notion of century storage − the Sudd, a huge area of floating vegetation and wetlands which physically blocks the river in southern Sudan, detaining and evaporating half of the inflow. The area of the Sudd fluctuates according to climatic conditions in the headwaters of the White Nile as Table 5.8 shows.

In 1925 the Egyptian government approved a scheme to cut through the Sudd in order to reduce detention and evaporation. The Egyptian irrigation service told the Sudan and the Governor of the Upper Nile nothing of their proposed Bor-Zaraf Cut and the scheme became politically impossible. Subsequently a large number of ways of breaking through the Sudd were evaluated and by 1938 the Jonglei Canal Diversion Scheme was selected by Egypt, though once again the British in Sudan were not consulted and no surveys were made of the impact the Canal might have on the large indigenous population (Collins, 1990).

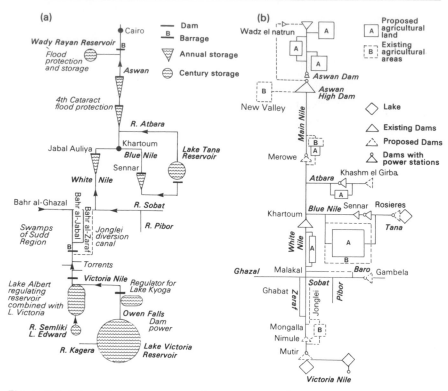

Figure 5.5 Nile water resources – dreams and reality:
(a) Hurst's plan for 'century storage', indicating the value of the upper White Nile (Collins, 1990)
(b) Actual developments in resources, showing the concentration on Egypt/Sudan (Fahim, 1981)

Table 5.8 Losses in the Sudd

	Precipitation 7.5 km^3	
Inflow 21 km^3	*Area (average) = 8300 km^2	Outflow 14.3 km^3
	so loss = 21 + 7.5 − 14.3	

Areas of floodplain	pre-1960	post-1960
Permanent swamp	2700 km^2	16100 km^2
Temporary swamp	10400 km^2	13600 km^2

5.3.3   Jonglei: long promised, incomplete through war

After the Second World War, Sudanese plans to develop the South and
H. E. Hurst's proposals for century storage and a canal from Jonglei to the
Sobat converged; British officials in Khartoum assembled a Jonglei Investigation Team which was to survey the desirability of reducing evaporative
loss with minimum impact on the living and economy of the people of the
Upper Nile, an early but unlabelled example of environmental impact
assessment. The Jonglei Investigation Team's four-volume report was published in 1954 but its findings have been refined and updated in a recent
book (Howell *et al.*, 1988). As part of the work undertaken by the Jonglei
Investigation Team, Sutcliffe (1974) surveyed the floodplain regions of the
Sudd in relation to inundation patterns and the resulting spatial distribution
of vegetation, the basis of the existing rural ecology. He concluded:

> In the absence of agricultural or pastoral improvement, the economy of
> the area is dependent on the natural environment, and especially on the
> grazing provided by the river through the annual cycle of river flow and
> the relative levels of the river, river bank and flood-plain ... any change
> in the relation of the river to the bank and flood-plain, or in the flow,
> will have an exaggerated effect on the vegetation.
>
> (Sutcliffe, 1974, p. 254)

Later Sutcliffe and Parks (1987) used a simple mathematical model
to predict the areas of inundation under various natural and modified
flow regimes. Howell *et al.* (1988), in their volume devoted to the Jonglei
Investigation Team's work, conclude:

> The fact of the matter is that water evaporated in the Sudd region is not
> a total loss; it has its vital local value in the subsistence economy and has
> done from time immemorial. It also has potential for future development
> in the Jonglei area. In this context there are fundamentally different per-
> ceptions of riparian rights. For downstream users, water saved from
> evaporation by major drainage or diversion works financed by them is
> 'new' or 'additional' water; it is water saved and theirs by right. For
> those who live in the Jonglei area ... in the process of seasonal inunda-
> tion of the floodplain valuable economic assets in pasture and fisheries
> are created.
>
> (Howell *et al.*, 1988, p. 468)

At the time of writing their book, Howell and his colleagues reported that,
as a result of the outbreak of civil war in Sudan in 1983, all work on the
Jonglei Canal had ceased. They conclude that a 260 km 'vast trench which
catches water during the rains' will need repairs and crossing points for
people and wildlife whatever the outcome of the Project once peace is
re-established.

Table 5.9 The Aswan High Dam debated: a summary sheet

Logistics	Benefits to date (1980)	Major side effcts	General assessment and prospects
Land development was a necessity to cope with the incredible imbalance between the country's population growth and agricultural production. Agriculture is basic to the Egyptian economy.	Controlled high floods and supplemented low ones; saved Egypt from the monetary cost to cover the damage from both high and low floods.	Water loss, through seepage and evaporation, is likely to affect the water supply needed for development plans; studies show that the water loss is within the predicted volume.	The Aswan High Dam is solid engineering work; more importantly it is fulfilling a vital need for 40 million people.
Egypt found no option but to increase the water supply for land development policies of both horizontal and vertical extension.	Allowed for increase in cultivated land area through reclamation, and increased the crop production of the existing land through conversion from basin to perennial irrigation.	Loss of the Nile silt would require costly use of fertilisers; it has also caused riverbed degradation and coastal erosion of the northern delta.	All dams have problems; some are recognised while others are unforeseen at the time of planning.
Building a dam and forming a water reservoir in an Egyptian territory minimises the risks of water control politics on the part of riparian countries.	Improved Nile navigation and changed it from seasonal to year-round.	Soil salinity is increasing and land in most areas is becoming waterlogged, due to delays in implementing drainage schemes.	The lesson learned from the Aswan project, however, is that dams may be built with missionary zeal but little careful planning and monitoring of side effects.
	Electric power generated by the dam supplies 50% of		As a result of the new semi-capitalist policies and also the technical and monetary

Egypt perceived the Aswan High Dam as a multipurpose project, basic to national development plans.

Egypt's current consumption, although the dam was built primarily not for power generation but for water conservation.

The new lake resources are potentially economic, including land cultivation and settlement, fishing, and tourist industries.

Increased contact with water through irrigation extension schemes is expected to affect schistosomiasis rates adversely; evidence exists that rates have not increased due to use of protected water supplies.

The Nile water quality has been deteriorating; studies indicate the occurrence of change in the water quality parameters; they do not consitute a health hazard at present.

aid that Egypt has lately been receiving from several Western countries, it is expected that several of the dam's problems will be efficiently controlled and monitored.

Dam-related studies have given recognition to present problems and have provided possible solutions. The dam would meet its expectations on several aspects providing that research findings are utilised.

The development potential and economic returns of this water project are expected to be very rewarding in the long run, if the project's developments are systematically studied and monitored.

Source: Fahim (1981)

5.3.4   Aswan and Lake Nasser: plus and minus

For the foreseeable future Egypt and Sudan will need to maximise the benefits of the Aswan High Dam. In order to carry through this project a second Nile Waters Agreement was signed in 1959, dividing 'the spoils'. It is fortunate that the Aswan scheme has been documented (e.g. by Fahim, 1981) in terms of construction and early impacts, both positive and negative. Fahim writes:

> As the controversy over the Aswan High Dam began to intensify during the early years of the 1970s and was especially aggravated by increasing conflicts between facts and fiction, science and politics, in both domestic and international circles, it became essential to tackle the dam's dilemma on a scientific basis and in a way that would realistically account for the technical and human issues combined.
>
> (Fahim, 1981, p. xiii)

Of the human issues, Fahim notes how closely the Dam came to President Nasser's ideals of a new social democracy and the abolition of feudalism; its scale (5 km long and 1 km thick at its base) was also important, Nasser remarking that, 'In antiquity we built pyramids for the dead. Now we will build pyramids for the living.'

How well has the pyramid performed? Four major problems are commonly identified:

(a) Water loss from Lake Nasser by seepage and evaporation.
(b) Sedimentation in the Lake and degradation below the Dam and in the Delta.
(c) Waterlogging and soil salinity from year-round irrigation.
(d) Increase in disease, especially schistosomiasis.

There is no sign of an end to controversy, rival sets of views and 'facts' offered freely on every topic (see Table 5.9). Egyptians are sure of the impact of the dam in preventing famine in 1972 and 1984 − for this they are prepared to accept some costs. Uptake of commercial farming is not yet complete and Fahim is critical of the unsystematic way in which human, community resources have remained uncoupled from the technical aspects of the Dam; he proposes Figure 5.6 as an integrating system for the proper consideration of such projects. For example, the Nubians displaced by the project (100,000 in both Egypt and Sudan) were resettled and have received the social benefits of modern living but without any infrastructure for community development, as if planners feared this. Many people chose to stay on or around Lake Nasser.

Fahim is convinced that it is water quality problems on the Nile that will eventually be the spur for basin integration. At present water quality data are extremely scarce; water quantity considerations prevail and tend to be

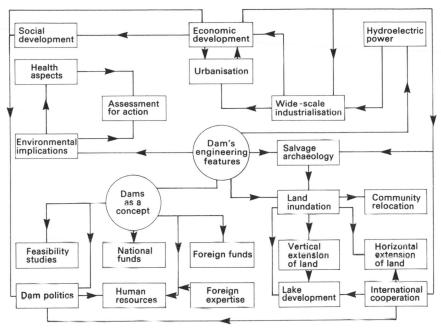

Figure 5.6 The development of a major dam scheme (e.g. Aswan) seen as an
interconnected socio-economic system (Fahim, 1981)

solved by large prestigious construction schemes:

> The Aswan experience has shown us that dam-related research, in terms
> of a canvass of impacts, was begun too late in most areas and is still too
> little in several fields; in general, research has been fragmented. An
> integrated approach to the dam's side effects, although recognised and
> advocated, is still limited in practice.
>
> (Fahim, 1981, p. 159)

Efforts continue to bring about political consensus on the planning of the
Nile as a basin resource. It is astounding that a river for which we have so
much data cannot utilise a fraction of that information, although more
rational irrigation modelling is promised if the Jonglei Canal is completed
(Stoner, 1990). The major hidden agenda on the Nile is development of the
major source of the river's flow − the Blue Nile. During negotiations over
the Nile Waters Agreement of 1959 Ethiopia launched a major study of
the river's potential through the agency of the United States Bureau of
Reclamation. This study proposed four major dams on the Blue Nile, producing three times more electricity than the Aswan High Dam, virtually
eliminating the seasonal fluctuations of flow into Sudan and reducing the
total flow by 8.5 per cent. The losses are accountable to evaporation but

Table 5.10 Divisive economic problems of major Nile basin partners

	Egypt	Sudan	Ethiopia
GNP/cap ($)	680.0	330.0	130.0
Annual growth (%)	3.5	−0.5	0.1
Debt bill (bn$)	40.2	11.1	2.6

they are, of course, much less on the Blue Nile in the mountains and these are optimal dam sites – the challenge of political consensus is therefore to throw much more of the Nile's control on to the Blue Nile. Post-revolutionary Ethiopia is unlikely to enter negotiations easily and has no capital (nor the desire for provincial development) to develop the Blue Nile unilaterally, preferring, it seems, to hold the potential to do so as a threat (see Table 5.10).

As for multinational forums in which use of the Nile can be discussed, the Nile Basin Commission (set up by the 1959 Agreement) is mainly a technical and hydrometric organisation but it has spawned a grouping of riparian nations (Egypt, Sudan, Uganda, Zaire and the Central African Republic) as the ENDUGU ('Brotherhood') group. Rwanda and Burundi have also joined; the aim is to encourage Kenya, Tanzania and Ethiopia to join, moving towards a Nile Basin Economic Community (Samir, 1990).

External interest in the Nile is represented by a UNDP Commission which has collated information on population growth and the expected loss of food and power security in the basin (as population doubles every twenty years). In fact a joint electricity grid may be a more tangible political expediency than an agreement on flow allocation.

Further organic progress in cooperation is however likely to need changes of international law governing river basins; the Nile needs a substitution of the principles of the International Law Association's *Helsinki Rules* for the myriad of *ad hoc* treaties currently in use (or abuse) in the basin (Okidi, 1990).

The most important Helsinki Rules comprise:

(a) Equity of distribution is the governing factor among riparians.
(b) Equity does not mean distribution by equal share, but by fair shares which can be decided by the following factors:
   —The topography of the basin, in particular, the size of the river's drainage area in each riparian state;
   —The climatic conditions affecting the basin in general;
   —The precedents about past utilisation of the waters of the basin, up to present-day usages;
   —The economic and social needs of each basin state;
   —The population factor;

—The comparative costs of alternative means of satisfying the economic and social needs of each basin state;

—The availability of other water resources to each basin state;

—The avoidance of undue waste and unnecessary damage to other riparian states.

5.4 RIVER BASIN DEVELOPMENT AUTHORITIES: EXPERIENCE ELSEWHERE IN AFRICA

Having considered the seemingly impossible task of integrated river basin management across nine nations' boundaries in the case of the Nile, we briefly investigate two 'model' river basin authorities wholly within national boundaries elsewhere in Africa: the Awash Valley Authority in Ethiopia (Winid, 1981) and the Tana and Athi Rivers Development Authority in Kenya (Rowntree, 1990). Both authorities are responsible for basin areas of approximately 120,000 km^2 but, whilst some of the lessons they teach us about development of power and irrigated agriculture are similar, their political context and structure illustrate the importance of individual national and regional development pathways in Africa.

5.4.1 The Awash Valley Authority, Ethiopia

The Awash Valley Authority was established in the pre-revolutionary Ethiopia of Emperor Haile Selassie in 1954. Ninety per cent of Ethiopia's 30 million people live in the central highland area where rainfed agriculture is feasible most years but where population pressure has led to huge soil erosion losses. Whilst 6m hectares are currently cultivated, half as much again could yield food and cash crops with irrigation. Rivers radiate from the highlands ('the water tower of Africa'). Situated in convenient proximity to the nation's capital, Addis Ababa, the Awash Valley stretches 700 km towards the Djibouti border across the Rift Valley, its flow sustained by fourteen tributaries but its course succumbing to aridity in the shallow Lake Abe (Figure 5.7). The highland rainfall of 1000 mm/yr decreases to 200 mm/yr in the Rift and rainfall is very unreliable; nevertheless irrigable soils constitute 24 per cent of the valley area. The indigenous agriculture consists of livestock, with cattle, sheep, goats and camels migrating in search of grass and water.

The Awash Valley Authority was set up to coordinate the activities of government ministries in the Valley, to charge for the use of water, to conduct surveys and to administer water rights.

The Development Plan followed by the Authority was highly ambitious prior to the Marxist revolution of 1974, itself a result of Sahelian drought. Winid (1981) describes the plan's objectives as including policy change to promote development, social and health surveys, feasibility studies for

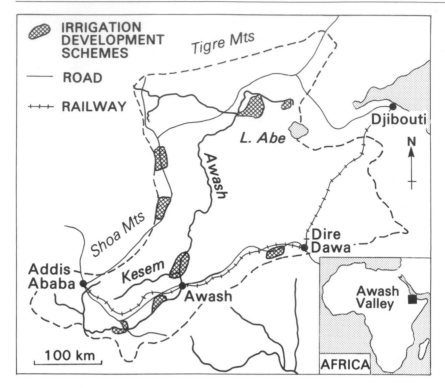

Figure 5.7 The Awash valley, Ethiopia and schemes developed by the former
Awash Valley Authority (after Winid, 1981)

irrigation, flood control and hydropower, establishment of agro-industries
and infrastructure improvements to permit tourism. Winid describes seven
run-of-river irrigation sites in the upper and middle Awash, together with
some smaller areas of the lower Awash (Figure 5.7); however, dam sites
to increase the scope of irrigation and to generate power for industry are
continually prospected.

The calculation of benefit/cost ratios for developments in the Awash is,
according to Winid, markedly influenced by the balance between the cultivation of food and cash/industrial crops. To date the latter dominate; this
in turn determines the fate, in development, of native nomadic pastoralists
who must be settled to form a labour force, joined by other migrants from
troubled regions of Ethiopia. However, the Awash schemes for resettlement
have been failures, with the true costs of resettlement soaring. No attempt
was made to integrate an improved traditional livestock sector with the
plantation irrigated agriculture.

Winid offers twelve reasons for the failures of the Awash Valley
Authority (Table 5.11), which was wound up by Ethiopia's centralist

Table 5.11 Reasons why the Awash Valley Development was not a success

1 Knowledge on the part of the French firm of consultants (SOGREAH) of the political, economical, social, cultural, scientific and technical aspects of the Awash valley region was lacking as a result of:
   (a) The short period during which the consultants were employed, namely, four years.
   (b) Their limited contacts with Awash Valley peoples which was mainly restricted to a small proportion of the population, the egoistic 'élite'.
   (c) The consultants living very much within the foreign UN community.
   (d) Frequent changes of advisers from different schools of thought.
   (e) Ineffective supervision policies (local counterparts were too young).
   (f) Relations with the home country and the international UNO bureaucracy.
   (g) The introduction of extensive techniques and excessive investments.
   (h) No interest in continental African 'integration' policy.
2 There were great differences in the Ethiopian technical levels between sectors, branches of the economy, industry, and infrastructural elements (services, education, health, science).
3 Small consideration was given to planning the future AVA situation in relation to Ethiopia, the African continent or the world (especially the Horn of Africa).
4 Foreign advisers were unaware of the true political and governmental obstacles to development activities.
5 There was little cooperation among those concerned with AVA development or between them and the countries adjacent to Ethiopia.
6 Advisers' preparation of plans were:
   (a) Not nationally integrated and were divided-up between specialised UN agencies.
   (b) Focused on the mining and consumptive industries.
   (c) Export-oriented in agricultural production.
   (d) Not related to existing locally trained manpower.
   (e) Minus much large-scale investment.
7 There were difficulties in the implementation stages, namely:
   (a) The existence of other advisory bodies/institutions (e.g. Australians were active in the AVA region).
   (b) The difficult financial situation – no domestic means were available.
   (c) There was instability, political and economic (both internally and externally to Ethiopia).
8 The creation and enlargement of the 'dual economy':
   (a) Weakened the links between the 'new economy' and the 'old' which had engaged 80–90% of the population.
   (b) Promoted a pattern of demand which required importation from industrialised countries.
9 New investments are very often owned or controlled by foreigners who view profit goals as the deciding factor.
10 Locational policies for industry were mostly drawn up in Addis Ababa, or the major Ethiopian ports which are in general the crystallisation or evolution of the colonial city.
11 The towns in AVA were only administrative centres for the exploitation of the countryside with the exclusion of the natives from government.
12 Production was in the form of goods and in quantities best suited to the ruling (minority) group.

Source: After Winid (1981)

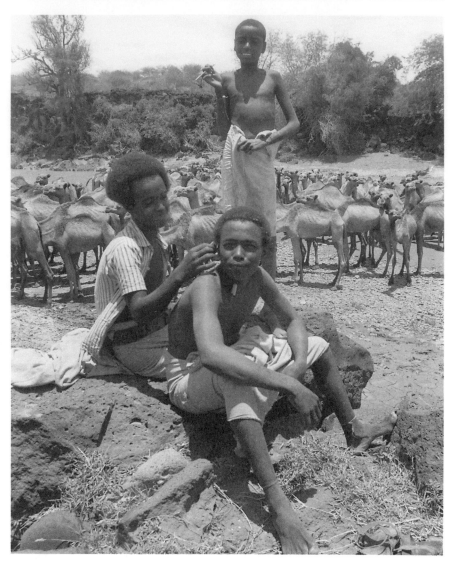

Plate 5.1a A herd of camels cared for by pastoralists in the Awash Valley, Ethiopia

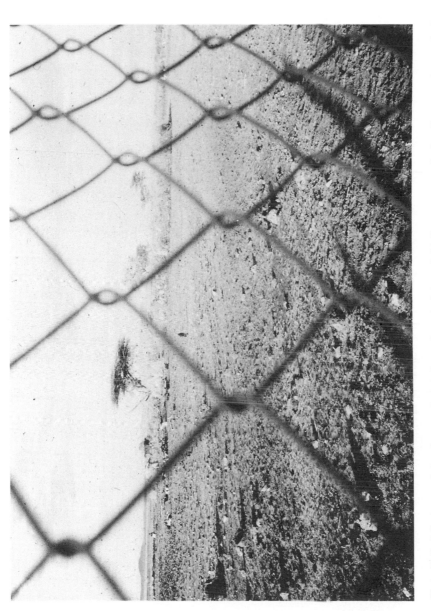

Plate 5.1b Life beyond the fence of an irrigated settled Awash Valley; a nomadic family camp beneath the tree

Marxist government in 1981 in favour of stronger ministerial roles in water developments.

In 1986 the present author was a member of the British team which investigated the feasibility of a dam on the Kesem tributary of the Awash, one of four dam sites suggested by the Awash Valley Authority in the 1960s. A Kesem Dam would irrigate 20,000 ha of land on the left bank of the Awash. Sir M. MacDonald and Partners, who carried out the Kesem study for FAO and UNDP, set out to use all resources to maximise agricultural potential under a balanced environmental and ecological system, producing cash and industrial crops for export and/or import substitution, plus food crops at least for local self-sufficiency. These objectives are much more broadly based than those of the Valley Authority's consultants in the 1960s, reflecting a new social and environmental conscience in river basin development. Referring to the demise of the Authority in 1981 the MacDonald report concluded that, whilst centrally the roles of ministries were now more defined, at local level there was 'frequent lack of communication, co-ordination and co-operation'. The pace of the proposals for a Kesem scheme was made compatible with the changing attitude of the Afar tribespeople; the Afar would be granted their own lands, avoiding a traditional plantation culture. Components of the new proposals, include roads, power supplies, housing, domestic water supply, offices and workshops, clinics and health services, schools and education, police and civil administration, and recreational facilities. Preferred crops are tobacco and citrus, with smaller areas of cotton, wheat and maize.

One problem with the proposed Kesem scheme is the high sediment yields of the river which would fill the reservoir in less than 100 years. Finally the recommendations concluded that the internal rate of return for the original scheme would be between 2 per cent and 4 per cent. A smaller scale scheme is recommended.

5.4.2 The Tana and Athi Rivers Development Authority, Kenya

Like Ethiopia, Kenya has a burgeoning population highly concentrated in its humid zones with an acute problem of peripheral aridity. However, it has a more pronounced and more recent colonial European past and, whilst currently a one-party state, has fewer problems of rebellious regionalism than has Ethiopia.

The Tana and Athi basins, whose joint Authority, TARDA, is reviewed by Rowntree (1990), total 132,700 km^2, containing a significant proportion of Kenya's population (62 per cent) including the capital, Nairobi (Figure 5.8). The principal water yield for both basins comes from the slopes of Mt Kenya and the Aberdares which receive 2000 mm of precipitation each year; out on the plains a potential evaporation of 1200 mm exceeds rainfall and

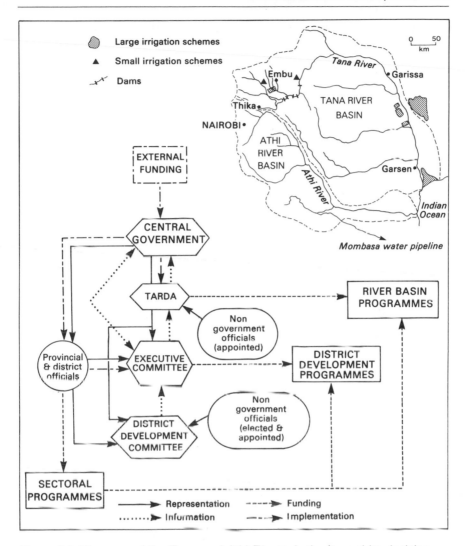

Figure 5.8 The area of the Tana and Athi Rivers Authority and its decision-
network diagram (after Rowntree, 1990)

irrigation forms the basis of most agriculture. An immediate problem of
this two-fold hydrological division is that, as in the case of the Kesem, the
desire to exploit *rainfed agriculture* in the uplands has led to deforestation
and soil erosion. Sediment yields of between $109\,\mathrm{t\,km^{-2}\,yr^{-1}}$ and
$433\,\mathrm{t\,km^{-2}\,yr^{-1}}$ are quoted by Rowntree. (Kenya is fortunate at least to
have had hydrometric surveys which include measurement of sediment
yields.) As well as threatening irrigation schemes downstream by excessive
sedimentation, the populous uplands also have a high demand for hydro-

electric power (coal and oil must be imported and exploitation of wood fuel leads to further erosion) and for domestic water supply/sanitation.

Like many other emerging nations, Kenya introduced strongly centralised planning in 1974 and set up a Ministry of Water Development; at the same time the Tana River Development Authority (the Athi was added in 1982) was instigated with aims as shown in Table 5.12. The Authority, like that of the Awash in Ethiopia, was designed to coordinate the work of ministries and to balance the competing demands of domestic water supply, hydropower and irrigation in the basin. Such coordination was vital in view of three major problems of development:

(a) Hydropower dams in the middle course appeared incompatible with irrigation in the lower reaches;
(b) Dry-season water supply abstraction in the upper catchment could reduce the hydropower potential;
(c) Siltation could only be controlled by a vast conservation programme.

The first major project of the Authority was the commissioning of the Masinga Dam in 1979. It was designed both to generate power itself and to

Table 5.12 Functions of the Tana River Development Authority

1 To advise the Government generally and the scheduled Ministries in particular on all matters affecting the development of the Area including the apportionment of water resources.
2 To draw up, and keep up to date, a long-range development plan for the Area.
3 To initiate such studies, and to carry out such surveys of the Area as it may consider necessary, and to assess alternative demands within the Area on the resources thereof, including electric power generation, irrigation, wildlife, land and other resources, and to recommend economic priorities.
4 To coordinate the various studies of, and schemes within, the Area so that human, water, animal, land and other resources are utilised to the best advantage, and to monitor the design and execution of planned projects within the Area.
5 To effect a programme of monitoring of the performance of projects within the Area so as to improve such performance and establish responsibility therefor, and to improve future planning.
6 To ensure close cooperation between all agencies concerned with the abstraction and use of water within the Area in the setting up of effective monitoring of such abstraction and use.
7 To collect, assemble and correlate all such data related to the use of water and other resources within the Area as may be necessary for the efficient planning of the Area.
8 To maintain a liaison between the Government, the private sector, and foreign agencies in the matter of the development of the Area with a view to limiting the duplication of effort and assuring the best use of technical resources.
9 To render assistance to operating agencies in their applications for loans fund if required.

Source: After Rowntree (1990)

improve the regime for existing downstream dams and irrigation schemes; as with the Awash settlement, plans for 40,000 people are part of the irrigation projects and once again social problems and climatic contrasts with the over-populated uplands are anticipated to give trouble. Nairobi is continuing to expand and to require power and water; its City Commission appears to Rowntree to act independently of TARDA.

Rowntree describes TARDA as an 'apparent failure', thanks partly to national and local factors of centralisation, a mismatch with overall development planning and a potential for political corruption largely avoided by the Tennessee Valley Authority, still the model for river basin development. However, the corollary of political freedom in such institutions appears to be technocratic rule of specialists (see Chapter 8) and these specialists are often foreign consultants. Faster progress can be achieved by the technocratic approach, at least up to the point where the people become forced to fit the scheme. It is instructive in this respect that the phasing of the Kesem project envisaged by the MacDonald team (Section 5.4.1) led to costs which threatened the economics of dam-building in favour of succouring a human-scale transition.

Rowntree's sad conclusion about TARDA is as follows:

> We are left with the conclusion that TARDA does not represent an effec tive framework for regional planning, neither on its own nor through integration with the district focus policy. Both are controlled by top-down planning, by political allegiance to the power élite and by the interests of foreign aid agencies. It may represent a forum through which technocratic solutions to resource development can be promulgated but it is unlikely to achieve the type of grass-roots development that is so essential to effective and lasting development programmes.
>
> (Rowntree, 1990, p. 39)

Linking Rowntree's criticisms to those of Winid (Section 5.4.1), we can draw out certain common constraints on institutional river basin management in those developing countries with a drylands settlement problem:

(a) In the last analysis the control is in the hands of those creating the new settlements and wealth; technocratic speed in the early stages of development (e.g. dam-building) is always liable to be forsaken once farming begins.

(b) If not overly centralised, multi-agency authorities can potentially deliver a unified picture to the people on the ground; however if they have been forcibly moved from the humid zone, or settled from a dryland nomadic lifestyle, there are still problems without much expensive attention to patterns of tenure, infrastructure and timing.

(c) Newly emerged nations, particularly facing problems of infant democracy or totalitarian control, often are troubled by regional rebellion verging on civil war. The present author has been held at gunpoint by rebels whilst sediment sampling in the Kesem. Local participation is therefore particularly difficult to 'release', there are cultural clashes within the local population and, within government, ministries are keener to compete than to collaborate.

(d) The use of foreign finance, foreign expertise and foreign personnel, often with the aim of growing exotic crops for foreign consumption or supplying electricity to distant cities, further threatens the local element of development schemes so widely seen as desirable.

Adams (1985) discussing the performance of River Basin Development Authorities in Nigeria (he cites eleven), reveals similar shortcomings:

(a) Over-reliance on large projects: dam construction and irrigation development.
(b) Inadequate economic, environmental and social appraisal.
(c) Ineffective population resettlement.
(d) Almost total lack of attention to watershed management and pollution control.

He quotes state/federal rivalry as a (now familiar) obstruction to progress and advocates both development from below and a concentration on improved operation of existing projects as priorities.

5.5   THE LAND-USE DIMENSION: AFRICA WAITS BUT THE GANGES RESPONDS

In our brief review of African river management problems we have touched little on the theme of 'hydrologic civilisations' (Chapter 1) in which upstream land use and land management practice is used to control downstream water resources. Rather, the African situation is one of 'hydraulic civilisations' using upstream water resources to control downstream land use. In the developed west and north we may well surmise 'their time will come', with particular reference to the inevitable pollution and conservation problems brought by development.

In Africa there is, as yet, only the thinnest body of empirical knowledge on the hydrological effects of land use and management. Of more than 50 papers presented at the Harare conference on African water resources (Walling et al., 1984) only four reported field measurements and all of these were in the area of erosion, which completely dominated the Harare Symposium. The books by Pereira (1973; 1989), whilst full of qualitative and extrapolated wisdom on the subject, are obviously short of experimental information and much reference is made to North American and European experimental material in both volumes.

One might argue that, until the mountain zones of Africa (outside the

Ethiopian Highlands) face population and land-use change pressures, little will be done, with the distributional philosophies (dominated by engineering) of irrigation and electricity- or water-supply prevailing. However, developments in Lesotho (Makhoalibe, 1984) suggest that monitoring schemes in Africa are needed urgently; recently the World Bank has financed studies designed to develop hydrometric and water-quality networks through sub-Saharan Africa.

The region to which we next turn has no waiting to do in terms of seeking a solution to the downstream impacts of headwater, mountain development. Like the Nile, the Ganges is a truly remarkable international river basin, 900,000 km^2 in area, with a dominant exploiting nation in the form of India for whom the river comprises a quarter of the available water resources, whose basin comprises 26 per cent of the nation's land and 43 per cent of its irrigated land. Additionally 'Ganga' has constituted a basis for successive dynasties in India's history and a firm religious theme of life-giving significance; the Hindu god Shiva collected Ganga's waters from heaven in his matted hair that the ashes of human dead might be purified for their return to heaven (Darian, 1978).

Indians bathe, water cattle, wash clothes and utensils, defecate, cremate their dead and conduct the other waste activities of 27 cities of over 100,000 people in the River Ganges; it is sacred in what we might call a 'prehygienic' way. Whilst the Indian government can control the activities of industrial polluters via the 1974 Water Pollution Control Act and, through the 1985 Ganges Action Plan, is improving urban sewerage and sewage purification, it is clear that a popular change in perception of the river's true role in an evolving society is required.

5.5.1   Nepal: a rush to judgement

However, pollution of the Ganges is not the major focus of international attention in the basin. This is divided between the international tension which exists as the result of India's prime role in exploiting the river (by comparison with its poorer riparian neighbours Nepal and Bangladesh) and the apparent recent increase in sedimentation and flooding in these countries, phenomena widely attributed to headwater land-use changes. When one considers that the headwaters of the Ganges are the Himalayas one might anticipate causes other than development pressures alone; one might also anticipate that 'solutions' to the 'problem' might be taken at a regional (Himalaya/Gangetic plain) level rather than locally or nationally. All of these latter themes have been strongly developed in writings on the Ganges basin in the last five years.

The link between the Ganges and the Nile is strengthened in a paper by Hellen and Bonn (1981) demonstrating that both Egypt and Nepal, central problem nations to the management of both basins, are experiencing population growth of 2–5 per cent per year. However, these authors express the dangers of assuming that the step from population growth to environmental degradation is inevitable and a one-dimensional problem.

In a recent book devoted entirely to the Ganges and the development of the mountain zone in Nepal (Ives and Pitt, 1988) Ives considers the elements of *'the perceived crisis'* in the Himalaya–Ganges region. They are:

(a) That a population explosion was initiated shortly after World War II due to the introduction of modern health care and medicine and the suppression of malaria and other diseases.
(b) That increased population in subsistence mountain societies has led to:
   —Reduced amount of land per family;
   —Deepening poverty;
   —Massive deforestation.
(c) That mountain deforestation, on such a scale, will result in total loss of all accessible forest cover by AD 2000 and is the cause of accelerating soil erosion and incidence of landsliding.
(d) That destabilised mountain slopes resulting from points (a)–(c) above cause:
   —Increased flooding on the Ganges and Brahmaputra plains;
   —Extension of the delta and formation of islands in the Bay of Bengal;
   —Massive siltation and drastic reduction in the useful life of highly expensive water resource projects;
   —Drying up of wells and springs in the hills and lower dry-season river levels downstream.
(e) That deforestation also leads to climatic change in general and reduced rainfall amounts in particular.

Newspaper and TV journalists, together with the World Bank, have keenly fallen upon the deforestation perception of cause with such statements as: 'at the present rate of cutting the Himalayas will be bald in 25 years, topsoil will have disappeared and the climatic effects threaten to turn the fertile plain into a new Sahel' (*Sunday Times*). Gilmour (1988) cites this as an example of the *'uncertainty principle'* (Thompson and Warburton, 1985) in Himalayan development, since, when conducting actual ground surveys, the Nepalese government and the hill farmers appear jointly to have reversed the loss of forests in the mountain zones – the problem is actually worse in the 'terai' or piedmont zone.

Ives and Pitt quote further direct survey evidence of the erosion problem from Nelson (1979):

The blanket indictment of Nepal for high erosion rates is obviously unwarranted. It is probable that, of the 14 Ecological Land Unit Associations, 3 or 4 will be the site of most of the watershed problems. This complex picture means that watershed management in Nepal must be a

(a)

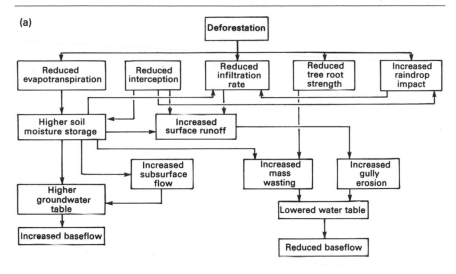

(b)

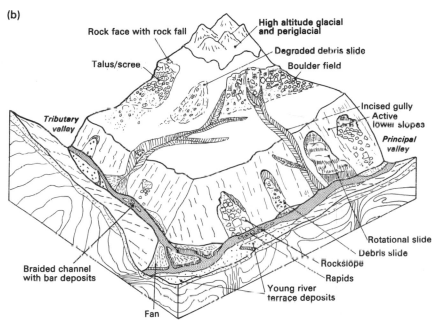

Figure 5.9 Problems of the Himalaya/Ganges region:
  (a) The deforestation problem
  (b) The physiographic instability problem – montane
      geomorphology and hazard (modified from Fookes and
      Vaughan, 1986)

mix of educational, remedial and protection activities which must vary
by geographic location.

(Ives and Pitt, 1988, p. 66)

Thus, whilst logic foretells a huge downstream impact for careless
deforestation of mountain lands (Figure 5.9a), the inherent local instability
of a very extreme physiographic and climatic setting has much to offer
as an explanation for the observed effects (Figure 5.9b). If one considers the
heavy, seasonally concentrated rainfalls, the very high altitudes, huge
floods and the 6 mm/yr rate of geological uplift of the region, the list of
causative factors becomes much broader than just deforestation (Sharma,
1987):

(a) Steep topography.
(b) Weak geology.
(c) Heavy and intensive rainfall.
(d) Glacial lake outburst floods.
(e) Deforestation.
(f) Seismicity.
(g) Human factors.

Nepal has suffered nine major landslide events since 1819 and fifteen major
earthquakes since 1866.

Nevertheless, land-use planning and management is worthwhile both for
its intrinsic benefit to Nepalese society and as an ameliorative policy in river
basin management. Gilmour *et al.* (1987), undertaking the all-too-rare factual field investigation in Nepal, point out that, whilst soil does become

Table 5.13 Erosion in various tropical moist forest and tree crop systems
(ton/ha/year)

Forest system	Erosion		
	Minimal	*Median*	*Maximal*
Multistoried tree gardens (4/4)[a]	0.01	0.06	0.14
Natural forests (18/27)	0.03	0.30	6.16
Shifting cultivation, fallow period (6/14)	0.05	0.15	7.40
Forest plantations, undisturbed (14/20)	0.02	0.58	6.20
Tree crops with cover crop/mulch (9/17)	0.10	0.75	5.60
Shifting cultivation, cropping period (7/22)	0.40	2.78	70.50
Taungya cultivation (2/6)	0.63	5.23	17.37
Tree crops, clean-weeded (10/17)	1.20	47.60	182.90
Forest plantations, burned/litter removed (7/7)	5.92	53.40	104.80

Source: From Wiersum (1984)
[a] (x/y) x = number of locations, y = number of treatments or observations.

compacted after deforestation and grazing, only 17 per cent of rainfall exceeds the infiltration capacity of such soils to become flood-producing, erosive surface runoff; they also point to the fact that deep-seated landslides are promoted by efficient infiltration, not surface flows (though under-cutting of slopes by stream incision must also be a factor). Hamilton (1988) stresses the importance of maintaining a litter layer in forests (Table 5.13).

Elsewhere in the Himalayas, successful land management schemes in India (Dhruva Narayana, 1987) have reduced the river impacts of deforestation (Figure 5.10) and the Chipko movement has popularised the environmental and local political benefits of forest covers.

Water is an important resource within Nepal's own boundaries; 25 per cent of cultivated land is irrigated and hydro-electric power (as yet only 0.15 per cent developed) perhaps offers the best chance to halt the wood-fuel crisis which threatens the forests of the terai. Sharma (1987) stresses that within Nepal aggradation has rendered river structures useless, ruling out the feasibility of dam-building, and has produced a substantial flood threat which extends, on the Kosi, into India. A review of the scanty sediment transport data for Nepal by Ramsay (1987) concluded that total erosion keeps pace with orogenic uplife (1–5 mm/yr), implying natural causes, but locally deforestation or poor grazing leads to surface erosion, gullying and shallow landsliding. Efficient delivery to channels sets up

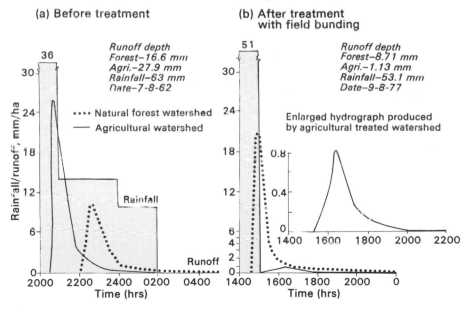

Figure 5.10 Sucessful management of land in the Indian Himalayan region has controlled runoff (Narayana, 1987)

positive feedbacks but Ramsay concludes that the loss to farmers is more serious than the 'gain' to rivers.

5.5.2   The Himalayas set new agendas for river basin management

The work of Ives and his colleagues in the region has had considerable benefits in the setting of new research agendas in watershed management, particularly relevant to developing mountainous zones, but equally applicable in principle to any large river basin. Ives *et al.* (1987) conclude that the Himalayan region 'is one of extreme complexity from both physical and human points of view, and panacea-type solutions of perceived and illusory problems will likely exacerbate growing human and environmental crises'. Further:

> Problems, though they do involve all sorts of real physical processes, are not defined by those processes. They are defined by people − people, moreover, who are embedded in very different social and cultural contexts and who naturally define their problems very differently. The system, in other words, is a system of mountains and people and we must do everything we can to avoid treating it as if it were two separate slices.
>
> (Ives *et al.*, 1987, p. 335)

Figure 5.11 emphasises this multi-faceted system; Ives and his colleagues demand a scaled, geographical approach to the search for solutions in which the people, the village, the region and international policies are reconciled through the flow of viewpoints and information.

As far as international activity is concerned, this is currently remote from environmental management, focusing on India's demands for water from the barrages erected across the river at Farakka and Gandak. Following the Farakka diversion of water to benefit Calcutta, India and Bangladesh set up a Joint Rivers Commission to study flows (Robinson, 1987); a treaty, resembling the Nile Waters Agreement, on 'Sharing of the Ganga Waters at Farakka and on augmenting its flows' was signed in 1977. The treaty with Nepal has little to do with that country's environmental and population problems, though it may come to have: the Gandak Barrage Treaty allows Nepal rights to withdraw water upstream until India's irrigation schemes downstream are threatened by shortage; the shortage is then shared! Robinson concludes that the knowledge base for a Ganges environment convention is not available, making the research agenda set by the Ives team yet more urgent if further tensions and damage are to be avoided.

Meanwhile Bangladesh is reacting to disastrous flooding in 1987 and 1988 (Brammer, 1990a). Floods are an integral part of Bangladeshi life but these were the worst on record, inundating 60 per cent of the nation's land. However, as one journalist put it, 'the world rallied round. It was open

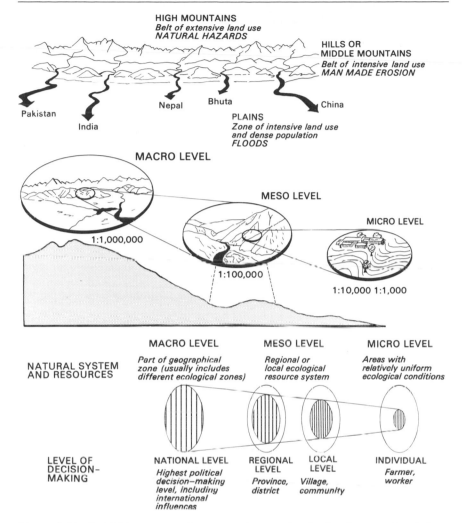

HIGH MOUNTAINS
Belt of extensive land use
NATURAL HAZARDS

HILLS OR
MIDDLE MOUNTAINS
Belt of intensive land use
MAN MADE EROSION

Pakistan

Nepal Bhuta China

India

PLAINS
Zone of intensive land use
and dense population
FLOODS

MACRO LEVEL

MESO LEVEL

MICRO LEVEL

1:1,000,000

1:100,000

1:10,000 1:1,000

	MACRO LEVEL	MESO LEVEL	MICRO LEVEL
NATURAL SYSTEM AND RESOURCES	*Part of geographical zone (usually includes different ecological zones)*	*Regional or local ecological resource system*	*Areas with relatively uniform ecological conditions*

LEVEL OF DECISION-MAKING	NATIONAL LEVEL	REGIONAL LEVEL	LOCAL LEVEL	INDIVIDUAL
	Highest political decision–making level, including international influences	*Province, district*	*Village, community*	*Farmer, worker*

Figure 5.11 Himalayan research: appropriate scales for implementation (after Ives *et al.*, 1987)

season for hydrologists and technologists and what emerged was a dog's breakfast of massive flood defence proposals'. The World Bank has now selected a coordinated scheme of the best proposals, avoiding large dams, but nevertheless having a large impact on people adapted to riparian or island livelihoods. The UNDP has stipulated that the flood control strategies adopted should research river morphology and justifies a 'small is beautiful' approach to irrigated food production in Bangladesh (Brammer, 1990b).

5.6   DAMS, ALTERNATIVES AND THE NEED FOR NEW INTERNATIONAL ORDER

Clearly one of the most compelling needs in the technological reappraisal of river basin development is a new look at large dams. Often the central, triumphal feature of a project, the large dam has a growing popular and political protest movement set against it. It is of note that Pakistan, for example, now has a Small Dams Directorate in the North West Frontier Province. Since the early 1980s the International Dams Newsletter (now International Rivers Network) has coordinated a campaign against such projects, not the least because of the large number of people relocated as a result of reservoir filling or of changes to local agriculture and infrastructures.

5.6.1   The case against large dams and associated developments

There are many technical problems in dam-building and dam operation, some of which are covered in Chapter 6, but in relation to development processes it is essential to remember the message of Fahim's study of Aswan.

> Since dams are often associated with development, which I conceive as an ultimate task involving a complex and longitudinal process of concept-making, strategy-building and implementation, people should present a central theme and a basic element in this process. Although capital and technology are important pre-requisites for development, people, in my view, represent a far more significant and non-depleting resource. A basic premise in this volume is that economic benefits and human welfare should constitute part and parcel of the development process of water projects. Otherwise, dams will result in situations of 'growth without development'.
>
> (Fahim, 1981, p. xv)

Goldsmith and Hildyard (1984) begin their litany of criticism of large dams with a poem by Kenneth Boulding, reproduced here instead of a table of environmental impacts!

A BALLAD OF ECOLOGICAL AWARENESS

The cost of building dams is always underestimated –
There's erosion of the delta that the river has created,
There's fertile soil below the dam that's likely to be looted,
And the tangled mat of forest that has got to be uprooted.

There's the breaking up of cultures with old haunts and habits loss,
There's the education program that just doesn't come across,
And the wasted fruits of progress that are seldom much enjoyed
By expelled subsistence farmers who are urban unemployed.

There's disappointing yield of fish, beyond the first explosion;
There's silting up, and drawing down, and watershed erosion.
Above the dam the water's lost by sheer evaporation;
Below, the river scours, and suffers dangerous alteration.

For engineers, however good, are likely to be guilty
Of quietly forgetting that a river can be silty,
While the irrigation people too are frequently forgetting
That water poured upon the land is likely to be wetting.

Then the water in the lake, and what the lake releases,
Is crawling with infected snails and water-born diseases.
There's a hideous locust breeding ground when water level's low,
And a million ecologic facts we really do not know.

There are benefits, of course, which may be countable, but which
Have a tendency to fall into the pockets of the rich,
While the costs are apt to fall upon the shoulders of the poor.
So cost-benefit analysis is nearly always sure,
To justify the building of a solid concrete fact,
While the Ecologic Truth is left behind in the Abstract.

Kenneth E. Boulding
(From T. Farvar and J. Milton [1973] *The Careless Technology*,
Tom Stacey, London)

After their extensive, and as yet incomplete, review Goldsmith and Hildyard claim to demonstrate:

(a) How little of the extra food grown through irrigation schemes ever reaches those who need it most; how, in the long run, those irrigation schemes are turning vast areas of fertile land into salt-encrusted deserts; and how, too, the industry powered by dams is further undermining food supplies through pollution and the destruction of agricultural land.

(b) How millions of people have been uprooted from their homes to make way for the reservoirs of large dams; how their social lives have been shattered and their cultures destroyed; and how, also, their health has been jeopardised by the water-borne diseases introduced by those reservoirs and their associated irrigation works.

(c) How dams are now suspected of triggering earthquakes; how they have failed to control floods and have actually served to increase the severity of flood damage; and how, in many instances, they have reduced the quality of drinking water for hundreds of millions of people.
(d) How the real beneficiaries of large-scale dams and water development schemes have invariably been large multi-national companies, the urban élites of the Third World, and the politicians who commissioned the projects in the first place.

Goldsmith and Hildyard's (1986) case studies involve 31 contributions from North America, Europe, the Soviet Union, Africa, South America, India and other Asian countries. One of these, the Narmada Valley Project (Kalpavriksh and the Hindu College Nature Club, 1986), involving two major reservoirs and up to 3,000 smaller structures, has now been the subject of an individual book of criticism (Alvares and Billorey, 1988). The key to the Narmada controversy, according to Alvares and Billorey, was that a 'majestic and sacred' river would be equipped with a plethora of dams which

> would, in addition to generating irreversible environmental changes, also uproot over a million people, including a large number of tribals, and submerge a total of 350,000 hectares of forest lands and 200,000 hectares of cultivated land.
>
> (Alvares and Billorey, 1988, p. 10)

The authors provide detailed scrutinies of 'the human tragedy' as well as of the adverse environmental impacts (notably sedimentation) and (on their calculation) minimal benefit/cost ratios of the project. The alternatives they propose are:

(a) Reducing the height of dams.
(b) Lift irrigation − direct from rivers.
(c) Small-scale, community-run dams.

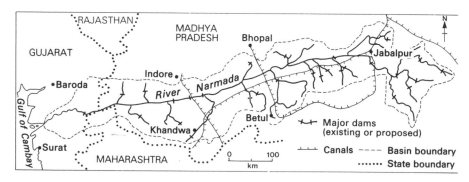

Figure 5.12 The Narmada scheme, western India, indicating the heavy reliance on dam construction (after Kalpavriksh, 1986)

Table 5.14 Villages and population to be submerged by Narmada Dams

Project	State	District	Villages	Population
Sardar	Gujarat	Bharuch	19	
Sarovar		Baroda		30,000
	Maharashtra	Dhulia	33	
	Madhya Pradesh	Dhar	80	
		Jhabua	26	70,000
		West Nimar	76	
Narmada	Madhya Pradesh	Khandwa	167	
Sagar		Dewas	39	170,000
		Hoshangabad	48	
Omkareshwar			27	13,000
Maheshwar			58	14,000
TOTAL			573	297,000
			Nearly	300,000

Source: Alvares and Billorey (1988)

Figure 5.12 and Table 5.14 point up the huge scale of the Narmada, a project in the tradition of the Tennessee Valley Authority but without its justification and having, if anything, the reverse impact.

Dislocations of traditional societies on such a scale have been relatively common in development schemes involving dam construction. Barrow (1987) tabulates more than twenty such schemes with resettlement costs ranging from $3.6 M to $100.2 M. The most recent concern of anti-dams activists in terms of dislocation has been the '2010 Plan' of the Brazilian government, involving 31 large dams on tributaries of the Amazon (Cummings, 1990). The Indian tribal people lose land both to permanent flooding above the dams and by lack of seasonal flooding below them.

Beauclerk *et al.* (1988) have listed the following characteristics of indigenous peoples:

(a) They make sustainable use of resources
(b) Their land is held in common.
(c) They have relatively unstratified economies; wealth is generally even.
(d) Their societies are rooted in kinship.
(e) They are highly vulnerable.

Turning finally to two international aspects of large dam schemes, their finance and cross-border impacts, the OECD has recently completed a review of the former (Carruthers, 1983) whilst Marchand and Toornstra (1986) also devote attention to the latter; cross-border water agreements are also seen as part of a general need for international environmental diplomacy by Carroll (1988).

Table 5.15 International river basin co-operation

Basin (and/or project)	Organisation	Sign	Countries concerned	Date of agreement
Senegal	Organisation pour la mise en valeur du fleuve Senegal	OMVS	Mali, Mauretania, Senegal	11. 5.72
Gambia	Organisation pour la mise en valeur du fleuve Gambia	OMVS	Gambia, Senegal	19. 4.67
Niger	Commission du fleuve Niger		Benin, Cameroon, Chad, Guinea, Ivory Coast, Mali, Niger, Nigeria, Burkina Faso	20.10.63
Lake Chad	Commission du Bassin du lac Chad		Cameroon, Niger, Nigeria, Chad	22. 5.64
Kagera	Organisation for the Management and Development of the Kagera River Basin		Tanzania, Rwanda, Burundi	24. 8.77
Mano	Mano River Union		Liberia, Sierra Leone	3.10.73
Nile	Permanent Joint Commission for Nile Waters		Egypt, Sudan	8.11.59
Plata	Comité Intergubernamental Coodinator de los Paises de la Cuenca del Plata	CIC	Argentina, Bolivia, Brazil, Paraguay, Uruguay	23. 4.69
Plata–Parana (Itaipu)	Itaipu		Brazil, Paraguay	26. 4.73
Plata–Parana	Comisón Técnica Mixta Argentino–Paraguaya del Rio Parana	COMIP	Argentina, Paraguay	16. 6.71
Plata–Parana	Ente Binaciónal Yacireta	EBY	Argentina, Paraguay	23. 1.58
Plata–Uruguay (Salto Grande)	Comisión Técnica Mixta del Salto Grande	CTM	Argentina, Paraguay	30.12.46
Plata–Uruguay	Comisión Administradora del Rio Uruguay	CARU	Argentina, Uruguay	7. 4.61
Puyango–Tumbes	Comisión Mixta Peruano–Equatoriana para el aprovechamiento de las cuencas hydrograficas binaciónales Puyango–Tumbes y Catamayo–Chira		Equador, Peru	27. 9.71
All water courses near border	Comisión internacional de Límites y Aguas		Guatemala, Mexico	21.12.61

Water courses	Commission	Abbr.	Countries	Date
All water courses near border	Comisión internacional de Límites y Aguas	IBWC	Mexico, USA	1. 3.1889
All water courses near border	International Joint Commission	IJC	Canada, USA	11. 1.09
Lower-Mekong	Comité pour la Coordination des Etudes sur le Bassin inférieur du Mekong		Laos, Thailand, Vietnam	31.10.57
Indus	Permanent Indus Commission		India, Pakistan	19. 9.60
All water courses near border	Indo-Bangladesh Joint Rivers Commission		India, Bangladesh	24.11.72
Ganges	Mixed Commission for the Ganges downstream of Farakka		India, Bangladesh	5.11.77
Rhine	Commission centrale pour la navigation du Rhin		Belgium, France, Netherlands, Germany, Switzerland	17.10.1868
Rhine	Commission internationale pour la protection du Rhin contre la pollution		Germany, France, Luxembourg, Netherlands, EC	29. 4.63
Danube	Commission du Danube		Austria, Bulgaria, Hungary, Romania, Czechoslovakia, Ukraine, USSR, Yugoslavia	18. 8.48
All water courses near border	Finnish–Swedish Frontier Rivers Commission		Finland, Sweden	16. 9.71
All water courses near border	Comisión Hispano–Portuguesa para la Reglamentacion del Uso y Desarrollo de las Aguas Fronterizas sobre los Tramos Comúnes a los dos países		Spain, Portugal	11. 8.27
Vardar–Axios	Joint Greek–Yugoslav Commission for the development of the Vardar–Axios		Greece, Yugoslavia	18. 6.59

Source: Translated by Marchand and Toornstra (1986)

Table 5.16 Tropical water resource development: problems, causes and possible relief

Problems	Causes	Possible relief
Data incomplete/uneven, i.e. geographically 'patchy' or lacks depth or continuity or collection has not progressed long enough to establish trends	Research largely in hands of expatriates	Train and encourage indigenous consultants
	Much knowledge/monitoring techniques based on temperate latitudes experience	Promote tropical research/monitoring
	Too few indigenous experts	Improved training/incentives encourage experts to stay in own country
	Useful research 'unfashionable', unattractive to researchers trained in the West	Promote vital research fields to discourage 'brain drain' to high-income nations
	Little exchange of information between (often environmentally similar) developing nations	Encourage exchange of ideas, data, personnel and promote shared research between developing nations
	Difficult environment, communications, political instability	
	Data not widely available (restricted by ministries/armed forces)	Better publicity; encourage flow of information between countries
	Data not standardised; difficult to compare between regions	Adopt internationally agreed standards; compile international registers and data banks

Inadequate use of data	Data not understood by planners, decision-makers, local people	Involve planners and public in research; publish data in simplified form to interest people
	Expedience, political or other pressures overrules sound advice of ecologists/planners	Improve public accountability; establish large powerful authorities to control water resources to avoid intimidation by other institutions
	Research too sectoral	Promote interdisciplinary research
Data unsatisfactory when applied to water resources development	Data inadequate or irrelevant to problem requiring solution	Adopt 'problem-orientated' research
	Data too site-specific; difficult to transfer experience between projects	Establish models, checklists, suitable environmental impact assessment procedures

Source: Barrow (1987)

In the volume edited by Carruthers, officials from major financing agencies such as the World Bank (which makes 38 per cent of agricultural sector loans to irrigation projects and has loaned over $10 billion to schemes since 1948) stress the need for all the improvements advocated in this chapter: participation, environmental appraisal, realistic benefit/cost accounts, long planning cycles, river basin scales, etc. In addition, Carruthers himself pleads for better assessment of whether irrigated or improved rainfed agriculture is more sustainable and for much more investment in operations and maintenance of existing schemes. The latter statement tacitly admits that benefit/costs have been poorly evaluated in the longer term: development 'lift-off' has been illusory. The former needs little technological elaboration – it simply builds on the lessons of traditional land and water use (Gilbertson, 1986). The long-term and broader scale considerations needed for investment in irrigation schemes are also stressed by Welbank (1978), who prefixes his reflections of two major schemes in the Sudan with the words, 'on the day of first water, dramatic changes take place in the project area'. Little thought and no investment, he claims, is available for *settlement* lay-out and planning, *social welfare* and the *multiplier effects* of the anticipated regional growth.

Marchand and Toornstra recognise that their ecosystem basis for the technological choices in river basin development applies all the new-found wisdom of experience across national boundaries, particularly in the developing world. Table 5.15 shows their summary of the existing institutional structures for such diplomacy. Carroll (1988) is, however, sceptical, citing the failure of the International Joint Commission to control pollution along the USA/Canada border as an example of failure to set and achieve the real objectives.

> I suggest we must start to measure such entities as boundary waters treaties and the institutions they spawn not on the basis of how much they seek to accomplish nor in how much they claim, but, in the final analysis, in the health of the environment they are meant to protect, and that means the long-term economic and political environment as well as the natural ecosystem – for they are all ultimately one.
>
> (Carroll, 1988, p. 276)

Barrow (1987) analyses a huge literature on irrigated agriculture in the tropics and pays attention to 'hindrances to water resources development due to management faults'. Barrow summarises these as a helpful table (see Table 5.16) and emphasises that

> Prediction of environmental and socio-economic impacts may even be seen as the work of 'soft science' and therefore get minimal attention. Concern for the aptitude, attitude and needs of the people affected by

development has often been inadequate, yet consideration of such factors is critical if water resources development is to succeed.

(Barrow, 1987, p. 74)

However, Barrow in this case offers only three paragraphs on river basin authorities and their role in bringing about his ideals (but see Saha and Barrow, 1981).

5.6.2   Respect for tradition: 'bottom-up' water development

Traditional forms of 'dry farming' cultivation are also worthy of encouragement by NGO aid or government extension services. The 'Khadin' system of cultivation in India uses basins of internal drainage in undulating semi-arid land to focus both surface and groundwater supplies; the ratio of catchment to the 'plain of accumulation' (Figure 5.13) is 11:1 (Tewari, 1988). Wheat and chickpeas are grown without irrigation after the summer rains have infiltrated the basin (also recharging wells for domestic supply and for livestock which manure the basin). Khadin farming may date back to 3000 BC but currently the Indian government has revived 500 Khadin farms under the Drought Prone Areas Programme.

Perhaps surprisingly a similar venture is being attempted around Tucson, Arizona, where groundwater irrigated agriculture is being 'retired' to be replaced by *water harvesting* via catchment basins (Karpiscak *et al.*, 1984). Runoff from the non-agricultural area is increased by removing weeds, compacting soil and adding salt to decrease infiltration. The resulting

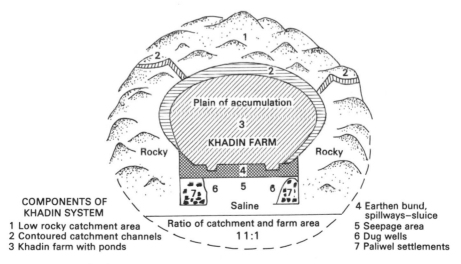

Figure 5.13 Traditional Indian dryland farming strategy: the Khadin irrigation system (after Tewari, 1988)

'agrisystem' is at its most efficient in small units of 0.2 ha. Runoff from catchment strips is concentrated in channels and flows into a sump. Annual average rainfall does not exceed 250 mm but evaporation reaches 2860 mm; consequently losses from storage are potentially ruinous but are curtailed by ingenious techniques such as the use of black film canisters which float on the reservoirs. High-yield, high-value and drought-tolerant crops such as grapes, jojoba, olives and pines are grown.

The aid agencies are coming to appreciate the lessons learned, mainly by NGO's operating on small budgets, that gaining acceptance for techniques is an innately socio-political process and that without it failure is likely however much capital is poured in. Conroy and Litvinoff (1988) describe, with case studies, 'sustainable rural livelihoods', including catchment protection in Indonesia and river basin development in Ecuador. These authors emphasise that sustainability entails 'staying with' projects well into the execution phase to avoid 'unravelling' of integration − it is at such a stage that regional development authorities can perform best.

Putting yet another slant on the sustainable water development conundrum, Dankelman and Davidson (1988) advocate a special role for women, 'the invisible water managers'. Women were mentioned specifically by the UN's Drinking Water Supply and Sanitation Decade. States and agencies were urged to 'promote full participation of women in the planning, implementation and application of technology for water supply projects'. Women in villages know where to find water, how to judge its quality and how to cope with shortages; however, much of their day needed for food production may be occupied in fetching water. Examples of women's schemes for local water development quoted by Dankelman and Davidson include a women's dam in Burkino Faso and two Kenyan schemes to improve water supplies. Chauhan *et al.* (1983) also develop the crucial role of women in community-based water supply and sanitation schemes.

There are supreme challenges in the management of development through the vehicle of improved water use. As Greenwell (1978) pointed out to us, our species originated on arid plains and has prospered, developing culturally through the hardships of dryland life. 'In fact, our very existence may be due to the now much-feared process of desertification' (p. 10). Greenwell sees many of the features of human life − bipedalism, binocular vision, birth of poorly developed infants, and communication − as being related to resource hardship.

Modern resource hardship has, however, other complications, of nation, politics, war and above all human numbers. It also has 'developmentalism'. Robert Lee sounds a warning about our perceptions of the development process:

the notion of reaching a universal model of economic, social and political change has failed. This failure, partially acknowledged in the

West, has not yet gained full recognition in the Third World, which limps along in pursuit of Western goals to which the West no longer subscribes.

(quoted in Fahim, 1981, p. 1)

The truth of his statement for the West is brought home by Eckerberg's (1990) study of Swedish forestry in which environmental protection is achieved mainly because non-professionals want it.

5.6.3   Avoiding modern 'water wars': the need for legal structures

Finally, the problem of developing world rivers which cross international boundaries appears to need a negotiated revision of international law; the agenda may well be set by a general need to bring about new forms of inter-national environmental diplomacy. During 1990, for example, Turkey closed the Ataturk Dam across the Euphrates, a culmination of the 'Pride of Turkey' project on both the Tigris and Euphrates designed to boost elec-tricity supplies by 70 per cent and to irrigate 1.6 million hectares of land; it is self-funded because of its political sensitivity (Hellier, 1990). Syria, next in line for the river's waters, anticipates flow reductions of 40–70 per cent volume; already electricity generation from its Assad Reservoir is reduced to one-third capacity (a fault also blamed on Russian technology). Iraq, next in line for the waters, fears not only reduced quantity but also reduced quality, since some of the flow reaching its own fields will have been salinised twice by upstream irrigation. With its own irrigation systems damaged by the Gulf War the prospects for resource tensions in the region clearly extend from oil to water in Iraq. Elsewhere in the Middle East, the abundance of energy reserves to power pumping has resulted in an over-reliance on groundwater reserves. The aquifers being 'mined' were recharged during the Pleistocene glaciations further north – this is 'fossil' water. With a current average annual rainfall of 90 mm, Saudi Arabia, the largest arid nation in the region, faces a future in which only demand management and recycling can avoid inevitable decline in agricultural production (Al-Ibrahim, 1991). Rowley (1990) describes how, within the general problems posed by Middle East aridity, competition occurs for groundwater resources on the West Bank. Since Israeli settlers entered the region in 1967 their numbers have expanded to 68,000 – representing a considerable water-supply burden. However, much of the water pumped from the region is destined for Israel proper and there are already signs of over-exploitation. The shallower wells and funnel systems of the Arab population are being depleted by the superior Israeli technology. Such problems are not unique to the developing world, as events on the Colorado and Danube prove, but negotiations are at least formal and ongoing in the latter cases.

Falkenmark (1989) uses the Turkey–Syria–Iraq grouping as one of three potential water conflicts in Middle East hydropolitics, the others being on the Nile and the Jordan. There are, however, some optimistic signs. Turkey has proposed a 'peace pipeline' for water, supplied from new sites in central Turkey, via Syria, Jordan, Israel and Saudi Arabia to the Gulf, a formidable distance of 3,000 km but one emulated by President Quaddafi's 'Great Man-Made River' in Libya (1,900 km). The peace pipeline could be completed in 8–10 years and could eventually serve 6–9 million people; it would not, of course, remove the potential for conflict – indeed it might strengthen the hand of terrorists. Pipelines once proved to be vulnerable to atack within the United Kingdom (e.g. Wales 1969).

Falkenmark (1989) actually doubts whether technology transfer from temperate zones unused to water shortage will ever meet the needs of the two-thirds of Africa now facing serious water scarcity. She develops a risk spiral of water demand now threatening Africa and calls for:

(a) Long-term national water master-plans.
(b) Water strategies for appropriate socio-economic development within supply limits.
(c) Top-level autonomous authorities for integrated land and water management.
(d) Possible use of local rain by integrating soil and water conservation on a catchment basis.
(e) Population control in relation to water resources.

The most pressing need is for developing indigenous expertise by prioritising national programmes of research, education and training.

Further exploitation of developed-world philosophies and technologies must clearly await a more introspective review of these, a process only recently begun (Gunnerson and Kalbermatten, 1978; Kruse *et al.*, 1982; Green and Eiker, 1983). Reforms in the education and training of engineers are also necessary and this is a theme returned to in Chapter 9.

5.7 DEVELOPMENT AND RIVERS: BROAD TRENDS

At the beginning of Chapter 4 we addressed two almost rhetorical questions about the size of large water-based development schemes, particularly those involving dams, and about the need to respect local variations in 'appropriate' technology. The two chapters can be viewed as a series of disparate national and regional case studies, hardly helping to answer these big questions. However, there seem to be certain threads in the material which indicate scenarios for better management of river basins.

The sequence of priorities listed by Table 4.1 is broadly accurate, the most challenging aspect being that, whilst issues such as conservation, recreation and pollution are the 'luxury' issues of a developed world, the care and attention they bespeak to river management practice brings benefits for all forms of water resource management. For example, whilst the USA, Canada, New Zealand and the UK hastily develop control strategies for non-point pollution sources, such as those for nitrate (not yet proven as a toxic threat), they indirectly incorporate measures which protect against soil erosion and encourage water recycling.

At earlier stages of national development these same nations made the sorts of gross errors about which we now criticise the least developed countries; indeed, in some cases the same technicians have been exported, their failings intact! In an environment of rapidly increasing population and urbanisation the developed nations felled their forests and let generations die from cholera; under the same conditions of growth but under the additional stress of dryland conditions it is likely to remain normal for large water development schemes to dominate, proportional in scale to the management of international finance. Since the monopoly of technical skill at such a scale is retained by expatriate experts we will rely very heavily on their steep learning curve to make such schemes more sensitive.

They appear to need to learn three important lessons:

(a) That the physical stability of river basins in drylands is finely balanced and likely to change rapidly in the next few decades.
(b) That the doctrine of 'sustainability' makes it necessary to anticipate the multiplier effects of development on the river system, e.g. future pollution patterns.
(c) That the indigenous population, whilst unlikely to participate in the design stage, from then on effectively control the future of that design.

Within these broad limits large schemes, including dam schemes, are likely to continue. However, a 'second front', mainly operated by non-government organisations, will deliberately exploit a knowledge of, and sympathy for, the local talents of indigenous peoples for environmental management – even when that environment is changing. Readers of Rowland Parker's *The Common Stream* (1976) (see Chapter 1) cannot deny that in the UK we have latterly realised that the by-laws of Foxton, 500 years ago, were correct!

Chapter 6

Technical issues in river basin management

Despite the power of holistic science to open up issues to interdisciplinary analysis, and despite the impression perhaps created in the book thus far that the role of the engineer should now be minimised in river management (see also Chapter 9), it is likely that *technocentric* solutions will remain influential, if not dominant, in a world of teeming population and widespread famine and disease.

We therefore now return to the technical aspects of the river basin system, having seen from Chapters 4 and 5 the dire consequences of the unsympathetic application of present technologies. Improving 'the sympathy' is one part of the research agenda; we also need to improve the technology of river basin management itself in order to stress the need for attention to the larger scale and longer term environmental elements, which has proved inadequate in both developed and developing worlds. Inevitably such improvements are brought about by 'normal science' – the conventional, experimental route championed by Francis Bacon and oriented to 'the relief of man's estate'; also inevitable for the foreseeable future is that research results will be applied by engineers – agricultural, civil and environmental. Nevertheless, at each stage of this chapter the 'people' issues are never far from the technical ones.

The first area of technical facilitation required by sustainable development of a basin's resources is that of controlling soil loss by erosion and salinisation. It is the crudest paradox that in order to develop plenty we tend to squander sufficient and, whilst erosion is a natural process, we must come to understand it well enough to work in balance with it. Another natural process, when achieved by lakes, floodplains and wetlands, is water storage; however, dam/reservoir construction, done to extend natural storage capacity, produces a hiatus in the river system and associated developments such as land drainage, flood control or irrigation can in fact reduce other parts of that capacity. It is unlikely that we have witnessed our last major dam scheme despite the protests illustrated in Chapter 5. However, by treating river basins in the ecosystem framework we have suggested that we can again work with the processes of nature, producing net, long-term gains rather than short-term gains ultimately exceeded by losses. One need not be a transcendental philosopher to hold this view, merely a well-trained engineer (see Chapter 9).

Finally, these important elements of any river basin development scheme must be refined to the point where they can be *interactively managed* through time to reflect the changing needs of society and the environment. On the latter count, therefore, the likely impact of climatic changes must be researched. This presents major problems to 'normal science', requiring highly public research ventures conducted urgently, without much prospect of a certain answer.

This chapter deals almost exclusively with the physical, sediment system of the basin (see Chapter 3), a partiality reflecting not only the research interests of the author but also the primacy of this system over the longer term. Furthermore, a system which is destabilised physically (one may say geomorphologically) is much more difficult to restore than a chemically polluted system. Once again therefore, as in Chapter 3, we will make relatively limited reference to water pollution as a technical problem in basin management. Restoration of unpolluted conditions is a challenge to law and to economics as much as it is to science; restoration of a physically degraded river system is a daunting task and the requirement to do so should be avoided by anticipation and good science. The issues selected here also relate logically together − soil erosion leads to reservoir siltation which leads to further degradation in the channels below dams; climate change brings threshold changes to the river transport system.

6.1 SOIL EROSION

The erosion of soils by running water (we do not here deal with wind erosion) is not in itself a problem; soils are produced from a bedrock or drift mineral base by weathering (and the incorporation of organic material) and are then eroded as part of the long-term evolution of landscapes. Soil erosion only becomes a problem when its rate is accelerated above that of other landscape development processes (see Table 6.1) − notably weathering − because it becomes visible; it becomes a river management problem when it constrains agricultural production and leads to river and reservoir sedimentation. Erosion is not the only way in which exploitation of river basins can damage soil. Mismanagement of this thin, interface system between lithosphere, biosphere and atmosphere takes many forms as Figure 6.1 illustrates.

Because soil erosion rates are *accelerated* most commonly by human intervention in the soil formation/denudation process its identification and control involves the social as well as the physical sciences; Hallsworth (1987) describes the 'anatomy, physiology and psychology' of erosion whilst a book by Blaikie (1985) explores the 'political economy of soil erosion in

Table 6.1 Recommended values for maximum permissible soil loss

	$kg\ m^{-2}\ y^{-1}$
Meso-scale (e.g. field level)	
Deep fertile loamy soils, values used in the Mid-West of USA	0.6–1.1
Thin, highly erodible soils	0.2–0.5
Very deep loamy soils derived from volcanic deposits, e.g. in Kenya	1.3–1.5
Soil depths: 0–25 cm	0.2
25–50 cm	0.2–0.5
50–100 cm	0.5–0.7
100–150 cm	0.7–0.9
over 150 cm	1.1
Probable realistic value for very erodible areas, e.g. mountains in the tropics	2.5
Macro-scale (e.g. drainage basins)	0.2
Micro-scale (e.g. construction sites)	2.5

Source: Morgan (1980)
Use of such rates under a 'permissible' heading implies a standardisation of practice; this, however, is misleading and the fixing of indicator rates is highly controversial.

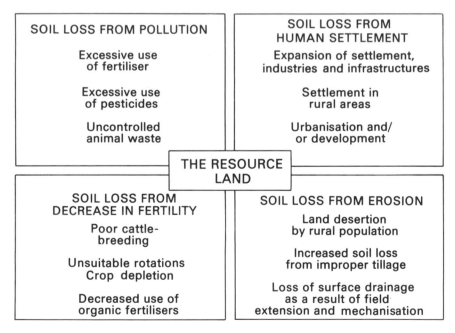

Figure 6.1 Mismanagement of land resources: soil erosion in context
(modified after Guerrieri and Vianello, 1990)

developing countries'. Boardman (1990) writes of the 'costs, attitudes and policies' in soil erosion control.

6.1.1   The physical processes of erosion: identifying controls

The need to control soil loss by interventionist measures, both agricultural and hydrological, was first perceived in terms of national crisis by the USA in the early 1930s following extremes which had created dust-bowls and badlands from essential pioneer farmland. This is not to deny that other civilisations have faced problems with the soil resource, as Seymour and Girardet (1986) draw out in a stimulating historical review.

The measures adopted in the USA during the modern era have, however, been exported across the globe, rightly or wrongly coming to dominate over the local, traditional measures practised by traditional agrarian communities. Equations to predict soil loss were developed on a rational basis to incorporate soil, slope and rainfall factors during the 1930s and 40s. However, these tended to be of only local or regional relevance and in the 1950s field research at the plot scale was combined to produce the USLE (Universal Soil Loss Equation), originally described by Wischmeier and Smith (1965).

The USLE is phrased as a simple multiplicative expression predicting a mass of soil removed from a unit area per annum, based on causative factors (see Figure 6.2) identified and measured at 36 locations in 21 states in the USA (totalling > 10000 plot-years of data).

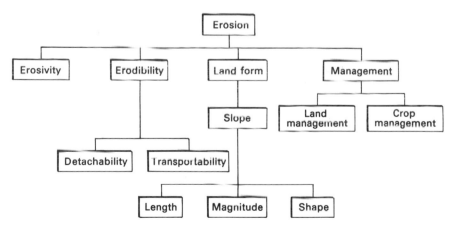

Figure 6.2 Controlling factors built into the calculations of the Universal Soil Loss Equation (USLE)

$$A = RKLSCP$$

where A = soil loss, kg.m^{-2}
  R = rainfall erosivity
  K = soil erodibility
  L = slope length
  S = slope gradient
  C = cropping management factor
  P = erosion control practice

The USLE is codified in a simple fashion, with nomographs to ease calculation of the basic factors from minimal data collection in the field. Clearly care and experience in applications are essential and as shortcomings have been identified in aspects of its operation further research has 'filled in the gaps'. The USLE has become much more 'universal' in a geographical sense than originally intended and is now applied well beyond its original range but has the great advantage of rationality and simplicity; scientists who may arrogantly claim that USLE is unsophisticated and outdated have seldom seen it in practice, supporting essential conservation schemes.

The USLE may be used to:

(a) Predict annual soil loss under specific land uses.
(b) Guide the selection of cropping and management options.
(c) Predict the effects of changing land use or management.
(d) Determine conservation practice.
(e) Estimate losses from non-agricultural developments (e.g. mine spoil).

Numerous authors have reviewed the refinements produced by the considerable research support that the USLE has achieved (e.g. Mitchell and Bubenzer, 1980). Two main components of research improvements have been made:

(a) Improvements to the rationality of the process mechanisms of the equation or to the way that it agglomerates processes.
(b) Improvements to the applicability of the equation in specific (often tropical) environments.

As it stands the Equation performs best for medium-textured soils on 3–18 per cent slopes less than 122 m in length. Improvements have, for example, sought to move from plot scale to field scale and thence to catchments; predictions for shorter time periods under variable input conditions are also desirable and have resulted in alternative approaches through dynamic models (see Morgan *et al.*, 1984). Such models seek to reproduce the process mechanisms of the soil detachment and transport processes (Figure 6.3).

Keeping strictly within the USLE structure, major research improvements have been made to extend the range of calibrations for slope form, for soil erodibility and, especially, for rainfall erosivity (to include refined estimates

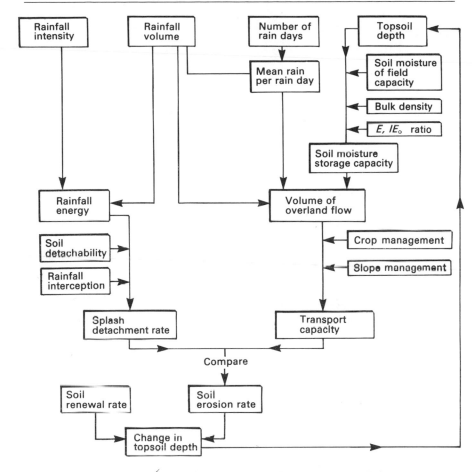

Figure 6.3 A dynamic model of soil erosion (Morgan *et al.*, 1984)

of raindrop size and the role of plant canopies — which tend to increase the kinetic energy of drops). A further problem has been to address *gully erosion* rather than *sheet erosion*. Rational equations, similar to the USLE, are available but tend to predict the rate of growth of gullying rather than initiation of this damaging process.

As examples of the often dire need to extend and apply the USLE to new conditions we may select the work described by Hurni (1983), who has improved the rainfall erosivity and slope components in Ethiopia, and Harper (1988), who additionally improved the C, K and P components for North Thailand.

Hurni's studies (Figure 6.4) contribute a basic statement of erosion as a long-term resource problem facing rainfed agriculture in the Ethiopian Highlands. His project led to the production of a simple field manual, using

Plate 6.1 Sheet (mid-foreground) and gully erosion, Ethiopian Plateau

cartoons to select appropriate estimates of erosion rates for different agroclimatic zones and to design simple protection strategies. Such advice in the hands of capable extension workers touring the farms achieves very rapid conservation results. The statistics of Ethiopian soil erosion and attempts to control it are impressive. Losses of soil from the Ethiopian Highlands exceed 20 tonnes per hectare; since this region comprises 40 per cent of the country but receives 90 per cent of the rainfall and is home to 88 per cent of the population, remedial action is urgent. Since 1978 the Ethiopian government has sponsored a national campaign of Food-for-Work; the 20,000 peasant associations formed after the revolution in 1974 are allocated extension workers and between 1978 and 1984 11 per cent of the land in need of protection was treated, with a total of 590,000 km of contour bunds; 600,000 km of diversion ditches; 1,100 check dams; and 470,000 km of afforestation terraces. These are merely locally practicable

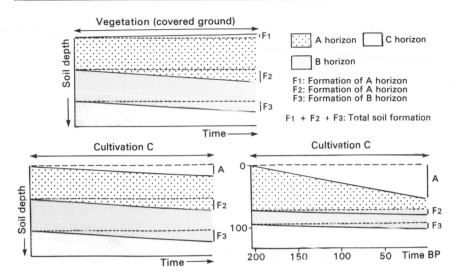

Figure 6.4 Soil erosion and sustainability; comparing the rate of soil production by weathering and loss by careless cultivations (Hurni, 1983)

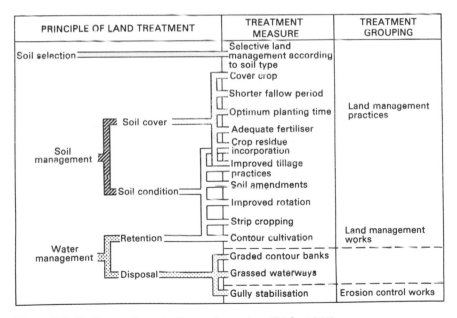

Figure 6.5 Methods of combating soil erosion (FAO, 1977)

examples from a wide range of available techniques for soil protection shown in Figure 6.5.

6.1.2   Sophistication and the role of research

Experience such as that of Hurni and his collaborators, together with that slowly emerging from other problem regions such as the Himalayas (Chapter 5) point to some interesting but daunting problems of effective erosion control.

In terms of scientific research the paradox becomes one of a need for increasing sophistication yet the virtual impossibility of applying it. For example, multi-parameter hydrological erosion models, either for sheet or gully erosion, require expensive instrumentation in the field. Whilst this is not impossible it is likely that such instrumentation can only be provided by foreign aid and only run by foreign experts, immediately breaking an important bond with local land users (Table 6.2 and Blaikie, 1985).

Boardman *et al.* (1990) reveal two fundamental elements of mismatch in research support for soil conservation. One is that research is often best supported in regions where there are few erosion problems: technology transfer has significant restrictions in land-use and land-management fields. Another is that 'problems in erosion studies' are not equivalent to 'erosion problems'; a mismatch can therefore occur between the intellectual satisfaction of process studies and the practical needs of application. Once again the USLE, or techniques with a similarly practical but validated orientation (e.g. Harris and Boardman's simple expert system, 1990), is seen to occupy an essential niche.

To quote Boardman *et al.*:

> Field scientists may need to become more imaginative in the types of questions posed at the beginning of a project; questions which may be tackled within a modelling framework. However, the research thrust in many countries is one of continually developing new kinds of model rather than exhaustively testing and improving the applicability of existing models.
>
> (Boardman *et al.*, 1990, p. 663)

Practical field experience in soil conservation reveals the true importance of social and cultural influences on the outcome; we should not consider this to be only a feature of the developing world. Napier (1990), reviewing the successes and failures of erosion control in the USA since the inception of the Soil Conservation Service in the 1930s, stresses the very high levels of financial and infrastructural support needed to achieve the initial, voluntary thrust by farmers. Such support found political approval because of the perception of the initial devastation of erosion and because of the strength of the economy: 13,000 advisers took to the fields on 23 million acres. An 'education-subsidy' approach to erosion broke down in the 1950s when 'soil

Table 6.2 Contradictions between foreign aid and soil conservation
programmes

Essential elements in conservation programmes	Objectives and limitations of foreign aid projects/ programmes	Results
Long maturing	Measurable benefits within 3–5 years	Emphasis on short-term and often peripheral objectives to soil conservation
Diverse, timely and highly coordinated inputs	Inability to deal with a large number of line ministries	Either disorganisation or attempts to set up independent foreign-staffed implementation agencies
Outputs diffuse, diverse and difficult to quantify	Quantifiable benefits need to be predicted at proposal stage for purposes of justification	Concentration on physical and often less important objectives of conservation
Implementation deeply involved in sensitive political issues	No overt inter-ference in internal political affairs of recipient country	Acute problems of implementation
In-depth analysis of political economic circumstances	Short-term consultants with the necessity to be tactful on political feasibility	Project documents full of rhetoric and technical details
Sustained political will at central government level	Short-term consult-ancies (1–3 years usual)	Uneven and uncertain back-up of project/ programme after aid finishes

Source: Blaikie (1985)

banking' schemes to reduce production in sensitive zones were often
abused; the Food Security Act of 1985 is much stricter in its Conservation
Title, a set of clauses which imposes penalties for the cultivation of, or
failure to protect, erodible soils. Napier's view is that: 'Societies wishing to
reduce soil erosion must be prepared to allocate necessary financial and
human resources to the problem. Vast economic resources are required
to finance permanent governmental agencies to implement national soil
conservation goals' (p. 640). He produces a list of twelve conditions to be
satisfied by effective soil conservation programmes (Table 6.3).

Table 6.3 The elements of a successful soil conservation programme

1 The development of a political constituency which supports action to reduce the social, economic and environmental costs of soil erosion.
2 The allocation of extensive human and economic resources on a long-term basis by national governments to finance soil conservation programmes.
3 The creation of government agencies commissioned to address soil erosion problems with sufficient autonomy to be immune from short-term political influences.
4 The development of well-trained professionals to staff soil-conservation agencies.
5 The development of an informed farm population which is aware of the causes and remedies of soil erosion.
6 The development of a stewardship orientation among land operators to protect soil and water resources.
7 The creation of national policies which place high priority on the protection of soil and water resources.
8 The creation of national development, agricultural and soil conservation policies and programmes which are consistent and complementary.
9 The creation of national environmental policies which are consistent and complementary.
10 The development of physical and social scientists who are committed to the generation of scientific information which will contribute to the creation, implementation and continual modification of soil and water conservation policies and programmes.
11 The creation of an interdisciplinary professional society committed to the maintenance of environmental integrity of soil and water resources.
12 The emergence of political leadership which will be willing to implement policies and programmes which some segments of the agricultural population will find oppressive.

Source: Napier (1990)

In the developing world the translation of soil conservation goals into practical agricultural action must bear Napier's assessment and the USA's experiences in mind but with the additional elements of local sensitivities. As Eckholm (1976) puts it: 'Land-use patterns are an expression of deep political, economic and cultural structures; they do not change overnight when an ecologist or forester sounds the alarm that a country is losing its resource base' (p. 54).

6.1.3 Social science and erosion

We are now closer to Hallsworth's 'psychology' and Blaikie's 'political economy' of erosion. Blaikie writes of the need for judgement as to whether an agrarian community can respond to the task of making good land degradation; he is sceptical as to whether 'induced innovations' can cope with the problem, particularly if the approach is technocratic and has foreign origins (Table 6.4).

Table 6.4 The technocratic perception: environmental protection

Problem	Symptoms	Causes	Solutions	Consequences
Kenya has an environmental crisis	→ Desertification	→ Overpopulation (overgrazing) (overcultivation)	→ Family planning	→ Lack of response
	Deforestation Soil erosion	Ignorance (tradition) (culture) (inappropriate practices)	→ Education Change attitudes	→ Inappropriate knowledge = frustration
	Catchment loss		Demonstrate new ideas	→ Short-term palliatives
	Silting			
	Decline of rivers	Lack of environmental awareness	→ Environmental education and impact analysis	→ Rationalising oppression
	Decline of food production			
		Inadequate legislation	→ Tougher legislation	→ Oppression and polarisation Protect environment against people
		Institutional weaknesses	→ Integration, e.g. Ministry of the Environment	→ New and more efficient ways of avoiding problem

Source: From Baker (1981)

Land tenure is an especially relevant element in erosion and its control. Whittenmore (1981) concludes that: 'unjust land tenure systems and the political, economic and social policies which enable these systems to prevail are the chief causes of hunger and poverty in the Third World today' (p. 1).

Stocking (1987) states, however, that part of the problem of introducing erosion controls in Africa is the tendency to hyperbole of specialists, mainly from outside the continent, who speak and write of an erosion 'crisis' – he quotes examples. The measurement of erosion rates for Africa reveals a huge variability inherent in the measurement techniques themselves. Furthermore, the essential participation of people on the ground is unlikely if their folk knowledge insists that there is no, or a very slow, acceleration of erosion rates over what is 'natural'.

Stocking's other conclusion is that whilst Africa may not have an 'erosion crisis' in terms of the depth of physical soil loss, the depletion of soil nutrients in a continent short of food is very serious. Zimbabwe loses 1,635,000 tonnes of nitrogen and 236,000 tonnes of phosphate each year through soil erosion; the cost of equivalent fertilisers would be $1.5 billion.

Hallsworth (1987) is optimistic that a balanced approach can be brought to soil erosion problems in the developing world. First he urges respect for traditional coping strategies such as:

(a) Terracing.
(b) Stone, soil or vegetation debris bunds along contours.
(c) Use of litter or mulch.
(d) Use of mixed crop banding along contours.
(e) Use of tree or brush cover during fallow.

For the modern, technological remedies in communities facing new erosion problems Hallsworth recommends:

(a) Advice provided by extension workers of the same racial stock.
(b) Financial authority for extension workers to support action by farmers.
(c) A large non-graduate force of support staff to keep up pressure.
(d) No support payments until work is approved and completed.
(e) Infrastructure improvements so that the requisite supplies are timely.

6.1.4   Tropical deforestation: a particular erosion problem

The cover type intervening between the very high rainfall intensities of the tropics (Table 6.5) and the underlying soil layer occupies a critical control on erosivity. In seasonal rainfall regimes such as those of the Ethiopian Highlands the present erosion 'crisis' has been precipitated by a mixture of deforestation and the extension of arable cropping into areas of steep slopes. However, in the remaining areas of tropical 'rain' forest, the rapid current rate of exploitation lays an extremely thin and sensitive soil cover

Table 6.5 Some examples of high intensity rainfall from tropical regions

Duration	Rainfall (cm)	Location	Date
15 min.	4.06	Ibadan, Nigeria	16 June 1972
15 min.	11.94	Monrovia, Liberia	1 Aug 1974
15 min.	19.81	Plumb Point, Jamaica	12 May 1916
90 min.	25.40	Colombo, Sri Lanka	1907
24 hr	50.80	Kalani Valley, Sri Lanka	May 1940
24 hr	116.81	Baguio, Philippines	14–15 July 1911
48 hr	167.10	Funkiko, Formosa	19–24 July 1913
63 hr	200.96	Baguio, Philippines	14–17 July 1911
96 hr	258.68	Cherrapunji, India	12–15 June 1876

whose fertility and stability depends on the rapid recycling possible with the forest cover intact.

Ross *et al.* (1990) point, however, to the danger of blanket conclusions about the erosional effects of tropical deforestation. In their Brazilian study site, erosion rates following virgin forest clearance varied according to soil texture, the presence of impermeable horizons, slope location and other variables. They further support the view that erosion is the more serious as a form of nutrient loss and that retention of soil organic matter is essential in management regimes.

Rates of soil erosion measured from various tropical cover types are shown in Table 6.6. Clearly, loss of the canopy cover involves a penalty of soil loss. It is generally assumed that traditional tropical farming practice, well adjusted to local conditions, can protect the soil and this has largely been borne out in plot experiments (e.g. Table 6.7a). However under field conditions, land pressure, for instance in small-holder cropping regions of southern Africa, leads to over-intensification of cultivation and erosion (Table 6.7b).

Table 6.6 Measurements of soil loss in Peninsular Malaysia

Land use	Rate $(kg\ m^{-2}\ y^{-1})$	Source
Rain forest	0.034	Cameron Highlands
Rain forest	0.004	Headwaters of R. Gombak[a]
Tea plantation	0.673	Cameron Highlands
Vegetables	1.009	Cameron Highlands
Mining	0.495	Ayer Batu, near Kuala Lumpur[a]

Source: Morgan, 1979

[a] Data have been converted using a bulk density value of $1.0g\ cm^{-2}$.

Table 6.7(a) The impact on soil erosion rates of
tropical deforestation

Treatment	% runoff	Soil erosion (kg ha^{-1})
1 Forest control	0.05	0.32
2 Cassava	3.27	29.49
3 Oilpalm and maize	15.78	170.10
4 Traditional farming	0.06	27.75
5 Alley cropping and rice	7.20	94.19
6 Plantain	8.69	157.34
7 Pasture and coconut	10.36	183.11
8 Improved forest	10.29	172.40

Souce: Mahoo (1989)

Table 6.7(b) Seasonal rainfall, runoff and soil loss totals

Catchment	Season	Rainfall (mm)	Runoff (mm)	Soil loss (t ha^{-1})
Bvumbwe (full land plan)	1981/2	957	29.7	0.12
	1982/3	822	19.0	0.21
	1983/4	836	6.7	0.03
	1984/5	1334	62.2	0.13
Mindawo I (traditional cultivation)	1981/2	890	81.0	10.06
	1982/3	910	156.7	13.70
	1983/4	865	42.0	4.44
	1984/5	1191	154.5	14.32
Mindawo II (physical conservation)	1981/2	–	–	–
	1982/3	975	54.8	2.31
	1983/4	914	17.4	1.18
	1984/5	1207	85.6	5.11
Mphezo (plantation)	1981/2	–	–	–
	1982/3	951	7.7	0.09
	1983/4	923	4.2	0.03
	1984/5	1137	8.4	0.06

Source: Amphlett (1990)

6.1.5 Soil erosion and protection in the UK

The situation regarding soil erosion in the UK is illustrative of possible
future agendas for a broader environmental approach to the soil resource
in a river basin framework. Until recently most studies of erosion conducted
in the UK were by geomorphologists concerned mainly with river channel
erosion but nevertheless identifying profound effects of land management,
particularly those of plantation forestry. Soil erosion as an agricultural
problem was often ignored, even denied by official agencies until work

by geographers exposed the extent of losses. Erosion of upland areas, notably fragile organic soils, has led to reservoir sedimentation problems but in 1986 it was revealed by the Soil Association that over a third of the arable area of Britain was experiencing accelerated erosion, the result of removal of field boundaries, increasing growth of winter crops, and untimely cultivation practices.

The off-site implications of soil erosion in the UK can be quantified in some instances. Boardman (1988) includes the costs of road clearance, drainage disruption, pollution and reservoir siltation; fisheries may also be adversely affected. Costs of erosion episodes on the South Downs are put at £100,000 to protect householders. Clearly the uptake of protective measures is likely to depend on a better estimate of these off-site costs, an estimate of the benefit to the farmer (via productivity) and the cost of various levels of control. Table 6.8 estimates the likelihood of take-up on two of these accounts. If cultivation practice and cropping are selected it is clear that farm price subsidies must be altered to reflect lower productivity in the public interest; devices such as Environmentally Sensitive Area status are available to the UK Government in this context.

R. Evans (1990) warns that the effects of global warming in England and Wales (on both agricultural practices and climatic variables) are likely to include an increase in the area of moderate to very high erosion from 24 per cent to 46 per cent of the land area.

The current trajectory of soil policy in the UK has seen a drastic reduction in resources for survey but an expanding interest in a much broader scope for soil erosion research under a heading of soil protection (Howard et al., 1989). There are many similarities between the concepts of soil protection and sustainable river basin management. Protection of soils against degradation implies protection for the quantity and quality of runoff over and through soils. Howard et al. see protection against heavy metals, agrochemicals, compaction, farm waste, acidification and erosion as comprising a 'total package'; they employ the concept of critical loads to define the maximum stress which the soil will bear without adverse changes in function.

As Stocking's (1987) views foretell, a similarly broad approach to the soil as a sensitive environmental indicator and moderator is desirable in the developing world. An approach through productivity would further reconcile soil degradation of all types with the financial approach to resource costs and benefits; sustainable economics would be necessary to avoid viewpoints in favour of short-term gains. With this trend to broader assessment processes, including risks of degradation, it may be that further research on predictive devices such as the USLE will become less concerned with numerical values for erosion, favouring instead a categorisation of soil sensitivities and the risks of both on-site and off-site impacts (for example see Dickinson et al., 1986).

Table 6.8 Assessment of erosion control techniques

Method	Likelihood of effective erosion control	Initial capital cost	Continuous annual cost	Likely[a] on-farm benefit
No action	Nil	Nil	£20ha^{-1} [b]	Nil
Contour cultivations	Low	£0.25ha^{-1} [c]	Nil	£5ha^{-1}
Change to coarser seedbeds	Low	Nil	£30ha^{-1} [d]	£5ha^{-1}
Change to all spring-sown crops	Low to moderate	Nil	£60ha^{-1}	£10ha^{-1}
Introducing grass to rotation:				
25% grass	Moderate	£370ha^{-1} [e]	£15/ha + £55ha^{-1} [f]	£10ha^{-1}
50% grass	High	£575ha^{-1} [e]	£0/ha + £85ha^{-1} [f]	£20ha^{-1}
100% grass	Very high	£1400ha^{-1} [e]	£35/ha + £210ha^{-1} [f]	£20ha^{-1}
Diversion terraces	High	£1000ha^{-1}	£28ha^{-1} [g] + £150[f]	£20ha^{-1}

Source: Frost et al. (1990)
a Direct effects of reducing loss of seedlings, etc.
b Direct yield loss by removal of seedlings, etc. Rarely exceeds 2.5% of potential yield.
c Cost of pneumatic fertiliser spreader (averaged over 200 ha).
d Increased costs of weed and slug control.
e Capital cost of stock plus buildings, improving fences, etc.
f Interest on borrowed capital.
g Loss of cropping land on terrace faces and in grassed waterways.

6.2   RIVER REGULATION

We have observed the popularity of dam construction as a means of moderating the natural extremes of flow which rivers exhibit in response to precipitation episodes. Since the first aim of reservoir storage is flow moderation, this is the first impact of dam construction; river habitat is adjusted to a natural pattern of flows (or 'regime'). The storage itself is also vulnerable from sedimentation in still-water conditions. Linking to the soil erosion problem we therefore here treat a major off-site cost of erosion. The dam is perhaps best seen as a simple hinge point in a disrupted erosion/ deposition system (Figure 6.6).

Because sediments as well as water are stored by reservoirs there are considerable changes in erosion and deposition downstream of dams; channel capacity is adjusted to the transport of both water and sediments (Chapter 2) and both are altered. Alterations also occur to water quality as a result of storage or of the uses to which the stored water is put. Impacts tend to decay downstream as natural tributaries restore the original flow regime and through time as a new equilibrium is reached, but not before primary effects of flow and sediment regulation have produced secondary and tertiary effects on the river environment (see Figure 6.9).

6.2.1   Soil erosion and reservoir sedimentation

In Chapter 2 we stressed the importance of natural processes of sediment storage in the basin sediment system; these tend to mitigate the impact of

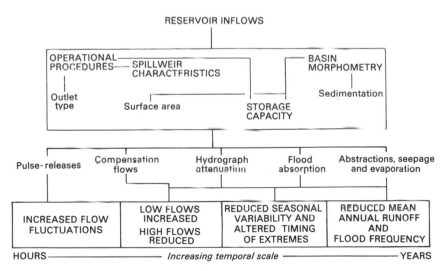

Figure 6.6 Influences of river regulation (by dam construction) on downstream flows (Petts, 1984)

erosion (natural or accelerated) in source areas. The process of sediment delivery is that which converts erosion products into a sediment yield and the sediment delivery ratio links the two (Walling 1983). Delivery ratios have been researched since the early 1950s with a view to allowing downstream impacts, notably reservoir sedimentation, to be calculated from erosion measurements (or predictions – using the USLE for example). The source area erosion rate is considered as unity (or 100 per cent) and the intervention of storage downstream reduces this value as area increases; area is the most common variable used in delivery ratio predictions (see Figure 6.7a) but multiple regression equations also exist and there have been many attempts to explain the variability shown in Figure 6.7a.

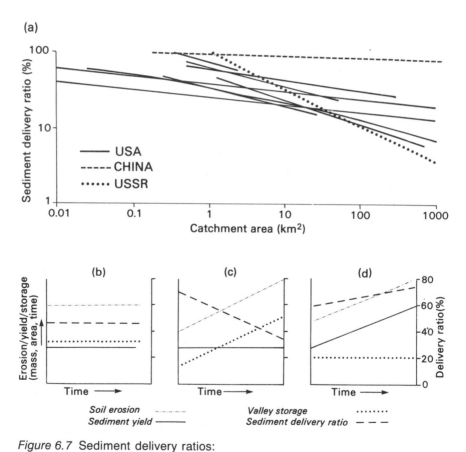

Figure 6.7 Sediment delivery ratios:
   (a) Variability of empirically derived curves (Walling, 1983)
   (b–d) Schematic illustration of the role of remobilised sediments
       in affecting delivery ratios. Periods of erosion lead to storage
       (c) and subsequently release (d) of eroded sediments
   (Boardman et al., 1990)

Walling (1983) attempts to shed some process 'light' on the black box model of catchment behaviour inherent in the delivery ratio. Ratios are subject to variability because of the sorting of different sediment sizes, inter-storm variability of erosive sources and re-mobilisation of previously stored sediment from sources downstream (see Figure 6.7b–d and Chapter 2).

A further property of the erosion-deposition system which is of critical importance to predicting reservoir sedimentation rates is the *trapping efficiency* of the impounded waters (Brune, 1958). Controlling variables include:

(a) Ratio of reservoir capacity to catchment size.
(b) Detention time of water in reservoir.
(c) Mixed variables such as
   —inflow volume/reservoir volume;
   —detention time/velocity of flow through system.

It is also important to calculate the location and thickness of deposited sediments within reservoirs. The successful operation of off-takes to supply, valves and power turbines, is fundamentally upset by sediment accumulation either because of the simple mechanical obstruction or because of abrasion damage. Upstream impacts are also produced by reservoir sedimentation – the backwater effects of deltaic deposition encourage deposition within the inflow channel and flooding may then occur through loss of channel capacity.

Increasingly, dams regulate sediment accumulation in their reservoirs by flushing and sluicing (Bruk, 1985). For example, on the Blue Nile the Roseires Dam forsakes the storage of water during the early part of the flood season to escape the first 'flush' of sediments; later the clearer inflows are stored as the valves close.

6.2.2   Regulated rivers below dams

We have already encountered many of the technical problems of regulating rivers (Chapters 4 and 5). It is difficult to ignore the recent prominence given to the construction and operation of large dams in relation to irrigation problems in the developing world; nevertheless river regulation has many purposes. There are many means of achieving it and it has a very long antecedence. Broadly speaking such a situation was inevitable for Man's habitation of earth, considering the very small proportion of usable water on the planet which flows in river systems (3 mm depth equivalent) and the very short residence time it has in those systems (2 weeks). If one further adds the need for Mankind to curtail major elements of natural storage such as wetlands and floodplains then the need to interrupt the natural flow of rivers and its pattern in space becomes inevitable. From the unsuccessful

Sadd el-Kafara dam onwards (i.e. for nearly five thousand years) the major form of river regulation – the dam – has spread to the point at which Lvovitch (1973) estimates that 15 per cent of the stable discharge of world rivers is provided by the 4000 km^3 of water now impounded behind them.

If one adds the extent of river margins protected by flood banks or in which groundwater or wetlands are manipulated (or indeed where profound changes to land use have modified flows) it would be difficult to find a 'natural' river. By the year 2000 it has been estimated that two-thirds of the world's runoff will be controlled even under the narrow definition of reservoir regulation. By that time the current potential availability to each of us of eight times more water than we need will have been halved by population growth, so measures to ensure its delivery will be crucial.

Beaumont (1978) catalogues the growth in the number of dams built across the world between 1840 and the 1970s; this assessment puts the peak of dam-building at 1968 but, since development is accelerating, as is the problem of food supply and aridity, the phenomenon is possibly one brought about by the increasing size of dam schemes. Changes to design have allowed earth-fill, a relatively cheap technique, to replace masonry or concrete structures. Unit costs are lower and maintenance less problematic with big dams. Finally, problems of gaining acceptance and land for dams is sometimes easier when a single dam is proposed and the prestige of size cannot be discounted in this respect. Nevertheless, some notable large dam proposals have, according to the International Rivers Network, recently been cancelled or delayed by the action of popular protest movements: for example, Silent Valley, Kerala, India; Franklin, Tasmania; Hainburg/Nagy Maros, Danube; Kings River, California; Serre de la Fare, Loire.

Dams are built for several purposes; most are multi-purpose or are adapted to be multi-purpose. They supply water from storage to domestic, industrial and agricultural users, either by feeding into *direct supply* pipelines or by *regulating* the flow of the river below the dam site (i.e. by using the river as a natural pipeline). Dams also house turbines for generating electric power from the controlled gravitational flow of water down a steep hydraulic gradient. They may also produce advantageous flow regimes for users of the river (navigation) or neighbouring land (flood control). Finally, they may have subsidiary aims of environmental enhancement, e.g. by aiding fisheries or maintaining wetlands but as yet only small dams are built to improve habitat conditions. Some large dams capable of regulating rivers have also produced episodic benefits for recreation (e.g. canoeing) and for pollution control (flushing accidental spills).

Whilst the regulation river flow regime has major benefits, especially for water suppliers, regulation brings environmental impacts whose full duration and scope are now being recognised and quantified. Use of the river as a 'cheap' pipeline permits a higher yield from a given storage volume because regulation patterns can be varied with natural conditions.

Regulation allows flood control to 'ride on the back' of other aims because both storage volume and downstream flows can be manipulated. Regulation encourages multiple use and re-use of water within the same river basin.

The environmental costs of regulation tend, however, to ruin the impression held formerly that rivers can be 'cheap' pipelines. Even without river regulation the obstruction represented by dam construction to the downstream system of water, sediment and solute transport and to the both-way migration of living matter can have serious consequences depending largely on the siting and operation of the dam in question; each is different and generalities are only now appearing as the literature grows and syntheses are made (e.g. Petts, 1984).

6.2.3   Impacts of regulation

The impact of a dam upon the physical, chemical and biological environment downstream varies mainly with the way in which the dam is operated with regard to the *timing* and *magnitude* of water releases (and partly with the depth from which releases are made). Since river channels tend to adjust to flood flows of a magnitude which occurs approximately annually it

Plate 6.2 (a) Clywedog Dam, mid-Wales, regulating the flow of the River Severn; (b) The Severn below Clywedog during valve testing at the dam; (c) The Severn below Clywedog: natural low flow; (d) The control of river flows by valves: inside Clywedog Dam

Plate 6.2 (Continued)

Plate 6.2 (Continued)

Plate 6.2 (*Continued*)

is important to note the general reduction of floods downstream of any storage (including natural lakes). Reviewing a large number of UK reservoir release strategies, Gustard *et al.* (1987) calculate a 26 per cent reduction of mean annual flood downstream.

However, where can this or any other flow distortion be measured on the downstream river reaches? We clearly need to consider an impact decay downstream as 'natural' tributaries gradually restore the original regime to the river. Petts (1979) provides considerable help in his depiction of the role of unregulated tributaries (in terms of both flow and sediment contributions) and the way in which a morphological response (channel capacity) responds through time (Figure 6.8). The time dimension is vitally important as the river system re-establishes a new steady state to reflect the balance of regulated and natural inputs at all points downstream (Petts suggests that morphological responses may be minimal by the stage at which the reservoir catchment area is less than 40 per cent of the total catchment area to that point). Figure 6.9 combines space and time in a conceptual framework for the range of physical, chemical, biological and off-stream impacts of regulation.

Returning to the temporal pattern of releases, Gustard *et al.* (1987) document the predominant types found in the UK (Figure 6.10a) and tabulate the frequency of use by reservoirs. They also graph the frequency of reservoirs by purpose and Figure 6.10b shows the domination of direct supply reservoirs, a legacy of the tendency to 'dam each valley' in parts of industrial Britain to obtain sufficient supply. Very little attention was given

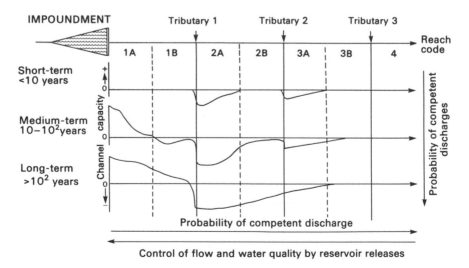

Figure 6.8 The role of tributary flow and sediment inputs in the adjustment of fluvial morphology to regulated flows below reservoirs (Petts, 1979)

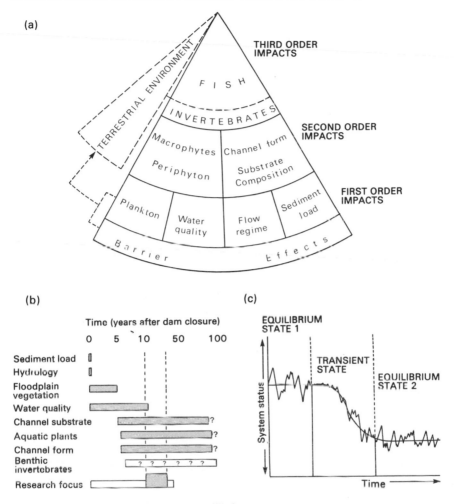

Figure 6.9 River regulation and equilibrium:
(a) Chained impacts – first, second and third orders (Petts, 1979)
(b) Reaction times recorded in the literature
(c) A hypothetical general model of adjustment through time
(Petts, 1987)

in the early approaches to setting compensation water rules (see Table 6.9 and Chapter 1) for the protection of fisheries or wildlife below such reservoirs. More recent, larger schemes have been dominated by a regulation operation (some of the older dams have also been modified in terms of operation) and some schemes have called in surveyors of impact downstream. For example an extremely comprehensive survey has been conducted on the River Wye, already the site of impounding reservoirs, to establish the

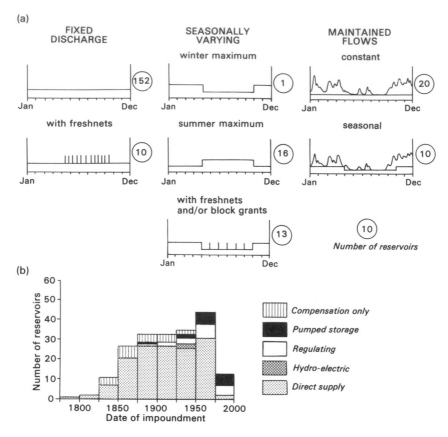

Figure 6.10 Patterns of UK river regulation:
(a) The river flow regime below typical schemes
(b) Changes in the aim of schemes built since 1750 (after
Gustard *et al.*, 1987)

Table 6.9 Summary of river uses which are considered when assessing
compensation flow requirements

1 Existing licence holders to abstract water for agriculture, industry and water supply.
2 Dilution of point source effluents; river quality objectives; public health.
3 Power generation – with regard to daily and seasonal demands.
4 Navigation – maintenance of adequate minimum depth and lockage.
5 Riparian rights, e.g. stock watering and household purposes.
6 Migratory and coarse fish.
7 Angling.
8 Plant and invertebrate ecology – nature conservation.
9 Amenity – canoeing, swimming, bank-side recreation.
10 Maintaining natural beauty.

baseline of biological habitats prior to a new dam which has not yet been built (Edwards and Brooker, 1982). In a book recording their results these authors establish the web of interrelationships between potential impacts (Figure 6.11).

However, such foresight is rare and is defined largely by the delay in dam construction; elsewhere in Britain little monitoring was commissioned before dam construction although major releases have produced *post-hoc* evaluations of the key processes at high flows after dam construction (e.g. Petts *et al.*, 1985; Leeks and Newson, 1989). Another notable exception to the lack of impact predictions in the UK is the case of Kielder Reservoir, Northumberland. Prior to its construction, surveys were conducted of the stability of the bed sediments under regulating flow conditions and of the invertebrates living above and below the dam site (Boon, 1987) mainly because of the importance of salmonid fisheries on the river.

A more recent *post-hoc* evaluation of Kielder's impacts was commissioned as the result of a change in the operation of the dam; because water supply demand has largely proved insufficient for the deployment of regulation releases for downstream transfers and off-takes, hydro-electric turbines were installed and a diurnal pattern of release waves is now the norm (Johnson, 1988; see Section 6.2.5 below).

The Kielder study is a vignette compared with the potential duration and extent of the eventual adjustments to regulation; full biological adjustments may take decades and be symptomatic of a 'complex response', particularly if the sediment system and channel morphology are involved (Petts, 1979). As Petts (1984) stresses: 'Completely adjusted systems have been observed only rarely and most studies relate to the period characterised by transient system states' (p. 258).

This conclusion has very serious implications because the decadal timescale is now seen as one over which both economic and climatic systems change profoundly; it is unlikely that Kielder will be the only dam to change its operating pattern in response to outside pressure, thereby initiating another transient phase. Another question raised by climatic change is the safety and permanence of dams; will future dam decommissioning require impact assessment? Impact studies of dam disasters are, regrettably, fairly common in the geomorphological literature (Costa, 1988).

6.2.4   Regulation in tropical catchments

Turning to river regulation in the developing world, Kariba Dam on the Zambezi River was the first large developing world scheme to involve river regulation (in 1958). Although Leopold and Maddock had written the first fundamental assessment of the physical impacts of regulation in 1954, Kariba has only been evaluated from an environmental viewpoint in retrospect, along with Volta (Ghana), Kainji (Nigeria) and the Aswan High Dam

(a)

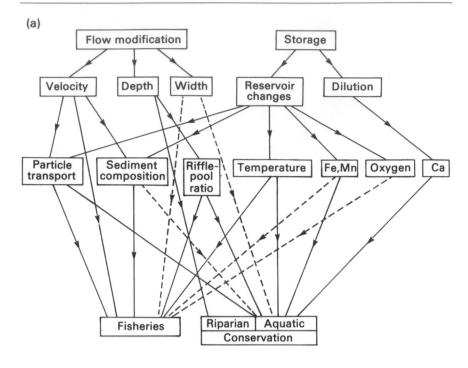

(b)

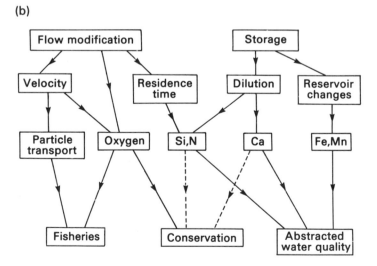

Figure 6.11 Impact webs for the development of a new regulating reservoir, River Wye, mid-Wales (after Edwards and Brooker, 1982)

(see Chapter 5) by Obeng (1978). Obeng's review of these impoundments deals with the more spectacular effects on communities, health, seismic activity, growth of macrophytes, and fisheries with only a passing mention of effects on channels. There is a perceptual point of difference here between developed and densely settled countries and the developing world: in the latter the types of impact described by Obeng dominate those of regulation, partly because they are major impacts but partly because the riparian zone downstream is not the densely owned, exploited, enjoyed zone it is in the developed world. The impacts of regulated flows downstream are more often quoted in terms of coastal sediments and coastal morphological change. For example, the Akosombo Dam on the Volta River in Ghana, 110 km from the coast, has reduced sediment inputs to the Guinea Current to the extent that in places 100 m of coastal retreat has occurred in five years.

Of the small collection of developing world studies of river regulation effects two are particularly valuable because they stress the importance of the environmental conditions of the tropics. Dealing with the savannah conditions of northern Nigeria (wet season June–September) Olofin (1984) describes the geomorphological response of gullies to regulation below the Tiga Dam (completed 1974). Because the Tiga reduces annual flows to a quarter of their natural value, gully tributaries have incised their beds to reflect the lowering of the effective base-level to their development; incision of almost a metre was achieved in three wet seasons with obvious effects on the sediment load of the river in the regulated reach and on the morphology of the floodplain, its habitat and communications.

Hughes (1990) reports that large areas of evergreen forest, a relatively common vegetation type in arid and semi-arid Africa, are vulnerable to the altered regime of regulated rivers. The Tana River of Kenya (see Section 5.4.2) has a 6 km-wide floodplain in its lower reaches upon which the forests are of conservation interest and of resource value to the tribal inhabitants. Both maximum and minimum flood levels and frequencies are found to control sensitively the occurrence of the forests; 'natural' rates of meander migration also help to maintain the floodplain vegetation. Consequently the impact of the water resource developments built and proposed on the Tana is likely to be adverse.

Reservoir sedimentation has proved a spectacular problem in India and China. Asia is the continent which yields more river sediment than any other to the oceans. The Nizamsagar reservoir in central India has lost over 60 per cent of its capacity (of $841.2 \times 10^6 \, m^3$) in 40 years and may no longer be capable of any effective storage in a further 30 years (Chettri and Bowonder, 1983). These authors blame the situation on four major factors:

(a) There was inadequate measurement of sediment yields before the scheme was implemented.

(b) The catchment extends over three states and no coherent approach can be taken to soil erosion control.
(c) A potentially protective control scheme upstream of Nizamsagar was cancelled.
(d) Silt build-up on the sluice gates has prevented reservoir flushing.

6.2.5   Improving the efficiency of regulation

A major technical problem encountered with river regulation is that of 'regulation losses'. Reservoir loss occurs because a large tract of open water is exposed to evaporation or because macrophyte plant communities colonise the reservoir and transpire without limitation. Regulation losses comprise 'operational losses', inherent in the time delay between the requirement for water use at a downstream site and the opening of a valve in the dam control room, and 'natural losses' which occur by seepage into the floodplains alongside the regulated river. Research in Britain (Central Water Planning Unit, 1979) has established from field experiments under drought conditions that natural losses are less than 20 per cent even in conditions and locations favourable to seepage through river banks. Whilst a release down the River Severn in 1975 was 'wasted' by approximately 20 per cent, another trial on the Tees in 1976 (a hard-rock and boulder clay basin) recorded only $2\frac{1}{2}$ per cent losses into the floodplain. As well as geological conditions differing between the two sites so did the height of the release wave (60 cm in the upper Severn, 20 cm in the upper Tees).

By varying the pattern of release waves it is also possible to predict the timing of downstream arrival and therefore reduce 'operational losses' (Figure 6.12). The CWPU research presents four methods of prediction of which the simplest is illustrative of the importance of the discharged flow from the dam, namely:

Wave speed $= 1.4 + 6Qpr/Qav$ (km hr^{-1})

where Qpr is the peak discharge of release
Qav is the average river discharge.

Clearly, therefore, 'tweaking' reservoir release patterns is in the interests of more efficient use of the river channel and 'playing tunes on' a suitably flexible arrangement of valves at a dam allows more equitable use of regulation flows. By 'equitable' one hopes to reconcile the different requirements of water management and the physical, chemical and biological elements of river habitat.

For example, recent research on the River Tyne UK has demonstrated that use of a scour valve (set low in the dam and therefore apt to discharge water which is silty and out of temperature regime with natural flows) to

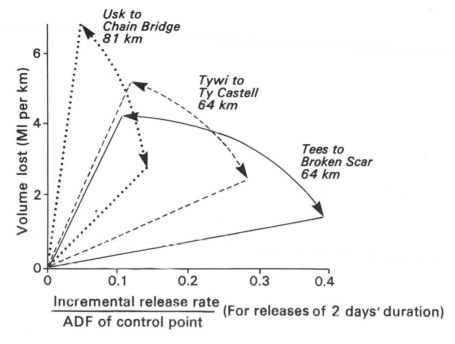

Figure 6.12 The relationship between release volume and timing and the operational loss of reservoir release water to floodplains and evaporation (ADF = average dry-weather flow) (Central Water Planning Unit, 1979)

generate hydropower can significantly influence habitat downstream:

(a) Fine deposits blanket the bed material, reducing the number and diversity of invertebrates.
(b) Warmer-than-ambient water emerges from the dam in spring, disrupting the normal seasonal pattern of fish emergence from eggs.

Releases from a valve nearer the reservoir surface might not produce these effects but would be much less efficient for power generation. The Tyne study also concludes that the diurnal pattern of releases, which rises in 2 hours and falls in 1.5 hours over a ten-fold flow range, produces fluctuating velocity conditions for micro-organisms and an oscillation of bed material significantly strengthening the fabric of gravel riffles; salmonid fish find greater difficulty in excavating egg-laying sites. Alongside these, albeit currently restricted effects, the North Tyne also shows degradation and armouring for 7 km downstream because of the obstruction of bedload supply and considerable growth of tributary bars where 'natural' inputs of gravels still occur into a flow of reduced competence (Petts and Thoms, 1987).

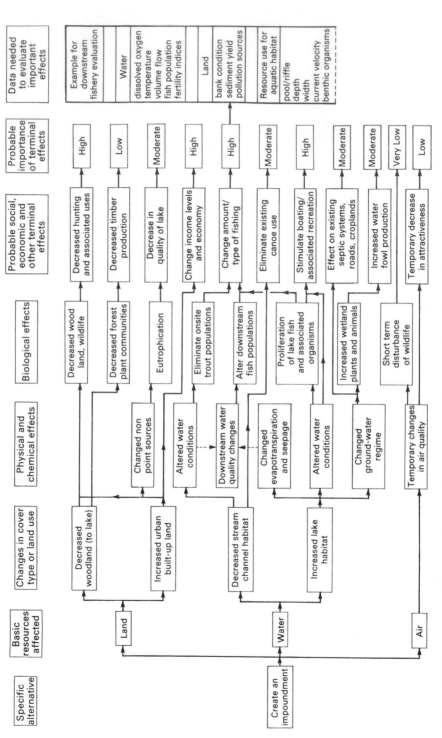

Figure 6.13 Environmental impact diagram for assessment of impoundment/regulation projects (Canter, 1985)

6.2.6   Future of regulation

Although many changes become apparent only after a period of years, much of the river system, including its floodplain, estuary or delta, and even the near-shore coastal zone, will, over time, be altered more or less drastically by any impoundment. The fundamental issue relates to the value which we give to these inevitable changes.

(Petts, 1984, p. xv)

It is unlikely that we can proceed to manage rivers without dams and, since we constantly explore the capacity of the environment to provide resources, we need, along with asking the questions, 'Is the scheme necessary?' and 'Is a dam the only answer?', to carry out very far-reaching proactive *impact assessments*. Engineers must be aware that virtually every site and system is different when local sensitivity to change and local requirements for operational patterns are superimposed. A modular approach may be possible but even this will work only if our knowledge is resourced by comprehensive and long-lasting *post-hoc* audits on regulated rivers, stretching even to the 'finer points' of river conditions under which certain operational patterns are permitted and to the siting of new dams in the optimum position with regard to 'natural' tributary inflows. Canter (1985) offers the impact matrix for impoundments modified here as Figure 6.13.

Finally, inevitably, *people* affected by dam schemes need an active and continuing role in management – beyond the flooded area and the irrigated area and including, especially, riparian interests. Lambert (1988) describes a prototype institutional framework; the Dee Consultative Committee, set up by Act of Parliament to influence the operation of a major regulating scheme in the UK, is dominated by technocrats but nevertheless admits that the operators of the scheme need inputs of advice (and even censure) from outside their ranks.

The dam is a perfect example of a large project with a long-term impact on the environment needing formal and public analysis (see also Chapter 7). It is hard to prescribe every potential impact in a sieving process for dams but Table 6.10, taken with Figure 6.13, goes a long way towards setting up classes of potential impact.

6.3   CLIMATIC CHANGE AND RIVER BASIN MANAGEMENT

Man-induced climatic change is a major issue for environmental science in the 1990s; identified as a by-product of the burning of fossil fuels as early as the 1930s, the crisis of confidence (in science) now facing the world's political leaders is one of trusting the evidence of progressive climatological trends and, furthermore, of taking actions which curtail economic growth by accepting the causal interpretations of change. At the World Climate

Table 6.10 Main ecological consequences of channel modification

Factor	Physical or chemical environmental effect	Potential ecological consequences	Probable severity	Remedial or ameliorative action	Comments
1 Enlargement of channel to provide increased flow capacity.	Change in physical dimensions of habitat to give: (a) Reduced depth under dry weather flow. (b) Greater channel width. (c) Change in water velocity for given discharge.	Removal of biota from existing channel by reconstruction work. High temporary turbidity reducing plant photosynthesis, blanketing substrate downstream and affecting macro-invertebrates and possibly feeding of fishes.	Often very variable but of short duration.	Reinstatement by reintroduction; working from downstream to upstream helps. Little can be done to avoid this but working short distances at any one time helps to reduce severity.	Recolonisation occurs by drift from upstream. High turbidity and suspended solids are 'natural' phenomena associated with floods but duration may be longer during engineering operations.
2 Modification of channel shape, in profile plan and cross-section.	Reduction in habitat diversity: (a) Smooth profile removes variation in depth (pool:riffle configuration) with tendency towards uniform substrate material.	Loss of many micro-habitats and their associated flora and fauna. Reduction in overall community diversity.	Severe.	Dig out deeper pools below level of designed profile.	Fortunately, tendency for channel to return to natural configuration unless constrained by massive structures (e.g. concrete channel or piling etc.).

(c) Trapezoidal cross-section destroys habitat diversity, especially shallower margins.	Loss of habitat diversity; marginal plants unable to establish foothold. Loss of some macro-invertebrates.	Severe.	Construct with an irregular channel cross-section and especially with marginal ledges ('berms') to allow reinstatement of marginal plants.	
(c) Straight channel removes meanders having deep fast water on outside and shallow on inside of bends, modifies velocity and suspended solid carrying capacity.	As above. Channel length reduced and even with increased width, habitat area may be lost.	Severe.	If flood channel must be straight, encourage dry weather channel to meander within its confines.	Not an ideal solution but will encourage some habitat diversity.
3 Bank modifications. (a) Removal of trees to provide access (mainly for machines) and reduce obstruction of floodplain.	Loss of shading so that increased light reaching water encourages algal and macrophyte growth. Loss of detrital input during leaf-fall and aerial insects for fish food.	Variable, usually moderate.	Remove only from one (preferably north) bank. Plant trees in rows parallel with flow to reduce risk of flood loss. Restrict control to portion of bank each season.	Tree loss is slow to recover but other vegetation may return within one or two seasons.
(b) Removal of bankside vegetation by mechanical means or herbicides.	As above. Herbicide spray drift may affect other plants.	Moderate.		

(Continued)

Table 6.10 (Continued)

Factor	Physical or chemical environmental effect	Potential ecological consequences	Probable severity	Remedial or ameliorative action	Comments
	(c) Construction of raised or flood-banks.	Increased carrying capacity of channel may modify habitat.	Probably insignificant.		
4 Maintenance of channels.	(a) Removal of substrate and vegetation by mechanical means.	Habitat modification, removal or loss of benthic fauna. Loss of flora and fauna associated with it.	Variable, moderate to severe.	Restrict to partial treatment in any one season.	
	(b) Removal or control of vegetation by means of herbicides.	Loss of plants and associated animals. Invasion of more resistant species leading to community changes.	Variable, usually mild to moderate.		
5 Abstraction of water from catchment: (a) Construction of regulating impoundment.	(a) Reduced (compensation) flow in river below dam.	Habitat modification by presence of dam; downstream habitat changes in silt, detritus, deposition. Loss of flushing action of floods.	Variable but may be very severe.	Allocate adequate proportion of stored water for variable compensation, including flushing.	

(b) Exposure of shore by drawdown.	Loss of marginal flora and fauna; reduced fish production.	Moderate.	Provide bunds to hold water and maintain shallow margins.	
(b) River abstraction. (a) Reduction in normal river flows.	Habitat modification (as above).			
(b) Diversion of water.	Loss of fish stocks especially young fish and salmonid smolts.	Moderate.		
	Confusion of returning migrant species, especially salmonids imprinted by natal stream pheromones.	Unknown, potentially serious.		Headwaters of receiving river may have no (or inadequate) spawning grounds.
6 Civil engineering construction and works for water transfer: (a) Channel capacity enlargement of donor and recipient rivers.				Donor stream enlargement applies if flows are augmented by regulation.
(b) Operation of connecting tunnels and pipes.	Intermittent releases of stored water, possibly low in dissolved oxygen and high in sulphides etc. when scheme is operated infrequently.	Death by asphyxiation of sensitive fish and invertebrates.	Severity depends on BOD etc. and duration of storage.	Inject oxygen or ensure pipes and tunnels are emptied when transfer ceases or continue some water movement at all times.
				Likely to be serious only in large schemes or when use is infrequent.

(Continued)

Table 6.10 (Continued)

Factor	Physical or chemical environmental effect	Potential ecological consequences	Probable severity	Remedial or ameliorative action	Comments
7 Release of water to recipient catchment.	(a) Change in normal hydrological regime (usually approaching an inversion).	Modification of normal biological communities through changes in bed stability, deposition of detritus (food for many invertebrates). Potential consequences for reproductive success of fish species.	Variable but potentially very severe.	Ensure augmentation is not excessive.	A seasonal high and low flows asynchronous with normal ecological cycles.
	(b) Changes in water velocity: (i) when flows augmented.	Fish (especially fry), invertebrates and plants displaced.	Potentially severe.	Ensure rates of change of flow do not exceed those in natural floods.	Accurate and fully variable control mechanisms required.
	(ii) when support ceases.	Less active species stranded.			
8 Modification of water quality:	(a) Chemical composition (e.g. hardness).	Loss or addition of species, depending upon tolerances.	Mild/moderate.	Little can be done.	Largely depends on geology of donor and recipient catchments.

(b) Temperature differences.	Modification of growth rates and timing of life cycles.	Mild.	Little can be done.	Depends on whether augmentation is from impounding reservoir and lower draw-off points used.
9 Transfer of biological material: (a) Organisms.	Transfer of phytoplankton, potential food source for invertebrates. Facilitates dispersion of species, including unwanted 'nuisance' species, 'trash fish', unwanted predators, fish diseases, parasites and their intermediate hosts.	Variable, potentially very serious.	Provision of screens, filters; use of biocides which quickly inactivate.	
(b) Fish pheromones.	Confusion of migratory salmonids returning to spawn in natal streams.	Potentially very serious.	Little can be done.	Politically a very sensitive issue. Owners of fisheries in donor streams where smolts raised, are naturally concerned when adults return to recipient stream. Population at risk if no suitable spawning grounds in recipient catchment.

Source: After Hellawell (1986)

Conference, in Geneva in 1990, there was a good measure of agreement between climatologists in 'scenario setting'; this is achieved by examining recorded trends (in CO_2 concentrations and global mean temperatures) and using global climate models (GCMs) to extrapolate into the next century.

The conclusions presented to the 1990 World Climate Conference and their implications for rivers and the coast are as shown in (Table 6.11).

Whilst hydrological predictions have been made from GCMs and some trends in river behaviour already appear conclusive to journalists (e.g. droughts in the USA and floods in Bangladesh), hydrologists find the incorporation of global water balancing in models very difficult indeed. Furthermore, the response by water managers to global change will produce feedback effects.

6.3.1   Asking questions of data and models

The most recent international meeting on the prediction of hydrological changes (Solomon *et al.*, 1987) raised the following apparently insoluble questions:

(a) Is climate variability distinct from climatic change?
(b) What are the causes of long- and short-term climatic change?
(c) To what extent are people inadvertently causing additional variability or triggering change?
(d) What are the best ways to treat data to detect and quantify variability and change?
(e) What are the quantitative relationships between climatic and hydrological variability/change?
(f) How can Mankind cope with change?

In dealing with the prime question of the inherent variability in elements of the hydrological cycle, McMahon *et al.* (1987) stress the sensitivity of Australia and Southern Africa to the variability of precipitation simply because of the high evaporative demand in those regions (Figure 6.14). These authors have used 30,800 station years of river gauge data (average 33 years from 938 stations worldwide) and the records of 424 raingauges. A much fuller analysis is in progress and is expected to reveal the importance of the large semi-arid interiors of Australia and Southern Africa in promoting efficient evaporation and of the indigenous plant and animal species in utilising episodic and extreme supplies of water.

The Vancouver conference at which McMahon *et al.* reported their study used six classifications of contribution:

(a) Identifiable hydrological patterns (such as those of McMahon *et al.*).
(b) Proxy (historical) data.

Table 6.11 Range of climate changes

Phenomenon	Projection of probable global annual average change	Distribution of change				Confidence of projection		Estimated years for research leading to consensus
		Regional average	Change in seasonality	Interannual variability	Significant transient	Global average	Regional average	
Temperature	+20 to +5°C	−3 to +10°C	Yes	Down?	Yes	High	Medium	0–5
Sea level	+10 to +100 cm		No	?	Unlikely	High	Medium	5–20
Precipitation	+7 to +15%	−20 to +20%	Yes	Up	Yes	High	Low	10–50
Direct solar radiation	−10 to +10%	−30 to +30%	Yes	?	Possible	Low	Low	10–50
Evapotranspiration	+5 to −10%	−10 to +10%	Yes	?	Possible	High	Low	10–50
Soil moisture	?	−50 to +50%	Yes	?	Yes	?	Medium	10–50
Runoff	Increase	−50 to +50%	Yes	?	Yes	Medium	Low	10–50
Severe storms	?	?	?	?	Yes	?	?	10–50

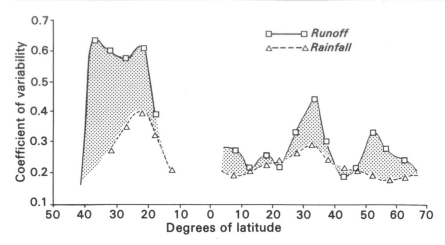

Figure 6.14 Rainfall and runoff variability by latitude (McMahon *et al.*, 1987)

(c) Stochastic models of change.
(d) Sensitivity of river basins to change.
(e) Sensitivity of water resource systems to change.
(f) Man's influence on change.

Each contribution appeared prepared to admit to the likelihood of a change in the hydrological cycle towards higher activity rates as a result of warming. Evaporation is likely to increase and therefore precipitation will also increase. There the consensus ends because there is no firm guidance on the regional variability of the changes, the timing of change and the importance of extreme conditions, the effects of the response to change in the atmosphere or by natural plant covers, crops or water management systems.

6.3.2   Reconstructing past changes

The basic river basin system of water and sediment/solute transport has proved sensitive in the past to climatic change (in so far as we can identify this from proxy data). Figure 6.15 shows the options available to reconstruct climates over periods up to 100,000 years before present, i.e. into the last glacial cycle. From records preserved in sediments, morphology and human cultures it is possible to invoke analogues in the past for those changes in major variables such as temperature now proposed for the immediate future. For example, Newson and Lewin (1991) use analogies between current trends and the warming in Britain following the Little Ice Age; this occurred during the eighteenth and nineteenth centuries and was accompanied by increased storminess and flooding. These authors refer to

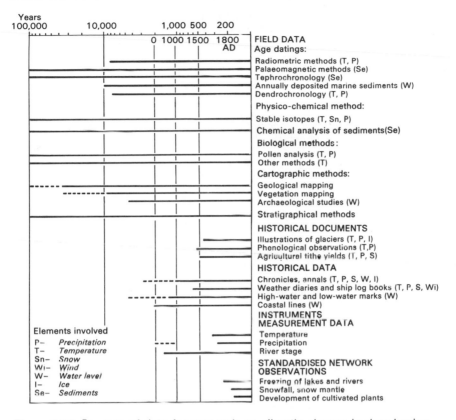

Figure 6.15 Sources of data for research on climatic change in river basins
(Liebscher, 1987)

the 'forcing function' of climate in controlling river basin evolution; land use tends to bear the imprint of climatic variability in which the record of extreme conditions is most marked.

Eybergen and Imeson (1989) are more cautious than Newson and Lewin, stressing the difficulty of using analogues but also listing the problems associated with monitoring and modelling the processes of river basin change (Table 6.12). Eybergen and Imeson set up a research agenda which urges attention to:

(a) A synthesis of the available knowledge of processes sensitive to climatic change.
(b) Quantification of the key interrelationships.
(c) Identification of the key meteorological variables.
(d) Identification of the role of extreme meteorological events.
(e) Specification of threshold effects.
(f) Reassessment of monitoring programmes.

Table 6.12 Evaluation of scientific approach methods for studying impacts of climatic change on abiotic processes

ANALOGUE STUDIES

Advantages
1 The (bio)geological record provides a solid base for establishing trends between the 'end-members' of process–response systems.
2 Paleogeomorphological data allows one to study the response time and recurrence time of a specific process and thus could indicate threshold values.
3 They are useful for validation and improvement of existing climatic models.

Disadvantages
1 Time resolution in the (bio)geological record is yet too small for impact assessment on a decenium scale.
2 Records made within contemporary time are too short to indicate the pattern of landscape evolution.
3 Short-term event sequences may provide a misleading impression of the long-term variability of a process.
4 Contemporary data do not cover the whole process–response period and thus do not offer information on threshold values.

PRESENT-DAY ON-SITE MONITORING STUDIES

Advantages
1 Possibilities of quantification and statistical manipulation.
2 They offer detailed knowledge of local significance on impact–process–response.
3 They provide knowledge about the physical basis of processes.

Disadvantages
1 Limited representation for larger regions and limited extrapolation in time.
2 Records are often too short with the possibility that extreme events with longer recurrence intervals are not covered.
3 Methods are time and money consuming.
4 Low representation.
5 Extrapolation in time and space is hard.

MODELLING AND SIMULATION

Advantages
1 It allows quantification and statistical manipulation of past, present and future climate patterns and their impact.
2 Relatively low costs are involved.
3 General insight can be obtained of process–responses to changes in climatic parameters.
4 Input of data and usage of parameters can easily be simulated if real figures are not available.
5 Quick results.

Disadvantages
1 Oversimplification, due to the limited number of parameters which can be simulated.
2 Output generally depends too strongly on how the input variables are chosen.

Source: Eybergen and Imeson, (1989)

(g) Quantification of response times and timescales of impacts.
(h) Identification of the main climate-sensitive river basins.
(i) Comparison of climate and anthropogenic signals.

6.3.3   Change, management and resource stress

The Vancouver symposium pointed up that whilst changes in the geomor-phological aspects of river systems are likely, bringing adaptive problems for flood control, reservoir design and irrigation, this may be a rather narrow perspective from a humid temperate standpoint. There will clearly be profound changes to glacierised river systems if melting increases, con-siderable movement in the boundaries of arid lands, extensive alterations in the volume of lakes and reservoirs and changes in water quality. Peterson *et al.* (1987) argue convincingly that the position of regional atmospheric systems off the west coast of North America exercises considerable control on runoff patterns; sequences of dry and wet seasons are especially impor-tant in explaining water quality variability.

In terms of the water resource management problems posed by climatic change, attention has inevitably focused on those regions which are already marginal in terms of coping with drought or flood; it is no accident that a comparison has been made between the Colorado basin, USA, with avail-able water supplies halved over fifty years, and the Ganges/Brahmaputra in Bangladesh with a markedly higher flood risk over the same period. Gleick (1987) considers that international conflict may well be the major result of CO_2-induced warming (Figure 6.16) with many international river basins the scene of potential warfare over scarce resources (see also Chapter 5).

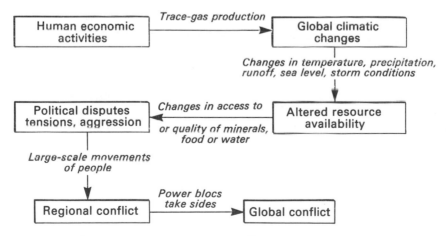

Figure 6.16 The critical path to global conflict over water and other major resources following climate change (after Gleick, 1987)

Tables 6.13a and b illustrate the inevitability of a water management crisis in many parts of the world: nearly 50 countries have more than three-quarters of their land area in international basins. Over 200 river basins are multi-national including 57 in Africa and 48 in Europe. In an adjacent article to Gleick's, Milliman *et al.* (1987) quantify the additional pressure on land and population likely to be suffered by Egypt and Bangladesh as the result of losses of delta land to sea-level rise. Between 15 per cent and 30 per cent of habitable land could be lost, especially where the rise of coastal waters is accelerated by depriving the deltas of sediments as the result of dam-building on the contributing rivers.

The Bangladesh floods of 1987/8 are briefly described in Chapter 5, together with the proposed engineering and environmental response. At the other extreme the drought which affected the USA in the same years is documented by Ross (1989); the extreme low flows reached across 60 per cent of the USA and into southern Canada with major river systems flowing 45 per cent below median discharge – exceeding the drought of 1934 during the 'dustbowl years'. The importance of the USA for grain production has a further influence on world flood resources (and hence water management) in the event of more frequent droughts of this severity, although some agronomists point to the improved conservation of water practised by plants in an atmosphere which contains double the present amount of carbon dioxide.

Perhaps the longest available records specific to an important, managed river system are those from the Nile. The Roda 'nilometer' (Figure 1.2) record dates back to AD 641; it has been shown to exhibit periodicities of

Table 6.13(a) Rivers with five or more nations
forming part of the basin

River	No. of nations	Watershed area (km^2)
Danube	12	817 000
Niger	10	2 200 000
Nile	9	3 030 700
Zaire	9	3 720 000
Rhine	8	168 757
Zambezi	8	1 419 960
Amazon	7	5 870 000
Mekong	6	786 000
Lake Chad	6	1 910 000
Volta	6	379 000
Ganges–Brahmaputra	5	1 600 400
Elbe	5	144 500
La Plata	5	3 200 000

Source: Gleick (1987)

Table 6.13(b) Per capita water availability in selected countries dominated by international river basins

Country	10^3m^3 per year per person[a]	Land area in international river basins (%)[b]
High water availability		
Bangladesh	12.1	86
Brazil	35.2	61
Burma	27.0	73
Cameroon	18.8	65
Colombia	34.3	64
Ecuador	29.9	51
Guatemala	13.0	54
Kampuchea	10.9	87
Lao People's Dem.	59.9	94
Nepal	9.4	100
Venezuela	44.5	80
Low water availability		
Afghanistan	2.5	91
Belgium	<1	96
Botswana	0.8	68
Bulgaria	2.0	79
Czechoslovakia	1.8	100
Egypt[b]	<1	30
Ethiopia	2.3	80
Germany (Dom. Rep.)	1.0	93
Germany (FRG)	1.3	88
Ghana	3.4	75
Hungary	0.6	100
India[b]	2.3	<30
Iraq	1.9	83
Israel[b]	0.4	6
Jordan[b]	0.2	6
Kenya	0.6	64
Luxembourg	2.8	100
Pakistan	2.7	>75
Peru	1.8	78
Poland	1.3	95
Portugal	3.3	56
Romania	1.6	98
Spain	2.8	57
Sudan	1.2	81
South Africa	1.4	66
Syria	0.6	72
Togo	3.4	77

Source: Gleick (1989)

[a] Data are for internally available renewable water resources. Some of the largest developed countries, such as the Soviet Union, Japan, Australia, New Zealand, Canada, and the United States have few or no internationally shared rivers.

[b] Note that some regions with tensions over water may have only small areas that are in international basins, for example, Israel, Jordan (the Jordan River). India and Egypt are other examples. Some developed countries such as the Federal Republic of Germany, Israel, and Belgium have very low per capita water availability, while some developing countries, such as Nicaragua, Ecuador, and Indonesia have high per capita water availability. A realistic assessment of water availability must consider total water supplies, timing of water availability, quality, location and political allocations.

small amplitude. However, a wider variability of flood levels dates from 1741 (T. E. Evans, 1990) and the period 1822–1921 shows the largest fluctuations of any of the 100-year periods. The fall flow records at Aswan date from 1871 and exhibit a falling mean discharge:

1871–1898	102 Mm³
1899–1971	88 Mm³
1972–1986	77 Mm³

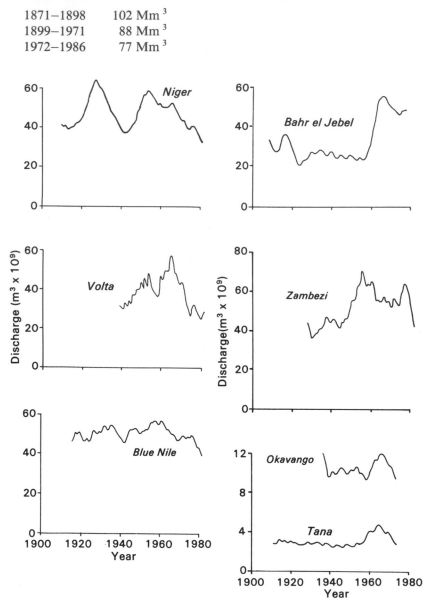

Figure 6.17 The variable evidence of climatic change in the river discharge records of Africa (from Sutcliffe and Knott, 1987)

Hulme (1990) uses general circulation models to construct future climatic scenarios for the Nile Basin; increased evaporation is likely to be a feature and more important than changes in precipitation, although these may well produce relative changes in the flows from the Blue and White Nile, requiring flexible management. Sutcliffe and Knott (1987) clearly indicate a considerable variability in the pace and direction of contemporary change in African hydrology (Figure 6.17).

In the UK the use of analogues of past cool and warm periods within the climatic database allows Palutikov (1987) to predict a general increase in wetness for the north of England (Figure 6.18a shows models of monthly river flows). However, as Figure 6.18b indicates, reduced river flows

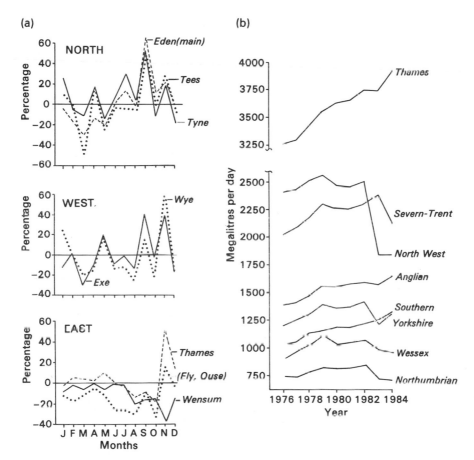

Figure 6.18 The problems of predicted climate change in England and Wales:
   (a) River flow changes by month
   (b) Trajectory of water demands by region (Palutikov, 1987)

Table 6.14(a) Dynamics of water consumption over continents and physiographic and economic regions of the world for 1900–2000

Region no.	Continent region	Mean annual runoff (mm)	Water consumption total/irretrievable (km^3 year^{-1})			
			1900	1950	1990	2000
	EUROPE	310	37.5/17.6	93.8/38.4	555/178	673/222
1	Northern	480	1.4/0.2	3.8/0.4	11.7/2.0	13.0/2.3
2	Central	380	12.8/2.7	32.0/6.0	176/27.8	205/33.0
3	Southern	320	16.0/11.0	37.4/25.2	184/64.4	226/73.0
4	North of European USSR	330	0.3/0.2	0.9/0.2	23.9/3.4	29.2/5.2
5	South of European USSR	150	6.9/3.5	20.2/6.6	159/80.6	200/108
	NORTH AMERICA	340	79.4/29.3	286/107	724/255	796/302
6	Canada and Alaska	390	2.6/0.5	13.2/2.3	57.1/10.6	97.2/14.6
7	USA	220	54.0/20.0	244/85.9	546/171	531/194
8	Central America	450	12.8/8.8	28.5/18.8	120/72.9	168/93
	AFRICA	150	41.0/34.0	56.2/44.4	232/165	317/211
9	Northern	17	37.0/30.4	43.2/34.6	125/97.0	150/112
10	Southern	68	1.9/1.5	6.5/5.0	36.0/20.9	62.0/34.0
11	Eastern	160	1.0/0.8	3.7/2.8	32.0/23.0	45.0/28.0
12	Western	190	1.0/0.7	2.3/1.7	33.0/23.0	51.0/34.0
13	Central (Equatorial)	470	0.1/0.05	0.5/0.18	4.8/2.1	8.4/3.4
	ASIA	330	414/323	860/654	2440/1660	3140/2020
14	North of China and Mongolia	160	53.4/42.0	141/103	527/314	677/360
15	Southern	490	201/160	367/293	857/638	1200/865
16	Western	72	42.8/34.0	90.0/71.2	220/165	262/190
17	South Eastern	1090	81.8/65.0	187/142	609/399	741/435

#	Region	Mean total annual runoff (km³)	Irretrievable additional water losses (km³ year⁻¹)	Total additional precipitation (km³ year⁻¹)		Volume of additional runoff (km³ year⁻¹)
18	Middle Asia and Kazakhstan	70	29.6/18.9	57.3/36.7	157/109	174/128
19	Siberia and Far East	230	0.7/0.4	6.0/1.0	39.8/16.8	49.3/25.0
20	Trans-Caucasus	410	4.2/2.1	11.4/7.1	25.9/18.3	32.6/20.8
	SOUTH AMERICA	640	15.1/11.3	59.4/44.7	150/86.5	216/116
21	Northern area	1230	1.6/1.3	6.4/5.0	23.2/15.5	32.9/19.5
22	Brazil	720	1.1/0.52	3.0/1.15	33.0/14.1	48.1/20.8
23	Western	740	8.8/6.9	36.7/29.0	45.3/32.5	64.5/44.4
24	Central	170	3.6/2.6	13.3/9.6	48.1/24.4	70.3/31.3
	AUSTRALIA and OCEANIA	270	1.6/0.6	10.3/5.1	37.6/17.4	46.8/22.0
25	Australia	39	1.6/0.6	9.7/4.7	34.3/15.6	42.3/19.7
26	Oceania	1560	0.0/0.0	0.6/0.4	3.3/1.8	4.5/2.3
	WORLD (rounded-off)		589/416	1360/894	4130/2360	5190/2900

Source: Shiklomanov (1989)

Table 6.14(b) Changes in precipitation and runoff from continents affected by human activity

Continent	Mean total annual runoff (km³)	Irretrievable additional water losses (km³ year⁻¹)		Total additional precipitation (km³ year⁻¹)		Volume of additional runoff (km³ year⁻¹)	
		1930	2000	1980	2000	1980	2000
Europe	3210	127	222	60	173	19	55
Asia	14410	1380	2020	790	1320	306	512
Africa	4750	127	211	185	245	21	36
North America	8200	224	302	110	338	34	104
South America	11760	71	116	0	0	0	0
Australia and Oceania	2390	14.6	22	0	0	0	0

Source: Shiklomanov (1989)

in Southern England may afflict those regions where, currently, there is a steep increase in demand for water resources – summer droughts may become the norm.

6.3.4   Global approaches

Clearly a global approach to predicting the effects of climate change on the hydrological cycle is desirable and it has been a tradition of Soviet hydrologists to provide worldwide assessments; their territory spans almost every world climate. In this tradition Shiklomanov (1989) develops the picture of future world water use first put forward in the *Global 2000 Report to the President* of the USA (Barney, 1982) which predicted 'serious water shortages in many nations or regions' (including Africa, North America, the Middle East, Latin America and South Asia).

Shiklomanov, besides providing estimates of the demand for water in the year 2000 for 26 regions of the world (Table 6.14a), deals separately with the extra evaporation brought about not only by global warming but also because of the increased 'irretrievable losses' of water through consumptive use in agriculture, especially in irrigated agriculture. As Table 6.14b shows, the extra evaporation effectively redistributes the extra use: the global cycle is conservative. However, regions gaining from extra precipitation and runoff are not necessarily those using most. Australia and South America do not recoup from the increased circulatory volumes which amount to 17–34 per cent. As the author observes:

> Thus a change in the evaporation regime resulting from human activity may lead in future to some transformation of the ratios between water balance components in various continents and large regions. The quantitative evaluation of these events relative to vast regions is of great scientific and practical importance for the future planning of large-scale projects for the national water resources development of a global nature [*sic*].
>
> (Shiklomanov, 1989, p. 515)

Clearly, since one of the themes of this book is the influence of land use, we cannot ignore the fact that changes in natural land covers brought about by climatic changes and the cultural response by agrarian and forest productive systems may be crucial to good predictions of river response. Canada has already drawn up comparative maps of ecoclimatic zones before and after a doubling of CO_2 (Rizzo, 1988) but it is as yet impossible to model river flows to incorporate such wholesale shifts in some of the controls.

Whilst the major control of river basin dynamics is climate the cultural influence on the hydrological cycle can be profound; in some scenarios painted of climatic change it is the 'knock-on' effects of changing settlement and food production patterns on river basins which are proving difficult to determine. For example, the change in patterns of global food production which would be brought about by the 'retirement' of the arid Midwest of the United States (Dallas, 1990) could have a degrading effect on river basins thousands of kilometres distant from those re-created 'buffalo commons'.

Chapter 7

Institutional issues in river basin management

The significance of modern science and technology is that we now know well the potential for degrading the water and for safeguarding it, and this sharpens the social and political challenge of water policies.

(Kinnersley, 1988, pp. 6–7)

Institutions are the embodiment of values in regularised patterns of behaviour.

The institutions and organisations that supply and distribute water resources reflect society's values towards equity, freedom and justice.

(Priscoli, 1989, pp. 33, 34)

We noted earlier (Chapter 1) that a feature of the hydraulic civilisations of prehistory, due mainly to their complete dependence upon irrigation, was a very strong social structure in which the most basic, vital commodity was a focus for human organisation. In *Oriental Despotism* Karl Wittfogel (1957) explains the origins of autocratic power through the development of water supply systems. One might speculate that such a strong structure produced:

(a) The technology to exploit the vital resource.
(b) A means of regulating rights to and use of the resource.
(c) Protection of the resource against those who had no rights.
(d) Protection of the resource against misuse and deterioration.

At the end of the twentieth century the role and relevance of social and institutional structures is under scrutiny in connection with the whole field of contemporary environmental management. Environmental politics and disputes over basic resources and their despoliation have ensured that societal structures are being re-examined in relation to environmental management of land, air and water. The essential thing about water management with an environmental objective is that the catchment or river basin is an easily appreciated plan projection of the ecosystem requiring management, an area within which the population have one form of common identity. Consequently, it is suggested that river basins are an ideal unit for many forms of environmental management and popular partici-pation. In introducing the new National Rivers Authority to England and Wales its Chairman described it as the strongest *environmental* organisa-tion in Europe.

The transition from engineering-dominated *distribution* philosophies to hydrology- (and environmental science-) dominated *collection* philosophies has accelerated in the developed world in the last decade; the American Society of Civil Engineers now speaks of the 'Life' agenda, i.e. the

Legal   Institutional   Financial and Environmental

aspects of each water scheme. Of these, the institutional framework is most important since it determines and channels the effectiveness of legal struc-tures and financial processes. Institutions are also important because of the increasing realisation of the necessity to consult widely with the population before environmental policies are implemented. Whilst, for example, purely economic analysis can produce an optimum solution to the allocation of resources in a river basin and purely hydraulic analysis can produce implementation technology, an 'appropriate' design has a host of qualitative aspects which, except in totalitarian hydraulic civilisations, can best be analysed in public.

Table 7.1a European Water Charter

---

1 There is no life without water. It is a treasure indispensable to all human activity.
2 Freshwater resources are not inexhaustible. It is essential to conserve, control and, wherever possible, to increase them.
3 To pollute water is to harm Man and other living creatures which are depen-dent on water.
4 The quality of water must be maintained at levels suitable for the use to be made of it and, in particular, must meet appropriate public health standards.
5 When water is returned to a common source it must not impair further uses, both public and private, to which the common source will be put.
6 The maintenance of an adequate vegetation cover, preferably forest land, is imperative for the conservation of water resources.
7 Water resources must be assessed.
8 The wise husbandry of water resources must be planned by the appropriate authorities.
9 Conservation of water calls for intensified scientific research, training of specialists and public information services.
10 Water is a common heritage, the values of which must be recognised by all. Everyone has the duty to use water carefully and economically.
11 The management of water resources should be based on their natural basins rather than on political and administrative boundaries.
12 Water knows no frontiers; as a common resource it demands international co-operation.

In this chapter we explore the pattern of institutions relevant to river basin management in the restricted sense of the organisations responsible for that activity. In order to judge the success or failure of specific river basin institutions it is appropriate to begin with some very general principles

Table 7.1b San Francisco Declaration

This declaration calls for a moratorium on all new large dam projects, either planned or under construction, which fail to satisfy all of the conditions listed below. A moratorium should be implemented by all those countries, agencies, and banking institutions involved in financing and building large dams either through loans, the sale of equipment, or the provision of services.

A large dam can only be built if:

1 The people affected are included in the planning process and have the power of veto over the project.
2 The people who finance the project (such as taxpayers) and those affected by the dams have total access to information on the project.
3 It does not threaten national parks, heritage sites, areas of scientific and educational importance, tropical rainforests, or areas inhabited by threatened or endangered species.
4 It improves public health and does not threaten to spread waterborne diseases.
5 It poses no threat to downstream fisheries.
6 It poses no threat to the water quality and water supplies of those living downstream.
7 It poses no threat to downstream agriculture, either through increasing salinity or through the deprivation of nutrients.
8 Its associated irrigation works can be guaranteed not to lead to salinisation or waterlogging.
9 It provides irrigation for local food production and not solely for export crops.
10 It benefits large sectors of the population rather than just the urban élite and export industries.
11 Its operation and maintenance is under community control.
12 Its energy produced will not be used to fuel environmentally damaging activities.
13 It poses no threat to public safety, such as inducing earthquakes or the collapse of a dam.
14 A full assessment of the short- and long-term environmental, social, and economic effects has been submitted for independent review by a body of experts approved by the communities involved.
15 Available energy-efficient improvements and water conservation measures, using the latest technology, have already been implemented.
16 Those people who have suffered the loss of homes and livelihood from completed projects are fully compensated with land and other means by the governments and banks that financed those dams.
17 The same governments and funding agencies implement an immediate program to reforest those watersheds that have been adversely affected by past water development projects.

about the management of water as a resource, preferably non-technical but derived from knowledgeable interest groups. We present here both the European Water Charter (Table 7.1a) and the San Francisco Declaration (Table 7.1b/c) as indicative of such statements of principle. Both include the requirement to set the river basin unit as the unit of management. Table 5.1 (p. 137) is also relevant as a statement of the ecological principles of river basin development.

Table 7.1c Watershed Management Declaration

1 International efforts must be increased to bring back the vegetation that once acted as a groundcover for the river catchment areas. The loss of this groundcover in the last century is a major reason for the depletion of groundwater, soil erosion, droughts and floods in many countries.

2 Groundwater must be considered a renewable resource and its use should not exceed its natural recharge.

3 The need for water must first be identified at the community level, and any solution devised to meet those needs must include the explicit identification of users and beneficiaries. Solutions must be appropriate to indigenous resource-use patterns.

4 Local production systems should be strengthened by phasing out use of capital-intensive, agricultural chemicals, fossil fuel derivatives, and excessive water in favor of low-cost, ecologically safe alternatives.

5 The timetable of a water project should be determined by donor-driven funding cycles. Appropriate development is an economic solution for the long term. Therefore, its planning and implementation must be determined by the cultural and economic aspects of the community in question.

6 Reinstitute traditional methods of water preservation and use. Rather than building reservoirs bring back methods such as those used in India where forested buffer zones around catchment systems, ponds, water tanks, and wells helped to protect water supplies.

7 Rainforest preservation of the earth's great watersheds, such as those of the Amazon and Congo regions, requires our most urgent attention. Rainforests play a crucial role maintaining the health of the biosphere.

8 Legal and political rights to protect the environment are simply not recognised in many countries. Therefore we request that all countries
  (a) Create and strengthen environmental regulations for water management.
  (b) Democratise and decentralise decision-making for environmental protection and natural resource management. This includes a public-hearings process for all project proposals.
  (c) Uphold the human rights of environmentalists and water project critics.

9 Create an International Code of Waters Resource Management that would provide the legal guidelines for water development and for public interest groups to challenge violations of the law.

10 A compilation of successful sustainable water programs should be prepared and published by the member organisations of IRN.[*] This can help to encourage the academic community and development experts to re-examine the traditional systems and help to rebuild the self-respect and self-reliance of indigenous peoples.

[*] International Rivers Network

7.1   BASIN AUTHORITIES: THE INFLUENCE OF THE TVA

It is appropriate to begin with the Tennessee Valley Authority (TVA) because:

(a) It was formed to ameliorate existing environmental problems.
(b) It has been influential across the world in promoting successor organisations.
(c) It has been the subject of studies which reveal that, by some definitions, it was and is largely unsuccessful.

A British observer of the Tennessee Valley after the American Civil War commented: 'The Tennessee Valley consists for the most part of plantations in a state of semi-decay and plantations of which the ruin is total and complete.'

The extent of the valley (it covers an area equivalent to 80 per cent of England and Wales) means that its environmental problems range from eroded hill farms of the East to malarial swamps in the West. Flat-bottomed boats could navigate much of the 652-mile-long channel except at Muscle Shoals where canal works were begun late last century. During the First World War Muscle Shoals was selected as a site for a hydropower dam and fertiliser plant; it is important to note that this proposal did not survive economic evaluation prior to the 'New Deal' conditions introduced in the 1930s by Franklin Roosevelt. Introducing the Tennessee Valley Authority in 1933, Roosevelt described it as: 'charged with the broadest duty of planning for the proper use, conservation and development of the natural resources of the Tennessee River drainage basin'.

Much of the criticism of the TVA and its achievements stems from a cultural distrust of large public authorities (as redolent of socialism), and a suggestion of duplicitous power- and finance-brokering by the leading lights (Arthur Morgan, Engineer, Harcourt Morgan, President, and David Lilienthal, Lawyer and Administrator). However, despite recent criticism of the heavy dependence upon dam-building, it is to the integration of land and water management that supporters of the TVA most look for praiseworthy achievements. The 'ruin' observed after the Civil War was largely repaired by improvements to land management and erosion control, with dams and navigation improvements bringing power and salience to a neglected peripheral region.

The TVA supporters would therefore claim that the Authority had trailblazed the field of *integrated basin management*, led by economic restoration. Recently Downs *et al.* (in press) have referred to the sometimes platitudinous or rhetorical use of the term 'integrated river basin management'. Of 21 different approaches analysed, five basic components of integrated schemes are derived: water, channel, land, ecology and human activity. Downs *et al.* prefer to separate the term *comprehensive* river basin management, where several components are involved, retaining *integrated* basin management for schemes where the components interact (though one may lead); they then interject *holistic* river basin management to cover both divisions but emphasising system energetics, change and human interactions.

7.2 DOES AN IDEAL RIVER BASIN INSTITUTION EXIST?

Much of the comment by analysts on the TVA and its many imitator river basin authorities has been negative in some respect; often criticism locates near the interface between the technological side of the institutions and the need to be publicly accountable. Clearly the institutions cannot take all the blame since they seldom operate outside the basic policy framework of the host nation, its laws and its financial plans. However, there are systematic problems involved with operating knowledge-based systems and, because all future environmental management will fall into this category, it is worth pausing to investigate the power of knowledge about the system to be managed before, in the next section, moving on to how the system is opened to public scrutiny.

If river basins are to be managed successfully there has to be knowledge: this must be both basic geographical knowledge and the technical knowledge needed to engineer, control, purify and provide basic resources. In Chapters 4 to 6 we gained the impression that the basic categories of knowledge required are:

(a) A complete description of, and database for, the catchment.
(b) An understanding of the physical processes operating under the boundary conditions specific to the basin.
(c) A breakdown of the resource needs and problems (including conservation) in the basin.
(d) Technological knowledge to manipulate the resources and hazards of the basin.

Whilst information may be regarded as interior in status to knowledge there is clearly a justifiable need for information on the current state of any system by those who manage it. The kinds of information available, and particularly the level of sophistication in its gathering, have a considerable bearing upon the flexibility of the institutions which manage river basins. One of the traditional problems of river basin management has been the *interdisciplinary* nature of the knowledge base; information on the basin has, therefore, always been tagged or coloured by a particular application rather than used to create a synoptic view.

There are also new demands upon the kind of information available to be presented to the public. To consult the public on what remain highly technical issues requires innovation in modelling, computing and interactive display. Flug and Ahmed (1990) describe a modelling scheme for reservoir-regulated flows which has a decision-support role in circumstances involving special interest groups. The model functions as a screening tool to identify good and bad flow alternatives.

In the report of a survey of integrated river basin management conducted by the Organisation for Economic Co-operation and Development (OECD 1989) the integration problem is given special attention. The report includes around 100 case studies and over 50 country reports, allowing OECD to conclude on the relative importance of thirteen administrative/institutional characteristics leading to effective integration of management. The Organisation remarks that this stress on institutions marks a major shift from its traditional emphasis upon economic approaches to achieving efficiency and legislative approaches to resolving environmental problems. In the case of water resource management, however, integration between such diverse strands as pollution control and transportation or hydropower and forestry must be achieved. OECD suggests that the perpetual danger is that of independent, fragmented groups with narrow mandates having a vested interest in a closed decision process.

The thirteen OECD guidelines were derived from four basic dimensions of the 'good' water resource organisation:

(a) Political credibility and legitimisation.
(b) Organisation structures relevant to a spatial hierarchy of issues and functions.
(c) Processes and mechanisms for bargaining, negotiating and planning.
(d) Organisational culture and participant attitudes which will communicate, educate, etc.

Nevertheless, even with the perfect set of attributes, an organisation designed to bring about successful integration and put proactive, anticipatory action foremost will need to improve legislation and also employ 'the economics of integration'. Resource pricing (including the cost of pollution control and water purification) is seen as a key element for driving integrated management.

The OECD study legitimises a strong movement away, however, from purely economic approaches to river basin management. These were strongly related to the development of resource systems rather than their sustainable management but reached a high degree of economic/mathematical sophistication prior to their demise. Krutilla and Eckstein's (1958) study applies economic efficiency as a criterion in three US basins developing integrated hydropower schemes. The generation of power is an ideal vehicle for conventional economic analysis and in such studies 'integration' often refers to the efficient conjunctive use of a number of reservoirs for generation. Even these early economic analyses admitted, however, that 'higher' criteria often applied, for example: 'complementary institutions for group decisions and collective action are required to meet adequately the needs of the members of a free society' (Krutilla and Eckstein, 1958, p. 267).

7.3   CASE STUDY: UK WATER INSTITUTIONS

There are many reasons for a special study of water institutions in the UK besides this author's nationality. As a result of being amongst the earliest nations to industrialise and simultaneously to urbanise, the UK has a century-and-a-half of institutional developments from which to select trends. It may well be that, despite the OECD's recommendations, institutional controls are always in flux and rapidly evolving; if so, a historical survey of one nation may repay our detailed attention. This history, recently much reviewed by protagonists and opponents alike of the 'privatisation' of the water authorities in England and Wales, illuminates a number of issues of general relevance to river basin management (Rees, 1989). They are:

(a) Policy responses to the growing list of activities attending the provision of public benefits from water.
(b) Attitudes to private, municipal or basin authorities (with attendant issues of commodification of values and public consultation.
(c) Scales of organisation.

The importance of cultural and traditional factors in river management systems may also be gathered from the UK example: there are entirely separate patterns of organisation in Scotland, Northern Ireland and England and Wales.

In Chapter 1 we briefly considered the history of the major evolutionary changes in river basin management in Britain. Rowland Parker's records for Foxton were quoted as an indication that sophisticated *local*, stream-based by-laws were in operation, each of which (whether for maintenance of the channel or pollution control) gave a boost to the integration of legal interests downstream (and, in navigable reaches, upstream too). Kinnersley (1988) also speaks of the Foxton records as illustrating a golden age of simple riparian principles.

Later, as part of the development of common law, this riparian principle required definition and implementation as pressures far greater than 'dunghills' and 'cess-pits' began to threaten the sharing of a fundamental resource. As Kinnersley puts it:

> the sharing of water has long been and will continue to be, in all communities, a matter requiring public and constitutional governance by lawyers, courts and community leaders at various levels.
>
> (Kinnersley, 1988, p. 34)

At the first stage of the Industrial Revolution in England it was the issue of navigation which forced the local by-laws into a larger scale of relevance. The construction and filling of canals also had a profound influence on rivers (Rolt, 1985).

Kinnersley views the canals as 'among the first privately financed large constructions intended for use by all comers' (p. 43). Their individual Acts of Parliament were 'cast in a statutory format setting out obligations which protected public and private interests as well as rights necessary for effective co-operation' (p. 43). The canal companies required water from rivers, interconnection with river users and the agreement of landowners for construction; the latter were well represented in Parliament and so the Canal Acts provided a balance between gaining and losing interests and wider public rights.

The extension of this institutional structure to municipal water supply and sewerage was, however, much less straightforward. Throughout the 18th century commentators made much of the critical problem of the emerging urban centres: a fair supply system of water for both fire fighting (the major physical urban hazard) and human health.

Whilst many authors document the problems of Victorian urban water supply and sanitation as a series of local cameos, two important books develop the critical themes of local institutional development (Rennison, 1979, for Tyneside) and the role of health reformers and engineers (Binnie, 1981).

It is impossible to exclude the influence of a class of social reformers and bureaucrats touched by a sense of shame at the health toll produced by the burgeoning industrial cities of early Victorian England. Among these Edwin Chadwick has been most notably selected for review (Kinnersley, 1988; Binnie, 1981). Chadwick's plans for organised systems of pure water supply (and for water-flushed, egg-shaped sewer pipes beneath the streets) at first ran foul of the existing monopoly of private suppliers. He was also a centralist; however public health was to become the single issue around which the emerging local democracies for cities – the municipalities – could form. Chadwick's 'Report on the Sanitary Condition of the Labouring Population of Great Britain' (1842) was followed by the facilitating legislation for private Bills developing corporate powers for water supply. This was in 1847; by 1878 there were 78 municipal water undertakings.

If urban water supply was identified as a major problem in the eighteenth century, it became a crisis in the nineteenth, principally because of the arrival of cholera from India in 1831. A further major urban development which added to the health crisis of the nineteenth century was the development of foul sewers.

It is worthwhile to examine briefly the reason for the adoption in Britain of water-borne sewerage systems. Whilst the open channels of early Victorian cities were heavily abused by the dumping of every form of waste, the early preference for disposal of human lavatory waste was to land, often outside the city, as in Edinburgh. Until 1818 the law prevented waste other than from surface and kitchen sources from entering sewers. However the perfection of the water closet (WC) allowed legislation making discharge of cesspool waste into urban drains obligatory (1847).

The rapid expansion of city buildings and roads led to a big surface water drainage problem, brought home frequently even today when street drains are blocked or surcharged in a downpour. It was logical to channel excess surface flow to the nearest natural river and a major saving in investment could be made if foul sewers were combined with the surface drains such that street drainage could flush the solids along the network of pipes (steep gradients were not available in most cities).

Rivers became the sink for the sewerage systems of the neighbouring cities. Even if the cholera epidemics became curtailed by the rise of municipal institutions for supply of water, what became of waste was to herald the next scandal — that of stinking rivers. Parliament itself, next to the Thames, had to meet behind sheets soaked in disinfectant in the 1870s and a series of Royal Commissions eventually led to the Public Health Act 1875 and the Rivers Pollution Prevention Act 1876.

These two years mark a very important stage in the development of British institutions for river management:

(a) We see the beginnings of a move from municipal units to river basin units (a law for water supply in rural areas was passed in 1878 and, as Kinnersley records, a geologist named Toplis suggested twelve new river basin authorities in 1879).

(b) The Rivers Pollution Prevention Act 1876 laid down principles of control which reflect a British cultural attitude to statutory law in environmental matters. Whilst it was now to be an offence to discharge waste into rivers (not only sewers but mines, gasworks and other features of industrial growth were also a threat), it was left to the municipal authorities to administer the Act and it was to be a defence that polluters had used the 'best practicable means' of preventing pollution. Since most municipalities were keen to promote further growth at the lowest cost to developers these three words became a polluters' charter.

At this stage, therefore, Britain reached back an era to reassess the common law principle of riparian rights; these could not empower the new institutions since they were property rights but, redefined by a series of key judgements, they were to provide some check to river-based developments.

There is argument over the classic definition of riparian rights. Kinnersley (1988) chooses Lord Macnaughton's judgement in 1893, whilst Wisdom (1979) chooses Lord Wensleydale's 1859 judgement in the case of

Chasemore v. Richards:

> the right to the enjoyment of a natural stream of water on the surface
> ... belongs to the proprietor of the adjoining lands as a natural incident
> to the right to the soil itself ... He has the right to have it come to him
> in its natural state, in flow, quantity and quality.' [For the full definition
> see p. 15, this volume.]
>
> (Wisdom, 1979, p. 83)

Importantly, groundwater rights were appropriative and judgements made
it clear that landowners could not win cases brought against the use of wells
or boreholes on a neighbour's land. Pollution of groundwater was also
unclear.

The separation of legal attitudes to surface waters and groundwater in the
UK, set down at this early stage, has had unwelcome effects on all aspects
of comprehensive water management ever since.

Kinnersley concludes his review with the opinion that Foxton's village
sense of local responsibility for water is the basic strength of the best
management institutions. However, as he admits, river basins are, even in
the UK, larger than the extent of most people's personal identification.
Furthermore, their boundaries do not coincide with those of other
important administrative units.

The subsequent sections of this chapter address mainly these problems of
scale which have attended the institutions of UK water management since
the Victorian reforms: water resources and supply, water quality and land
drainage. We may, in fact, consider them in reverse since it was reorganisations in the management of land drainage (and previously fisheries) which
formed a pattern for the growth of multi-functional institutions based upon
basin outlines.

The 1930s and 1940s saw, therefore:

(a) The beginnings of a move from municipal to river basin authorities.
(b) The incorporation of public representation to encompass all relevant
    related interests.
(c) An increasing role for central planning (and therefore a separation
    in arrangements for Scotland and Northern Ireland from those for
    England and Wales).

7.4   RIVER BASIN UNITS: LAND DRAINAGE LEADS THE WAY

An international audience might find it difficult to appreciate the importance of land drainage in the UK without consulting both rainfall and
geology maps. The island of Great Britain can be divided into a very wet
west and an eastern half which, whilst markedly drier, has a predominance
of low-lying clay land. England and Wales are especially prone to water-

logged agricultural soils and to flooding (Figure 7.1) from both rivers and the sea; the first 'Commissions of sewers' to control local drainage date back to the thirteenth century.

Drainage has, therefore, been of paramount importance in the settlement of and optimum agricultural use of the land in the UK; only recently have

████   **Land areas dependent upon complete systems for flood defence and land drainage**

Figure 7.1 The drainage problem in England and Wales: flood-prone rivers and wetlands (from Newbold *et al.*, 1989)

conservation pressures forced new attitudes in favour of the retention of remaining wetlands and the new official title for the activity originally (and proudly!) called *land drainage* is now *flood protection* (or flood prevention as Hall (1989) and some journalists wrongly record it).

The scientific logic of drainage basin systems makes, as we saw in Chapter 2, the act of draining land in one part of a basin antagonistic in principle to that of protecting downstream areas against flooding. However, the rationality of the process, which has seen both activities funded from the same budget, with designs by the same engineer, has never been perfect in the UK, great store being put on 'getting the water away' to field boundary, stream, river and the sea.

Land drainage interests are powerful enough in England and Wales to have led to the creation of special local institutions. For the 214 Internal Drainage Boards (IDBs) in England and Wales the security of life and economy still centres around efficient land drainage. Their power to levy rates in order to create and maintain arterial drains date back to medieval times but their formal inception came with the 1930 Land Drainage Act. They have been criticised for being slow to adopt more conservation-orientated practices (Purseglove, 1988) and for being 'exclusive clubs' (Hall, 1989).

Amongst several acts of Parliament between the World Wars which attempted to reduce the Victorian legacy in UK water policy, the most far-reaching was the Land Drainage Act (1930) which established 47 Catchment Boards. Here at last was, for each major river catchment, an institutional context free of the compartmental strictures of local government yet very widely representative and able to devote investment according to specialist engineering designs across whole catchment areas. The Ministry of Agriculture, which has continued to control land drainage (flood protection) in England and Wales, also ensured a central, specialist coordinating interest.

At the same time the Ministry was also organising catchment-wide Fisheries Boards (from 1923). Fishery interests are a continuing thread in UK river basin management, mainly because they combine the interests of the unpolluted environment (fish act as 'miners' canaries' for pollution) and property rights. They are a valued (in the economic sense) aspect of riparian ownership and rights to fisheries may be sold or leased. Consequently fisheries, after milling and minor navigations became less important, came to be a major platform from which landed interests intervened in river management.

Kinnersley (1988) records the importance of these developments:

> in membership and financing. These new (or in some cases reshaped) boards were bringing together various local interests or lobbies such as elected councillors, landowners, anglers and others directly engaged in

river basin activities, in a close relationship with central government also, but in each case for a river-related territory. The significance of the systematic revision of legislation and administration in this way was that, while local influence was being kept very strong, the central government (in the shape of the Ministry of Agriculture and Fisheries) was becoming committed in the 1920's and 1930's to a coherent pattern covering these specialist water functions across England and Wales.

(Kinnersley, 1988, pp. 71–2)

7.5 ISSUES OF RESOURCES AND POLLUTION

The basin-wide needs of fisheries and land drainage for coordinated action to manage resources and hazards led in the UK to strong and purposeful specialist institutions working clear legal and financial systems. It is interesting therefore to see how the much more generally important themes of water resources and pollution control became administered at the river basin scale.

The 1948 River Boards Act set up 32 Boards (plus the Thames and Lea Conservancies). These Boards were to become the administrators of the system of licences introduced first for discharging pollutants to rivers (1951 Rivers, Prevention of Pollution, Act) and, after a further reorganisation into River Authorities, licences to abstract water resources (Water Resource Act 1963). Whilst the concept of integrated basin management therefore began to grow, the extensions beyond land drainage (flood protection) and fisheries powers for the basin authorities were to be weak, especially in the field of pollution control. Existing dischargers were exempt from licensing, the 'consents' procedures were kept secret (even though the public had a fundamental right to know the sources of river drainage) and the municipal council representation on the Boards often led to a muted approach to improving sewage discharges (mainly from municipal sources!).

For water resources there was a much more positive grouping of interests; few politicians, whether local or national, doubted the wisdom of economic growth in the 1960s. Growth required water resources and the rapidly developing applied science of hydrology was now prepared to assess the UK's needs. The 1945 Water Act had regrouped the supply industry and the supply sector was ready and able to distribute large volumes to domestic users (automation and cleanliness in the home was the advertisers' dream), to industry (new large plants placed a huge demand for process and cooling waters) and to agriculture (the drought of 1959 spectacularly checked the post-war productivity surge).

Until the 1960s there were no specialist agencies dealing with water resources. From the Victorian period of health reforms, during which seeking the purity and clarity of upland waters had taken on an almost religious fervour for municipal suppliers, each city wishing to dam an upland valley and pipe its supplies merely took a private Act of Parliament through Westminster.

Not only did the Water Resources Act (1963) perpetuate river basin institutions which were broadly representative in decision-making (34 Boards became 29 Authorities) but water became a resource or raw material like any other: abstractions required consents for which a charge was levied. The scene became set for the commodification of water which was to end in privatisation in 1989. Licensing of abstractions became a public process with advertisement of proposals in newspapers.

The rise of centralism and the continued rise of technocrats in the water industry both received a boost in the Act. It set up the Water Resources Board, a national agency but with non-executive functions, to coordinate water resource policy by advising the River Authorities and collating material from them. The Board began a systematic archive of hydrometric information (the 1963 Act had begun the process of instrumentation in river basins, especially the measurement of river flows). A list of some of the WRB's reports gives a flavour of the activities of what became a highly influential organisation (Table 7.2).

Reviewing the procedures by which water resource planning was achieved during this centralist phase, Rees (1969) pointed to the remoteness and technical domination of the schemes proposed. She revealed the lack of published data on demand and supply, without which, 'no definitive statements can be made on ... future demands for water, or the characteristics of water users, on the possible effects of resource planning and controls, or on the influence of water as a location factor' (p. 2). Her own survey revealed the irony of central planning for a burgeoning demand but the failure of water supply or effluent disposal to influence industrial activity in any major way. Effectively, water supply provision had become an industry in itself. Politically the centralised era was doomed by demands for more strenuous, more localised, provision of and accounting for water use and a multitude of other river basin activities.

Between the years 1974 and 1989 England and Wales had ten multifunctional Regional Water Authorities charged with operating the human use of the hydrological cycle within river basin boundaries. Once again the decision-making lacked transparency (Kinnersley, 1988 and Hall, 1989). However, during a period of changing political stewardship it is remarkable that a consensus prevailed. Two reforms were seen as necessary in the early 1970s, one to local government boundaries and the other to control of environmental issues. Almost overnight it seemed that the burden of the UK's water problems had shifted from *quantity* to *quality* of supply. In Scotland, where the abundant rainfall and low (mainly dispersed) population density had never thrown up a major resource problem, the water supply function had been rationalised into thirteen Boards in 1967 and there was less to change. Furthermore, the separation of regulatory functions

such as hydrometry, fisheries and pollution control to the Scottish River
Purification Boards became a model for the reorganisation in 1989 south
of the Border. After local government reorganisation in Scotland water
supply and sewerage became concentrated in the hands of the Regional
Councils (and hence a local government function, with public representation) whilst the Purification Boards also have local government representatives as well as the nominees of the Secretary of State for Scotland

Table 7.2 Reports and hydrological data produced by the Water Resources
Board

Reports

1 Water Supplies in South East England 1966
2 Morecambe Bay Barrage: Desk Study: Report of Consultants (HMSO 1966)
3 Solway Barrage: Desk Study: Report of Consultants (HMSO 1966)
4 Morecambe and Solway Barrages: Report on Desk Studies 1966
5 Interim Report on Water Resources in the North (HMSO 1967)
6 Report on Desalination for England and Wales (HMSO 1969)
7 Water Resources in the North: Northern Technical Working Party Report
   (HMSO 1970)
8 Water Resources in the North: Report by the Water Resources Board (HMSO
   1970)
9 The Groundwater Hydrology of the Lincolnshire Limestone 1969
10 The Wash: Estuary Storage: Report of the Desk Study (HMSO 1970)
11 Water Resources in Wales and the Midlands: Report by the Water Resources
   Board (HMSO 1971)
12 Morecambe Bay: Estuary Storage: Report by the Water Resources Board
   (HMSO 1972)
13 Morecambe Bay: Estuary Storage: Report by the Water Resources Board
   (HMSO 1972)
14 Artificial Recharge of the London Basin I – Hydrogeology 1972
15 The Generation of Synthetic River Flow Data 1972
16 Modelling of Groundwater and Surface Water Systems I – Theoretical
   Relationships between Groundwater Abstraction and Base Flow 1972
17 Desalination 1972 (HMSO 1972)
18 The Trent Research Programme Volume I: Report by the Water Resources
   Board (HMSO 1973)
19 Artificial Recharge of the London Basin II – Electrical Analogue Model
   Studies
20 Groundwater Resources of the Vale of Clwyd
21 A Simulation Model of the Upstream Movement of Anadromous Salmonid
   Fish

Hydrological data

The Surface Water Year Book of Great Britain Supplement 1965
The Surface Water Year Book of Great Britain 1965–66
The Groundwater Year Book 1964–66
The Groundwater Year Book 1967
The Hydrogeology of the London Basin

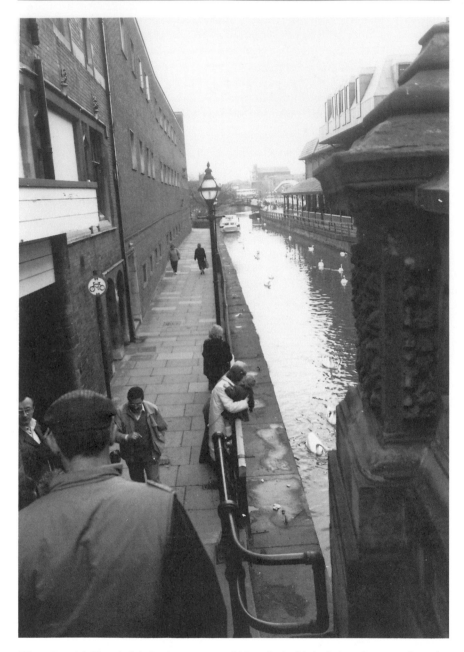

Plate 7.1 (a) Flood risk in the centre of Lincoln is high. It has been reduced by creative use of farmland upstream; (b) At high flows water which would normally flood Lincoln is now released onto farmland

Plate 7.1 (Continued)

to influence policy (such as whether to bring pollution charges against a Regional Council).

In Scotland the relationship between those responsible for waste-water management (i.e. local authorities) and those regulating river pollution (the River Purification Boards) has also attracted political attention. In this case the heavy representation of local councillors on the regulatory body was seen as dangerous in cases where prosecution was required for pollution offences. Recent recommendations (Scottish Development Dept, 1990) have unanimously retained the Purification Boards but have reduced local government representation; the Boards were, in any case, unwieldy in size.

In England and Wales local government reorganisation represented the opportunity needed by central government (according to Kinnersley) to intervene in the notably poor performance of councils in carrying out sewage disposal. Kinnersley adopts a 'great man hypothesis' for the process of creating Regional Water Authorities – the key actor being Jack Beddoe – head of the Department of Environment's Water Division. Environmental interests were, apparently, well protected in the new arrangements if the public put their trust in the technological and spending power of the new Authorities. If they did not have such trust they might suspect an organisational framework which put polluters and prosecutors under the same roof; however, Beddoe helped to ensure a very generous system of *local government representation* on the RWAs. As an additional reassurance the Control of Pollution Act, passed in the same year as the RWAs began work, made public the consent registers and pollution monitoring data; unfortunately this did not become reality until 1985.

As with most reorganisations, not all of the 'boat' was 'rocked' with equal energy. For example, some district councils retained their sewerage interests under licence from their RWA and the British Waterways Board retained control of canals and navigation.

In a celebrated piece of ministerial infighting the Ministry of Agriculture, Fisheries and Food (MAFF) retained control of land drainage (flood protection). The battle between MAFF and DOE, described by Richardson *et al.* (1978), is critical for this review of institutional roles since it effectively prevented complete integration of management and denied an overall environmental 'flavour' to the RWAs. Some of the biggest political battles in their 15-year lifetime were to be fought over the production-orientation and farmer-control of the land drainage function within RWAs.

Ironically, in the light of the strong political and technical movement away from water resources, the first major practical test of the RWAs was the drought of 1976 (Doornkamp *et al.*, 1980). They came through the water supply crisis 'with flying colours', thanks to some over-provision of storage, to a general neglect of river ecology in seeking Drought Orders (the amount of 'compensation water' allowed from reservoirs to maintain downstream life was much diminished under these Orders) and to some old-fashioned engineering ingenuity in temporarily linking neighbouring supply systems. The only centralised function in the new structure – the National Water Council (which had a pensions and pay negotiating role) – was able to proclaim, 'We didn't wait for the rain' (National Water Council, 1976).

When the newly elected Conservative government of 1979 began its long campaign for executive efficiency in public life (which became a battle against many aspects of local government) it abolished the National Water Council, feeling that the RWAs were now sufficiently competent to manage alone. In a further gesture towards technocratic water management the Water Act 1983 also reduced local government representation (replacing it with consumer consultative bodies), closed meetings to press and public and appointed managerial personalities to key vacancies on RWAs. It would be easy to think that privatisation had begun six years before its enactment.

7.6   POLITICAL ANALYSIS OF THE REGIONAL WATER AUTHORITIES

It is no secret that the concept of integrating river management was championed by the professionals in the RWAs; many made explicitly antagonistic statements during the run-up to privatisation, mourning the proposed loss of total functional integration. However, the RWAs also attracted some detailed political science scrutiny which was less favourable.

Saunders (1985) placed the Regional Water Authorities alongside the Regional Health Authorities in order to examine the divergence between what he calls the 'politics of production' and the 'politics of consumption'. Local government lost control of both water and community health in 1974 yet, claims Saunders, there was no political analysis of the 'regional state' which was being thereby empowered. He goes on to use the dual politics thesis (production, consumption) and to select the water authorities as examples of the former, subject to influence from those enjoying property rights yet with a large degree of managerial autonomy.

Patterson (1987) is yet more critical of the removal of water management from its democratic, municipal (Victorian) roots in favour of regionalisation in technocratic, remote agencies upon which was then forced the commodification of water in an ill-disguised lead-up to privatisation (following a spell of minimal investment and labour-shedding – see Figure 7.2). In terms of our argument here, over basin management, Patterson claims that whilst the authorities had integrated control of the water cycle they made little or no attempt to link it to local authority planning.

By the mid 1980s the regular surveys of river water quality carried out by the RWAs were beginning to cause concern: a deterioration had replaced the steadily improving trend since the first surveys in 1975. New sources of pollution were partly to blame, such as spillage of slurry and silage liquor from livestock farms and nitrate from arable land; groundwater was becoming polluted and the European Community was steadily tightening the standards for river water, supply water and coastal water. However, a major component of the RWAs' problem remained their own decaying infrastructure of sewerage and sewage disposal. The legacy of the Victorian reformers, when not maintained and replaced by modern investment, became a liability and the progress made by Mrs Thatcher's government in reducing public investment had badly hit the RWAs (see Figure 7.2).

The Thatcher government had another doctrine in pursuit of economic efficiency: privatisation of large public corporations. Kinnersley (1988) suggests that the government 'stumbled' into privatisation of the RWAs in England and Wales, though Table 7.3 indicates a large number of apparently rational arguments made by government for the policy. In Scotland local government owns the water supply and sewerage assets and so there is little profit to be made in privatisation. Indeed it is debatable whether public profit or an improvement in competitiveness drove on the privatisation of the ten RWAs south of the border. Competitiveness is a difficult concept in terms of public goods.

As Kinnersley points out, private companies can produce very efficient water supply and sewerage services but in nations where they do so the infrastructure remains in local government ownership (e.g. France) and

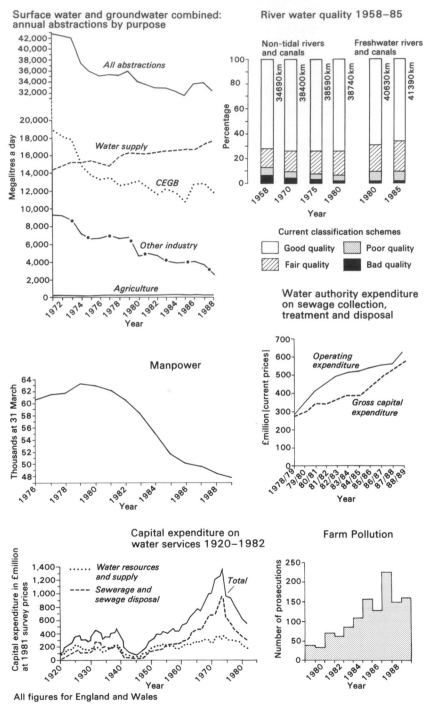

Figure 7.2 Trends in investment, labour and problem abatement in the water
industry of England and Wales at the time of privatisation (1989)
(sources: water industry/DoE)

Table 7.3 Why private ownership?

The Government believes that the privatisation of the water authorities will benefit their customers and employees, and indeed the nation as a whole, in the following ways:

1 The authorities will be free of Government intervention in day-to-day management and protected from fluctuating political pressures.
2 The authorities will be released from the constraints on financing which public ownership imposes.
3 Access to private capital markets will make it easier for the authorities to pursue effective investment strategies for cutting costs and improving standards of service.
4 The financial markets will be able to compare the performance of individual water authorities against each other and against other sectors of the economy. This will provide the financial spur to improved performance.
5 A system of economic regulation will be designed to ensure that the benefits of greater efficiency are systematically passed on to customers in the form of lower prices and better service than would otherwise have occurred.
6 Measures will be introduced to provide a clearer strategic framework for the protection of the water environment.
7 Private water authorities will have greater incentive to ascertain the needs and preferences of customers, and to tailor their services and tariffs accordingly.
8 Private authorities will be better able to compete in the provision of various commercial services, notably in consultancy abroad.
9 Privatised authorities will be better able to attract high quality managers from other parts of the private sector.
10 There will be the opportunity for wide ownership of shares both among employees and among local customers.
11 Most employees will be more closely involved with their business through their ownership of shares, and motivated to ensure its success.

Source: Department of the Environment (1988)

there are strong regulatory agencies to maintain standards and to run integrated river basin management. In fact EC rules do not permit private companies to operate the regulatory rules contained in EC Directives.

Rees (1989) develops, at length, the lead-up to privatisation but her main focus is on the way in which true resource economics will impinge on water supply, rather than the impact of regulatory, environmental operations. She is doubtful that the privatised water and sewerage enterprises can achieve improved quality service, renew assets, respond to growth, improve water quality and protect customers against price rises. With so many objectives and so much regulation Rees cannot foresee the pricing of water services as operating any control over demand, even if metering were introduced.

It is said that the EC influence was conducive in forcing the UK Government to abandon plans for outright privatisation of the RWAs (excepting flood protection which had already been recognised as a public good). The privatisation was first mentioned in Parliamentary business in February

1985, was widely regarded as a non-starter by water industry professionals (with the notable exception of Thames Water) and was withdrawn from the Conservative manifesto for the 1987 General Election. Afterwards a Discussion Paper from the Department of the Environment, MAFF and the Welsh Office put forward a National Rivers Authority to carry out the regulatory, environmental and flood defence functions for the same river basin areas as the privatised water supply and sewerage authorities. The full list of duties proposed for the NRA is shown in Table 7.4.

When the National Rivers Authority inherited its new role on 1 September 1989 its staff were described as 'Guardians of the Water Environment'. It had leapt from being a hastily designed alternative to full privatisation to being a vanguard of the rapidly 'greening' Conservative government. It had ten regional units, each with a large measure of public consultations including Regional Rivers Committees, Regional Fisheries Committees and Regional Flood Defence Committees. It also had a firm central administration in London (60 staff, compared with 6,500 in the regions). Its annual spend was set at £300 million of which £80 million came in from the Department of the Environment direct.

On 1 September 1989 two major problems confronted the NRA: resources (and it was awarded an extra £30 million very quickly after establishment) and the ability to raise the profile of river quality control. At last an organisation had been set up to use the full power of the 1974 Control

Table 7.4 Duties proposed for the National Rivers Authority

(a) Water resources – water resource planning, licensing of abstractions and impoundments, monitoring of licences.
(b) Environmental quality and pollution control – maintaining or improving water quality in rivers, estuaries and coastal seas in accordance with standards and objectives set by the Secretary of State; conservation, granting of discharge consents; maintaining registers (open for public inspection); monitoring of water quality and of compliance with consents; enforcement of consents; recommendation of protection zones; granting of consents for prescribed activities within protection zones and associated monitoring and enforcement; advice on measures to prevent pollution; public information and education.
(c) Land Drainage and Flood Protection – the general supervision of land drainage, the carrying out of works on main rivers, sea defence.
(d) Fisheries – the maintenance, improvement and development of fisheries in inland waters, including all licensing, restocking and enforcement functions at present the responsibility of the water authorities.
(e) Conservation and Recreation – the present duties of water authorities in these respects would apply both to the NRA and to the privatised utilities.
(f) Navigation – 3 water authorities have navigation responsibilities which would transfer to the NRA.

Source: Dept of the Environment, MAFF, Welsh Office (1987)

of Pollution Act. Clearly the NRA had to be seen to 'police' UK rivers and by January 1990 they had brought 500 prosecutions for river pollution, including 27 against the water plc's and a celebrated £1M case against Shell UK for an oil spillage in the Mersey.

7.7   RIVER BASIN INSTITUTIONS AND DEVELOPING NATIONS

The historical survey of institutional change in UK river management can be said to have taken the nation's rivers from rural low-density usage to urban, industrial exploitation.

In addition to the trends in scale, control structure and political basis observed in Figure 7.3 one may also select those trends which are characteristic of river basin development as a process:

(a) Early private enterprise: opportunist, local and mainly urban (with, in rural areas, characteristic self-sufficiency).
(b) Urban centres of population extend their needs for water supply to rural hinterlands and by private acts of Parliament secure rights to build

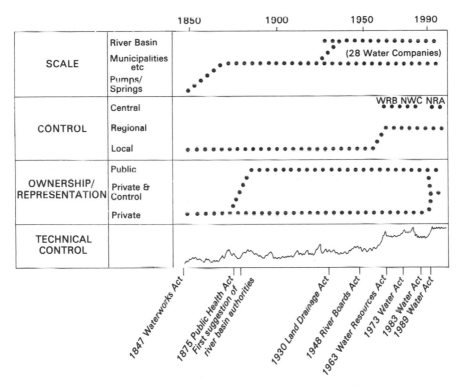

Figure 7.3 Trends of scale, ownership and control in river basin management in England and Wales

dams. Political reaction by the population displaced from dam sites but riparian rights of e.g. mill-owners protected (see Chapter 1).

(c) Transition to river basin development as the basic unit to give a coordinated systematic theme to management. In the UK land drainage was the theme of the first moves but subsequently pollution control took over.

(d) Commodification of water supply and sewerage once all population served, partly to control demand and to encourage high standards.

(e) Increasing interest in environmental management and regulatory control; environmental assessment for all new developments.

There are ways in which this sequence is unlikely to apply to nations experiencing contemporary development of their river basins in the developing world:

(a) The UK is unusual, in that erosion problems are not a contemporary corollary of settlement.

(b) The UK's industrial revolution was powered by fossil fuel not by hydro-electric power: the remaining water power interest in fact led to legal protection which is now seen as beneficial.

(c) The earliest movements towards integrated basin-scale management came from land drainage (which is not a problem in most developing countries) and pollution (which becomes a basin-wide problem only after development).

The two most pressing river basin development problems in the developing world are irrigation, to permit rural development, and power generation, largely for urban populations. Both are served best under existing technologies by the construction of dams. Because erosion problems are a frequent accompaniment to land pressure problems in the developing world, it is to river basins as sediment transport systems that we should look for guidance (Chapter 2).

The lesson of these differences should be that UK water professionals enter an entirely new world when they work on development projects. Elliot (1982) points to this confusion of identities but also to the intellectual training of single discipline excellence which is the European tradition in water technology. This, he considers, is a threat to communication between disciplines; therefore we may have *multi*-disciplinary project teams but very little of the *inter*-disciplinary work which is now shown as necessary in both developed world and developing world river management. Whilst the powerful leaders of developing nations often have very little room for public participation in river basin development, they should at least expect a good project. Elliot says:

It is important to emphasise the losses in efficiency that result from this failure of communication. Resources are misallocated and specifications or operating schedules are suboptimal precisely because one discipline cannot fully internalise the complexities and requirements of the other.

(Elliot, 1982, p. 22)

The importance of the signals given by project team operation is that they become embodied in the river basin institutions that are left to manage the systems post-project. Barrow (1987) presents the desiderata for those developing tropical catchments; they are rationalised here in Table 7.5 which demonstrates why the traditional lead discipline − engineering − in water projects needs the support of other skills in education or the inter-disciplinary breadth and dialogue requested by Elliot.

Some items on Barrow's list appear to be wishful thinking and clearly represent a view from the cultural background of the developed world. Local consultation may be laudable in the Thames basin but is highly improbable in the Awash. However, properly conducted environmental assessment, matched with economic analyses which include the principles of sustainability (WCED, 1987) and intergenerational equity (Dixon *et al.*,

Table 7.5 Guidelines to tropical river basin development

Procedures

1 Institute comprehensive water resource planning.
2 Institute sound economic analysis of projects.
3 Conduct thorough environmental analysis at the same time as technical design.
4 Open up planning process to the public.
5 Indigenous people affected by the project should be included in the planning process.
6 Provide for independent technical review of projects.
7 Establish links in the international scientific and academic community.
8 Establish links between environmental, human rights and indigenous people's support groups.
9 Establish watershed management and rehabilitation as a priority.
10 Establish enhancement of traditional food crop agriculture as a priority.
11 Educate decision-makers on emerging problems with large dams.

Natural sensitivities

Rainfall	Heavy: canopy cover of plants critical to protect soil, even where rain is seasonal. Phreatophytes, however, 'waste' water.
Soil	Leaching rapidly depletes exposed soils; erosion danger (drylands) plus landslides (humid). Care required in cultivation. Terracing etc. required.
Natural vegetation	Often needs to be left unless crop can be chosen to replicate soil protection. Tropical forest ecosystems require conservation.
Land use	Local systems well adapted until land pressure builds up. Resource conservation must replace this indigenous skill.

Source: Barrow (1987)

1986), can be further matched with ethnographic observation to moderate rates of change to those appropriate to the cultural environment as a whole.

Once established and under local control a tropical river basin development authority can make many mistakes. Despite its mandate to advise the Government on 'all matters affecting the development of the Area' and to 'coordinate the various studies of, and schemes within, the Area so that human, water, animal, land and other resources are utilised to the best advantage', the Tana River Development Authority in Kenya has failed to prevent interference between hydropower generation in the upper basin and irrigation in the lower basin and has succeeded in supplying most of the generated power to Nairobi. The most recent Development Plan passes the focus of activity to the Districts as a move from resource conservation to rural development (Rowntree, 1990).

7.8   ENVIRONMENTAL ASSESSMENT OF WATER PROJECTS: WORLDWIDE PANACEA?

Environmental (impact) assessments must be more than a cipher in order to free up development funds (it is now the practice of the World Bank and other agencies to insist on EA before funding projects), as is shown by Abracosa and Ortolano (1988) for the Bicol River Basin Development Program in the Philippines. The assessment failed to identify problems of flooding in the reservoir basin, fisheries deterioration and the growth of water hyacinth. Failure to include public hearings and to involve the public in assessment are identified by these authors as leading to a very large amount of post-project modification and maintenance.

At the United Nations Water Conference in Mar del Plata in 1977 the Mexican delegation proposed the following:

> It is recommended that the effective participation of the public is the key for success of programs of water management and that the lack of local participation has frequently resulted in ineffective programs.
>
> (in Elmendorf, 1978)

Mexico has been well served by community-based development since the revolution of 1910; even so, as reported by Elmendorf (1978), 30 per cent of small village water supply systems are inoperative. Maintenance is a key problem and failure to fund maintenance or to equip people in the project community with the necessary expertise once again recall the need for adherence to sustainable development.

Warford and Saunders summarise the problem in this way:

> No matter how badly (in the opinion of an external appraiser) a village 'needs' a better water supply system, if the population itself does not perceive the value of the system, the usage rate will be low, system

maintenance and local administration will be inadequate and vandalism could be a problem.

(in Elmendorf, 1978)

Elmendorf concludes that 'vicariousness' — an ability to imagine how the project will feel to the people of the project area — is a neglected aspect of planning, given that full consultation is seldom possible and that values will need translation into a factual form for the rational choice between alternatives.

Barbier (1991) suggests that comprehensive identification of components of a watershed system (such as may be identified by EIA) make a very suitable basis for applying the emerging factual basis of environmental economics. In terms of development projects, environmental economics present the opportunity to refine cost/benefit evaluations of project worth. Barbier quotes examples of the cost of soil erosion in Java (both on-site and downstream remedial actions are costed). He further suggests river basin projects as suitable for applying the 'environmentally compensating project' to parallel the main project and bring enhancement or rehabilitation to the basin affected.

It is very clear that a huge responsibility for effective environmental assessment and the embodiment of precautions revealed as necessary rests with the engineering profession. As Kalbermatten and Gunnerson (1978),

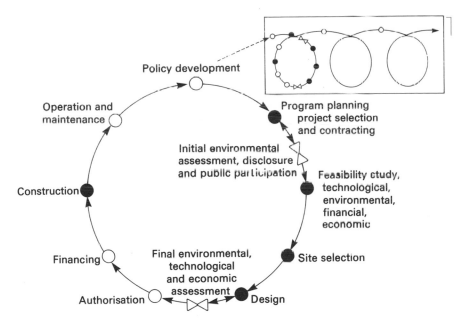

Figure 1.4 The engineering programme planning helix (Kalbermatten and Gunnerson, 1978)

introducing the proceedings of a professional workshop on the topic, conclude, it is essential to analyse the pattern of the project 'helix' (Figure 7.4). The engineer needs to 'enter into and support programs for early public disclosure and public participation in the conceptual planning and implementation stages of civil engineering projects' (p. 241) (see also Section 7.10).

Wertz (1982) counsels against a headlong rush to interdisciplinary fusion. From experience with land-use planning in connection with water issues in West Germany, Wertz concludes that open conflict is the best way to 'settle' rival professional interests and responsibilities. Within such a field of creative tension it would be of value to the water interest to adopt standards to be attained by land-use interests 'even if those standards are not always scientifically dependable' (p. 292). Interestingly for an author representing a successful developed economy, Wertz also concludes that 'it is not advisable to commercialise public interests in water supply and sewage

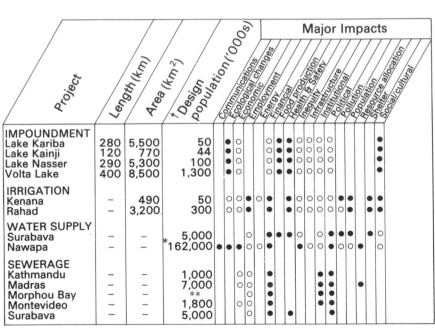

IDENTIFIED [●] AND PROBABLE [○]

MAJOR IMPACTS OF CASE STUDIES OF WATER DEVELOPMENT

NOTES

† Includes resettlement ** Industrial discharge

* Assuming 90% of Canada, 60% of United States and 20% of Mexico populations for 1974. Estimated corresponding figure for 2025 is 342m population.

Figure 7.5 Retrospective environmental assessment of major water resources schemes (Kalbermatten and Gunnerson, 1978)

treatment ... public administration and management should, therefore, be given priority over private forms of organisation' (pp. 292–3).

Within the appropriate institutional framework, claims Wertz, the one remaining problem is to integrate research knowledge in relation to specific courses of action rather than in abstract:

> Only if exchanges between scientists and practitioners are related to actual projects, while they are being implemented, rather than being treated theoretically, can they be of greatest value. Land-use planners and decision-makers should be included in educational activities and in the exchange of information.
>
> (Wertz, 1982, p. 293)

This voice of experience is echoed by Hellen and Bonn (1981) with their rueful quote that 'the best interdisciplinary activity is often that which goes on in one person's head' (p. 333). In this context, thorough (even bruising!) environmental assessments, which are very broadly scoped, appear to be central to institutional management of developing river basins (see Figure 7.5).

7.9 INTERNATIONAL RIVER BASIN MANAGEMENT

It is appropriate, once more, to differentiate between problems and policies in the developed world and those in the developing world.

Ten factors which influence the likelihood of achieving workable inter-governmental agreements are:

(a) Severity of the problem.
(b) Degree of technical agreement on the solution.
(c) Geographical balance of the problem.
(d) Law standards and access allowable to foreigners.
(e) Domestic interests and pressures.
(f) Level of preparedness of appropriate institutions.
(g) History of cooperation/conflict.
(h) Relative economic strength/military power.
(i) Third party involvement, e.g. United Nations.
(j) Timing – agreement must precede entrenchment.

Taking two developed world problem basins (the North American Great Lakes and the Rhine) and two developing world basins (the Nile and the Ganges/Brahmaputra), it is easy to see how these factors work slightly differently in the two situations.

In the Great Lakes the situation is covered by an International Joint Commission dating back to 1909. It is a neutral adviser and factfinder staffed by impartial professionals. Since the USA accounts for 87 per cent of the water used from the Great Lakes basin and discharges 80 per cent of the pollution load, it is clear that Canada has a vested interest in the impartiality of the IJC; special boards and advisory groups were grafted on to the Commission to deal with cross-border tensions over pollution. Manifestations of these tensions included environment groups from Canada fighting in the US courts (backed by Canadian Government funds) to control toxic dumping and the effects of a stark contrast in pollution control laws (US control at source, Canada uses receiving water standards). However, working in favour of the IJC are the parallel arrangement of the two nations on either side of the water (rather than upstream/downstream) and their similar levels of development.

Whilst the nations of Europe have similar levels of development the River Rhine basin is one in which there are clear source (Switzerland) and receptor (Netherlands) nations and two traditionally antagonistic nations (France and Germany) with intervening riparian interests. Treaties controlling the management of the river date back, through two World Wars fought across it, to 1868. Fisheries and navigation have been regularised for more than a century; however, pollution has proved problematic for several reasons. First, of the four participating nations Switzerland is not a member of the European Community and therefore not bound by EC Directives on the control of pollution. Second, the basin includes extremely important mining and industrial zones relatively high up (e.g. potash mining in Alsace which contributes a third of the Rhine's huge salt load) and very important agriculture low down (in river and altitude terms) in the Netherlands. Nevertheless, the four nations established the International Commission for the Protection of the Rhine against Pollution in 1963 and two important conventions (chemical pollution, chloride pollution) in 1976.

Whilst the Netherlands is highly dependent on good management of the Rhine upstream it is in no way as vulnerable as Egypt on the Nile. The life of Egypt (and its burgeoning population) is highly dependent on irrigated agriculture (see Chapter 5). A cornerstone to Egypt's survival has been, therefore, friendly relations with the Sudan immediately upstream, with whom the first Nile Waters Agreement was signed in 1929. In 1959 a Permanent Joint Commission was set up, gathering data, planning and coordinating. It was this Commission which facilitated the Jonglei Canal project (p. 151). To the Sudan the Canal is an equally prestigious contribution to the water resource conservation of the Nile as is Egypt's Aswan High Dam. However, the real problem of Nile management is that whilst the six headwater nations on the White Nile (Uganda, Kenya, Tanzania, Rwanda, Burundi and Zaire) are apparently amenable to joining a UN compact on the basin, they control only 14 per cent of the flow. Ethiopia, responsible for the 86 per cent from the Blue Nile, is politically, culturally and economically very distinct and refuses to join moves towards integrated basin management.

Cultural and political differences also confuse moves to manage the huge basins of the Ganges and Brahmaputra. In the 1950s India 'stole' water from the Ganges above the Bangladesh (East Pakistan) border to keep open the port of Calcutta by flushing silt into the Bay of Bengal. As Bangladesh became independent in 1971 a Joint Rivers Commission was established but apart from aiding flood control in Bangladesh the Commission has been largely unsuccessful. In 1976 India 'stole' more of the low flow of the Ganges at the Farakka barrage. There is a perennial proposal to divert the Brahmaputra in India across to the Ganges. Bangladesh countered with proposals to dam tributaries on Nepalese territory.

7.10 CURRENT UK TRAJECTORIES IN RIVER BASIN ASSESSMENT AND CONSULTATION: LESSONS FOR INSTITUTIONS

In Britain Thames Water Authority (NRA Thames region, post-1989) began to formalise public consultation in the late 1980s, particularly in connection with flood protection projects. A handbook of their experiences is now available (Gardiner, 1991). The Thames was quoted by the Government as exemplifying a British triumph of management:

> The River Thames is a classic example of integrated river-basin manage-ment. The catchment area supports 3,500 abstractions — 1,200 for agri-culture, 500 for water supplies (by statutory water companies and the Thames Water Authority itself) and 1,800 for industrial and other uses. The river receives 6,500 discharges from industry and 450 discharges from the Authority's own sewage treatment works. In addition, the river is used for fishing (193,000 rod licences are issued annually) and for boating (19,000 boats are registered and a million passages a year recorded through the river's 45 locks). The river and its tributaries are regulated and managed to ensure that discharges do not pollute water supplies and abstractions do not lower the level of the river and put at risk natural life or the enjoyment of those who use the river for recreation.
>
> (Department of the Environment, 1988, p. 5)

The essence of the Thames approach is *appraisal* and *review* which, fol-lowing the definition of a project, are applied at every stage to the evalu-ation of options in three fields: economics, engineering and environment. Thames believe that it is the responsibility of a public authority to:

(a) Demonstrate that all relevant factors have been properly considered at the appropriate stage.
(b) Provide an appreciation of the important impacts of a proposal and its alternatives.
(c) Improve the quality of decision-making.
(d) Ensure efficient implementation of the project.

'Project appraisal must be set within the context of integrated river basin management, wherein the changes induced by man tend to change system morphology and the balance of the river environment'. Clearly Thames Water, and now the NRA, have faced costs in this approach, not the least in recruiting the relevant disciplines for the promotion of each project. In fact it is, in the view of Gardiner (1988), the *inter*disciplinary, holistic view of river basins (Figure 7.6) which becomes the major drive for vesting the rejuvenated field of river engineering in the context of project appraisal and management of system equilibria.

Further encouragement to the civil engineering profession to formalise public participation in water projects is provided by Priscoli (1989) who sees a continuum between PI (public involvement) and CM (conflict management) – see Figure 7.7. Priscoli reiterates the view that:

Frequently the major problems that engineers and scientists face are not technical. They are problems of reaching agreement on facts, alternatives or solutions.

The engineer, trained and rewarded for technical excellence is frequently frustrated by what are perceived as extra social or environmental design constraints. However, far from constraints, broadening the social

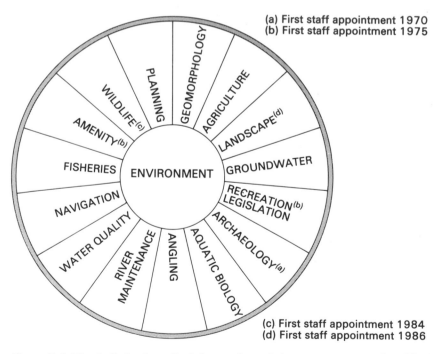

(a) First staff appointment 1970
(b) First staff appointment 1975

(c) First staff appointment 1984
(d) First staff appointment 1986

Figure 7.6 The holistic, interdisciplinary view of river management (modified from Gardiner, 1988)

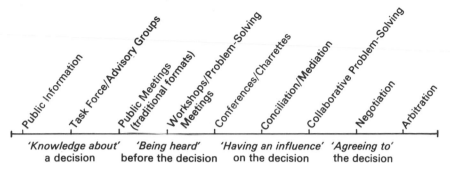

'Knowledge about'   'Being heard'   'Having an influence' 'Agreeing to'
    a decision   before the decision   on the decision   the decision

Figure 7.7 Conciliation procedures and public consultation (Priscoli, 1989)

objectives of engineering presents new opportunities for engineering service if one makes the effort to look.

(Priscoli, 1989, pp. 31, 36)

Priscoli attempts to guide the engineer through a simple definition of the values which public consulters might bring to discussion of a water scheme (Figure 7.7) and to emphasise that an essential step for the professional is to admit the interactive bias of the situation. Once open for discussion the project loses its Newtonian, mechanistic simplicity and the professional, too, feels lost. 'You need to give the project away,' says one experienced British flood control engineer. Once the interests of the consultees are established by exploring the salience of values to the particular project, formal methods of interest-based bargaining (e.g. Fisher and Ury, 1981) can be employed to progress to a solution which is both feasible and broadly acceptable.

Returning to the experience of flood control personnel at the Thames Water Authority, their approach to controlling land use in relation to river management objectives has been further developed under the Water Act 1989. The National Rivers Authority (Thames Region), to whom the flood protection role has passed, is being given the opportunity to:

(a) Have a more formal and influential role in local development planning (mirroring recent legislation in Ontario and New Zealand).
(b) Carry out 'catchment planning', an activity as yet variously defined by engineering, water resources, water quality and conservation/recreation staff.

If catchment planning becomes the vehicle for the NRA as an institution to advance the holistic appraisal of river basin development, the procedures described by Gardiner (1991) and his colleagues could well become a model technology. Their 'manual for holistic appraisal' incorporates nineteen specialist sections as well as eight showing how the interdisciplinary

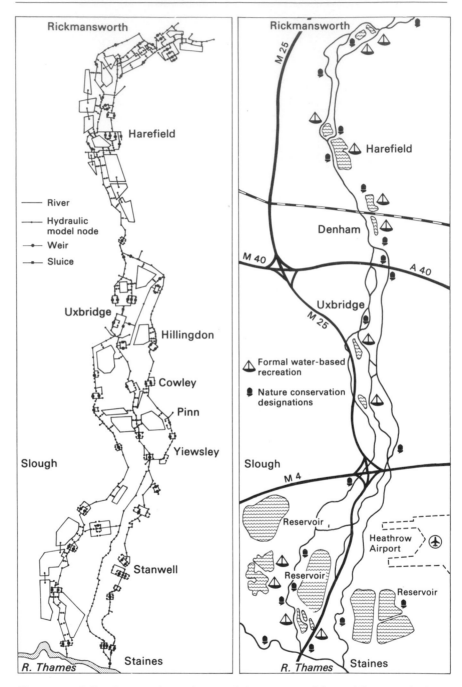

Figure 7.8 A flood protection scheme of the type used for public consultation by Thames division of the UK National Rivers Authority (modified from Gardiner, 1988). Both the hydraulic model (left) and the contentions sites (right) are presented to the public

structure is coordinated and presented to the public. Despite the recruitment by the former Thames Water Authority of diverse technical skills in-house (Figure 7.6), it is clear that the role of consultants and academic advisers is crucial to the success of even such a catholic and multi-functional organisation as the National Rivers Authority. So, too, is the process of public consultation and the interaction achieved with the planners developing zoning policies over strategic timescales (as well as the planners responsible for large river developments).

Figure 7.8 indicates the complexity of the urban environment tackled by Thames NRA in the London area. The Colne valley flood protection plan involved a very extensive public consultation, which, however, was cost-beneficial in curtailing delays in implementation. The maps also indicate the complexity of the channel networks whose flood flows were simulated by the essential hydraulic modelling.

Woolhouse (1989) confirms the need for both modelling the hydrological effects of new urban developments in Thames Region (where development of Luton, Stevenage and Harlow have had costly effects on flooding) and interaction with planning authorities. The former becomes the vehicle for the latter.

7.11   CONCLUSIONS: INFLUENCE OVER LAND – AN ESSENTIAL PREREQUISITE

We have seen that, in addition to decisions over funding and representation, river basin organisations also face profound problems of scale. Paradoxically they can operate best by owning land and/or influencing people to concur with their wishes on land when the scale is very small. That is why many conferences, books and papers are addressed to 'catchment management' or 'catchment control', where the word catchment infers the diminutive of 'basin' (see Chapter 1). Possibly this sense of involvement and understanding is what lies behind the views of those in Britain who feel that the age of municipal control was right for water resources.

Paradoxically, as geographical scale increases to the natural drainage basin outline, including sources and users of water, polluters and conservationists of the aquatic environment, there is a better job which can be done but far fewer means of tackling that task. Schramm (1980) concludes that there is a negative relationship between basin size and the scope of work undertaken by planning institutions. It may, therefore, be an essential feature of large basin management to set goals for small areas e.g. the 'Priority Watershed Approach' in Wisconsin, USA (Konrad et al., 1986). The message of the successes won at small scale is that 'ownership rules OK', at least in much of the developed world and it is no accident that the Ontario Conservation Authorities are encouraged at grass roots and can then purchase land over which they want management control. The case of the UK,

Table 7.6 Conclusions and recommendations of the UNEP/UNESCO study of 'large water projects' and the environment

1 Water resources projects needed for socio-economic development and the resulting environmental changes are inseparable. Recent procedures for the planning of water resources projects and their assessment have promoted a better understanding of the conflicting nature of this problem and have contributed to improved decision-making as far as the development and management of water projects are concerned.
2 A large number of ecological, financial, social, economic and technical difficulties must be overcome. It is necessary not only to assess but also to manage the environmental impacts of these water projects on both a short and long-term basis. This can only be done if environmental considerations become an integrated part of the decision-making process.
3 It has been recognised that water resources projects have a dual objective nature, namely, to serve both socio-economic development and ecological-environmental development. These dual but sometimes conflicting objectives require trade-offs between them. To do this, alternative options should be considered at various levels of water resources decision-making (policy formulation, planning, design, construction, operation, maintenance, rehabilitation). To obtain the most appropriate option, a compromise between the dual objectives has to be made. This can be achieved by the environmentally sound management of water resources projects which should be oriented towards the establishment of a long-term, dynamic equilibrium between the water project and its environment.

4 The environmentally sound management of water resources projects should be implemented by an active interdisciplinary and intersectorial learning process. Representatives of various interest groups (socio-economic, ecological, technical, legal, local, regional and national) should be involved in the development and management of these projects. A proper institutional and legal framework should be established according to specific conditions. Monetary, measureable and qualitative aspects should be considered on an equal basis.
5 The interaction between water projects and their host river basins should be studied in depth. Both the basin-wide and the regional approach should be basic components of environmentally sound water management.
6 It was agreed that the success of a project is not necessarily related to its size. Both large and small projects have positive and negative elements depending on specific conditions. If the size of the project is one of the reasons for considering an alternative option, a comprehensive analysis of both small and large projects should be undertaken taking into consideration all social, economic and ecological aspects. Both types of project should be developed, planned, operated, maintained and rehabilitated in an environmentally sound manner.
7 To develop alternative options, several specific approaches were suggested. Water demand and consumption control was suggested as an alternative measure for water transfer. The local and regional beneficiaries and the people likely to be harmed by the project should be identified more precisely. Income distribution should also be considered. Land-use planning should be

Table 7.6 (Continued)

combined with water resources planning. Incentives to attract people to other areas can also be considered as alternative options. To develop and compare alternative options, the decision support system planned by IIASA [International Institute of Applied Systems Analysis, Vienna] has been supported as a possible tool for the environmentally sound management of water.

8 The costing of environmental impact management as identified by EIA should be integrated into the planning procedure. The application of this approach should be supported by environmental legislation especially in countries where such legislation does not yet exist. In this respect, the overall recommendations of the UN/ECE task force on the application of EIA was supported. It reads: 'EIA should be viewed as an integral part of the project planning process, beginning with an early identification of project alternatives and the potentially significant environmental impacts associated with them and continuing through the planning cycle to include an external review of the assessment document and involvement of the public.'

9 Continuous monitoring of the socio-economic and ecological aspects of water project development and management is strongly recommended with emphasis on pre-project and long-term follow-up monitoring.

10 The UNEP/UNESCO draft methodology on integrated environmental evaluation of water resources development was considered to be appropriate for evaluating the state of environmentally sound management of water projects and river basins. It was recommended that UNESCO and UNEP should finalise this draft methodology and support its further development and application.

11 Better co-operation and understanding between specialists from various disciplines dealing with water projects and problems are needed and strongly recommended.

12 It was recommended that a systematic review of existing methods of evaluating all possible interaction between water management activities and environmental components be undertaken, for example, in the form of a matrix and referring to existing literature.

13 Although in most cases it is not possible or advisable to transfer methodologies for public information and participation from one social environment to another, it is recommended to collect and exchange information on national experiences.

14 As no environmentally sound planning and management is possible without the active positive involvement of professionals including planners, UNEP and UNESCO are recommended to continue and expand their activities related to the incorporation of environmental aspects in the formal education and post-graduate training programmes of engineers and planners. This education should not only relate to the scientific and technical aspects but also to the social and ecological ones.

Source: UNEP/UNESCO (1990)

however, and the recent trajectory of the Catchment Authorities in New Zealand, is that the land planning process is an essential element at the broader scale.

It may not be through the priority interest of the river basin organisation that planning influence is achieved; for example, it was the fisheries and conservation interests in the UK who first persuaded the Forestry Commission to plan and manage plantations with stream sensitivity in mind, yet the water losses by interception are more costly but had had no influence. Similarly, the nitrate pollution issue has forced the identification of 'sensitive areas' in the UK agricultural landscape; nitrate is of unproven toxicity yet has achieved a policy change impossible to arrange for the more serious issue of land drainage and flood protection.

No government is going to allow a primacy to its water management organisations; they must achieve influence by various means and it appears that 'sensitive areas' are a good way to publicise the interests of good basin management; they also have a profound educational value.

In time, too, there are problems of scale. Many of the strongest precautionary regulatory activities (e.g. environmental assessment) apply to projects, but not to routines. Recent advice from the United Nations Environment Project (UNEP) and UNESCO (1990) offers an extensive guide to sympathetic management of 'large water projects' – summarised on Table 7.6. Thus, whilst a large development may be carefully considered by all with a legitimate interest and carefully 'nested' into its environment, a rash of smaller developments over a long time period may escape scrutiny.

Despite the practicalities of an approach to control via small areas and large projects, therefore, much broader goals must be achieved by good river basin authorities. We have seen that these include:

(a) Conservation (and distribution of the benefits thereby achieved) of the water resource. This requires a huge knowledge base.
(b) Protection of rights, legal and human, including the democratic right to be consulted.
(c) Use of an ecosystem principle which forces management to be basin-wide.

Thus, to follow these principles, it becomes essential for water managers to understand land, its uses, management and planning. To intervene in land issues is a large political step in any system of government; the intervention is highly determined by the context of the information held about land and the policy framework surrounding land. These matters are worth a chapter on their own (Chapter 8).

Chapter 8

Sustainable river basin management
Issues of the knowledge base

Although the river and the hillside ... do not resemble each other at first
sight ... one may fairly extend the river all over its basin and up to its
very divides.

W. M. Davis (1899)

The word 'sustainable' is hard to define; however, many agree that working
towards a practical definition is an essential technical and political venture
in all fields of environmental management at the close of the twentieth century. It is, however, an appropriate adjective for the type of management
which Chapter 7 implicitly prescribes for the river basin system. Pezzey
(1989) describes 61 versions of a definition and the political, philosophical
and scientific doubts which attend the broad notion of *sustainable development*, first widely publicised by the World Conservation Strategy (IUCN,
1980) but mainly boosted by the Brundtland Report (WCED, 1987) which
defines it as: 'development that meets the needs of the present without
compromising the ability of future generations to meet their own needs'
(p. 43).

Sustainability has not been specifically defined for river basin development and management but put broadly would encompass:

(a) Use by those developing resources of space and time scales appropriate
    to the optimum functioning of river basins as natural systems.
(b) Assessment, using these scales, of the impact of both technical and
    policy developments.
(c) Monitoring the state of both pristine and developed basin systems and
    of both channel and catchment processes.

8.1 SCIENCE IN THE 'NEW ENVIRONMENTAL AGE'

Whilst Chapter 7 has extolled the virtues of a rebalancing between technical
and popular inputs to river basin management it is clear that basic guidance
will continue to come from scientific research. The burden of this chapter
is to explore the appropriateness of the knowledge base available for the

conjunctive use of the land and water resources of large basins but, before this exploration, we need to address more general problems of the nature of *environmental sciences* and how they interact with the *institutions* whose critical role is now understood (i.e. from Chapter 7).

In one sense sustainable river basin management is a vanguard project in the critical quest for all ecosystem management systems; other than the few world examples of urban 'air basin' management to curtail pollution (recently extended to the European Community in terms of critical air pollution loads for acidification) and ecosystem management in nature reserves, the river basin is uniquely a process–response system with definable, meaningful boundaries often coincident with existing social and administrative limits. The popularity of rivers for recreation in the developed world (see Chapter 9) means that popular environmental campaigns are directed at river managers before the appropriate institutions are aware of problems or at least before they are prepared to take mitigating action.

The high cost of taking mitigating action or of error in proactive action means that from the outset environmental policies in many nations have been cautionary rather than precautionary (see Section 8.3).

For example, in Victorian Britain clear principles were laid down to guide public policy responses to pollution (Dept of the Environment/Welsh Office, 1988):

(a) Controls would be applied when the scientific evidence justified it.
(b) Pollution should be prevented at source.
(c) The best commercially viable technology should be used to effect abatement of emissions or discharges.
(d) The polluter should bear the costs of the necessary controls.

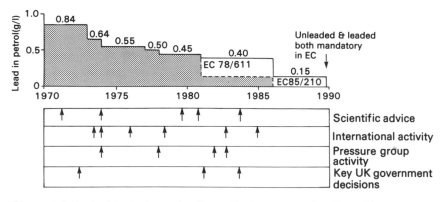

Figure 8.1 Typical trajectory of policy adjustment to scientific evidence, pressure from the public and political opportunity (the case of lead additives in petrol) (modified from Haigh, 1986)

Thus scientific evidence is codified as a key factor in prompting response but debate, of course, rages about the stage at which the evidence is 'conclusive'. Haigh (1986) describes the pattern of policy responses to the pollution threat from the lead content of petrol; he describes Figure 8.1 as indicating a 'majestic descent' of the lead content in response to a complex interplay of scientific evidence and political and technical activity at a variety of scales. Ashby (1978) has also noted a repeatable pattern of 'ignition' from public opinion, 'examination' by scientists and 'formulation' of political action by a combination of evidence and advocacy.

At this stage we may note the ironic situation in which science is credited with a key role but not as an anticipatory and radical force in the same way as technology. For these reasons we need to examine environmental science.

8.2 THE ENVIRONMENTAL SCIENCES

The popular definition of science plays up its objectivity and exactness; science has become in the twentieth century utterly confused with technology, to a point where 'technocentrist' positions on environmental management (O'Riordan, 1977) are optimistic that the continued success of research and development will ensure technical solutions to resource and hazard problems.

Environmental sciences fall into the popular and political images built for the laboratory sciences and this leads to considerable confusion over the incorporation of research results into policy; by comparison, the incorporation of laboratory science into technology is extremely simple and is mainly concealed from public scrutiny. Conventional research and development processes have tended to support the growth of economies, diversifying, extending and modernising the range and capability of manufactures and services. The short history of the environmental sciences has, however, shown them to be markedly different:

(a) They have tended to be identified with the sounding of alarms about the effects of economic development.
(b) Their stated results, or the conclusions made from them, have been contentious and much of the resulting public debate is between scientists with opposing results or interpretation.
(c) Environmental sciences have lacked the methodological rigour of the established sciences, being forced often into extensive modes of inquiry, and uncontrolled or at best statistically validated frameworks.
(d) Environmental sciences have tended to group together in pursuit of trans-boundary problems, particularly during the late 1980s with the rise of global scale environmental challenges. Headings such as 'Earth and Atmospheric' or 'Terrestrial and Freshwater' sciences have appeared on doors and on letterheads. In addition, the social

sciences have been drawn into an increasingly holistic framework widely regarded as appropriate by both philosophers (Bunyard and Goldsmith, 1988) and managers (Gardiner, 1988) of environmental systems.

How well-equipped is environmental science to provide knowledge for practical management of natural systems? Because river basins are, and have been, in the vanguard of system management we can partly answer this question by following the development of hydraulics and hydrology (see Chapter 1). However, it is first necessary to consider the relationship between providers and users of knowledge and therefore between science and society.

8.3 'SCIENCE SPEAKS TO POWER'

The field of metascience (the science of science) has been a very popular area of enquiry for philosophers in recent years. Perhaps initially inspired by the environmental damage brought about by some facets of applied science and technology (e.g. nuclear power) but also by the way in which positivist approaches to social systems were applied in an unquestioning way by policy-makers, the metascientists have been able to capitalise on a period of profound introspection on the part of scientists themselves, largely brought on by a rapidly falling resource base for research.

Ziman (1984) attempts a guide to the contemporary status and problems of *applied science*, though without any special attention to environmental science. Ziman's view is that, despite a treasured perspective of science as a distinctive and wholly objective philosophy, independent of its material base, this perspective has never been representative outside higher education. He suggests that epistemological, occupational and societal functions are always combined in a scientist. For long periods (e.g. 1850–1950) societal functions of science are stable; an important aspect of stability is autonomy. However, *external steerage* has now largely taken over (Kogan and Henkel, 1983) and this has implications for what is researched, the manner of research and the interface with policy.

Collingridge and Reeve (1986) are even more dubious of the role of science in relation to policy rather than technology. In a study which gives its title to this section, they unpick what they call 'the myth of the power of science' in relation to policy-making, i.e. that 'whatever information is needed to reduce uncertainty in making a particular policy choice, science can meet the challenge'. (p. 2).

They claim that this myth is perpetuated as recently as the introduction of environmental assessment in development programmes and conclude that:

Contrary to the myth of the power of science there is a fundamental and

profound mis-match between the needs of policy and the requirements
for efficient research within science which forbids science any real
influence on decision-making.

(Collingridge and Reeve, 1986, p. 5)

Collingridge and Reeve see research proceeding best when scientists are
allowed autonomy in their choice of problem, allowed to work in single disciplines and allowed to reach a consensus with low error costs. However,
the more relevant the policy field, the more likely will be criticism of technical arguments. The status of scientific knowledge as simply a stage of
negotiation amongst scientists which has reached consensus is therefore
directly threatened. Similarly scientists become frustrated with the fact that
policy-making does not involve a synoptic rationality in which exact bricks
are built into a carefully planned wall of knowledge. Policy-making therefore becomes incremental (see Figure 8.1) rather than fundamental and this
aspect of the political filtering of research results is poorly appreciated by
scientists, including the present author.

Three years after the acceptance of a paper by Calder and Newson (1979)
by the hydrological community, the Secretary of State for the Environment
in the UK Government made the following statement in Parliament: 'As
regards afforestation, its percentage and its effect on catchment areas ... I
am advised there is a lack of clear scientific evidence' (Hansard, 21 March
1980). In later papers (Newson, 1990; 1991; 1992 [b]), therefore, the author
has tried to put the knowledge base of hydrology into a policy context.
These papers illustrated a slow but measurable policy readjustment to the
original scientific research.

One weakness of Collingridge and Reeve's arguments for the field of
research on the natural environment is that they ignore the interdisciplinary
nature of a science like hydrology; contributions by generalists in this field
have been far more important than those in the medical and psychological
research fields they cover. Nevertheless, it is highly appropriate to the subject matter of this chapter to consider the need for knowledge in
river basin management to be constrained by the restrictions raised by
Collingridge and Reeve. It is especially pertinent to consider the concept of
managing the uncertainty which applies to all scientific findings; we may
speak, therefore, of the *error costs* of changing policy in response to faulty
scientific guidance. This will apply particularly in river basins to problems
of scale and of experimental control which arise in hydrology.

As a final element of our considerable prologue to investigating the
knowledge base for sustainable river basin development and management,
we investigate a recent innovation in West German public policy-making
which has caught the attention of the Royal Commission on Environmental
Pollution (1988).

The German *Vorsorgeprinzip* (*precautionary principle*) may be defined as taking integrated steps to protect the environment from processes of degradation which can be identified by research but about whose precise operation and impact there is still scientific uncertainty.

If applied to river basin management the precautionary principle could have no other outcome than land-use planning because it would be important to apply anticipatory controls to maintaining both quantity and quality of river flows. Such planning is already part of public policy in some countries (see Chapter 9).

8.4 ENVIRONMENTALISM, ENVIRONMENTAL SCIENCE AND RIVER BASIN SYSTEMS

Many of the oft-quoted visionaries of the environmental movement have made observations which describe the relationship between the land and water resources, and their human exploitation, within river basins. As explained by Chapter 1, what allowed them to bring out the connectivity of basin systems (before aerial and satellite photography and environmental science 'revealed all') was the depiction of land and channel components as integral on plans and maps – dating back to Leonardo da Vinci and beyond.

The origin of the modern phase of 'basin scale environmentalism' is reputed by many writers to have been 'The Alpine Torrents' controversy (Glacken, 1956) of the nineteenth century in Europe. In 1797 a French engineer (Fabre) linked the sequence of damaging floods from rivers draining the Alps to deforestation of the headwaters. Fabre listed seven kinds of disaster which resulted in:

(a) The ruin of the forests themselves.
(b) The erosion of mountain soils and consequent destruction of mountain pastures.
(c) The ruin of settlements near streams.
(d) Instability of channels.
(e) Litigation over channel migration.
(f) Siltation lower down rivers.
(g) Diminution of runoff from springs and subsoil.

Fabre's work produced a series of studies in France which eventually evoked a policy response from the French government. It introduced a project of *reboisement* (reafforestation) during the nineteenth century (1860 and 1882). The Austrians and Italians also faced the same problem. Alexander von Humboldt pronounced on the causative link between catchment mismanagement and environmental stress, using lake levels in the New World, Asia and South America as evidence:

by felling the trees which cover the tops and sides of mountains, men in every climate prepare at once two calamities for future generations: want of fuel and scarcity of water.

(von Humboldt, 1852, quoted in Kittredge, 1948, p. 9)

A further profound influence at about this time was the landmark volume, *Man and Nature: or physical geography as modified by human action* by George Perkins Marsh (1864). Widely acknowledged as the first major influence on western environmental concern, especially by geographers, this book records Marsh's extensive travels in the Alps. He was despatched by President Lincoln as an American ambassador to several countries with environmental problems in the Mediterranean and in Alpine Europe. He gave very high prominence to the dangers of deforestation and became instrumental as a diplomat and bureaucrat in drafting laws on irrigation (in France and in California); he also influenced the British Parliament in a policy of reafforestation for India.

Marsh focused much of his factual reporting of deforestation on the Alpine zone of Europe, linking deforestation with both flood and drought; in places his observational data and bibliographic enquiries appear to yield contradictory evidence on the precise hydrological effects of a forest cover but concluded overwhelmingly that they were beneficial. It is interesting to note a recent and contentious entry into the debate over deforestation; Metailie (1987) concludes, from a study of the Pyrenees, that nineteenth century catastrophes from flooding can be blamed on exceptional climatic sequences and natural geological and geomorphological proclivities rather than 'anthropic' erosion which was limited in extent. The same sort of battle between alternative explanations rages in connection with the Ganges (see Chapter 5).

The Swiss established a paired catchment study in 1900 to investigate the effect of forest cover on runoff. They concluded almost entirely beneficial effects of tree cover – balancing the extremes of flow and attracting precipitation. The results were reported in the USA by Zon (1912), two years after the establishment of the Wagon Wheel Gap paired catchment experiment (including forest felling – whereas the Swiss had compared catchments with 98 per cent and 30 per cent covers). Zon reported that: 'Accurate observations … established with certainty … Forests increase both the abundance and frequency of local precipitation over the areas they occupy' (quoted by Kittredge, 1948). After less than 50 years of a plethora of US paired catchment experiments, Hibbert (1967) summarised the results of 39 such studies as concluding that forest reduction increases water yield, and reforestation decreases water yield.

Clearly these early observers did not have the benefit of quantitative data; these did not become available until the systematic hydrological monitoring of a wide range of land uses in a wide range of climatic and physiographic conditions began during the International Hydrological Decade (1965–74).

The Decade established a key distinction for scientists researching options in river basin management: between *representative* and *experimental* basins.

8.5 THE HYDROLOGISTS' STOCK-IN-TRADE: CATCHMENT RESEARCH

Even within the autonomy of science under internal controls there is a profound debate about the appropriateness of one of the basic forms of research used to input to river basin management. We have already referred to the systematic problems of environmental science in framing experiments. One of these is that it has no unique theories to test but rather explores the boundary conditions which constrain the application of theory within significant combinations of climate and physiography. Enter, therefore, traditional geographical and biological tendencies to induction and classification (Burt and Walling, 1984), which become combined in catchment research frequently being carried out as a series of case studies (Church, 1984). Burt and Walling are very critical of this tendency and, following Kuhn, claim that: 'protracted attachment to the methodological directive "Go ye forth and measure" may well prove an invitation to waste time' (p. 7).

Nevertheless, these authors are hopeful that the phases of classification of catchments and of the identification of processes and their controls are now complete. An experimental approach to catchments can now mean, therefore, the careful testing of models incorporating processes. Church eases this sentiment into two avenues for catchment studies – *exploratory* and *confirmatory*.

It is unlikely that catchment research will avoid a continuing plethora of case studies, simply because land-use and land management effects often require opportunistic research, especially where a manipulation of land is required (part of the original definition of a true experimental catchment). We here begin to move towards the true crux of catchment experimentation – it is almost inevitably an applied science and has, therefore, in addition to the problems of experimental control, problems of relevance (increasingly as funds become scarcer) and the infrequently assessed problem of scale.

During the International Hydrological Decade (1965–74), Ward (1971) produced a concise evaluation of the catchment framework for hydrological work; he wrote from experience, having been amongst the earliest academic geographers in Britain to set up field hydrological studies. Ward quotes a Texas Congressman who proclaimed that an experimental catchment was 'an area drained by a creek of the size that a coon dog could jump across'. More seriously, Ward centres his critical evaluation of the catchment approach on the relationship between the purely empirical findings it provides and two much sterner tests – the ability to extrapolate those findings and an understanding of the processes underlying them. In all, Ward lists five practical problems of catchment experimentation:

(a) Lack of control.
(b) Representativeness.
(c) Accuracy of data.
(d) Data manipulation.
(e) Costs.

In terms of extrapolation, there had been early optimism amongst field hydrologists that research catchments could be seen as modules, with results being merged and grouped according to relief, soil, climate or land-use protocols, 'grossing up' to the scale of river basin for which management predictions are required. Most of them became less optimistic after their first practical attempts; Amerman (1965) concluded that processes related to the areal pattern of runoff from slopes (such as throughflow in soils and groundwater recharge on slopes of different lengths and geometries) produced an inherent, scale-dependent geographical variability in catchment performance. A further, more obvious source of scale-dependent behaviour is that of the proportion of its travel time spent by an element of runoff on slopes and in channels – the channel proportion increasing with distance from the headwaters. It is no accident that the most successful extrapolations from catchment research have been those determined by atmospheric processes, such as interception loss (see Calder and Newson, 1979). As one 'goes deeper' in the hydrological process cascade, extrapolation becomes much more complex. Turning to problems of providing basic understanding through catchment research, Reynolds and Leyton (1967) were very clear that even smaller experimental areas are needed: 'Watershed experiments cannot provide understanding of the physical processes, for which plot studies must be conducted' (quoted by Ward, 1971, p. 131).

Reynolds and Leyton do not specify the location for plot studies but clearly there is much to be gained from a *nested* approach to scales of study; the geomorphologist's technique of stream ordering can offer a basic principle for this hierarchical approach, one which was to be critical to the UK Institute of Hydrology's Plynlimon research catchments (Kirby *et al.*, 1992). As Ward says:

> None of these ... useful ways of supplementing small watershed experiments ... is a replacement for the small experimental watershed, however, since ultimately all other methods must be verified and assessed in relation to watershed data.
>
> (Ward, 1971, p. 131)

This conclusion is valid within the confines of the research approach but still neglects the problem of the next quantum leap – to application. In this

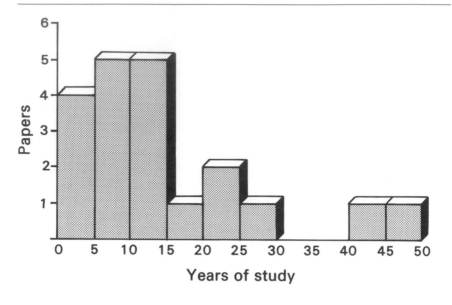

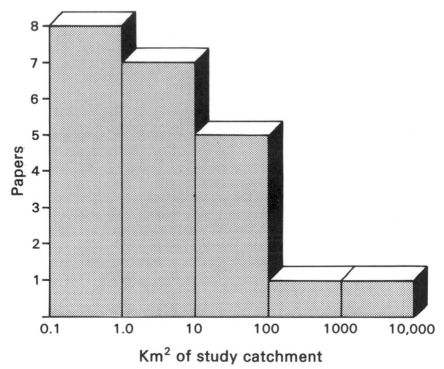

Figure 8.2 The scale and duration of catchment experimentation on land-use effects: data included in papers presented to the 1980 Helsinki Symposium of the International Association of Hydrological Sciences (IAHS)

respect it is relevant to note that, at the start of the IHD, Da Costa and Jacquet (1965) reviewed 252 catchment studies, of which 188 were of areas less than 25 km^2. The size of catchments and the duration of research on them revealed by the Helsinki Symposium in 1980 is shown in Figure 8.2 – they are mainly small and operate for around a decade.

At the conclusion of the IHD in 1974, UNESCO implemented an indefinite extension to coordinate further experimental hydrology: the International Hydrological Programme (IHP). Arnell (1989a) reviews the accumulated catchment studies from eighteen nations under the 'FREND' programme (Flow Regimes from Experimental and Network Data). It is important here that 'N' for Network has been included. At the time of the IHD, routine hydrological measurement and data collection were often local and low-tech. Thus catchment experiments were, in addition to their major role, a test-bed for instrumentation techniques and data processing routines. Twenty years later the 'routine' catchment is as well-equipped as

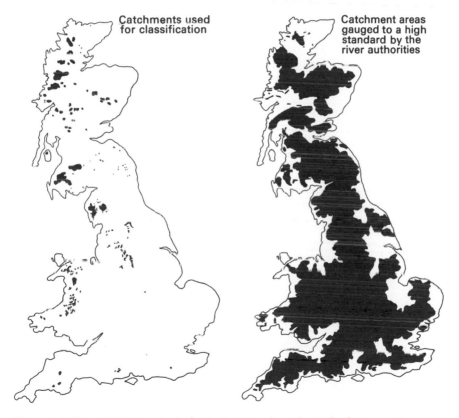

Figure 8.3 Great Britain – hydrological research and monitoring:
    (a) The research scale – small, dispersed catchments
    (b) The monitoring scale – large, cohesive basins

the early experimental sites, with data processed, checked, used and archived as part of national information systems such as the UK Surface Water Archive Programme (SWAP).

Thus it is now to network data that river managers can look, at least for vindication of an effect first isolated by researchers; the research catchment is still the more likely venue for a true experiment, i.e. manipulation of a control such as land use, and has increasing value as a monitoring device as the duration of its records grows and circumstances in policy (and now climate) change.

The relative spatial coverage attained by research catchments and by network measurements is shown in Figure 8.3 for Britain. A further indication of the growth of network power in the field of land and water management comes from the volume edited by Solbé (1986). Of 46 pieces of work reported only two make detailed use of research catchment data; seven use plot experiments or lysimeters and the remainder which report data collection programmes utilise network monitoring data, especially in connection with water quality data.

Arnell (1989a) further indicates a shift in scientific attention between the IHD and the IHP. The theme of the Decade, he says in his Preface, was that 'Rational water management ... should be founded upon a thorough understanding of water availability and movement' whilst in the IHP 'the objectives have shifted slightly towards a multidisciplinary approach to the assessment, planning and rational management of water resources'.

Figure 8.4 conceptualises the position of catchment research as offering an intermediate domain between penetrating investigations of process and the much broader scale of routine monitoring.

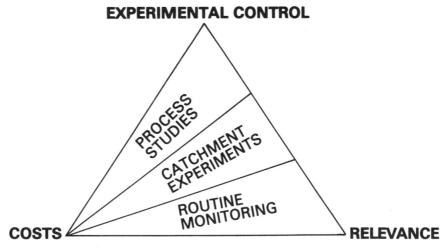

Figure 8.4 The catchment research dilemma: cost v. control v. relevance

8.6 ALTERNATIVES TO CATCHMENT RESEARCH

Rational management, of course, asks similar questions to those of scientific enquiry but often a preoccupation of the scientist with 'how?' becomes the familiar 'what if?' of the manager.

In an era of fast computation and an explosion in data availability, the conventional answer to such a question is 'simulation'; the mathematical model is in theory capable of replacing the research catchment for a fraction of the hardware investment. Arnell (1989a) includes modelling alongside experimental basins in a list of current hydrological techniques used to predict the effects of land-use change. Also listed are analysis of time series data to detect significant changes of trend (severely constrained by the gradual change characteristic of anthropogenic effects) and regional comparisons, substituting space for time. Both rely on statistical tests for which management tends to have a blind spot; the latter approach is also subject to the problem of transferability faced by catchment results.

Huff and Swank (1985) describe the PROSPER model, incorporating both canopy and (multiple) soil layers which essentially see climate as powering a flux of moisture away from the evaporating surface (the canopy). Interception storage is modelled as an alternative source of the evaporated moisture. The performance of the model on one of the Cowceta forest catchments through a number of years of felling and regrowth demonstrated significant problems of calibrating the leaf area of forest regrowth but as a bulked tool for predicting the increase of water yield on felled catchments in the first year it was more successful. Huff and Swank, however, conclude that the model cannot achieve comparable accuracy to field measurements.

Turning to models of whole catchments, the most usual incorporation of a land-use effect is via a tank concept, one which can be incorporated into a hardware model for educational purposes (Figure 8.5). The parameters of such a model therefore scale the size of the storages in the hydrological cascade from canopy to channel and the catchment is simply seen as a 'lumped' system of these tanks (Blackie and Eeles, 1985). The interception store is particularly amenable to this treatment but overall there is, of course, the need to fit the model to an actual flow record so as to set the parameters.

By contrast, distributed models are more frequently physically based (Beven, 1985); their parameters are the variables determining the operation of process equations which determine the routeing of rainfall to runoff. Distributed models are therefore useful to land-use hydrology and particularly to catchment experiments because they incorporate a detailed knowledge of actual catchment behaviour and can operate in data-sparse environments and on land-use impacts whose main interest may be in their spatial organisation: seldom will afforestation, or urbanisation, be the 'lumped' phenomenon considered best by 'lumped' models.

(a)

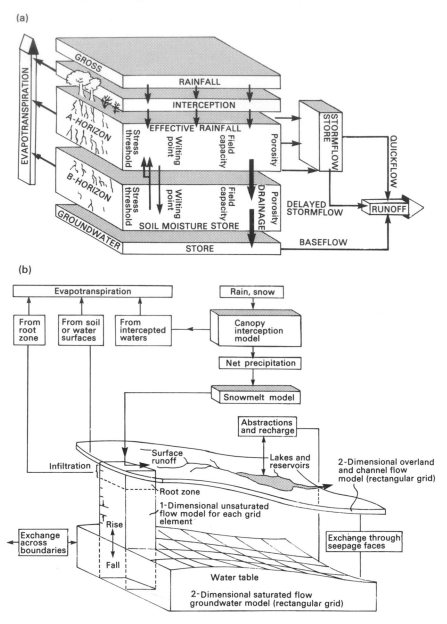

(b)

Figure 8.5 Deterministic hydrological models, an alternative to catchment research?

8.7 SCIENCE AND POLICY: LAND-USE MANAGEMENT IN RIVER BASINS

It was important to the progress of integrated land and water management in the USA that Yale established a graduate school of forestry in 1900 and that it promoted the doctrine (attributable to Gifford Pinchot) of 'scientific resource management'. An important graduate of the school in 1909 was Aldo Leopold (Tanner, 1987) who went on to work for the US Forest Service under Pinchot and to develop an holistic approach to land management, a practical evocation of the 'green' attitude of this time. He drew inspiration from the intact landscape and clear, tree-lined rivers of the Sierra Madre and sought to develop a 'biotic view of land' which led him to produce ethical guidance to public policy developments. He was successful as a generalist, claims Callicott (1987), because he provided an impeccable scientific basis for an holistic, systems approach to all landscapes but particularly to those of river basins. As a result land management for the benefit of water resources has taken on an almost evangelical nature in the USA (see Plate 8.1), a point which British foresters, faced with undesirable hydrological implications of their plantations, must find hard to understand and to bear.

The recent compendia of catchment, plot and policy material by Solbé (1986) and Arnell (1989b) allow an insight into the status of hydrological

Plate 8.1 The American Way: forests in support of resource conservation

research on issues of land management. The specific problems of environmental science in achieving public credibility, except under a 'precautionary principle', have already been dissected but there are extra difficulties within the phrase 'science speaks to power'. In many ways the case of hydrological research into land use and land management is a case of 'science speaks to the power*less*' since it is only rarely that rational management of water has been given the political power to extend to issues of land. In Chapter 7 we discussed that one reason might be the quest for the perfect river basin institution; in many ways this issue is peripheral, however, to rivalry between resource managers and property interests.

We have no opportunity to investigate the translation into the nineteenth century French policy of *reboisement* (reafforestation) of the observations by many of changes in the flow of Alpine rivers. Kittredge (1948) lists the many books and papers published in Europe prior to the policy decision; in an environmental age we have earlier in this chapter referenced the work of von Humboldt and Marsh in this connection. However, the telling work, according to Kittredge was not by an environmentalist but by the engineer Surell who, in 1841, published a book confirming the observations of his predecessor Fabre (see Glacken, 1956). We may therefore conclude that almost half a century of influential, official persuasion was necessary before policies relating to land were changed. It is also important to note that the agent of that change was the French government's Forest Department; Kittredge refers to the Department as being given 'the mission of controlling the torrents'. It is interesting to note that in neighbouring nations with a problem of flood-prone Alpine rivers the approach to control was more direct and structural. Vischer (1989) describes how Switzerland coped with the apparent increase in river instability in the eighteenth and nineteenth centuries: here was the birthplace of river 'training' (by analogy one might call land-use controls 'river education'!).

The gauntlet of responsibility for managing land in relation to the aims of flow regulation passed quickly to the USA where the 1902 Forest Reserve Manual listed the aims of forest reserves as 'to furnish timber' but also 'to regulate the flow of water'. The Wagon Wheel Gap catchment studies in Colorado did not begin until 1909, so this indicates a simple acceptance on faith of the European conclusion. It is perhaps no accident that Kittredge refers to 1877–1912 as the 'period of propaganda'. There were counter-claims against a widespread hydrological influence for forests but in the Eastern USA, the region most affected by the activities of the early settlers in clearing trees, the Week's Law of 1911 provided the crucial right to acquire land for afforestation 'for the protection of the watershed of navigable streams' and to 'appoint a commission for the acquisition of lands for the purpose of conserving the navigability of navigable rivers' (Kittredge, 1948, p. 13)

The ability to alter land use and to control land management techniques depends critically on the approach of land-owning democracies to state intervention; the USA became necessarily adept at Federal ownership for the purposes of forest, conservation and erosion management. We must also remember the great importance of river navigation to the spread of the Union and cannot underestimate the undesirable effect of the early felling of forests by European settlers on the erosion of the eastern USA.

From the small amount of historical evidence available on major land policy changes in relation to water management we may conclude that the following issues may be important:

(a) The spread of the observed change in river regime or water quality and the extent to which such changes reflex upon the land interest itself (e.g. through flooding, influence on navigation and trade in land products).

(b) The disciplinary origins of the work establishing the causal links. Government engineers and foresters clearly work from within the policy framework.

(c) The traditions of land ownership and planning in the region/nation affected and the role of federal agencies and corporations as vehicles for change.

These factors may be unique to the problem of forest and water, even to those cases where afforestation has a benign effect on water properties (cf UK uplands). It is perhaps worthwhile to bring this treatment up to date via the reviews by Solbé (1986) and Arnell (1989b).

Solbé's book is divided into four areas of inter-relationship between land and water:

(a) Urbanisation   (6 papers)
(b) Mineral exploitation   (4 papers)
(c) Agriculture   (13 papers)
(d) Forestry   (6 papers)

Arnell's table (modified here as Table 8.1) goes into more detail to reflect the considerable geographical spread of his eighteen nations:

(a) Urbanisation   (11 countries)
(b) Mining   (6 countries)
(c) Agriculture — land restructuring   (7 countries)
                 — field drainage   (6 countries)
                 — fertiliser application   (13 countries)
(d) Forestry   — vegetation change   (15 countries)
                 — acid precipitation   (4 countries)
     plus:
(e) Waste fill leakage   (1 country)

The impacts considered by Arnell's authors also include those of the water

Table 8.1 Land-use effects on hydrology: an international survey

(a) Nations where land-use effect noted

	Canada	China	Finland	France	FR Germany	Hungary	Ireland	Japan	Rep. of Korea	Netherlands	Norway	Poland	Romania	Sweden	Switzerland	UK	USA	Vietnam
Acid precipitation	×																	
Vegetation change		×	×	×	×	×		×	×	×	×	×	×	×		×	×	×
Urbanisation					×	×		×	×	×	×	×		×		×	×	×
Land restructuring			×	×	×			×		×	×			×		×	×	
Field drainage			×	×			×				×		×	×				
Mining												×	×					
Fertiliser application	×		×	×	×	×	×	×	×	×	×			×		×	×	×
Waste fill leakage	×				×			×	×							×		

(b) Specific impact of land-use effect

	Inputs to catchment	Evaporation/ transpiration	Surface/ subsurface interaction	Subsurface processes	In-channel processes	Soil water quality	Groundwater quality	Channel water quality
Acid precipitation	×					×	×	×
Vegetation change	×	×	×			×	×	×
Urbanisation	×	×	×	×				×
Land restructuring		×	×	×				
Field drainage			×	×		×		×
Mining			×		×			×
Fertiliser application	×					×	×	×
Waste fill leakage	×					×	×	×

Source: After Arnell (1989a)

managers themselves:

(a) Cloud seeding.
(b) Channel modification.
(c) Water use and return.
(d) Impoundment.

Since all eighteen nations, bar China, report some impact of these 'in-house' activities by water managers it is clear that in the development of public policy a particular perception is one of engineers 'in sole charge' of river behaviour. The land users and managers, it would seem, have a ready excuse for inaction through pointing an accusing finger at the water managers; this is particularly true in the case of nations such as the UK in which water quality debates include the added dimension of official responsibility for sewage pollution. The influence of climatic change is also now a potential confusion to policy-makers since it can dominate over both land-use and water-use effects on river regime. Climatic change also bespeaks new land uses and management techniques (see Chapter 6).

8.8 POLICY RESPONSES

Arnell's overview of his national reports from catchment research makes interesting reading in relation to public policy reactions to the findings. He concludes that the most widespread human impacts on hydrological characteristics are:

(a) Deforestation.
(b) Irrigation.
(c) Urbanisation.
(d) River regulation.
(c) Use of agricultural chemicals.

He reports: 'The reviews received from the international hydrological community have shown that although there is a general consensus about the types of change resulting from a given activity, the actual degree of change is very variable' (p. 15).

He also concludes that major river basins perform a kind of smoothing process on the hydrological signals from individual anthropogenic activity:

> Not only do the physical and climatic conditions of basins vary but similarly-titled impacts also take many forms. One activity is rarely performed in isolation, and the hydrological characteristics at a basin outlet are an integration of the effects of different activities operating at different scales.
>
> (Arnell, 1989a, p. 15)

Yet earlier in his review Arnell considers different orders of impact –
immediate or 'first order' and others triggered by it, for example hydrological change which evolves a hydraulic response and thence substrate,
temperature, water quality and eventually fish population changes.

The policy-maker has, therefore, some excuse for confusion: either land-
use effects are confused and overlapping or clear and the source of an
insidious chain of 'knock-on' deteriorations in the river environment.

The key to the confusion is twofold: first, land-use effects are regionally
adjusted in their impact by major variables such as climate (e.g. forests
behave differently in wet, dry and snowy climates) and second, their impact
will depend on the sensitivity of the river basin resource system considered
(e.g. in relation to the degree of control on basin behaviour already exerted
by climate and water management).

Hydrologists have been slow to make their findings clear to policy-
makers; it is not just a case of there being few appropriate laws or institutions to bring about land/water control in most developed nations. None of
Arnell's authors puts their reports of hydrological experiments in the context of policy, though the report from Germany at least begins with a tabu-
lation of national land-use categories and recent rates of change. With the
exceptions of Australia and New Zealand, the choice of research catchments as far back as the launch of the IHD in 1965 was without reference
to the potential use of results in a policy context.

A typical outcome of the neglect of policy links in the UK is the retrospective multivariate analysis of over 300 research catchments in which
acidification has been studied (Bull and Hall, 1989). This study groups
the catchments statistically so that six groups are linked for future data
collection programmes.

Whilst Arnell's authors report as scientists to a scientific peer group in
UNESCO, those contributing to Solbé's (1986) volume, whilst also scientists, reflect far more the results of the relationship with policy (i.e. power)
described by Collingridge and Reeve (Section 8.3). They also contain a high
proportion of applied scientists, engineers and managers. Thus, under
urbanisation, we read of tests of control structures (Coombes; Hellawell
and Green). Hamerton lists the Acts of Parliament relevant to his water
quality study, Howells and Marriman list legal difficulties as well as
chemical determinands and Worthington seeks regulatory remedies to halt
farm pollution.

Interestingly this largely British book contains 'the farmer's view' as a
chapter whilst the contribution by Phillips suggests that better engineering
will clean up rivers draining farming regions. A similar theme of 'managing
through' is set by British contributions on the (deleterious) effects of conifer
afforestation (chapters by Binns and by Mills).

In complete contrast, chapters from the USA on farm pollution control
(Konrad, Baumann and Ott) and forest management (Ponce) are much

more prescriptive and describe rational policy structures reflecting the impact of those activities on river basin management.

Clearly Solbé's collection is of more direct use to policy-making and equally clearly contains controversies and contradictions of exactly the type predicted by Collingridge and Reeve for work produced in a policy context. Possibly the knowledge base for river basin management is destined to remain divided into a set of concentric rings around the core of policy implementation.

8.9 THE STRUCTURE OF IMPLEMENTATION: BRITISH EXAMPLES

There are two essential prerequisites of policy information before investigating the uptake of hydrological guidance in land use and land management in Britain.

(a) Land use policy is not achieved directly but by market interventions for produce.
(b) Outside towns there is little land-use planning, exceptions being national parks and land for nature conservation.

Thus, in a sense, the UK cannot use hydrological advice except and unless the government forestry and agriculture agencies take action (mainly fiscal action via grant control) or the planning process for towns incorporates the professional guidance of water managers. Movement is now brisk on both fronts and this brief review explores the factors which lie behind recent policy developments (see also Newson, 1988, 1990).

If precedence were a principle and land allocation a policy in the British uplands, the arrival of water-gathering in the uplands during the Victorian era of public health improvement would give the modern water industry a powerful say in the allocation of land for commercial coniferous forestry, a need which has largely arisen since the creation by government of the Forestry Commission in 1919. Two major inconsistencies in the attitude to land use taken by the water industry itself, however, spoil this simple argument. First, British water engineers and scientists are not accustomed to invoking catchment area processes to explain river dynamics. Second, and more specifically, for at least forty years the water industry gave a cautious welcome to conifer plantations on catchment areas. Newson (1986) reviews the history of attitudes within the water industry and how research results, principally those of Law (1956), eventually impinged on decision-making.

Prefacing the 'era of trees on catchments', the Gathering Grounds Committee (Ministry of Health, 1948) decided that whilst trees did not attract rainfall they did protect upland reservoir catchments against erosion. The Committee reached this conclusion on the basis of a trawl of the qualitative opinions of experts, much of the information coming from abroad. Much of it was inappropriate but several well-known reservoirs became surrounded by conifers in an effort to blanket them off from human and livestock influences.

Thirty years ago Frank Law's (1956) studies at Stocks Reservoir were to preface (with great accuracy, as we now appreciate) the era of a presumption against upland catchment afforestation by water engineers – especially by those like Law himself – who managed direct-supply reservoirs in regions of growing water demand. His simple translation of the scientific results into an economic equation for forest rentals brought opprobrium on his science from those whose real objection was to the naïvety of the economics. Law argued for a £200 per acre rental to be charged by the water industry for conifer forests (compared to an existing £0.125 per acre) as compensation to allow new water storage reservoirs to be built: forests, he concluded, increased the evaporative loss of water very seriously indeed.

Law's results, which 'proved' that trees 'use' more water than rough moorland, did not lead to a change of policy but to an intensification of research. Indeed there was no public policy to change, catchment area land use being mainly decided by individual water suppliers, who desired to own whole catchment areas in order to prevent public access and agricultural improvement.

A chronology of events surrounding a second phase of the conflict in the late 1970s points up further salient features of the relationship between publication of research results and the development of public policy. In September 1977 the Centre for Agricultural Strategy (CAS) at the University of Reading held a symposium on 'The Future of Upland Britain' (Tranter, 1978). Water resources topics provided 10 per cent of the input to this potentially influential forum. Only the contribution from Devenay (1978) mentioned land use conflict with forestry, 'because afforestation reduces runoff which in turn affects the water supplied by a given reservoir or intake'. Baldwin (1978) contributed the opposite view: 'The Forestry Commission strives continuously to increase afforestation in upland Britain. In the author's opinion this activity is wholly beneficial to water supplies interests'. Shearer (1978) was even deferential to forestry, writing of the proposal to create the Kielder Reservoir that, 'the land is heavily wooded with conifer ... the Forestry Commission ... do not object to the proposal'. The symposium took the view, therefore, that forestry and water were compatible harvests from our bleak uplands.

In 1979 the results of the important Plynlimon (mid-Wales) catchment experiments were published, confirming and extending Law's adverse conclusions about the reduction of water yields when the uplands are covered by mature conifer plantations (Calder and Newson, 1979). The lesson of the criticism heaped upon Law's work by foresters was further confirmed at the 1979 Royal Scottish Geographical Society's meeting on land use in Scotland, which concluded that hydrology must be mindful of the unique nature of those land-use and land management issues upon which its science impinges.

In the late 1970s the outlook for timber production (Forestry Commission, 1979) suggested that Scotland would bear the brunt of new planting. Already the Scottish local councils and hydro-electric boards were identifying local hydrological problems in connection with afforestation. Since research results were not available in Britain on the effects of a 'natural' vegetation dominated by heather or of frequent snowfall (both conditions likely to make Scottish afforestation unique in its hydrological effect), the Institute of Hydrology set up a paired catchment study on the Plynlimon model at Balquhidder, Perthshire. Work began in 1980.

As can be gathered from Figure 8.6a, by now the water quality dimension was becoming much more important to water industry perceptions of land use and land management (see Youngman and Lack, 1981). Issues not strictly related to water supply, such as fisheries, also began to surface (Harriman, 1978) and none of these research results was favourable to forestry.

The last ten years have brought further research results which sustain a critical attitude by the water industry to proposals for upland afforestation, principally on the grounds of erosion, acidification and discoloration. They have also brought several changes of the context in which land use policy can utilise these research results:

(a) Many upland plantations have reached the stage of harvesting; research results are only slowly emerging on the hydrological effects of this and therefore the water industry is only now able to take a 'whole cycle' attitude to the timber crop.

(b) The water industry in the UK is beginning to take on a much broader environmental remit to include a heavier emphasis on water quality throughout drainage basins, and care of the amenity, recreation and conservation aspects of rivers. Afforestation proposals at various scales have recently been made for lowland areas as an alternative use for agricultural land; the issue itself is now broader.

(c) Legislative support for land-use control in the UK has grown, principally in other contexts (e.g. to reduce nitrate pollution from agriculture). It is now possible to consider protection zones and environmental quality standards (for certain pollutants). In addition, and in contrast, voluntary guidelines for foresters have been published to reduce conflict. These standards (Forestry Commission, 1988, 1991) are used directly by the Commission but also indirectly in the Commission's judgements on the suitability of applications by private forestry for government grants. They are also likely to be used by forest developers facing the new legal requirement in the UK for an environmental assessment on new plantations larger than 200 ha.

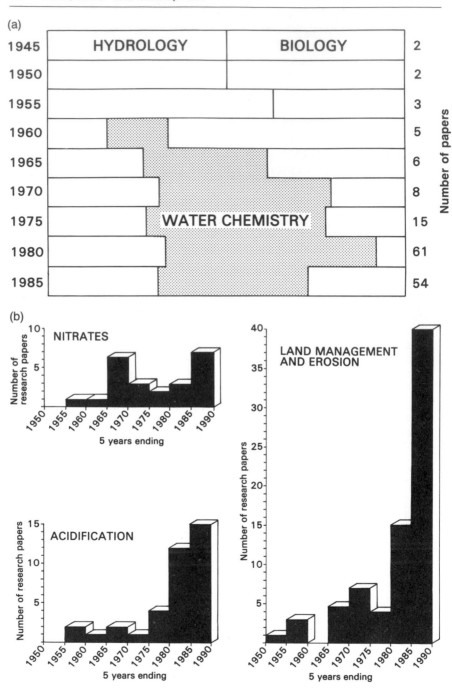

Figure 8.6 Continuing problems of basin land use control:
(a) Rise of water chemistry in the scientific literature
(b) Patterns of literature in the UK for nitrates, acidity and soil erosion

It is useful to maintain and develop the dichotomy between issues of land allocation and issues capable of resolution through existing legal or technical fixes, allowing a harvest of both water and timber from the same land in the uplands; we may set up two scenarios for decision-making:

(a) The *allocation* option, whereby a 'keep-off' attitude to catchment areas may be followed by the water industry, armed with maps of sensitive areas. A refinement of this approach might be to plan catchment land use rationally on the basis of land capability assessments and hydrological predictions. This approach is likely to flourish if *catchment planning* becomes a major policy plank of the National Rivers Authority.
(b) The *accommodation* option, whereby land is allocated by a combination of 'free' market forces and a technical dialogue between the forest and water industries. Both water and timber are harvested from the same land but both industries accept that higher costs may be involved, e.g. for greater care in preparing ground for afforestation, for leaving large strips of land unplanted or for higher levels of water treatment from upland sources.

In practice a third, 'middle way' is more likely, the precise balance between options being determined by local factors, not the least of which is pressure from outside interests using their own formal or informal means of applying pressure, e.g. conservation and recreation. The 'middle way' is also more likely because water quality issues now dominate the debate and because the debate is going on in the UK. Enforcement of environmental pollution laws and directives in the UK is an exercise in the art of the possible. Thus 'keep off' attitudes will only prevail for very sensitive sites or for persistent and, if it can be proved, deliberate contributions to the deterioration of upland water quality.

The salient features of the present state of the upland management debate indicate that at the stage where there is no policy, for example on rural land-use planning, there will be considerable rejection of research results. O'Riordan (1976) suggests that 'Where problems pose solutions which challenge the dominant values and rules of political consensus, substantial power may be directed simply at keeping this challenge out of the political arena'. Under such circumstances the researcher may well feel jealous of the effect evoked by qualitative rather than quantitative evidence, such as in the case of the high impact of the conservation lobby in the uplands (see publications by Nature Conservancy Council [1986] and Tomkins [1986]). O'Riordan (1976) finds society's fears of rationality predictable; as a direct result, 'policy making is basically a political process'.

At a second stage one can detect that society 'feels a policy coming on'. Hydrologists may well feel resentment that moves towards policy will be led by other issues, principally nature conservation and agricultural production. Thus, once again, numerical inputs to a rational model for land use are swept aside by fiscal, social and even ideological considerations. In the uplands the activities of single-interest agencies clearly need to become broadened and coordinated whilst the value of land is manipulated to achieve some form of planning. Roome (1984) concludes that there must be 'fundamental change to the distribution of rights, whether voluntarily accepted or legally enforced'. Clearly we are some distance now, both conceptually and methodologically, from the interception of rainfall!

Even if public policy in the UK embraces the precautionary principle, there is clearly a continuing need for research to reflect forest effects at different scales, parts of the crop cycle, regional conditions, namely:

(a) To continue to research the hydrological and water quality effects of timber harvesting, including, for example, the effects of whole-tree harvesting on nutrient yields.
(b) To research the hydrological and water quality effects of lowland and hardwood forests, particularly in England where there is now a severe policy restriction on upland conifer plantations.
(c) To research the success of the 'riparian policy'; can buffer strips really solve most of our problems?

The policy arena additionally suggests, however, other urgent needs:

(d) To research the scale of forestry effects on river basins and the importance of location of land-use change within larger basins (physical science is well served by small-scale experiments, but society is not!).
(e) To incorporate the geographical variation of causative variables and the link to effects which may invalidate certain of our current 'universal truths' about forest hydrology; it is a regional science but is still being practised at a local scale. Compilations and extrapolations after the fashion of Calder and Newson (1979) are now required on a much greater range of water quality and environmental topics and at a much greater level of sophistication (computers, geographical information systems, etc. provide the technology).
(f) To research further the tolerances of the aquatic environment to those parameters of flow and water quality known to be influenced at each stage of the forest cycle. Such research would enable a more credible approach to policy procedures which might set environmental objectives (or standards if the need arose). Chemical assessment techniques may well need to be subordinated to multivariate biological indicators.

Figure 8.6b suggests that if an 'issue-attention cycle' exists for catchment land use it has not yet begun to subside, judged by the publication in the UK of scientific books and papers.

8.10   CONCLUSIONS: INTERVENING IN LAND – A POLITICAL TEST OF KNOWLEDGE

The author well remembers the chill realisation that his work was politically unrecognised and, perhaps, unknown to an otherwise successful politician (see Section 8.3). We may conclude that the location of the research effort within water management, the degree to which it is funded and the degree to which it is 'controlled' (towards practical answers) is a critical aspect of the ideals of this book. If we wish for 'hydrologic civilisation', hydrology must be done, well done and exposed to political scrutiny. As many scientists would conclude, this requires an educational movement amongst politicians; many of the conclusions from hydrological research are as difficult to comprehend by politicians as 'sustainable development'. In other words, whilst spectacular results may convince the politician they are seldom forthcoming; instead hydrology tends to produce 'depth charges' or a 'delayed fuse' when it comes to impact.

Because hydrology is a regional science, results often differ between research sites – notably true of forest hydrology (Newson and Calder, 1989). A far larger problem is that land-use influences are apparently subordinate to climatic change in gross effect on rivers. The scientific agenda is moving strongly to changing environments at present and away from man-made manipulations. However, the polluting effects of unwise land use are well known, as is the conservation loss produced by some forms of catchment 'abuse'. In addition, catchment land use or management can be used to mitigate the effects of climate change – but the processes involved must be understood and deployed.

The lessons are surely that hydrologists must start with policy in mind; just as engineering hydrology was adjusted to the service of society, so

Table 8.2 Linking small-area research to large-area application

Methods of extrapolation[a]	Methods of incorporation[a]
1 Replication of research in other environments	1 Education – broad approach
2 Pooling data from individual research efforts; synthesis	2 Technical education of practitioners – 'good practice'
3 Use of geographical predictions	3 Fiscal manipulation of land-use financial support
4 Mathematical modelling of processes	4 Proscription of damaging operations (plus prescription of beneficial ones)
5 Natural 'demonstration' of effect – hazardous event	5 Protection zones → whole-basin planning

[a] Whilst the columns do not cross-correlate, they both represent an ascending sequence of demonstration and action.

environmental hydrology must agree a certain subordination to human needs. It must anticipate needs. For example, at the time of writing it would seem obvious to put more effort into groundwater research since, during periods of environmental change, the groundwater store provides continuity and survival.

Finally, as Table 8.2 shows, there must be a continuing research field which attempts to link the outputs of research from small catchments to devices and structures which control the processes of accommodation or allocation in large basins.

Chapter 9

Land and water

Towards systems of management in a period of change

9.1 FUTURE OF THE RIVER BASIN IDEA

This book follows in the footsteps of a Geography text, *Water, Earth and Man* (Chorley, 1969), which brought together authors from the physical science, social science and humanities areas of Geography to set down what were at that stage separate agenda items, components of an integrated approach to river basins. In the final chapter of *Water, Earth and Man*, O'Riordan and More (1969) describe the power of two technical innovations, sophisticated resource economics and dynamic physical modelling, in bringing about integrated and adaptive management. Their words were written at a time when geographers were fascinated by quantification and at the beginning of the 'New Environmental Age' (environmental issues and policies have arguably done much to frustrate the simple positivist views of economists and modellers). However, they presaged one of the important tensions in the development of water resources which endures to this day:

> Thus, whereas the vehicles of water-resources planning are becoming more massive and complex, the requirement for their manoeuvrability is also increasing, and the aim of all future planning is to produce a large-scale and completely integrated scheme capable of constant re-evaluation.
>
> (O'Riordan and More, 1969, p. 572)

Without super-human foresight the authors could not have judged how great the need for manoeuvrability might become; for example, in 1969 climatic change was being written of but was mainly played down by official agencies. *Water, Earth and Man* was published four years before Schumacher (1973) brought out *Small is Beautiful*, a herald call to a generation to begin thinking in terms of the organisation of human society in units which its members understand and can practically manage with low technologies. Nevertheless, O'Riordan and More are concerned with the institutional aspects of river basin management and list eight constraints facing the decision-maker: physical, fiscal, policy, legal, administrative, ownership, quantification and perception. The word 'environmental' is missing from the list; we might now use it instead of 'physical'.

The river basin idea, therefore, needs modifications to take it beyond that of an academically justifiable unit within which geographers work. Scale problems are particularly acute when operationalising the concept; O'Riordan and More seem pleased with the notion of large-scale river basin schemes because they break the mould of short-term engineering solutions to point problems. However, new thinking on environmental issues, on the role of those affected in decision-making and on the need for sustainable, long-lasting options illustrates in 1991 the need for an emphasis on flexibility; 'you need to give the project away' said one engineer ruefully of public consultation! We must not allow ourselves the illusion that technology transfer will achieve the uniformity in river basin management that has been achieved in the appearance of airport lounges! A scheme which will be successful for the River Tyne will not work well on the Nile, and one which works for the Nile (solutions are urgently needed – see Chapter 5) would not be appropriate for the Ganges.

The reasons for this inherent geographical variability of options for river basin management include:

(a) Differences in scale. In successful river basin management the flow of information is critical (see below) and so scale does not merely become a boundary condition to physical and chemical processes in rivers but a central institutional issue. One of the critical contrasts between the Tyne and the Nile is the presence of nine national boundaries in the latter river's basin.

(b) Differences in trajectory. Here we may include changes through time in water needs, the development process, climatic controls and political controls. Successful river basin management will be the result of considering a range of options to suit the often unique combination of these variables for each basin, though admittedly there will be some basins in which the water stress is so great that emergency, monolithic action is considered essential.

The practical future of the river basin unit as one in which environmental management is practised therefore might be summed up in the word 'interactive', implying built-in operational responses to changing conditions and a carefully planned consultation phase before the management algorithm is applied in the first place. There is a considerable challenge for the application of new technology in both components of interaction; it is wrong to assume that the humanistic connotations of adaptability and consultation force us into the Schumacher mould (though in many river basins they will guide us into it!).

9.2   THE MUTUAL CONSIDERATION OF LAND WITH WATER

One of the major commendations for a river basin approach to water resource issues is that land resources are considered conjunctively with water resources, whether the approach taken by water technology is essentially distributive (major irrigation or power schemes) or collective (runoff management and pollution control). It is easy, however, to move from the fact that 98 per cent of rainfall passes over or through land on its way to the river (Chapter 3) to an assumption that land use and management is axiomatic to those who set up water schemes, even where their chosen scale is the river basin.

A major problem here is that of ownership and the history of land use and management; water agencies seldom own land in the river basin and therefore have only indirect controls. We may, in fact, divide the routes for influence over land into 'catchment control' and 'catchment planning' (Newson, 1991). Control implies ownership or legislative circumscription of land use (e.g. South Africa's Mountain Catchment Areas Act, which allows direct intervention in catchments vital to water conservation) whilst planning describes the consultative indirect manipulation of land management rather than land use. The water interest is sometimes weak, entering the land political ring late, and therefore needs to accommodate to existing patterns in the basin; where it has entered early it has earned a poor reputation for land planning of its own holdings (e.g. careless afforestation, disruption of traditional land rights, salinised irrigation fields, etc.).

Of more direct importance to the theme of this book, however, is that land issues, whilst all-pervasive and conceptually logical, have many rivals in the perception of water managers interested in the degree of control exercised by all the relevant variables in the river basin environment. Thus land use and management may mean little in some basins compared with tectonic activity (e.g. the Ganges – see Chapter 5); in others climate changes are the main concern. In yet others only urban land use may be important and so the problem of conjunctive management of resources is contained within a small area of point pollution controls or flood runoff detention.

Land use and management therefore has rivals for the attention of river managers, including the strongest of all, namely the influence of river regulation in bringing about fundamental changes to the flow and water quality patterns of up to two-thirds of the flow of world rivers (Chapter 6). This immediately facilitates the traditional engineering approach to river management in which manipulation, 'training' and other interventionist, structural measures come to be preferred because of the degree and certainty of control they offer.

In terms of catchment management we have, to date, been able to advocate 'suitable' land uses for river basin management and in some cases national planning has concurred, although not at a very large scale. We have been much less successful, however, at removing 'unsuitable' land uses. Nevertheless there are many signs that, for small and *sensitive areas* (both whole catchments and riparian zones of all rivers), there is a tendency for the indirect, non-structural approach to be gaining momentum. This book has been written at a time when public concern for the prevention of pollution is being rapidly translated into schemes of monitoring and control; it is apparent, for example from the Nitrate Sensitive Areas of the UK, that land issues (including rural land uses) will not gain greater prominence in basin management (Newson, 1991). In countries undergoing rapid development and embarking on major water schemes it should not be beyond our wit to warn that a concern for supplies, power, crops and other water benefits bespeaks a relatively rapid (140 years in the UK) transition to the hygienic and then ecological concerns of an urbanised population.

9.3 LAND, WATER AND DEVELOPMENT

Development continues. Some 'green' politicians are against it; many have stressed the need to make it sustainable. Because of its continuity, albeit at different rates and taking different forms, it is tempting to say that the problems faced by those developing river basin resources in a 'developing country' are no different to those in a 'developed country'. There are good reasons, discussed below, for looking for common institutional problems (see also Chapter 7) but at the outset we may illustrate some typical differences brought about by the physical environment of 'typical situations' – see Figure 9.1.

Chapter 5 emphasises that problems of water development in the developing world surround:

(a) The least developed countries.
(b) The drylands and their wetter hinterlands, often mountains.
(c) Major international river basins.
(d) Inter- and intra-national political tension.
(e) Institutional problems of integration and application.

These problems are shown in Figure 9.1(a).

In the developed world, outside drylands (which makes the case of the USA's drylands so intriguing) we have the following problems, shown in Figure 9.1(b):

(a) Pollution controls permissive to further development.
(b) Hazard management.
(c) Recreational and conservational priorities.
(d) Problems of inadequate data; decisions must appear rational.
(e) Institutional problems of integration and planning.

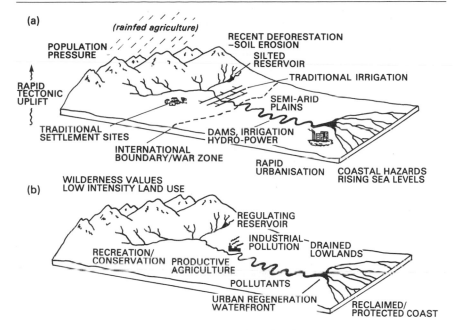

Figure 9.1 Cartoon river basins summarising the development and
management problems of:
(a) A developing tropical/semi-arid basin
(b) A developed humid–temperate basin

Covergence in the last two items of each list is deliberate, despite the
dangers to a physical scientist of admitting that the common thread is
social! However, since integration, planning and application issues are
genuinely interdisciplinary the physical scientist has a right, even a duty, to
intervene. This author does so from a background of considerable disap-
pointment at the institutional rejection of certain of his own research contributions, the result of a previously ingenuous attitude to the practicalities
of applying knowledge. The real issue, therefore, of sustainable river basin
management, wherever it is required, is that of the application of
knowledge.

9.4   TECHNOCRACY AND DEMOCRACY: PLANNING AND PEOPLE

The horns of the river basin dilemma are as follows. As soon as one leaves
the realms of traditional, local environmental management of the water
resource or hazard, i.e. when one embarks on development, there is an
immediate need for technology and for experts. Society, if it identifies with
the project, supports the experts; in the hydraulic civilisations their power

was considerable and society was structured around the need to achieve the goals of development. Whilst environmental scientists, including hydrologists, enjoy considerably less certainty in their technology they need the support of society for their agenda by that anticipation or reclamation (see Section 9.5).

Environmental science is highly technical and its proponents find it no easier to communicate simply with those affected by their proposals than their specialist, reductionist colleagues and forebears; there are, however, signs of increasing freedom of environmental information and an increasing effort by specialists and their institutions to provide environmental education. The bridging of the information gulf is essential to the acceptance by those affected by river basin management of the schemes its technologists employ. We cannot dispense with the pure scientist, nor with the engineer. The engineering discipline has dominated water development and basin management throughout history (de Camp, 1990); its support has been tacit because its achievements have been spectacular. However, engineers in particular need to explore a new relationship with people and the education and training of engineers should emphasise this. As Kirpich (1990) remarks: 'the poor performance of engineers in management results to a considerable degree from inadequate education requirements, i.e. insufficient attention to non-engineering but pertinent subjects such as economics, sociology and business management' (p. 846). Most geographers would want another subject added to the list and the present author has often mused on the valency of two disciplines which at first appear to compete on issues of depth and breadth!

It is, of course, also a duty for the rest of us to understand the position of the *engineer in society* (a compulsory paper in the qualification procedure for UK Civil Engineers). As Cosgrove (1990) has stressed, 'the need for visionary engineering is still with us' (p. 11). Society must realise that, outside the prison of its reliable, practical reputation, engineering is speculative and as open to flair and passion as the arts. The world became modernised by engineers and water engineering is often the hallmark of the process. This progress represented an amalgam of engineering skill and the support of society; there is no reason at all why the same combination cannot achieve the new agenda items of environmental management.

Consultation over river basin management may be inevitable but it should also be formal; it is a particularly dangerous assumption by environmentalists that consultation does not need rules! Protest movements can often set their own rules, but for an official agency to consult widely needs the formality of the emerging field of *conciliation* (see Chapter 7).

Furthermore, it should not be assumed that consultation is possible under all political conditions. This is a particular difficulty in the politics of development. Nations undergoing rapid development are often one-party states with major regional problems of opposition, even civil war. The

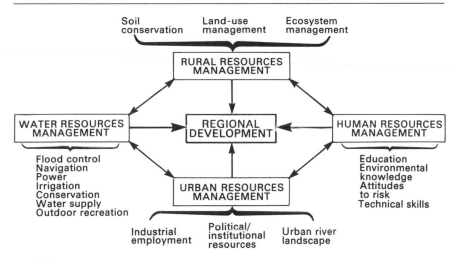

Figure 9.2 The complex of projects involved in river basin development

consultation process also, of course, needs the information to supply from the technocratic to the democratic process or body. As Chapter 5 shows, research agendas need to change to respect the eventual use of the information which is gained. Important here is the need for truly interdisciplinary research activity.

The whole system may be considered, as in Figure 9.2, as a complex of resources, including rural, urban, water and human resources, each requiring management and impact assessment.

9.5 ANTICIPATION AND RESTORATION: A PRACTICAL AGENDA

Environmental Impact Assessment (EIA, or simply EA) has been mentioned frequently in this book, both in a positive and in a negative vein. It is far too early to pronounce EA procedures a success or a failure; they were introduced in 1969 in the USA, from the same stable as an earlier litmus test for development: cost-benefit analysis. Ingram (1990) concludes that the National Environmental Protection Act (NEPA) which established the legal need for EA rang the death knell of the large water project in the USA. The addition of EA to project evaluation by the World Bank (in March 1989) may have a similar effect on developing world schemes; the United Nations Environment Programme (UNEP) has a programme devoted to the environmentally sound management of inland waters. EA procedures differ wherever they are applied and there is a current clamour for more uniformity, if only among technical practitioners. They are essentially conciliation procedures in which knowledge plays a very large part, if allowed to and if available. Ingram cites the cost of achieving the knowledge for EA as one nail in the coffin of US water development.

There are also humanistic issues in the use of EA; like its simpler predecessor, cost-benefit analysis, it can be used as an alternative to true consultation and may be equally unable to include local factors and values (see Sagoff, 1989). In polarised cases there must be considerable room for the triumph of passion over knowledge as Petts (1990) hints:

> decisions on new water projects will continue to be made without adequate baseline data. Arguably the existence of an undisturbed river valley should be cause enough to guarantee its protection from development, at least until such baseline data are available.
>
> (Petts, 1990, pp. 199–200)

A further, more technical problem with river basin EA is that in river basin management long timescales are essential; Chapter 2 drives home a message from the basic physical science of river systems – geomorphology – that the longer view is essential for basic stability and that stability is a steady state, not equilibrium. Predictions of future changes in the river transport system are extremely difficult to make, especially under conditions of climatic change; the best way in which EA processes can respond is by building in monitoring and evaluation procedures where doubt is honestly expressed in the scientific evidence.

Antle (1983) has suggested that *post hoc* impact analyses will always be necessary in order to refine the process of forward planning in water development, though an intractable element of such analysis is the 'what if not?' question (i.e. what would have happened had not the scheme been built?).

Whilst, in 1978, Kalbermatten and Gunnerson were able to describe EA as exhibiting 'newness and unfamiliarity', they nevertheless prescribe two aspects of the procedure which are still relevant to the success of the principle:

(a) Public involvement and participation is essential to a project's success.
(b) Environmental constraints constitute performance standards.

However, by 1985, Canter's annotated bibliography of published environmental impact analyses (formal and informal) reveals that only 10 per cent were connected with baseline studies or indicators of environmental viability; a similar proportion were relevant to public participation and decision-making, but not at a scale relevant to major international problems of river basin development, nor to the conjunctive consideration of land and water. Only very recently have formal, technical procedures such as decision support modelling been brought to bear on the problem of EA for large international rivers (e.g. Kovacs, 1990; Hartmann, 1990). These authors use techniques such as database management, impact modelling and decision algorithms as a means of producing a flexible-scale and interactive procedure for cross-disciplinary exploration of options.

River restoration has a short history (Gore, 1985) but is experiencing a steep growth curve. Restoration capitalises on the innate ability of fresh-water biotic systems to recover from damage; Gore labels it recovery enhancement. The indirect methods of restoration include, obviously, restoration of hydrological stability and the improvement of water quality but direct methods are becoming prominent too: instream habitat structures and management of the riparian zone. Restoration is largely successful because it:

(a) Involves a committed professional and public approach.
(b) Uses a systems approach, tackling quite extensive reaches.
(c) Is feasible in terms of land-take and therefore of ownership and control.

The latter point is critical in river basins where ownership confers rights, simply because water agencies, conservation and amenity agencies have very little ownership of land. The valley floor cross-section shown in Figure 2.8 represents a policy agenda for extending restoration campaigns from the open flow channel to the catchment as a whole (this agenda has its spatial implications and controlling functions depicted in Figure 9.3).

Widespread public involvement is also critical to restoration; there are now a number of metropolitan restoration schemes in the UK motivated either by those who in increasing numbers live in waterfront locations taken up by developers as part of civic regeneration schemes or by those who are seeking to improve riverside amenity or conservation. The most

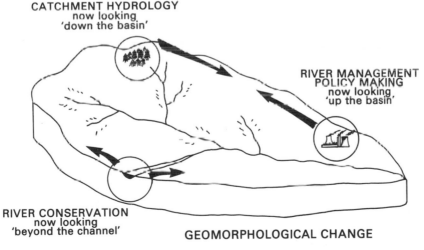

CATCHMENT HYDROLOGY
now looking
'down the basin'

RIVER MANAGEMENT
POLICY MAKING
now looking
'up the basin'

RIVER CONSERVATION
now looking
'beyond the channel'

GEOMORPHOLOGICAL CHANGE

Figure 9.3 The extensification of professional interests in the river basin

comprehensive restoration scheme is that for the Mersey Basin; because it takes the basin approach it is multi-agency as well as public (through the voluntary sector). Having spent half a billion pounds on structural improvements during the 1980s the water authorities, local authorities and Shell UK have now come together to make the improvements sustainable; special posts include a 'Waterwatch Officer' and there are joint committees with executive power over interagency action (Mersey Basin Campaign, 1988).

9.6 CATCHMENTS, BASINS, CORRIDORS AND VALLEYS: A FINAL NOTE ON SCALE

I have frequently claimed in this book that the river basin concept has been promoted mainly by geographers; however the topic of stream restoration introduces the very important, hitherto latent role of the biologist. Academic biologists have for many years stressed the continuity of the river basin system (e.g. Hynes, 1975; Vannote *et al.*, 1980); issues of conservation and restoration have brought biologists and fluvial geomorphologists together, if not in research programmes on contentious sites. Their contribution is particularly noteworthy, for example, in the new journal *Regulated Rivers: Research and Management*. Biologists have achieved many of the senior posts in the reorganised water industry in England and Wales. Biological assessment of water quality standards is becoming formally incorporated in UK monitoring systems. Definitions of land-take for conservation of wetlands are increasingly 'bullish', particularly as doubts are raised by economists and politicians about the validity of production-orientated farming. Figure 9.3 emphasises the extensification of interest in land/water issues inherent in the debate which now often centres on holistic biology and political conservation (Newson, 1992 [a]).

Petersen *et al.* (1987) first pointed out to river managers the centrality of the riparian zone; huge costs involved with river purification can be saved by what the authors call a 'holistic, ecosystem approach' in which the first goal is not catchment control but riparian control. In many countries of Europe stream restoration is now associated with the achievement of water quality objectives and, where relevant, compliance with EC legislation – a fusion of idealistic conservation and hard-nosed economics. In Denmark, for example, formerly straightened streams are being 're-meandered' and *buffer strips*, akin to those used in US forestry activities (Chapter 4), are legally applied to prevent soil erosion and nutrient leaching from polluting streams. Germany, the Netherlands and Denmark are close behind. Petersen and colleagues set down five principles of 'repeated patterns of stream management':

(a) Watershed management is the goal, riparian control the starting point.

(b) The riparian zone is the important interface between the terrestrial and stream ecosystem.
(c) Short-term events may be far more damaging than average conditions.
(d) Good management requires holistic approaches.
(e) Some stream management problems are the result of global environmental problems.

The final point will inevitably be borne out by events in the next decade. Predictions by the United Nations for AD 2000 (UN, 1990) make depressing reading for water managers in some regions:

> In North Africa and the Middle East ... meeting the expected demands by the year 2000 could require virtually all of their usable fresh-water supplies

but

> contamination of water supplies is posing health risks and is drastically increasing the cost of water treatment facilities. Polluted inland water bodies and seas are reducing the productivity of fisheries ... Polluted irrigation water poses health risks, undermines long-term crop productivity, and degrades the recreational use and aesthetic aspects of surface water.
>
> (UN, 1990, pp. 89, 90)

Here, then, is an obvious point for technology transfer. If a practical agenda of riparian control can be introduced as part of developed-world stream restoration projects it can be introduced as part of international environmental management for those 200 major river basins whose boundaries cross national boundaries, including the 'water crisis' zone.

Petersen (in press) has now developed a management sequence for the riparian zone, effectively the valley floor:

(a) Buffer strips.
(b) Revegetation (natural cf agricultural species).
(c) Horseshoe wetlands (where productive agriculture discharges drainage waters to the valley floor).
(d) Reduction of channel bank slopes to reduce erosion.
(e) Restoration of meanders.
(f) Restoration of riffle/pool sequences in channels.
(g) Restoration of wetland valley floors and swamp forests.

The future is one of great interest. It represents, as I have stressed, a pattern of the application of knowledge within an increasingly public context. The compromise will exist between two extremes, the traditional one of water power, as quoted by Ingram (1990):

> Water still symbolizes such values as opportunity, security and self-determination. Water represents these values less because the water itself

has economic value than because control over it signals social organiz-ation and political power ... Strong communities are able to hold on to their water and put it to work.

(Ingram, 1990, p. 5)

and the new context of crisis and opportunity provided by water as an element of our natural environment for which we require sustainable management strategies, compliance with which will depend on public acceptability. The slogan 'think globally, act locally' is by no means irrelevant. Whilst this book has tried to tease out the generalities for students and practitioners worldwide, the final word must go to the particular, as enunciated by Kenneth Grahame's Mole and Rat:

You must think me very rude; but all this is so new to me. So − this − is − a − River!'

'*The* River', corrected the Rat.

(from *The Wind in the Willows*, 1908, which
first inclined the ear of the author to the gurgle
and slap of a 'proper' river)

Bibliography

Abracosa, R. and Ortolano, L. (1988) 'Lessons from EIA for bicol river development in Philippines', *Journal of Water Resource Planning and Management*, Proceedings of the American Society of Civil Engineers, 114(5), 517–29.

Adams, W. M. (1985) 'River basin planning in Nigeria', *Applied Geography*, 5, 297–308.

Agarwal, A., Kimondo, J., Moreno, G., and Tinker, J. (1980) *Water, Sanitation, Health – For All? Prospects for the International Drinking Water Supply and Sanitation Decade, 1981–90*. Earthscan, London and Washington.

Alabaster, J. S. (1972) 'Suspended solids and fisheries', *Proceedings of the Royal Society of London, Series B*, 180, 395–406.

Al-Ibrahim, A. A. (1991) 'Excessive use of groundwater resources in Saudi Arabia: impacts and policy options', *Ambio*, 20(1), 34–7.

Alvares, C. and Billorey, R. (1988) *Damming the Narmada: India's Greatest Planned Environmental Disaster*. Third World Network/Appen, Penang, Malaysia.

Amerman, C. R. (1965) 'The use of unit-source watershed data for runoff prediction', *Water Resources Research*, 1, 499–507.

Amoros, C., Roux, A. L., Raygrobellet, J. L., Brayard, J. P., and Paton, G. (1987) 'A method for applied ecological studies of fluvial hydrosystems', *Regulated Rivers: Research and Management*, 1 (1), 17–36.

Amphlett, M. B. (1990) 'A field study to assess the benefits of land husbandry in Malawi', in J. Boardman, I. D. L. Foster and J. A. Dearing (eds) *Soil Erosion on Agricultural Land*, Wiley, Chichester, 575–88.

Antle, L. G. (1983) 'Evaluation of completed projects: why is it necessary?', in G. G. Green and E. E. Eiker (eds) *Accomplishments and Impacts of Reservoirs*. American Society of Civil Engineers, New York, 6–19.

Arnell, N. (1989a) 'The influence of human activities on hydrological characteristics: an introduction', in N. Arnell (ed.) *Human Influences on Hydrological Behaviour: an International Literature Survey*. UNESCO, Paris, 1–18.

Arnell, N. (ed.) (1989b) *Human Influences on Hydrological Behaviour: an International Literature Survey*. UNESCO, Paris.

ASCE (1988a) *Evaluation Procedures for Hydrologic Safety of Dams*. American Society of Civil Engineers, New York.

ASCE (1988b) *Lessons from Dam Incidents USA II*. American Society of Civil Engineers, New York.

Ashby, E. (1978) *Reconciling Man with the Environment*, Oxford University Press, Oxford.

Ashworth, P. J. and Ferguson, R. I. (1986) 'Interrelationships of channel processes, changes and sediments in a proglacial braided river', *Geografiska Annale*, 68A, 361–71.

Atkinson, T. C. (1978) 'Techniques for measuring subsurface flow on hillslopes', in M. J. Kirkby (ed.) *Hillslope Hydrology*. Wiley, Chichester, 73–120.

Bagnold, R. A. (1977) 'Bedload transport by natural rivers', *Water Resources Research*, 13, 302–12.

Baker, D. R. (1981) *Environmental Crisis in Kenya: Social Crisis or Environmental Crisis?* DEV Discussion Paper 82, School of Development Studies, University of East Anglia, Norwich.

Baldwin, A. B. (1978) 'Quality aspects of water in upland Britain', in R. B. Tranter (ed.) *The Future of Upland Britain*. Centre for Agricultural Strategy, University of Reading, 322–7.

Barbier, E. (1991) 'Environmental degradation in the Third World', in D. Pearce (ed.) *Blueprint 2: Greening the World Economy*. Earthscan, London, 75–108.

Barney, G. O. (Study Director) (1982) *The Global 2000 Report to the President*. Penguin Books, Harmondsworth.

Barrow, C. (1987) *Water Resources and Agricultural Development in the Tropics*. Longman, Harlow.

Beauclerk, J., Narby, J., and Townsend, J. (1988) *Indigenous Peoples: a Fieldguide for Development*. Oxfam, Oxford.

Beaumont, P. (1978) 'Man's impact on river systems: a world-wide view', *Area*, 10, 38–41

Beaumont, P. (1989) *Environmental Management and Development in Drylands*. Routledge, London.

Beven, K. (1985) 'Distributed models', in M. G. Anderson and T. P. Burt (eds) *Hydrological Forecasting*. Wiley, Chichester, 405–35.

Binnie, G. M. (1981) *Early Victorian Water Engineers*. Thomas Telford, London.

Binnie, G. M. (1987) *Early Dam Builders in Britain*. Thomas Telford, London.

Binns, A. (1990) 'Is desertification a myth?', *Geography*, 75(2), 106–13.

Bissio, B. (ed.) (1988) *Third World Guide*. Third World Editors, Montevideo.

Biswas, A. K. (1967) 'Hydrologic engineering prior to 600 BC', *Proceedings of the American Society of Civil Engineers Journal, Hydraulics Division*, HY5, 118–31.

Black, P. E. (1970) 'The watershed in principle', *Water Resources Bulletin*, 6(2), 153–62.

Black, P. E. (1982) *Conservation of Water and Related Land Resources*. Praeger, Westport, CT.

Blackie, J. R. and Eeles, C. W. O. (1985) 'Lumped catchment models', in M. G. Anderson and T. P. Burt (eds) *Hydrological Forecasting*. Wiley, Chichester, 311–45.

Blaikie, P. (1985) *The Political Economy of Soil Erosion in Developing Countries*. Longman, Harlow.

Blench, T. (1952) 'Regime theory for self-formed sediment-bearing channels', *Transactions of the American Society of Civil Engineers*, 117, 383–400.

Boardman, J. (1988) 'Public policy and soil erosion in Britain', in J. M. Hooke (ed.) *Geomorphology in Environmental Planning*. Wiley, Chichester, 33–50.

Boardman, J. (1990) *Soil Erosion in Britain: Costs, Attitudes and Policies*. Social Audit Paper 1, Education Network for Environment and Development, Brighton.

Boardman, J., Dearing, J. A., and Foster, I. D. L. (1990) 'Soil erosion studies: some assessments', in J. Boardman, I. D. L. Foster and J. A. Dearing (eds) *Soil Erosion on Agricultural Land*. Wiley, Chichester, 659–72.

Boon, P. J. (1987) 'The influence of Kielder Water on Trichopteran (caddisfly) populations in the River North Tyne (northern England)', *Regulated Rivers: Research and Management*, 1, 95–109.

Bord, J. and Bord, C. (1986) *Sacred Waters: Holy Wells and Water Lore in Britain and Ireland*. Paladin, London.

Bordas, M. P. and Walling, D. E. (1988) *Sediment budgets*. International Association of Hydrological Sciences, Publication 174.

Bosch, J. M. and Hewlett, J. D. (1982) 'A review of catchment experiments to determine the effect of vegetation changes on water yield and evapotranspiration', *Journal of Hydrology*, 55, 3–23.

Bowman, J. A. (1990) 'Ground-water-management areas in United States', *Journal of Water Resources Planning and Management*, ASCE, 116(4), 484–502.

Brammer, H. (1990a) 'Floods in Bangladesh. I Geographical background to the 1987 and 1988 floods', *Geographical Journal*, 156(1), 12–22.

Brammer, H. (1990b) 'Floods in Bangladesh. II Flood mitigation and environmental aspects', *Geographical Journal*, 156(2), 158–65.

Broen, A. G. (1987) 'Long-term sediment storage in the Severn and Wye catchments', in K. J. Gregory, J. Lewin and J. B. Thornes (eds) *Palaeohydrology in Practice*, Wiley, Chichester, 307–32.

Brown, B. W. and Shelton, R. A. (1983) 'Fifty years of operation of the TVA reservoir system', in G. G. Green and E. E. Eiker (eds) *Accomplishments and Impacts of Reservoirs*. ASCE, New York, 138–51.

Bruk, S. (Rapporteur) (1985) *Methods of Computing Sedimentation in Lakes and Reservoirs*. UNESCO, Paris.

Brune, G. M. (1953) 'Trap efficiency of reservoirs', *American Geophysical Union Transactions*, 34(3), 407–17.

Bull, K. R. and Hall, J. R. (1989) *Classification and Comparison of River and Lake Catchments*. Institute of Terrestrial Ecology, Monks Wood Research Station, UK.

Bunyard, P. and Goldsmith, E. (1988) *GAIA, the Thesis, the Mechanisms and the Implications*. Wadebridge Ecological Centre, Camelford.

Burt, J. P. and Walling, D. E. (1984) 'Catchment experiments in fluvial geomorphology: a review of objectives and methodology', in T. P. Burt and D. E. Walling (eds) *Catchment Experiments in Fluvial Geomorphology*. Geo Books, Norwich, 3–18.

Burt, T. P. (1986) 'Runoff processes and solute denudation rates on humid-temperate hillslopes', in S. T. Trudgill (ed.) *Solute Processes*. Wiley, Chichester, 193–249.

Calder, I. R. (1990) *Evaporation in the Uplands*. Wiley, Chichester.

Calder, I. R. and Newson, M. D. (1979) 'Land use and upland water resources in Britain – a strategic look', *Water Resources Bulletin*, 15(6), 1628–39.

Callicott, J. B. (1987) 'The scientific substance of the land ethic', in T. Tanner (ed.) *Aldo Leopold: the Man and his Legacy*. Soil Conservation Society of America, Ankeny, IA, 87–104.

de Camp, L. S. (1990) *The Ancient Engineers*. Dorset Press, New York.

Canadian Council of Resource and Environment Ministers (1987) *Canadian Water Quality Guidelines*. Environment Canada, Montreal.

Canter, L. (1985) *Environmental Impact of Water Resources Projects*. Lewis Publishers, Chelsea, MI.

Carroll, J. E. (1988) *International Environmental diplomacy*. Cambridge University Press, Cambridge.

Carruthers, I. D. (1983) *Aid for the Development of Irrigation*. OECD, Paris.

Carson, M. A. (1984) 'The meandering-braided threshold: a reappraisal', *Journal of Hydrology*, 73, 315–34.

Central Water Planning Unit (1979) *River Regulation Losses in England and Wales.* CWPU, Reading.

Chandler, W. V. (1984) *The Myth of the TVA Conservation and Development in the Tennessee Valley, 1933–1983.* Ballinger, Cambridge, MA.

Charlton, F. C., Brown, P. M., and Benson, R. W. (1978) 'The hydraulic geometry of some gravel rivers in Britain', *Report IT180, Hydraulics Research*, Wallingford, UK.

Chauhan, S. K., Bihua, Z., Gopalakrishnan, K., Lala Rukh, H., Yeboak-Afari, A., and Leal, F. (1983) *Who Puts the Water in the Taps? Community Participation in Third World Drinking Water, Sanitation and Health.* Earthscan, London and Washington.

Chesworth, P. M. (1990) 'The history of water use in Sudan and Egypt', in P. P. Howell and J. A. Allan (eds) *The Nile.* SOAS/RGS, London, 41–58.

Chettri, R. and Bowonder, B. (1983) 'Siltation in Nizamsagar reservoir: environmental management issues', *Applied Geography*, 3, 193–204.

Chorley, R. J. (ed.) (1969) *Water, Earth and Man.* Methuen, London.

Church, M. (1984) 'On experimental method in geomorphology', in T. P. Burt and D. E. Walling (eds) *Catchment Experiments in Geomorphology.* Geo Books, Norwich, 563–80.

Collingridge, D. and Reeve, C. (1986) *Science Speaks to Power.* Francis Pinter, London.

Collins, R. O. (1990) *The Waters of the Nile, Hydropolitics and the Jonglei Canal 1900–1988.* Clarendon Press, Oxford.

Conroy, C. and Litvinoff, M. (1988) *The Greening of Aid: Sustainable Livelihoods in Practice.* Earthscan, London.

Conway, V. M. and Millar, A. (1960) 'The hydrology of some small peat covered catchments in the north Pennines', *Journal of the Institution of Water Engineers*, 14, 415–24.

Cooke, A. (1973) *America.* BBC Publications, London.

Cooke, R. U., Brunsden, D., Doornkamp, J. C., and Jones, D. K. C. (1982) *Urban Geomorphology in Drylands.* Oxford University Press, Oxford.

Cosgrove, D. (1990) 'An elemental division: water control and engineered landscape', in D. Cosgrove and G. Petts (eds) *Water, Engineering and Landscape.* Belhaven Press, London, 1–11.

da Costa, J. A. and Jacquet, J. (1965) 'Présentation des résultats de l'enquête UNESCO-AIHS sur les bassins représentatifs et expérimentaux dans le monde', *IAHS Bulletin*, X(4), 107–19.

Costa, J. E. (1988) 'Floods from dam failures', in V. R. Baker, R. C. Kochel and P. C. Patton (eds) *Flood Geomorphology.* Wiley, New York, 439–63.

Cummings, B. J. (1990) *Dam the Rivers, Damn the People.* Earthscan, London.

Dankelman, I. and Davidson, J. (1988) *Women and Environment in the Third World.* Earthscan, London.

Dallas, R. (1990) 'The agricultural collapse of the arid midwest', *Geographical Magazine* (October), 16–20.

Darby, H. C. (1983) *The Changing Fenland.* Cambridge University Press, Cambridge.

Darian, S. G. (1978) *The Ganges in Myth and History.* University of Hawaii Press, Honolulu.

Davis, W. M. (1899) 'The geographical cycle', *Geographical Journal*, 14, 481–504.

Day, J. C. (1985) 'Canadian interbasin diversions. Inquiry on Federal Water Policy', Research Paper 6, Simon Fraser University BC.

Department of the Environment (1988) *Privatisation of the Water Authorities in England and Wales*, Cmnd 9734. HMSO, London.

Department of the Environment/Welsh Office (1988) *Integrated Pollution Control, A Consultation Paper.*

Department of the Environment/Ministry of Agriculture Fisheries and Food/Welsh Office (1987) *The National Rivers Authority: The Government's Proposals for a Public Regulatory Body in a Privatised Water Industry.* London.

Devenay, W. T. (1978) 'Water supply in upland Scotland', in R. B. Tranter (ed.) *The Future of Upland Britain.* Centre for Agricultural Strategy, University of Reading, 328–35.

Dhruva Narayana, V. V. (1987) 'Downstream impacts of soil conservation in the Himalayan region', *Mountain Research and Development*, 7(3), 287–98.

Dickinson, N. W. T., Rudra, R. P., and Wall, G. J. (1986) 'Identification of soil erosion and fluvial sediment problems', *Hydrological Processes*, 1, 111–24.

Dixon, J. A., Carpenter, R. A., Fallon, L. A., Sherman, P. B., and Manipomoke, S. (1986) *Economic Analysis of the Environmental Impacts of Development Projects.* Earthscan, London.

Dooge, J. C. I. (1974) 'The development of hydrological concepts in Britain and Ireland between 1674 and 1874', *Hydrological Sciences Bulletin*, 19, 279–302.

Doornkamp, J. C., Gregory, K. J., and Burn, A. S. (1980) *Atlas of Drought in Britain 1975–76.* Institute of British Geographers, London.

Douglass, J. E. (1983) 'The potential for water yield augmentation from forest management in the eastern United States', *Water Resources Bulletin*, 19(3), 351–8.

Downs, P. W., Gregory, K. J., and Brookes, A. (in press) *How Integrated is River Basin Management?*

Dunne, T. and Leopold, L. B. (1978) *Water in Environmental Planning.* W. H. Freeman, San Francisco.

Eckerberg, K. (1990) *Environmental Protection in Swedish Forestry.* Gower, Aldershot.

Eckholm, E. (1976) 'The politics of soil conservation', *The Ecologist*, 6(2), 54–9.

Edwards, R. W. and Brooker, M. P. (1982) 'The ecology of the Wye', *Monographiae Biologicae*, 50, Junk, The Hague.

Elliot, C. (1982) *Making Excellence Useful.* Royal Society of Arts Conference on Technical Assistance Overseas and the Environment (16 November), London, 20–5.

Elmendorf, M. (1978) 'Public participation and acceptance', in C. G. Gunnerson and J. M. Kalbermatten (eds) *Environmental Impacts of International Civil Engineering Projects and Practices.* American Society of Civil Engineers, New York, 184–201.

Englebert, G. A. and Scheuring, A. F. (1984) *Water Scarcity – Impacts on Western Agriculture.* University of California Press, Berkeley, CA.

Environment Canada (1989) *Federal Water Policy.* Ottawa.

Environment Ontario (1988) *Controlling Industrial Discharges to Sewers.* Queens Printer.

Ericksen, N. J. (1986) 'Creating flood disasters?', Water and Soil Miscellaneous Publication 77, NWASCA, Wellington, New Zealand.

Ericksen, N. J. (1990) 'New Zealand water planning and management: evolution or revolution?', in B. Mitchell (ed.) *Integrated Water Management.* Belhaven, London, 45–87.

Ericksen, N. J., Handmer, J. W., and Smith, D. I. (1988) 'ANUFLOOD: Evaluation of a computerised urban flood-loss assessment policy for New Zealand', Water and Soil Miscellaneous Publication 115, NWASCA, Wellington, New Zealand.

Evans, R. (1990) 'Soils at risk of accelerated erosion in England and Wales', *Soil Use and Management*, 6(3), 125–31.

Evans, T. E. (1990) 'History of Nile flows', in P. P. Howell and J. A. Allan (eds) *The Nile*. School of Oriental and African Studies/Royal Geographical Society, London, 5–39.

Eybergen, F. A. and Imeson, A. C. (1989) 'Geomorphological processes and climatic change', *Catena*, 16(4), 307–20.

Fahim, H. M. (1981) *Dams, People and Development: The Aswan High Dam Case*. Pergamon, New York.

Falkenmark, M. (1986) 'Fresh water – time for a modified approach', *Ambio*, 15(4) 192–200.

Falkenmark, M. (1989) 'The massive water scarcity now threatening Africa – why isn't it being addressed?', Ambio, 18(2), 112–18.

FAO (1986) *World Agricultural Statistics*. FAO, Rome.

FAO (1977) *Assessing Soils Degradation*. FAO Soils Bulletin no. 34. FAO, Rome.

Farrimond, M. S. (1980) 'Impact of man in catchments. (iii) Domestic and industrial wastes', in A. M. Gower (ed.) *Water Quality in Catchment Ecosystems*. Wiley, Chichester, 113–44.

Ferguson, R. I. (1981) 'Channel form and channel changes', in J. Lewin (ed.) *British Rivers*. Allen & Unwin, London, 90–125.

Ferguson, R. (1987) 'Hydraulic and sedimentary controls of channel pattern', in K. S. Richards (ed.) *River Channels: Environment and Process*. Blackwells, Oxford, 129–58.

Finkel, H. J. (ed.) (1977) *Handbook of Irrigation Technology Vol 1*. CRC Press, Boca Raton, Florida.

Fisher, R. and Ury, W. (1981) *Getting to Yes*. Houghton Mifflin Co, Boston, MA.

Fleming, G. (1969) 'Design curves for suspended load estimation', *Proceedings of the Institution of Civil Engineers*, 43.

Flug, M. and Ahmed, J. (1990) 'Prioritizing flow alternatives for social objectives', *Journal of Water Resource Planning and Management*, 116(5), 610–24.

Fookes, P. G. and Vaughan, P. R. (1986) *A Handbook of Engineering Geomorphology*. Surrey University Press, London.

Forestry Commission (1979) *The Wood Production Outlook in Britain*. Forestry Commission, Edinburgh.

Forestry Commission (1988) *Forests and Water Guidelines*. Forestry Commission. Edinburgh.

Forestry Commission (1991) *Forests and Water Guidelines* (Second Edition), HMSO, London.

Foster, I. D. L., Dearing, J. A., and Grew, R. (1988) 'Lake-catchments: an evaluation of their contribution to studies of sediment yield and delivery processes', in M. P. Bordas and D. E. Walling (eds) *Sediment Budgets*. International Association of Hydrological Sciences Publication 174, 413–29.

Frost, C. A., Speirs, R. B., and McLean, J. (1990) 'Erosion control for the UK: Strategies and short-term costs and benefits', in J. Boardman, I. D. L. Foster and J. A. Dearing (eds) *Soil Erosion on Agricultural Land*. Wiley, Chichester, 559–67.

Gardiner, J. L. (1988) 'Environmentally sensitive river engineering: examples from the Thames catchment', in G. Petts (ed.) *Regulated Rivers Research and Management*, 2.

Gardiner, J. L. (ed.) (1991) *River Projects and Conservation: a Manual for Holistic Appraisal*. Wiley, Chichester.

Gibbs, R. (1970) 'Mechanisms controlling world water chemistry', *Science*, 170, 1088–90.

Gilbertson, D. D. (1986) 'Runoff (floodwater) farming and rural water supply in arid lands', *Applied Geography*, 6, 5–11.

Gilmour, D. A. (1988) 'Not seeing the trees for the forest: a reappraisal of the deforestation crisis in two hill districts of Nepal', *Mountain Research and Development*, 8(4), 343–50.

Gilmour, D. A., Bonell, M., and Cassells, D. S. (1987) 'The effects of forestation on soil hydraulic properties in the Middle Hills of Nepal: a preliminary assessment', *Mountain Research and Development*, 7(3), 239–49.

Glacken, C. J. (1956) 'Changing ideas of the habitable world', in W. L. Thomas (ed.) *Man's Role in Changing the Face of the Earth*. University of Chicago Press, Chicago, IL, 70–92.

Gleick, P. H. (1987) *Global Climatic Changes and Regional Hydrology: Impacts and Responses*. International Association of Scientific Hydrology Publication 168, 389–402.

Goldsmith, E. and Hildyard, N. (eds) (1984) *The Social and Environmental Effects of Large Dams. Volume 1: Overview*. Wadebridge Ecological Centre, Cornwall.

Goldsmith, E. and Hildyard, N. (eds) (1986) *The Social and Environmental Effects of Large Dams. Volume 2: Case studies*. Wadebridge Ecological Centre, Cornwall.

Gomez, B. and Church, M. (1989) 'An assessment of bed load sediment transport formulae for gravel bed rivers', *Water Resources Research*, 25(6), 1161–86.

Goodell, L. L. (1988) 'Water management in the Delaware river basin', in S. K. Majumdar, E. W. Miller, and L. E. Sage (eds), *Ecology and Restoration of the Delaware River Basin*. Pennsylvania Academy of Science, 286–94.

Gore, J. A. (1985) *The Restoration of Rivers and Streams. Theories and Experience*. Ann Arbor Science (Butterworth), Stoneham, MA.

Graf, W. L. (1985) *The Colorado River: Instability and Basin Management*. Association of American Geographers, Washington, DC.

Grainger, A. (1990) *The Threatening Desert: Controlling Desertification*. Earthscan, London.

Green, G. G. and Eiker, E. E. (eds) (1983) *Accomplishments and Impacts of Reservoirs*. American Society of Civil Engineers, New York.

Greenwell, J. R. (1978) 'Aridity, human evolution and desert primate ecology', *Arid Lands Newsletter*, 8, 10–18.

Gregory, K. J. (ed.) (1977) *River Channel Changes*. Wiley, Chichester.

Guerrieri, F. and Vianello, G. (1990) 'Identification and reclamation of erosion-affected lands in the Emilia-Romagna region, Italy', in J. Boardman, I. D. L. Foster and J. A. Dearing (eds) *Soil Erosion on Agricultural Land*. Wiley, Chichester, 621–5.

Guest, P. (1987) 'Who values our waterways?', *Soil and Water* 23(3), 8–12.

Gunnerson, C. G. and Kalbermatten, J. M. (eds) (1978) *Environmental Impacts of International Civil Engineering Projects and Practices*. American Society of Civil Engineers, New York.

Gustard, A., Cole, G., Marshall, D., and Bayliss, A. (1987) (eds) *A Study of Compensation Flows in the UK*. Institute of Hydrology, Wallingford, UK, Report No. 99.

Haigh, N. (1986) 'Public perceptions and international influences', in G. Conway (ed.) *The Assessment of Environmental Problems*. Imperial College Centre for Environmental Technology, London, 73–83.

Hall, C. (1989) *Running Water*. Robertson McCarta, London.

Hallsworth, E. G. (1987) *Anatomy, Physiology and Psychology of Erosion*. Wiley, Chichester.

Hamilton, L. S. (1988) 'Forestry and watershed management', in J. Ives and D. C. Pitt (eds) *Social Dynamics in Watersheds and Mountain Ecosystems*. Routledge, London, 99–131.

Hamley, W. (1990) 'Hydrotechnology, wilderness and culture in Quebec', in D. Cosgrove and G. E. Petts (eds) *Water, Engineering and Landscape*. Belhaven Press, London, 144–58.

Hare, F. K. (1984) 'The impact of human activities on water in Canada', Trinity College, University of Toronto Inquiry on Federal Water Policy Research, Paper 2.

Harper, D. E. (1988) 'Improving the accuracy of the Universal Soil Loss Equation in Thailand', in S. Runwanich (ed.) *Land Conservation for Future Generations*. Department of Land Development, Bangkok, 531–40.

Harriman, R. (1978) 'Nutrient leaching from fertilised forest watersheds in Scotland', *Journal of Applied Ecology*, 15, 933–42.

Harris, T. and Boardman, J. (1990) 'A rule-based expert system approach to predicting waterborne soil erosion', in J. Boardman, I. D. L. Foster and J. A. Dearing (eds) *Soil Erosion on Agricultural Land*. Wiley, Chichester, 401–12.

Hartmann, L. (1990) 'Methodological guidelines for integrated environmental evaluation of water resources development', in UNEP/UNESCO *The Impact of Large Water Projects on the Environment*. UNESCO, Paris, 467–86.

Hauck, G. F. W. and Novak, R. A. (1987) 'Interaction of flow and incrustation in the Roman Aqueduct of Nimes', *Journal of Hydraulic Engineering*, 113(2), 141–57.

Hawkes, J. (1976) *The Atlas of Early Man*. Macmillan, London.

Heede, B. H. and King, R. M. (1990) 'State-of-the-art timber harvest in an Arizona mixed conifer forest has minimal effect on overland flow and erosion', *Hydrological Sciences Journal*, 35(6), 623–35.

Hellawell, J. M. (1986) *Biological Indicators of Freshwater Pollution and Environmental Management*. Elsevier, London.

Hellen, J. A. and Bonn, P. (1981) 'Demographic change and public policy in Egypt and Nepal: some long-term implications for development planning', *Science and Public Policy*, 308–36.

Helley, E. J. and Smith, W. (1971) 'Development and calibration of a pressure-difference bedload sampler', *US Geological Survey Open File Report*, 8037-01, Menlo Park, CA.

Hellier, C. (1990) 'Running the rivers dry', *Geographical Magazine*, July, 32–5.

Hewlett, J. D. and Nutter, W. L. (1970) 'The varying source area of streamflow from upland basins. Interdisciplinary aspects of watershed management', American Society of Civil Engineers, New York, 65–83.

Hibbert, (1967) 'Forest treatment effects on water yield', in W. E. Soppen and H. W. Lull (eds) *International Symposium on Forest Hydrology*. Pergamon, New York, 527–43.

Hickin, E. J. (1983) 'River channel changes: retrospect and prospect', Special Publications International Association of Sedimentologists, 6, 61–83.

Higgs, G. and Petts, G. E. (1988) 'Hydrological changes and river regulation in the UK', *Regulated Rivers: Research and Management*, 2, 349–68.

Higgins, G. M., Dielman, P. J., and Abernethy, C. L. (1988) 'Trends in irrigation development and their implications for hydrologists and water resource engineers', *Hydrological Sciences Journal*, 33(1/2), 43–59.

Hill, A. R. (1990) 'Groundwater cation concentrations in the riparian zone of a forested headwater stream', *Hydrological Processes*, 4, 121–30.

Hjulstrom, F. (1935) 'Studies of the morphological activity of rivers as illustrated by the River Fyris', *Bulletin of the Geological Institute*, University of Uppsala, 25, 221–527.

Hodges, R. D. and Arden-Clarke, C. (1986) *Soil Erosion in Britain: Levels of Soil Damage and their Relationship to Farming Practices*. The Soil Association, Bristol.

Holeman, J. N. (1968) 'The sediment yield of major rivers of the world', *Water Resources Research*, 4(4), 737–47.

Hollis, G. E. (1988) 'Rain, roads, roofs and runoff: hydrology in cities', *Geography*, 73(1), 9–18.

Hooke, J. M. and Kain, R. J. P. (1982) *Historical Change in the Physical Environment*. Butterworth, London.

Horberry, J. (1983) *Environmental Guidelines Survey. An Analysis of Environmental Procedures and Guidelines Governing Development Aid*. International Institute for Environment and Development, Washington and London.

Horton, R. E. (1933) 'The role of infiltration in the hydrologic cycle', *American Geophysical Union Transactions*, 14, 446–60.

Horton, R. E. (1945) 'Erosional development of streams: quantitative physiographic factors', *Bulletin of the Geological Society of America*, LVI.

Howard, P. J. A., Thompson, T. R. E., Hornung, M., and Beard, G. R. (cds) (1989) *An Assessment of the Principles of Soil Protection in the UK* (3 volumes). Institute of Terrestrial Ecology, HMSO, London.

Howarth, W. (1988) *Water Pollution Law*. Shaw & Sons, London.

Howell, P. P. and Allan, J. A. (eds) (1990) *The Nile: Resource Evaluation, Resource Management, Hydropolitics and Legal Issues*. Conference Proceedings, Royal Geographical Society, School of Oriental and African Studies, London.

Howell, P., Lock, M., and Cobb, S. (1988) *The Jonglei Canal: Impact and Opportunity*. Cambridge University Press, Cambridge.

Huff, D. D. and Swank, W. T. (1985) 'Modelling changes in forest evapotranspiration', in M. G. Anderson and T. P. Burt (eds) *Hydrological Forecasting*. Wiley, Chichester, 125–51.

Hughes, F. M. R. (1990) 'The influence of flooding regimes on forest distribution and composition in the Tana River floodplain, Kenya', *Journal of Applied Ecology*, 27, 475–91.

Hulme, M. (1990) 'Global climate change and the Nile Basin', in P. P. Howell and J. A. Allan (eds) *The Nile*. SOAS/RGS, London, 59–82.

Hurni, H. (1983) 'Soil erosion and soil formation in agricultural ecosystems: Ethiopia and Northern Thailand', *Mountain Research and Development*, 3(2), 131–42.

Huxley, J. (1943) *TVA: Adventure in Planning*. Architectural Press, London.

Hynes, H. B. N. (1975) 'The stream and its valley', *Verh Internat Verein Limnol*, 19, 1–15.

IAHS ( ) *Proceedings of the Wellington Symposium*, 2 volumes. Wallingford, UK.

IAHS (1980) 'The influence of man on the hydrological regime with special reference to representative and experimental basins', *Proceedings of the Helsinki Symposium*. Wallingford, UK.

IAHS-UNESCO (1970) *Results of Research on Representative and Experimental Basins*. UNESCO, Paris.

Independent Commission on International Development Issues (1980) *North-South: a Programme for Survival*. Pan Books, London.

Ingram, H. (1990) *Water Politics: Continuity and Change*. University of New Mexico Press, Albuquerque.

Institute of Hydrology (1980) *Low Flow Studies*. Wallingford, UK.

IUCN (1980) *World Conservation Strategy*. IUCN-UNEP-WWF, Gland, Switzerland.

Ives, J. D. (1988) 'Development in the face of uncertainty', in J. Ives and D. C. Pitt (eds) *Deforestation: Social Dynamics in Watersheds and Mountain Ecosystems*. Routledge, London, 54–74.

Ives, J. and Pitt, D. C. (eds) (1988) *Deforestation: Social Dynamics in Watersheds and Mountain Ecosystems*. Routledge, London.

Ives, J., Messerli, B., and Thompson, M. (1987) 'Research strategy for the Himalayan region', *Mountain Research and Development*, 7(3), 332–44.

Jansen, J. M. L. and Painter, R. B. (1974) 'Predicting sediment yield from climate and topography', *Journal of Hydrology*, 21, 371–80.

Johnson, P. (1988) 'River regulation: a regional perspective – Northumbrian Water Authority', *Regulated Rivers: Research and Management*, 2, 233–55.

Johnston, W. B. (1985) 'Sector and place: the place of environment in government administration', *Proceedings of the 13th New Zealand Geography Conference*, Hamilton, 96–8.

Kalbermatten, J. M. and Gunnerson, C. A. (1978) 'Environmental impacts of international engineering practice', in C. G. Gunnerson and J. M. Kalbermatten (eds) *Environmental Impacts of International Civil Engineering Projects and Practices*. American Society of Civil Engineers, New York, 232–54.

Kalpavriksh and The Hindu College Nature Club (1986) 'The Narmada Valley Project: development or destruction?', in E. Goldsmith and N. Hildyard (eds) *The Social and Environmental Effects of Large Dams*. Cambridge University Press, Cambridge, 224–44.

Karpiscak, M. M., Foster, K. E., and Rawles, R. L. (1984) 'Water harvesting and evaporation suppression', *Arid Lands Newsletter*, 21, 11–17.

Kellerhals, R. (1967) 'Stable channels with gravel-paved beds', *Journal of the Waterways and Harbours Division*, Proceedings of the American Society of Civil Engineers, 93, 63–84.

Kinnersley, D. (1988) *Troubled Water: Rivers, Politics and Pollution*. Hilary Shipman, London.

Kirby, C., Newson, M. D. and Gilman, K. (1992) *Plynlimon Research: the First Two Decades*. Institute of Hydrology, Report 109, Wallingford, UK.

Kirpich, P. Z. (1990) 'Technology, society and water management – discussion', (of a paper by W. Viessman), *Journal of Water Resource Planning and Management*, 116(6), 846–7.

Kittredge, J. 1948 (1973) *Forest Influences*. Dover, New York.

Knight, D. W. (1987) Dissemination of information to practising engineers and researchers in the water industry, *Journal of the Institution of Water & Environmental Management*, 1(3), 315–24.

Knight, M. S. and Tuckwell, S. B. (1988) 'Controlling nitrate leaching in water supply catchments', *Journal of the Institution of Water and Environmental Management*, 2, 248–52.

Knighton, A. D. (1984) *Fluvial forms and processes*. Edward Arnold.

Knox, J. C. (1989) *Long- and Short-term Episodic Storage and Removal of Sediment in Watersheds of Southwestern Wisconsin and Northwestern Illinois*. IAHS Publication 184, 157–64.

Kogan, M. and Henkel, M. (1983) *Government and Research*. Heinemann, London.

Konrad, J. A., Baumann, J. S., and Ott, J. A. (1986) 'Non-point source planning and implementation in Wisconsin', in J. F. Solbe (ed.) *Effects of Land Use on Fresh Waters*. Ellis Horwood, Chichester, 283–95.

Kovacs, G. (1990) 'Decision support systems for managing large international rivers', in UNEP/UNESCO *The Impact of Large Water Projects on the Environment*. UNESCO, Paris, 435–48.

Kruse, E. G., Burdick, C. R., and Yousef, Y. A. (eds) (1982) *Environmentally Sound Water and Soil Management*. American Society of Civil Engineers, New York.

Krutilla, J. V. and Eckstein, O. (1958) *Multiple Purpose River Development – Studies in Applied Economic Analysis*. Johns Hopkins University Press, Baltimore, MD.

Lambert, A. (1988) 'Regulation of the River Dee', *Regulated Rivers: Research and Management*, 2, 293–308.

Lambert, C. P. and Walling, D. E. (1988) 'Measurement of channel storage of suspended sediment in a gravel-bed river', *Catena*, 15, i, 65–80.

Law, F. (1956) 'The effect of afforestation upon the yield of water catchment areas', *Journal of the British Waterworks Association*, 38, 484–94.

Leeks, G. J. L. and Newson, M. D. (1989) 'Responses of the sediment system of a regulated river to a scour valve release: Llyn Clywedog, Mid-Wales, UK', *Regulated Rivers: Research and Management*, 3, 93–106.

Leopold, L. B. (1968) 'Hydrology for urban land planning', US Geological Survey, Circular 554.

Leopold, L. B. (1974) *Water: A Primer*. W. H. Freeman, San Francisco, CA.

Leopold, L. B. and Langbein, W. B. (1962) 'The concept of entropy in landscape evolution', US Geological Survey Professional Paper 500-A, Menlo Park, CA.

Leopold, L. B. and Maddock, T. (1954) *The Flood Control Controversy*. Donald, New York.

Leopold, L. B. and Wolman, M. G. (1957) 'River channel patterns: braided, meandering and straight', US Geological Survey Professional Paper 282-B, Menlo Park, CA.

Leopold, L. B., Wolman, M. G., and Miller, J. P. (1964) *Fluvial Processes in Geomorphology* W H Freeman, San Francisco, CA.

Lewin, J., Macklin, M. G., and Newson, M. D. (1988) 'Regime theory and environmental change – irreconcilable concepts?', in W. R. White (ed.) *International Conference on River Regime*. Wiley, Chichester, UK, 431–45.

Liebscher, H. J. (1987) *Palaeohydrologic Studies Using Proxy Data and Observations*. IAHS Publication 168, 111–21.

Likens, G. E., Bormann, F. H., Pierce, R. S., and Reiners, W. A. (1978) 'Recovery of a deforested ecosystem', *Science*, 199, 192–6.

Livingstone (1963) 'Chemical composition of rivers and lakes: data of geochemistry', US Geological Survey, Prof Paper 440-9.

Lvovitch, M. I. (1973) 'The global water balance', *US International Hydrological Decade Bulletin*, 23, 28–42.

Lynch-Stewart, P., Wiken, E. B., and Ironside, G. R. (1986) *Acid Deposition on Prime Resource Lands in Eastern Canada*. Canada Land Inventory, Report 18. Environment Canada, Ottowa.

McClimans, J. (1980) 'Best management practices for forestry activities', *Watershed Management 1980*. American Society of Civil Engineers, New York, 694–705.

McColl, R. H. S. and Gibson, A. R. (1979) 'Downslope movement of nutrients in hill pasture, Taita, New Zealand. III Amounts involved and management implication', *Journal of Agricultural Research*, 22, 279–86.

Macklin, M. G. and Dowsett, R. B. (1989) 'The chemical and physical speciation of trace metals in fine grained overbank flood sediments in the Tyne basin, North East England', *Catena*, 16(2), 135–51.

McMahon, T. A., Finlayson, B. L., Haines, A., and Srikanthan, R. (1987) *Runoff Variability: a Global Perspective*. International Association of Scientific Hydrology Publication 168, 3–11.

Mahoo, H. (1989) 'Deforestation of a tropical humid rainforest and resulting effects on soil properties, surface and subsurface flow, water quality and crop evapotranspiration', Unpublished Ph.D. Thesis, University of Sokoine, Tanzania.

Majumdar, S. K., Miller, E. W., and Sage, L. E. (1988) *Ecology and Restoration of the Delaware River Basin*. Pennsylvania Academy of Science.

Makhoalibe, S. (1984) *Suspended Sediment Transport Measurement in Lesotho*. International Association of Hydrological Sciences Publication 144, 313–21.

Marchand, M. and Toornstra, F. H. (1986) *Ecological Guidelines for River Basin Development*. Centrum voor Milienkunde, Dept 28, Rijksuniversiteit, Leiden.

Marsh, G. P. 1864 (1965) *Man and Nature. Physical Geography as Modified by Human Action*. (reprinted) Belknap Press of Harvard Univesity Press, Cambridge, MA.

Mas'ud, A. F. (1987) 'Land use and physical hydrology of selected mesoscale catchments in Wales', Unpublished Ph.D. Thesis, University College North Wales, Bangor.

Meade, R. H. (1982) 'Sources, sinks and storage of river sediment in the Atlantic drainage of the United States', *Journal of Geology*, 90(3), 235, 252.

Melton, M. A. (1957) *An Analysis of the Relations among Elements of Climate, Surface Properties and Geomorphology*. US Office of Naval Research, Project NR389-042, Columbia University, New York.

Mensching, H. (1986) 'Is the desert spreading? Desertification in the Sahel zone of Africa', *Applied Geography and Development*, 27, 7–18.

Mersey Basin Campaign (1988) *Reviving the Regions Rivers*. Department of the Environment, Manchester (information pack).

Metallie, J. P. (1987) 'The degradation of the Pyrenees in the nineteenth century', in V. Gardiner (ed.) *International Geomorphology*. Wiley, London, 533–44.

Meybeck, M. (1979) 'Concentrations des eaux fluviales en éléments majeurs, et apports en solution aux océans', *Revue de Geologie Dynamique et de Geographie Physique*, 21, 215–46.

Meybeck, M. (1983) *Atmospheric Inputs and River Transport of Dissolved Substances*. IAHS Publication 141, 173–92.

Michener, J. A. (1975) *Centennial*. Corgi Books, London.

Milliman, J. D., Broadus, J. M. and Gable, F. (1987) 'Environmental and economic implication of rising sea level and subsiding deltas: the Nile and Bengal examples', *Ambio*, 18(6), 340–5.

Ministry for the Environment New Zealand (1989) *Update on the Resource Management Law Reform*. Wellington, New Zealand.

Ministry of Health (1948) *Gathering Grounds. Public Access to Gathering Grounds, Afforestation and Agriculture on Gathering Grounds*. HMSO, London.

Ministry of Natural Resources Ontario (1986) *Conservation Areas Guide*. Government Bookstore, Toronto.

Mitchell, J. K. and Bubenzer, G. D. (1980) 'Soil loss estimation', in M. J. Kirkby and R. P. C. Morgan (eds) *Soil Erosion*. Wiley, Chichester, 17–62.

Moore, D. J. (ed.) (1982) 'Catchment management for optimum use of land and water resources: Documents from an ESCAP seminar, Part 2: New Zealand contributions', Water and Soil Miscellaneous Publication 45, NWASCA, Wellington, New Zealand.

Moorehead, A. (1973) *The White Nile*. Penguin Books, Harmondsworth.

Moorehead, A. (1983) *The Blue Nile*. Penguin Books, Harmondsworth.

Morgan, R. P. C. (1979) *Soil Erosion*. Longman, London.

Morgan, R. P. C. (1980) 'Implications', in M. J. Kirkby and R. P. C. Morgan (eds) *Soil Erosion*. Wiley, Chichester, 253–301.

Morgan, R. P. C., Morgan, D. D. V., and Finney, H. J. (1984) 'A predictive model for the assessment of soil erosion risk', *Journal of Agricultural Engineering Research*, 30, 245–53.

Muckleston, K. W. (1990) 'Integrated water management in the United States', in B. Mitchell (ed.) *Integrated Water Management*. Belhaven Press, London, 22–44.

Nace, R. (1974) *General Evolution of the Concept of the Hydrological Cycle*. UNESCO/WMO/IAHS, Paris, 40–51.

Napier, T. L. (1990) 'The evolution of US soil conservation policy: from voluntary adoption to coercion', in J. Boardman, I. D. L. Foster and J. A. Dearing (eds) *Soil Erosion on Agricultural Land*. Wiley, Chichester, 627–44.

National Water Council (1973) *Water Policies for the Future*. Water Information Center Inc, Port Washington, New York.

National Water Council (1976) *We Didn't Wait for the Rain*. National Water Council, London.

National Water and Soil Conservation Authority (NWASCA) (NZ) (1987) *Farming the Hills – Mining or Sustaining the Resource?* Streamland 62, Wellington, New Zealand.

Nature Conservancy Council (1986) *Nature Conservation and Afforestation in Britain*. NCC, Peterborough.

Nelson, D. (1979) 'A national watershed inventory', *Journal of Nepal Research Centre*. 2/3, 81–96.

NERC (1975) *Flood Studies Report* (5 volumes). Institute of Hydrology, Wallingford, UK.

Newbold, C., Honnor, J., and Buckley, K. (1989) *Nature Conservation and the Management of Drainage Channels*. Nature Conservancy Council, Peterborough.

Newson, M. D. (1979) *Hydrology: Measurement and Application*. Macmillan, Basingstoke.

Newson, M. D. (1980) 'The geomorphological effectiveness of floods – a contribution stimulated by two recent events in mid-Wales', *Earth Surface Processes*, 5, 1–16.

Newson, M. D. (1986) 'River basin engineering – fluvial geomorphology', *Journal of the Institution of Water Engineers and Scientists*, 40(4), 307–24.

Newson, M. D. (1988) 'Upland land use and land management – policy and research aspects of the effects on water', in J. M. Hooke (ed.) *Geomorphology in Environmental Planning*. Wiley, Chichester, 19–32.

Newson, M. D. (1989) 'Flood effectiveness in river basins: progress in Britain in a decade of drought', in K. Beven and P. Carling (eds) *Floods: Hydrological, Sedimentological and Geomorphological Implications*. Wiley, Chichester, UK, 151–69.

Newson, M. D. (1990) 'Forestry and water, 'good practice' and UK catchment policy', *Land Use Policy*, 7(1), 53–8.

Newson, M. D. (1991) 'Catchment control and planning: emerging patterns of definition, policy and legislation in UK water management', *Land Use Policy*, 9(1), 9–15.

Newson M. D. (in press) *Geomorphic Thresholds in Gravel-bed Rivers – Refinements for an Era of Environmental Change. Gravel-bed rivers.* Wiley, Chichester, UK.

Newson, M. D. (1992[a]) 'River conservation and catchment management: UK perspective', in P. Boon, P. Calow and G. Petts (eds) *River Conservation and Management.* Wiley, Chichester, UK, 385–96.

Newson, M. D. (1992[b]) 'Land and water: convergence, divergence and progress in the UK policy', *Land Use Policy*, 9(2), 111–21.

Newson, M. D. and Calder, I. R. (1989) 'Forests and water resources: problems of prediction on a regional scale', *Philosophical Transactions Royal Society of London*, B324, 283–98.

Newson, M. D. and Leeks, G. J. (1987) 'Transport processes at the catchment scale', in C. R. Thorne, J. C. Bathurst and R. D. Hey (eds) *Sediment Transport in Gravel-bed Rivers.* Wiley, Chichester, UK, 187–223.

Newson, M. D. and Lewin, J. (1991) 'Climatic change, river flow extremes and fluvial erosion – scenarios for England and Wales', *Progress in Physical Geography*, 15(1), 1–17.

Newson, M. D. and Robinson, M. (1983) 'Effects of agricultural drainage on upland streamflow: case studies in mid-Wales', *Journal of Environmental Management*, 17, 333–48.

Obeng, L. E. (1978) 'Environmental impacts of four African impoundments', in C. G. Gunnerson and J. M. Kalbermatten (eds) *Environmental Impacts of International Civil Engineering Projects and Practices.* American Society of Civil Engineers, New York, 29–43.

OECD (1989) *Water Resource Management: Integrated Policies.* OECD, Paris.

Okidi, C. O. (1990) 'History of the Nile and Lake Victoria Basins through treaties', in P. P. Howell and J. A. Allan (eds) *The Nile.* SOAS/RGS, London, 193–224.

Olofin, E. A. (1984) 'Some effects of the Tiga Dam on valleyside erosion in downstream reaches of the River Kano', *Applied Geography*, 4, 321–32.

O'Riordan, J. (1986) 'Some examples of land and water use planning in British Columbia, Canada', in F. T. Last, M. C. B. Hotz and B. G. Bell (eds) *Land and its Uses – Actual and Potential.* Plenum, New York, 193–211.

O'Riordan, T. (1976) 'Policy making and environmental management: some thoughts on purposes and research issues', *Natural Resources Journal*, 16, 55–72.

O'Riordan, T. (1977) 'Environmental ideologies', *Environment and Planning*, Series A, 9, 3–14.

O'Riordan, T. and More, R. J. (1969) 'Choice in water use', in R. J. Chorley (ed.) *Water, Earth and Man.* Methuen, London, 547–73.

Palmer, T. (1986) *Endangered Rivers and the Conservation Movement.* University of California Press, Berkeley, CA.

Palutikov, J. P. (1987) *Some Possible Impacts of Greenhouse Gas Induced Climatic Change on Water Resources of England and Wales.* International Association of Scientific Hydrology Publication 168, 585–96.

Park, C. C. (1977) 'World-wide variations in hydraulic geometry exponents of stream channels: an analysis and some observations', *Journal of Hydrology*, 35, 133–46.

Parker, R. (1976) *The Common Stream.* Paladin, London.

Patterson, A. (1987) *Water and the State.* Geographical Paper No. 98, Department of Geography, University of Reading, Reading.

Paylore, P. and Greenwell, J. R. (1979) 'Fools rush in: pinpointing the arid zone', *Arid Lands Newsletter*, 10, 17–18.

Pearse, P. H., Bertrand, F., and Maclaren, J. W. (1985) *Currents of Change*. Environment Canada, Ottawa.

Pereira, H. C. (1973) *Land Use and Water Resources*. Cambridge University Press, Cambridge.

Pereira, H. C. (1989) *Policy and Practice in the Management of Tropical Watersheds*. Belhaven, London.

Petersen, R. C., Peterson, B-M. and Lacoursiére, J. (1992) 'A building-block model for stream restoration', in P. Boon, G. Petts and P. Calow (eds) *River Conservation and Management*. Wiley, Chichester, 293–309.

Petersen, R. C., Madsen, B. L., Wilzbach, M. A., Magadza, C. H. D., Paarlberg, A., Kullberg, A., and Cummins, K. W. (1987) 'Stream management: emerging global similarities', *Ambio*, 16(4), 166–79.

Peterson, D. H., Cayan, D. R., Dileo-Stephens, J. and Ross, T. G. (1987) *Some Effects of Climate Variability on Hydrology in Western North America*. International Association of Scientific Hydrology Publication 168, 45–62.

Petts, G. E. (1979) 'Complex response of river channel morphology subsequent to reservoir construction', *Progress in Physical Geography*, 3(3), 329–62.

Petts, G. E. (1984) *Impounded Rivers: Perspectives for Ecological Management*. Wiley, Chichester, UK.

Petts, G. E. (1987) 'Timescales for ecological change in regulated rivers', in J. Craig and J. B. Kemper (eds) *Regulated Streams: Advances in Ecology*. Plenum, New York, 257–66.

Petts, G. (1990) 'Water, engineering and landscape: development, protection and restoration', in D. Cosgrove and G. Petts (eds) *Water, Engineering and Landscape*. Belhaven Press, London.

Petts, G. E. and Thoms, M. C. (1987) 'Morphology and sedimentology of a tributary confluence bar in a regulated river', *Earth Surface Processes*, 12(4), 433–40.

Petts, G. E., Foulger, T. R., Gilvear, D. J., Pratts, J. D., and Thoms, M. C. (1985) 'Wave-movement and water quality variations during a controlled release from Kielder Reservoir, North Tyne River, UK', *Journal of Hydrology*, 80, 371–89.

Pezzey, J. (1989) *Definitions of Sustainability*. CEED Discussion Paper 9, Centre for Economic and Environmental Development, London.

Pinay, A. and Decamps, H. (1988) 'The role of riparian woods in regulating nitrogen fluxes between the alluvial aquifer and surface water: a conceptual model', *Regulated Rivers: Research and Management*, 2, 507–16.

Platt, R. H., Macinko, G., and Hammond, K. (1983) 'Federal environmental management: some land-use legacies of the 1970s', in J. W. House (ed.) *United States Public Policy: a Geographical Review*. Clarendon Press, Oxford, 125–66.

Playfair, J. (1802) *Illustrations of the Huttonian Theory of the Earth*. William Creech, Edinburgh.

Pollemus, Van Dyke (1988) 'Delaware River Basin Commission's river management role: the interface between water users and managing entities', in S. K. Majunder, E. W. Miller and L. E. Sage (eds) *Ecology and Restoration of the Delaware River Basin*. Pennysylvania Academy of Science, Easton, PA, 312–22.

Polls, I. and Lanyon, R. (1980) 'Pollutant concentrations from homogenous land uses', *Journal of Environmental Engineering Division*, Proceedings of the American Society of Civil Engineers, 106, 69–80.

Poole, A. L. (1983) 'Catchment control in New Zealand', Water and Soil Miscellaneous Publication 48, Ministry of Works and Development, Wellington, New Zealand.

Pope, W. (1980) 'Impact of man in catchments (II) road and urbanisation', in A. M. Gower (ed.) *Water Quality in Catchment Ecosystems*. Wiley, Chichester, 73–112.

Popham, A. E. (1946) *The Drawings of Leonardo da Vinci*. Jonathan Cape, London.

Priscoli, J. D. (1989) 'Public involvement, conflict management: means to EQ and social objectives', *Journal of Water Resource Planning and Management*, Proceedings of the American Society of Civil Engineers, 115(1), 31–42.

Purseglove, J. (1988) *Taming the Flood*. Oxford University Press, Oxford.

Quinn, J. M. and Hickey, W. (1987) 'How well are we protecting the life in our rivers?', *Soil and Water*, 23(4), 7–12.

Raikes, R. (1967) *Water, Weather and Prehistory*. John Baker, London.

Ramsay, W. J. H. (1987) *Deforestation and Erosion in the Nepalese Himalaya – is the Link Myth or Reality?* IAHS Publication 167, 239–50.

Rees, J. (1989) *Water Privatisation*. Research Papers, Department of Geography, London School of Economics, London.

Rees, J. A. (1969) *Industrial Demand for Water: a Study of South East England*. London School of Economics/Weidenfeld and Nicholson, London.

Reid, I. and Frostick, L. E. (1986) 'Dynamics of bedload transport in Turkey Brook', *Earth Surface Processes and Landforms*, 11, 143–55.

Reid, I. and Parkinson, R. J. (1984) 'The nature of the tile-drain outfall hydrograph in heavy clay soils', *Journal of Hydrology*, 72, 289–305.

Reisner, M. (1990) *Cadillac Desert. The American West and its Disappearing Water*. Secker & Warburg, London.

Rennison, R. W. (1979) *Water to Tyneside*. Newcastle and Gateshead Water Co., Newcastle upon Tyne.

Reynolds, E. R. C. and Leyton, L. (1967) 'Research data for forest policy: the purpose, methods and progress of forest hydrology', Proceedings of the 9th Br Commonwealth Forestry Conference, University of Oxford.

Richards, K. S. (1982) 'Channel adjustment to sediment pollution by the china clay industry in Cornwall, England', in D. D. Rhodes and G. P. Williams (eds) *Adjustments of the Fluvial System*. Allen & Unwin, 309–31.

Richardson, J. J., Jordan, A. G. and Kimber, R. H. (1978) 'Lobbying, administrative reform and policy style: the case for land drainage', *Political Studies*, 26(1), 47–64.

Rizzo, B. (1988) *The Sensitivity of Canada's Ecosystems to Climatic Change*. Newsletter 17, 10–15, Canada Committee on Ecological Land Clarification, Environment Canada, Ottawa.

Roberts, C. R. (1989) 'Flood frequency and urban-induced channel change: some British examples', in K. Beven and P. Carling (eds) *Floods: Hydrological, Sedimentological and Geomorphological Implications*. Wiley, Chichester, UK, 57–82.

Roberts, G. and Marsh, T. (1987) *The Effects of Agricultural practices on the Nitrate Concentrations in the Surface Water Domestic Supply Sources of Western Europe*. IAHS Publication 164.

Roberts, J. (1983) 'Forest transpiration: a conservative hydrological process?', *Journal of Hydrology*, 66, 133–41.

Robinson, M. and Beven. K. J. (1983) 'The effect of mole drainage on the hydrological response of a swelling clay soil', *Journal of Hydrology*, 64, 205–23.

Robinson, M., Ryder, E. L., and Ward, R. C. (1985) 'Influence on streamflow of field drainage in a small agricultural catchment', *Agricultural Water Management*, 10, 145–58.

Robinson, N. A. (1987) 'Marshalling environmental law to resolve the Himalaya-Ganges problem', *Mountain Research and Development*, 7(3), 305–15.

Rolt, L. T. C. (1985) *Navigable Waters*. Penguin Books, Harmondsworth.

Roome, N. (1984) 'A better future for the uplands – a planning critique', *Planning Outlook*, 27(1), 12–17.

Ross, S. M., Thornes, J. B., and Nortcliff, S. (1990) 'Soil hydrology nutrient and erosional response to the clearance of terra firme forest, Maraca Island, Roraima, Northern Brazil', *Geographical Journal*, 156(3), 267–82.

Ross, T. A. (1989) 'Drought in the US 1987–8', *US Geological Survey Yearbook 1988*. US Government Printing Office, Washington DC, 24–7.

Rowley, G. (1990) 'The West Bank: native water-resource systems and competition', *Political Geography Quarterly*, 9(1), 39–52.

Rowntree, K. (1990) 'Political and administrative constraints on integrated river basin development: an evaluation of the Jana and Athi Rivers Development Authority, Kenya', *Applied Geography*, 10, 21–41.

Royal Commission on Environmental Pollution (1988) *12th Report, Best Practicable Environmental Option*. HMSO, London.

Ryckborst, H. (1980) 'Geomorphological changes after river meander surgery', *Geologie in Mijnbouw*, 59(2), 121–8.

Sagoff, M. (1989) *The Economy of the Earth*, Cambridge University Press, Cambridge.

Saha, S. K. and Barrow, C. J. (eds) (1981) *River Basin Planning, Theory and Practice*. Wiley, Chichester.

Samir, A. (1990) 'Principles and precedents in international law governing the sharing of Nile waters', in P. P. Howell and J. A. Allan (eds) *The Nile*. SOAS/RGS, London, 225–38.

Saunders, I. and Young, A. (1983) 'Rates of surface processes on slopes, slope retreat and denudation', *Earth Surface Processes and Landforms*, 8, 473–501.

Saunders, P. (1985) 'The forgotten dimension of central-local relations: theorising the "regional state"', *Environment and Planning*, C, 3, 149–62.

Schramm, G. (1980) 'Integrated river basin planning in a holistic universe', *Natural Resources Journal*, 20(4), 787–806.

Schumacher, E. F. (1973) *Small is Beautiful*. Abacus, London.

Schumm, S. A. (1963) 'A tentative classification of alluvial river channels', *US Geological Survey*, Circular 477, Menlo Park, CA.

Schumm, S. A. (1969) 'River metamorphosis', *Journal of Hydraulics Division*, American Society of Civil Engineers, 95, 255–73.

Schumm, S. A. (1977) *The Fluvial System*. Wiley, New York.

Schumm, S. A. (1985) 'Patterns of alluvial rivers', *Annual Review of Earth/Planet Sciences*, 13, 5–27.

Schumm, S. A. and Lichty, R. W. (1965) 'Time, space and causality in geomorphology', *American Journal of Science*, 263, 110–19.

Schumm, S. A., Harvey, M. D., and Watson, C. C. (1984) *Incised Channels: Morphology, Dynamics and Control*. Water Resources Publications, Littleton, CO.

Scottish Development Department (1990) *First Policy Review of the River Purification Boards*. Edinburgh.

Sear, D. A. (in press) 'The effects of river regulation for hydro electric power on the sediment and sediment transport within riffle pool sequences', in R. Hey and Billi, P. (eds) *Dynamics of Gravel Bed River*. Wiley, Chichester.

Seymour, J. and Girardet, H. (1986) *Far from Paradise*. BBC Books, London.

Sharma, C. K. (1987) 'The problem of sediment load in the development of water resources in Nepal', *Mountain Research and Development*, 7(3), 316–18.

Sheail, J. (1988) 'River regulation in the United Kingdom: an historical perspective', *Regulated Rivers: Research and Management*, 2, 221–32.

Shearer, D. M. (1978) 'Water resource development in upland Britain', in R. B. Tranter (ed.) *The Future of Upland Britain*. Centre for Agricultural Strategy, University of Reading, 294–306.

Shiklomanov, J. A. (1989) 'Climate and water resources', *Hydrological Sciences Journal*, 34(5), 495–529.

Shrubsole, D. A. (1990) 'Integrated water management strategies in Canada', in B. Mitchell (ed.) *Integrated Water Management*. Belhaven Press, London, 88–118.

Slaymaker, O. (1982) 'Land use effects on sediment yield and quality', *Hydrobiologia*, 91–2, 93–109.

Smith, C. T. (1969) 'The drainage basin as an historical basis for human activity', in R. J. Chorley (ed.), *Water, Earth and Man*. Methuen, London, 101–10.

Smith, D. A. (1987) 'Water quality indices for use in New Zealand's rivers and streams', Water Quality Centre Publication 12, Ministry of Works and Development, Hamilton, New Zealand.

Smith, N. (1972) *A History of Dams*. Citadel Press, Secaucus, NJ.

Smith, T. R. (1974) 'A derivation of the hydraulic geometry of steady-state channels from conservation principles and sediment transport laws', *Journal of Geology*, 82, 98–104.

Snyder, G. (1980) 'Evaluating silvicultural impacts on water resources', *Watershed Management 1980*. American Society of Civil Engineers, New York, 682–93.

Solbe, J. F. de L. G. (ed.) (1986) *Effects of Land use on Fresh Waters – Agriculture, Forestry, Mineral Exploitation, Urbanisation*. Ellis Horwood, Chichester.

Solley, W. B. (1989) 'Reflections on water use in the United States', *US Geological Survey 1988 Yearbook*, Denver, CO, 28–30.

Solomon, S. I., Beran, M., and Hogg, W. (eds) (1987) *The Influence of Climate Change and Climatic Variability on the Hydrologic Regime and Water Resources*. International Association of Scientific Hydrology Publication 168.

Soons, J. M. (1986) 'Erosion rates in a superhumid environment', in V. Gardiner (ed.) *International Geomorphology, Volume I*. Wiley, Chichester, 885–96.

Stephens, H. G. and Shoemaker, E. M. (1987) *In the Footsteps of John Wesley Powell*. Johnson Books, Boulder, CO.

Stocking, M. (1987) *Environmental Crises in Developing Countries: How Much, for Whom and by Whom?* Developing Areas Research Group, Institute of British Geographers, Swansea.

Stoner, R. F. (1990) 'Further irrigation planning in Egypt', in P. P. Howell and J. A. Allan (eds) *The Nile*. SOAS/RGS, London, 83–105.

Strahler, A. N. (1957) 'Quantitative analysis of watershed geomorphology', *Transactions of the American Geophysical Union*, 38, 913–20.

Sutcliffe, J. V. (1974) 'A hydrological study of the Southern Sudd region of the Upper Nile', *Hydrological Sciences Bulletin*, 19, 237–55.

Sutcliffe, J. V. and Knott, D. G. (1987) *Historical Variations in African Water Resources*. International Association of Scientific Hydrology Publication 168, 463–75.

Sutcliffe, J. V. and Parks, Y. P. (1987) 'Hydrological modelling of the Sudd and Jonglei Canal', *Hydrological Sciences Journal*, 32(2), 143–59.

Swanson, R. H., Bernier, P. Y., and Woodard, P. D. (eds) (1987) *Forest Hydrology and Watershed Management*. IAHS Publication 167, Proceedings of the Vancouver Symposium. Wallingford, UK.

Tanner, T. (ed.) (1987) *Aldo Leopold: The Man and His Legacy*. Soil Conservation Society of America, Ankeny, IA.

Taylor, A. and Patrick, M. (1987) 'Looking at water through different eyes – the Maori perspective', *Soil and Water*, 23(4), 22–4.

Tewari, A. K. (1988) 'Revival of water harvesting methods in the Indian Desert', *Arid Lands Newsletter*, 26, 3–8.

Thompson, M. and Warburton, M. (1985) 'Uncertainty on a Himalayan scale', *Mountain Research and Development*, 5(2), 115–35.

Thorne, C. R. and Lewin, J. (1982) 'Bank process, bed material movement and planform development in a meandering river', in D. D. Rhodes and G. P. Williams (eds) *Adjustments of the Fluvial System*. Allen & Unwin, London, 117–37.

Tomkins, S. C. (1986) *The Theft of the Hills: Afforestation in Scotland*. Ramblers' Association, London.

Toynbee, A. (1976) *Mankind and Mother Earth*. Oxford University Press, Oxford.

Tranter, R. B. (ed.) (1978) *The Future of Upland Britain*. Centre for Agricultural Strategy, University of Reading (2 volumes).

Trudgill, S. T. (1986) 'Introduction', in S. T. Trudgill (ed.) *Solute Processes*. Wiley, Chichester, 1–14.

Tyler, S. (1987) 'River birds and acid water', *RSPB Conservation Review*, 1, 68–70.

UNCOD (1977) *Desertification: its Causes and Consequences*. Pergamon, Nairobi.

UNEP/UNESCO (1990) *The Impact of Large Water Projects on the Environment*. UNESCO, Paris.

United Nations (1990) *Global Outlook 2000. Economic, Social, Environmental*. United Nations Publications, New York.

United States Environmental Protection Agency (1986) *Water Quality Program Highlights: Arkansas Ecoregion Program*. USEPA, Washington DC.

US National Water Commission (1973) *Water Policies for the Future*. Water Information Center, Port Washington, New York.

Vallentine, H. R. (1967) *Water in the Service of Man*. Penguin Books, Harmondsworth.

Vannote, R. L., Minshall, G. W., Cummins, K. W., Sedell, J. R., and Cushing, C. E. (1980) 'The river continuum concept', *Canadian Journal of Fish and Aquatic Sciences*, 37, 130–7.

Vischer, D. (1989) 'Impact of 18th and 19th century river training works: three case studies from Switzerland', in G. E. Petts (ed.) *Historical Change of Large Alluvial Rivers: Western Europe*. Wiley, Chichester, 19–40.

de Voto, B. (1953) *The Journals of Lewis and Clark*. Houghton Mifflin, Boston, MA.

Walling, D. E. (1977) 'Assessing the accuracy of suspended sediment rating curves for a small basin', *Water Resources Research*, 13(3), 531–8.

Walling, D. E. (1979) 'The hydrological impact of building activity – a study near Exeter', in G. E. Hollis (ed.) *Man's Impact on the Hydrological Cycle in the UK*. Geo Books, Norwich, 135–51.

Walling, D. E. (1983) 'The sediment delivery problem', *Journal of Hydrology*, 65, 209–37.

Walling, D. E. (1990) 'Linking the field to the river: sediment delivery from agricultural land', in J. Boardman, I. D. L. Foster and J. A. Dearing (eds) *Soil Erosion on Agricultural Land*. Wiley, Chichester, 129–52.

Walling, D. E. and Webb, B. (1986) 'Solutes in river systems', in S. T. Trudgill (ed.) *Solute Processes*. Wiley, Chichester, 281–327.

Walling, D. E., Foster, S. D. D., and Wurzel, P. (eds) (1984) *Challenges in African Hydrology and Water Resources*. IAHS Publication 144, Proceedings of the Harare Symposium.

Ward, R. C. (1967) *Principles of Hydrology*. McGraw Hill, New York.

Ward, R. C. (1971) *Small Watershed Experiments, An Appraisal of Concepts and Research Developments*. Occasional Papers in Geography 18, University of Hull.

Ward, R. C. (1982) *The Fountains of the Deep and the Windows of Heaven*. University of Hull, Hull.

Watson, C. (1980) 'Watershed management: the California experience', *Watershed Management 1980*. American Society of Civil Engineers, New York, 1048–59.

Welbank, M. (1978) 'Irrigation and people', in C. G. Gunnerson and J. M. Kalbermatten (eds) *Environmental Impacts of International Civil Engineering Projects and Practices*. American Society of Civil Engineers, New York, 44–70.

Wertz, A. (1982) 'Integration of land and water management: political, administrative and planning problems', in P. Laconte and Y. Y. Haimes (eds) *Water Resources and Land-Use Planning: a Systems approach*. Nijhoff, The Hague, 283–95.

Weyman, D. R. (1975) *Runoff Processes and Streamflow Modelling*. Oxford University Press, Oxford.

Whipple, W. Jr and Van Abs, D. J. (1990) 'Principles of a ground-water strategy', *Journal of Water Resources Planning and Management*, American Society of Civil Engineers, 116(4), 503–16.

White, W. R. (1982) *Sedimentation Problems in River Basins. Studies and Reports in Hydrology*. UNESCO, Paris.

Whittenmore, C. (1981) *Land for People: Land Tenure and the Very Poor*. Oxfam, Oxford.

Wiersum, K. F. (1984) 'Surface erosion under various tropical agroforestry systems', in C. O'Loughlin and A. Pearce (eds) *Effects of Forest Land Use on Erosion and Slope Stability*. East-West Center, Honolulu, 231–9.

Winid, B. (1981) 'Comments on the development of the Awash Valley, Ethiopia', in S. K. Saha and C. J. Barrow (eds) *River Basin Planning, Theory and Practice*. Wiley, Chichester, 147–65.

Wischmeier, W. H. and Smith, D. D. (1965) *Predicting Rainfall Erosion from Cropland East of the Rocky Mountains*. Agriculture Handbook No. 282. United States Department of Agriculture, Washington DC.

Wisdom, A. S. (1979) *The Law of Rivers and Watercourses*, Shaw & Sons, London.

Wittfogel, K. A. (1956) 'The hydraulic civilisations', in W. L. Thomas (ed.) *Man's Role in Changing the Face of the Earth*. University of Chicago Press, Chicago, 152–64.

Wittfogel, K. A. (1957) *Oriental Despotism*. Yale University Press, New Haven and London.

Wolman, M. G. (1967) 'A cycle of sedimentation and erosion in urban river channels', *Geografiska Annale*, 49A, 385–95.

Woolhouse, C. H. (1989) *Managing the Effects of Urbanisation in the Upper Lee*. 2nd National Hydrology Symposium, British Hydrological Society, Wallingford, 2.9–2.17.

World Commission on Environment and Development (1987) *Our Common Future*. Oxford University Press, Oxford.

Youngman, R. E. and Lack, J. (1981) 'New problems with upland waters', *Water Services*, 85, 13–14.

Ziman, J. R. (1984) *An Introduction to Science Studies*. Cambridge University Press, Cambridge.

Zon, R. (1912) *Forests and Water in the Light of Scientific Investigation*. US Senate, Document 469.

Index

abstractions of water 224–5, 256
accommodation policy option 305
acidification: Canada 121; trend 84, 85; UK research 303, 304
Afar tribespeople 162
Africa: climatic change 236, 237; desertification 143–5; development authorities 157–66, drought problems 139, 140, 186; land use 166–7; soil erosion 200; Southern and precipitation 228; *see also under individual countries and rivers*
agriculture: dry cultivation methods 183–4; effects on runoff 64–5, 67; and soil erosion 201–2, 203, 204; *see also* forestry
aid, foreign 196, 197
Akosombo Dam 217
allocation policy option 305
'Alpine Torrents' controversy 286
Alvares, C. 176, 177
American Society of Civil Engineers (ASCE) 100, 102–3, 243
American Way 295
analogue studies 232
ANUFLOOD model 125
applied science 284; *see also* research; science
aquifers 43–4
Arizona 94, 95, 183–4
Arnell, N. 291, 292, 293, 297–9, 299–300
Arno River 9, 10
Assad Reservoir 185
Aswan dam scheme 148, 149, 152–3, 154–7
Aswan fall flow records 236
Ataturk Dam 185

Atbara River 148
Australia 228
Awash Valley Authority 157–62

Bahr el Jebel River 236
Balquhidder study 303
Bangladesh: floods 172–3, 233, 234; sharing Ganges 172, 272–3
bank modifications 223–4
Barrow, C. 180–1, 182–3, 267
Beddoe, Jack 259
bedload 25, 26, 51; sampling 47, 48
bedload formulae 28
Bible, The 9
Bicol River Basin Development Program 268
Billorey, R. 176, 177
Binns, A. 145
biologists 318
Biswas, A. K. 3, 5, 6
Black, P. E. xxix–xxxi
Blue Nile 148, 207, 272; boundaries 145–6; climatic change 236, 237; proposed development 155–6; *see also* Nile River
Boardman, J. 196
Bor-Zaraf Cut 149
'bottom-up' development 183–5
Boulder Canyon Project 92
Boulding, Kenneth E. 174–5
Brahmaputra River 233, 272–3
British Columbia 119
British Waterways Board 260
buffer strips 318

calcium ions 78, 79
Calder, I. R. 85–7
California 92, 94, 106